Sound Commitments

Sound Commitments

Avant-garde Music and the Sixties

Edited by Robert Adlington

OXFORD

UNIVERSITY PRESS

2009

OXFORD
UNIVERSITY PRESS

Oxford University Press, Inc., publishes works that further
Oxford University's objective of excellence
in research, scholarship, and education.

Oxford   New York
Auckland   Cape Town   Dar es Salaam   Hong Kong   Karachi
Kuala Lumpur   Madrid   Melbourne   Mexico City   Nairobi
New Delhi   Shanghai   Taipei   Toronto

With offices in
Argentina   Austria   Brazil   Chile   Czech Republic   France   Greece
Guatemala   Hungary   Italy   Japan   Poland   Portugal   Singapore
South Korea   Switzerland   Thailand   Turkey   Ukraine   Vietnam

© 2009 by Oxford University Press, Inc.

Published by Oxford University Press, Inc.
198 Madison Avenue, New York, New York 10016

www.oup.com

Oxford is a registered trademark of Oxford University Press

Library of Congress Cataloging-in-Publication Data
Sound commitments : avant-garde music and the sixties / edited by Robert Adlington.
p.   cm.
Includes bibliographical references and index.
ISBN 978-0-19-533664-1; 978-0-19-533665-8 (pbk.)
1. Music—Political aspects—History—20th century.   2. Avant-garde (Music).
3. Nineteen sixties.   I. Adlington, Robert.
ML3916.O84 2008
780.9'04—dc22 2008017865

9 8 7 6 5 4 3 2 1
Printed in the United States of America
on acid-free paper

Acknowledgments

This volume has been a collaborative project from the start. It originated in meetings with Amy Beal, Eric Drott, and Peter Schmelz at the 2004 annual meeting of the American Musicological Society in Seattle. Over the next year, suggestions for further possible contributors were exchanged, and newly approached contributors in turn made their own suggestions. I am immensely grateful to all the contributors for their enthusiasm, their ideas, and their patience as the volume has taken its final shape. I hope they will be pleased with the outcome.

Our editor at Oxford University Press, Suzanne Ryan, has been just as influential a collaborator. She commissioned anonymous reviewers whose insightful reports helped to improve the volume immeasurably, and added her own encouragement and sound advice at many stages along the way. Her assistants, Norm Hirschy and Lora Dunn, have also been unfailingly helpful and efficient in their responses to my numerous queries.

Acknowledgments for permission granted to reproduce copyright material are included with the reproductions themselves.

Contents

Contributors

Robert Adlington is associate professor in music at the University of Nottingham. He has written extensively on contemporary classical music, including monographs on Harrison Birtwistle (2000) and Louis Andriessen (2004). His current research explores music and politics in Amsterdam between 1966 and 1973, and has resulted in book chapters and articles in *Journal of Musicology* and *Cambridge Opera Journal*.

Amy C. Beal is associate professor at the University of California, Santa Cruz. Her primary research and recent publications (in *Journal of the American Musicological Society, American Music, Musical Quarterly, Contemporary Music Review*, and elsewhere) explore the history and historiography of American experimental music. She has written a book on American music in West Germany between 1945 and 1990: *New Music, New Allies: American Experimental Music in West Germany from the Zero Hour to Reunification* (2006). She has been the recipient of the Society for American Music's Wiley Housewright Dissertation Award and the American Musicological Society's Einstein Award.

Hubert F. van den Berg is researcher in the Groningen Research Institute for the Study of Culture and the Dutch Department of the University of Groningen (Netherlands). He has published on literature and politics, the social history of literature and art, Dada and the European avant-garde, as well as the literary representation and the cultural history of nature. His books include *Avantgarde und*

Anarchismus: Dada in Zürich und Berlin (1998), *Avantgarde! Voorhoede? Vernieuwingsbewegingen in Noord en Zuid opnieuw beschouwd* (coedited with Gillis J. Dorleijn; 2002), *The Import of Nothing: How Dada Came, Saw and Vanished in the Low Countries* (2002). Together with Walter Fähnders he is preparing a dictionary of the European avant-garde of the twentieth century.

Ralf Dietrich studied philosophy and musicology at the University in Mainz, Germany, and since 1990 has worked as a freelance music journalist for German public radio Hessischer Rundfunk. After moving to Ann Arbor, Michigan, in 1993 he embarked on extensive research on the ONCE Festival and the ONCE group, and has since published on related topics, including Eric Dolphy's appearance at the 1964 Festival (*SEMJA Newsletter*, 2000) and Robert Ashley's early works (*MusikTexte*, 2001). Currently, he is editing and translating the collected writings of Robert Ashley for Edition MusikTexte (Cologne) and preparing a book-length study on ONCE.

Eric Drott is an assistant professor at the University of Texas at Austin. His research focuses on European and American avant-garde music from the 1960s to the present, addressing in particular questions of cultural politics and aesthetics. Recent publications include articles on composers including Ligeti, Nancarrow, and Scelsi in *Musical Quarterly, Music Analysis, Journal of Musicology, and American Music*. He is currently working on a book on the interaction of music and politics in France after May '68.

Yayoi Uno Everett is a native of Yokohama, Japan. She is currently associate professor at Emory University in Atlanta, Georgia. Everett's research has focused on the analysis of postwar art music through the perspectives of cultural studies, semiotics, East Asian aesthetics, and mathematical modeling. Her recent publications include "Gesture and Calligraphy in the Late Works by Chou Wen-chung" in *Contemporary Music Review* (2007), *The Music of Louis Andriessen* (2006), and *Locating East Asia in Western Art Music* (2004).

Danielle Fosler-Lussier teaches music history at The Ohio State University School of Music. Her research on music's engagement with cold war politics in Eastern and Western Europe and the United States has been supported by an AMS-50 dissertation fellowship as well as fellowships from the American Council of Learned Societies, the International Research and Exchanges Board, and the Eisenhower Foundation. She is the author of *Music Divided: Bartók's Legacy in Cold War Culture* (2007).

Bernard Gendron is professor emeritus of philosophy at the University of Wisconsin-Milwaukee. He has taught in the areas of aesthetics, continental philosophy, and popular and experimental music. He is the author of *Technology and the Human Condition* (1976) and *Between Montmartre and the Mudd Club: Popular Music and the Avant-Garde* (2002), and articles including "Theodor Adorno Meets the Cadillacs" and "Pop Aesthetics: The Very Idea." He is presently at work on two book projects: *Aesthetics in Turmoil: Experimental Music in New York's Downtown* and *Why Jazz Lost to Rock 'n Soul.*

Sumanth Gopinath is assistant professor of music theory at the University of Minnesota. His research interests include post-WWII (American) art and popular musics, cultural theory (especially Marxism), the intersections of politics and music, and the globalization of cultural production. He is currently working on two book projects, one addressing issues of race and ethnicity in the music of Steve Reich and another on the global ringtone industry.

Beate Kutschke studied musicology and cultural history in Berlin, receiving her PhD in 2000. Since 2003, she has been Wissenschaftliche Mitarbeiterin (assistant professor) at the Universität der Künste in Berlin. Her dissertation on the idea of the end of history in the musical works of Theodor Adorno and Wolfgang Rihm was published as *Wildes Denken in der Neuen Musik* (2002). More recently her research has focused upon "1968" and avant-garde music, in which field she has published numerous journal and book articles, and a monograph, *Neue Linke/Neue Musik* (2007). Currently, she is working on her third monograph, on music and ethics around 1700.

Benjamin Piekut completed graduate studies at Columbia University, and is currently Lecturer in Music at the University of Southampton. His dissertation examines four case studies at the margins of experimentalism in the 1960s: Henry Flynt, Charlotte Moorman, the New York Philharmonic, and the Jazz Composers Guild. His research interests include music in the United States after 1950, critical studies, improvisation, and theories of performativity. He is coauthoring a book on posthumous duets with Jason Stanyek.

Peter J. Schmelz is assistant professor in the Music Department at Washington University in St. Louis. He has recently completed a book for Oxford University Press titled *Such Freedom, If Only Musical: Unofficial Soviet Music and Society during the Thaw*, for which he received a 2004 National Endowment for the Humanities Summer Stipend. Professor Schmelz is also founder and chair of the American Musicological Society's Cold War and Music Study Group, and has published on music and politics in both American and Russian popular genres.

Sound Commitments

Introduction

Avant-garde Music and the Sixties

Robert Adlington

The artistic avant-garde, many of its theorists seem to agree, is a culture of subversion. Conceiving itself as the radical leading edge of creative endeavor, it exists in a state of rebellion against the cultural mainstream, a state expressed in its dedication to provocation, controversy, and shock. This conception of art as "an instrument for social action and reform, a means of revolutionary propaganda and agitation"[1] can be traced back to nineteenth-century France, where art was perceived by utopian and anarchist thinkers as a crucial element of the movement for social progress.[2] The alliance of political and artistic radicalism was embodied in the bohemianism of *fin de siècle* Paris, whose nonconformism expressed opposition to both the government and artistic institutions of the bourgeoisie.[3] The socially critical function of progressive art was intensified in the early decades of the twentieth century, when a number of highly influential movements, including Dada, surrealism, futurism, and the left avant-garde in Russia and Germany, sought to overcome the separation of art from life—the position of critical distance—that had characterized the nineteenth-century avant-garde. Instead of commenting critically on mass culture, artists turned to attack the very institutions of art that continued to "set [art] off from the praxis of life," and thereby constrained its unsettling power.[4] This subversive attitude, in turn, entailed a departure from the established formal principle of "organicity," in which all parts of an artwork were subordinated to the whole; for avant-gardists the effect of such formal integration was to encourage perception as "a 'mere'

3

art product," thus detracting from its emancipatory potential.[5] The truly avant-garde work had to be "nonorganic."[6] In this way, formal experimentation—including the techniques of montage, quotation, and abrupt dissociation—came to be seen as integral to the avant-gardists' understanding that "art can be crucial to a transformation of society."[7]

Contrast this picture, however, with that given of avant-garde music by recent Anglo-American musicology. This has dwelt precisely upon its *disavowal* of issues of social and political concern. The apparent focus of postwar avant-garde composers upon questions of compositional technique and the creation of novel sound worlds appears to indicate a decided rejection of worldly engagement; Georgina Born, for instance, has referred to avant-garde music's "autarchy."[8] The pursuit of rarefied compositional or conceptual procedures effectively confines its appeal to an initiated social elite, and implies a rejection of a more democratic musical practice.[9] Indeed, the "difficulty" of avant-garde music, in the view of one influential commentator, signals an aloof "incorruptibility in one's resistance to the blandishments and debasements of modern life."[10] In place of popular demand, postwar avant-garde music has survived through the support of state institutions such as culture ministries, broadcasters, or educational organizations, and thus acts to offer covert endorsement of the societal status quo.[11] In ways such as these, it is argued, the rhetoric of dissidence and subversion that often surrounds avant-garde music is fatally undermined through its failure, in practice, to alter mind-sets and social structures.[12] Instead, for many commentators, it is popular music that has most successfully given voice to radical political views, the plight of the oppressed, and the desire for social change. Nowhere does this appear to be more clearly the case than in the 1960s, when the protest songs of Bob Dylan and Joan Baez gained a large audience, psychedelic rock flaunted alternative lifestyles, soul music emerged as a vehicle for racial commentary, and huge festivals advocated peace, love, and understanding.[13]

This view, however, increasingly risks obscuring the intense involvement of many avant-garde musicians in the tumultuous cultural and political developments of the sixties.[14] This involvement was widespread and took many forms. For instance, avant-garde composers—including figures closely associated with the 1950s' Darmstadt school, seen by many later commentators as epitomizing the postwar avant-garde's preoccupation with matters of compositional technique at the expense of worldly engagement—devised musical responses to the Paris protests of May 1968, to the assassination of Martin Luther King, and to anti-imperialist struggles in Latin America.[15] John Cage's well-established commitment to erasing the boundaries separating life and art—a commitment shared with the early twentieth-century avant-garde[16]—inspired new generations of musicians, for whom the values of immediacy and spontaneity offered a point of connection with youth counterculture, and who viewed performative freedoms, collaborative creative processes, and audience participation as consonant with the antiauthoritarian and democratizing movements of the era.[17] For musicians working under repressive state regimes, avant-garde techniques held a dissident appeal by virtue of being the object of official disapproval, and thus came to act as a symbol of resistance.[18] In jazz, it was frequently the most "progressive" artists who were the most visibly politically engaged, not least because of a growing understanding among African American musicians that "free jazz" signified freedom from "weak Western [meaning European] forms," and thus was consistent with the imperatives of the Black Arts Movement.[19] Rock musicians of the period were also moved to introduce experimental techniques as a cipher of liberation from convention and the market, in the process creating some of the most fêted avant-garde moments in popular music, precisely as the era of protest reached its height.[20]

For many musicians, engagement with the pressing social issues of the time did not require relinquishing an abiding preoccupation with technical advance and conceptual innovation. Indeed, there was a widespread conviction that aesthetic experiment and social progressiveness made natural bedfellows. At the same time, this stance inevitably threw up some sharp dilemmas; and while some avant-garde musicians were content simply to graft a political element onto their existing musical preoccupations in a manner that could be viewed as essentially self-congratulatory and condescending—"radical chic" was the term coined by the writer Tom Wolfe—others felt compelled to question the very principles of their creative practice.[21] Thus the point of departure for Hansjörg Pauli's 1971 volume of interviews with prominent avant-garde composers was Heinz-Klaus Metzger's grave query as to whether one should compose music at all "while the world burns"; the composers' responses, Pauli suggests, offer not solutions but "a record of difficulties."[22] The difficulties were many and various. For instance, could the cultural baggage of established performance institutions (such as concert halls, symphony orchestras, and broadcasting organizations) be reconciled with the contemporary critique of bourgeois values? As Hans Werner Henze noted, the composer of orchestral music appeared "to depend for everything on what the system has to offer"[23]; and this problem extended to musicians reliant upon institutional support of any kind. Then there was the question of whether novel approaches to musical language and technology could be meaningfully considered "revolutionary" when very real struggles against authoritarian state and economic systems were being visibly waged around the world. For Luigi Nono, to place undue emphasis purely upon the subversion of *musical* systems risked a powerless experimentalism "quite acceptable to the most cultivated bourgeoisie"; and the fetishization of technology signaled "the most logical capitalist or late capitalist ideological position" of all.[24] Most fundamentally, how could avant-garde musicians make a meaningful contribution to social change if their music remained the preserve of a tiny, initiated clique? Experimental ventures intended as a "reaction against elitism," such as Cornelius Cardew's Scratch Orchestra, tended to encounter the troubling difficulty that (as Cardew noted) "only a handful of people wanted to hear us play ... the only section of the public to take us seriously were the very elite we were rebelling against."[25]

The essays in this volume examine, from a diversity of perspectives, the encounter of avant-garde music and the "long" sixties, across a range of genres, aesthetic positions, and geographical locations. Rather than providing a comprehensive survey, the intention is to give an indication of the richness of avant-garde musicians' response to the decade's cultural and political upheavals, and of the complex and often ambivalent status of their efforts when viewed in the wider social context. The contributors address music intended for the concert hall; tape and electronic music; jazz and improvisation; participatory "events" and performance art; and experimental popular music; and explore developments in the United States, France, West Germany, Italy, the Netherlands, the Soviet Union, Japan, and parts of the so-called Third World. The activities of a number of figures subsequently to gain a substantial public following—including Louis Andriessen, Yoko Ono, Steve Reich, and Archie Shepp—are examined, but the volume also presents groundbreaking work on a number of less well-known individuals and developments. Each chapter draws on new archival research and/or interviews with significant figures of the period.

In his interview with Hansjörg Pauli, Hans Werner Henze observed sardonically that "no one seems to know any more where and how 'avant-garde' takes place."[26] The question of what counted as avant-garde in the 1960s is indeed a complex and many-faceted one. Prominent theorists of the avant-garde tend to support the view of recent musicologists that postwar developments betrayed the fundamental radicalism of the early twentieth-century avant-garde.[27] As a number of the chapters in this volume testify, the 1960s also saw the consolidation of aesthetic divergences among progressive musicians, divergences that were increasingly interpreted in terms of reaction against the serial avant-garde of the previous decade—a development encapsulated in the influential distinction between an academic avant-garde and a more free-spirited experimentalism.[28] At the same time, as Hubert van den Berg notes in the opening chapter of this volume, the term "avant-garde" was gaining increasingly widespread acceptance as a colloquial label, one that paid little heed to the fine distinctions of theorists or artists. The point of departure for van den Berg's overview of the history of the term in the historiography of art is precisely the lack of shared agreement as to its meaning; his historical reflections thereby serve to contextualize the particular problems attendant upon the idea of the avant-garde in the 1960s. Noting the almost complete absence of the term in the statements of the early twentieth-century artists more recently viewed as representing the avant-garde's apogee, van den Berg emphasizes instead the role of the 1960s avant-garde in retrospectively constructing a "historical avantgarde" to serve as their legitimating forebears. The nineteenth-century association of the term with the service of political ideology was, van den Berg argues, essential to its appeal in the 1960s, but this putative radicalism was muddied by the later, early twentieth-century understanding that progressive artists should lead, not serve.

In keeping both with van den Berg's image of the avant-garde as a fundamentally heterogeneous, "rhizomatic" entity, and with the varied usage of the time, the term is employed flexibly by the contributors to this volume, referring variously to music shaped by a sense of radical departure from tradition, by opposition to both established canons and contemporary commercial production, and by appeal (intended or unintended) to various kinds of specialized audience. The headings under which the remaining chapters have been grouped are intended to draw attention to shared concerns among the contributions, rather than indicating mutually exclusive areas of focus (many chapters could have been differently placed). Chapters 2 to 4 comprise three studies of avant-garde musicians particularly deeply affected by leftist ideology. Benjamin Piekut's discussion of the maverick composer, philosopher, and activist Henry Flynt traces the path taken by his career in the early 1960s, from a position at the heart of New York's downtown avant-garde community, to his radical repudiation of the avant-garde under the influence of the Marxist-Leninist Workers World Party (WWP). Piekut shows how the WWP both shaped the rhetoric of his attacks on the avant-garde, and (through its militant advocacy of civil rights) encouraged Flynt's growing interest in black popular music. Paradoxically, this was to lead to tension with the WWP itself, which shared the culturally conservative outlook of Soviet communism. Flynt, by contrast, viewed "street-Negro music" as representing (in Piekut's words) "the vanguard of musical evolution" through its resourceful use of electric instruments and recording and broadcasting technology.

My chapter focuses on a singular event in the musical life of late-1960s Amsterdam: a "political-demonstrative experimental concert" that brought together many of the leading lights of the Dutch musical avant-garde. At the time of the concert, its organizers—like many other avant-garde musicians of the period—were newly in thrall to the social and cultural model of Castro's Cuba.[29] Yet coexistent with this commitment was an equally strongly held belief in the apolitical nature of music itself. Closer investigation of the works performed at the concert reveals, however, that their musical processes were significantly shaped by the composers' earlier interest in anarchism. The resulting "forms of opposition" were not easily reconciled with their creators' new passion for communism. The West German composers examined in Beate Kutschke's chapter were far less reticent about attaching political meanings to their work. Kutschke's finely nuanced discussion revolves around a public controversy over the commissioning of a piece by the composer Nikolaus A. Huber, a controversy that illustrates the shift of avant-gardists away from the imperatives of Adorno's highly influential aesthetic theory and toward the New Left's emphasis upon praxis. This inevitably raised the awkward question of how avant-garde composers might be able to contribute to "praxis," when their music had such limited public appeal.

Chapters 5 to 7 highlight the desire on the part of many avant-garde musicians to connect with the popular, whether by seeking to establish new relationships with wider, less specialized audiences, or by engaging directly with popular activism. Amy Beal offers an evocative account, based largely on previously unexplored archive material, of the early years of the American-Italian improvisation group Musica Elettronica Viva (MEV). Central to their practice was a radical democratizing of music making, an expression of their belief that music was a "universal human right." In a series of public events in Rome, MEV invited anyone and everyone to participate in their musical "research," and sought to make overt connections with the spirit of protest gripping Italy at the time. At the same time, as Beal shows, the attempt at an unfettered implementation of "freedom" gave rise to tension between the musicians, and moreover did not always sit happily with the aspiration of contributing concretely to the social struggle.

There follow two studies of groundbreaking "documentary" tape pieces. Sumanth Gopinath gives a detailed account of the historical circumstances of the creation of Steve Reich's well-known tape piece *Come Out* (1966), which takes as its sole source material a declaration by a black youth (Daniel Hamm, one of the so-called Harlem Six) wrongly accused of murder. The civil rights struggle naturally features as the primary backdrop to this discussion, but Gopinath also draws on broader contexts relevant to the period, including contemporary discourses on paranoia and on the violence wrought upon and against language. Gopinath is not blind to the problematic aspects of Reich's creation, which arise in no small part from the experimental compositional processes to which Hamm's voice is subjected, but he closes by suggesting it nonetheless contains a powerful contemporary relevance. Luc Ferrari's *Presque Rien* (1970), which presents an apparently unembellished soundscape of a fishing village by the Black Sea, exemplifies the avant-gardist desire to dismantle the boundaries between art and life. Eric Drott's account explores the local social and political context for Ferrari's approach, a context that includes state endeavors to promote cultural democratization in the wake of May 1968, contemporaneous theories of musical listening by Pierre Bourdieu, and the situationist critique of the reifying effect of reproductive technology.

Drott questions the extent to which the piece succeeded in its attempt to escape "the sphere of cultivated apprehension," but proposes that it nonetheless offered a model for a type of avant-garde composition that anyone armed with a tape recorder could emulate.

For many creative musicians, the decade's spirit of activism gave new significance to the public act of musical performance. In the case of the ONCE group of musicians and artists—so-named after the festival they organised in Ann Arbor, Michigan, which showcased their work—performance was an arena both for addressing the hard political issues of the time and for enacting the liberation of the group's composer-performers. Ralf Dietrich's chapter emphasizes the importance of electronics and multimedia theatrics to both of these aims. The adventurous use of technology in many ONCE pieces was at once a reflection of the cold war investment by the United States in technological innovation (for a period, ONCE founder Gordon Mumma worked in a military-funded science laboratory), and an attempt to comment critically upon it. Dietrich also examines the tensions that arose at later ONCE performances with younger musicians and audiences set on their own radical paths, and thus reminds us that the sixties were witness to several generations of avant-gardists. Yayoi Uno Everett places the distinctive avant-garde scene in Japan in the context of anti-U.S. protests early in the decade, in which many musicians took part. John Cage was a crucial influence on avant-garde musicians associated with the Sôgetsu Arts Center in Tokyo, but indeterminacy and Dadaesque performance were here turned to distinctive ends that related to Japan's troubled past and present. Everett draws on rare primary sources to throw new light on the controversial performances of musicians including Toshi Ichiyanagi, Yûji Takahashi, and Yoko Ono. She argues that avant-garde techniques continued to be important in later Japanese music that, by incorporating traditional musics and instruments from across Asia, was more obviously focused on "embracing the premodern Japan."

By definition the avant-garde has a marginal positional in relation to mainstream culture. But this marginality is also a potential source of prestige for patrons and institutions wishing to demonstrate their discerning and progressive taste. Such parties can offer valuable enabling resources to the avant-garde artist, but by serving the interests of powerful patrons the socially subversive function of avant-garde art is also threatened. Musicians' negotiation of these competing aesthetic, social, and economic imperatives looms large in Bernard Gendron's analysis of the resurgence of the jazz avant-garde in New York in 1964–65. Through a detailed investigation of shifting patterns of reception in the jazz press, Gendron traces a complex set of factors that lifted the jazz avant-garde from near obscurity in the early years of the decade, to a canonized status by 1965. Prominent among these factors was the politically radical discourse promoted by figures associated with the

Black Arts Movement such as Amiri Baraka and Larry Neal, which conceived black avant-garde musicians as "shaping the spiritual foundation for revolutionary change."[30] The articulation of a radical social purpose thus assisted the process of canonization, although as Gendron notes, this canonization brought no parallel economic success.

Danielle Fosler-Lussier's chapter assesses the role of avant-garde music in the U.S. State Department's Cultural Presentations program, through which American musicians were funded to tour overseas as part of the cold war propaganda effort. By the sixties, avant-garde musicians from classical and jazz worlds formed a regular part of this program. Fosler-Lussier shows that the reasons for this inclusion differed according to the destination country concerned, and assesses the sometimes compromising impact of the institutional context upon the perceived meaning of avant-garde music, both in the visited nation and with the musicians' home audience. Peter Schmelz's discussion of the ANS synthesizer and the Moscow studio that housed it transplants us to the other side of the cultural cold war. In the early years of the decade, the ANS synthesizer was toured overseas as a symbol of the Soviet Union's technological prowess, but official interest soon waned and both the synthesizer and its studio, although continuing to be supported by official subsidies, fell into the hands of the musical underground. The studio thereby became a center for unofficial concerts that, in Schmelz's words, "undercut the dominant Soviet Realist aesthetic codes." It also witnessed a generational shift within the underground, from the older academic avant-gardists to a younger generation fascinated by progressive rock. The multimedia happenings staged at the studio in the early seventies finally precipitated the studio's closure, although it was the synthesizer's brief association with avant-garde composers such as Schnittke, Denisov, and Gubaidulina that figured most prominently in the official justification.

In his introductory chapter, Hubert van den Berg notes that the much-reported death of the avant-garde during the 1980s and 1990s was in part to be explained by its association during the sixties and earlier with radical political movements, whose failings seemed to be epitomized by the collapse of socialist states. The long-term legacy of the sixties is as widely disputed as that of the musical avant-garde. Conservative commentators, especially in America, have taken a disparaging view ever since the decade drew to a close—a view epitomized by Roger Kimball's 2000 book *The Long March*, which argues that "we owe to the 1960s the ultimate institutionalization of immoralist radicalism: the institutionalization of drugs, pseudo-spirituality, promiscuous sex, virulent anti-Americanism, naïve anti-capitalism, and the precipitous decline of artistic and intellectual standards."[31] Even historians sympathetic to the profound cultural shifts—racial, sexual, generational—wrought by the sixties have typically pointed to the era's paradoxes: the confinement of the decade's more radical behavior to a tiny and often socially privileged minority; the entrepreneurialism underlying putatively anticapitalist countercultural initiatives; the tendencies to hubris and individualistic indulgence.[32] A number of the chapters in this volume identify precisely these traits in the era's avant-garde music, which, as we have already observed, hardly unproblematically reflected the prevailing concerns of democratizing and participation. The volume's title similarly seeks to evoke the tension that frequently arose between tenaciously held political or social beliefs on the one hand, and a (sometimes frankly solipsistic) commitment to the possibilities of "sound" itself—with its potential to distract from broader cultural engagement—on the other. All of the volume's contributors are sensitive to the fault lines affecting particular musicians' activities, but they reach differing conclusions, pointing to a striking degree of success in the endeavors of some musicians, outright failure in others. Rather than striking a single position in the debate about sixties' radicalism, then, the book aims to contribute to a more finely nuanced history of avant-garde music, upon which such polemical debates might be more securely founded. As such, it is hoped it will make a contribution to the ongoing reassessment of the significance and cultural place of the postwar musical avant-garde, as well as to our understanding of the decade that saw some of its most singular and provocative manifestations.

I am grateful to a number of the contributors to this volume for their comments on earlier drafts of this introduction.

Notes

1. Gabriel-Désiré Laverdant, cited in Renato Poggioli, *The Theory of the Avant-Garde*, trans. Gerald Fitzgerald (Cambridge, Mass.: Harvard University Press, 1968), 9.

2. See Donald D. Egbert, *Social Radicalism and the Arts: Western Europe* (London: Duckworth, 1970); and Egbert, "The Idea of the 'Avant-garde' in Art and Politics," *American Historical Review* 73 (1967): 339–66.

3. Poggioli, *The Theory of the Avant-Garde*, 11.

4. Peter Bürger, *Theory of the Avant-Garde*, trans. Michael Shaw (Minneapolis: University of Minnesota Press, 1984), 83.

5. Ibid., 90.

6. Ibid., 84.

7. Andreas Huyssen, *After the Great Divide: Modernism, Mass Culture, Postmodernism* (Basingstoke: Macmillan, 1988), 7.

8. Georgina Born (with David Hesmondhalgh), "Introduction: On Difference, Representation, and Appropriation in Music," in *Western Music and Its Others: Difference, Representation, and Appropriation in Music*, ed. Born and Hesmondhalgh (Berkeley and Los Angeles: University of California Press, 2000), 1–58. See also Born's *Rationalizing Culture: IRCAM, Boulez, and the Institutionalization of the Musical Avant-Garde* (Berkeley and Los Angeles: University of California Press, 1995).

9. Richard Taruskin, for instance, alludes to the Darmstadt school's "use of a wilfully difficult style to create a social elite that excluded the noninitiated" in *The Oxford History of Western Music*, vol. 5 (Oxford: Oxford University Press, 2005), 37.

10. Lawrence Kramer, cited in Björn Heile, "Darmstadt as Other: British and American Responses to Musical Modernism," *Twentieth-Century Music* 1, no. 2 (September 2004): 161–78, esp. 165. For a more recent attack by Kramer on the musical avant-garde's "fiction of transgression," see "'Au-delà d'une musique informelle': Nostalgia, Obsolence, and the Avant-garde," in Lawrence Kramer, *Critical Musicology and the Responsibility of Response: Selected Essays* (Aldershot: Ashgate, 2006), 303–16.

11. See Susan McClary, "Terminal Prestige: The Case of Avant-garde Music Composition," *Cultural Critique* 12 (1989): 57–81.

12. For related arguments, see Dai Griffiths, "Grammar Schoolboy Music" [1995], in *Music, Culture, and Society: A Reader*, ed. Derek B. Scott (Oxford: Oxford University Press, 2002), 143–45; Christopher Small, *Music of the Common Tongue: Survival and Celebration in Afro-American Music* (London: Calder, 1987); Rose Rosengard Subotnik, "Toward a Deconstruction of Structural Listening: A Critique of Schoenberg, Adorno, and Stravinsky" [1988], in *Deconstructive Variations: Music and Reason in Western Society* (Minneapolis: University of Minnesota Press, 1996), 148–76. For a summary and critique of the negative stance of such writers toward the musical avant-garde, see Heile, "Darmstadt as Other," and Martin Scherzinger, "In Memory of a Receding Dialectic: The Political Relevance of Autonomy and Formalism in Modernist Musical Aesthetics," in *The Pleasure of Modernist Music: Listening, Meaning, Intention, Ideology*, ed. Arved Ashby (Rochester: University of Rochester Press, 2004), 68–100.

13. See Ian MacDonald, *The People's Music* (London: Pimlico, 2003); and James E. Perone, *Music of the Counterculture Era* (Westport, Conn.: Greenwood, 2004); also Ian Peddie, ed., *The Resisting Muse: Popular Music and Social Protest* (Aldershot: Ashgate, 2006).

14. At least in the English-language musicological world. In German musicology the countercultural status of the musical avant-garde is more widely accepted. Two recent volumes published in Germany appraise a wide range of music—including avant-garde—that engages with the upheavals of the sixties: Arnold Jacobshagen and Markus Leniger, eds., *Rebellische Musik: Gesellschaftlicher Protest und kultureller Wandel um 1968* (Cologne: Verlag Dohr, 2007); Beate Kutschke, ed., *Musikkulturen in der Revolte* (Stuttgart: Franz Steiner, 2008). See also Richard Toop, "Expanding Horizons: The International Avant-garde, 1962–75," in *The Cambridge History of Twentieth-Century Music*, ed. Nicholas Cook and Anthony Pople (Cambridge: Cambridge University Press, 2004), 453–77.

15. For a brief survey (one not limited to French music, despite the title), see Pierre Albert Castanet, "1968: A Cultural and Social Survey of Its Influences on French Music," *Contemporary Music Review* 8, no. 1 (1993): 19–43. A detailed examination of the impact of the emerging "New Left" on avant-garde composers in Europe and the United States is given in Beate Kutschke, *Neue Linke/ Neue Musik: Kulturtheorien und künstlerische Avantgarde in den 1960er und 70er Jahren* (Cologne: Böhlau, 2007).

16. See Bürger, *Theory of the Avant-Garde*, 55–59.

17. For an indication of the (varied) extent of such connections, see the survey conducted in 1969 by the journal *Source* among a number of leading American experimental musicians, each of whom was asked, "Have you, or has anyone ever used your music for political or social ends?" See *Source: Music of the Avant-Garde* 3, no. 2 (July 1969): 7–9, 90–91. (I am indebted to Virginia Anderson for loaning me a copy of this issue.) Musicians in Europe also saw Cage's "staged anarchy" as calling for "political action"; see Amy C. Beal, *New Music, New Allies: American Experimental Music in West Germany from the Zero Hour to Reunification* (Berkeley and Los Angeles: University of California Press, 2006), 105–30. For more on Cage's own relationship to politics, see David W. Bernstein, "John Cage and the 'Aesthetic of Indifference,'" in *The New York Schools of Music and Visual Arts,* ed. Steven Johnson (New York: Routledge, 2002), 113–33; and William Brooks, "Music and Society," in *The Cambridge Companion to John Cage,* ed. David Nicholls (Cambridge: Cambridge University Press, 2002), 214–26.

18. For two contrasting cases see Christopher Dunn, *Brutality Garden: Tropicália and the Emergence of a Brazilian Counterculture* (Chapel Hill: University of North Carolina Press, 2001); and Peter J. Schmelz, *Such Freedom, if Only Musical: Unofficial Soviet Music and Society in the Thaw* (New York: Oxford University Press, 2009).

19. Amiri Baraka, cited in Peter Townsend, "Free Jazz: Musical Style and Liberationist Ethic, 1956–1965," in *Media, Culture and the Modern African American Struggle,* ed. Brian Ward (Gainesville: Florida University Press, 2001), 145–60, esp. 150. See also Iain Anderson, *This Is Our Music: Free Jazz, the Sixties, and American Culture* (Philadelphia: University of Pennsylvania Press, 2007); and Bernard Gendron's chapter in this volume.

20. See Gianmario Borio, "Avantgarde als pluralistisches Konzept: Musik um 1968," in *Rebellische Musik,* ed. Jacobshagen and Leniger, 15–33. For further reflections upon the politics of avant-garde rock of the late sixties and early seventies, see Bernard Gendron, *Between Montmartre and the Mudd Club: Popular Music and the Avant-Garde* (Chicago: University of Chicago Press, 2002), 161–247; John Platoff, "John Lennon, 'Revolution' and the Politics of Musical Reception," *Journal of Musicology* 22, no. 2 (2005): 241–67; and Peter Wicke, "AvantgardeRock—RockAvantgarde: Crossover als politisches Programm—Ein (pop)historischer Exkurs,"*Positionen: Beiträge zur Neuen Musik* 71 (May 2007): 10–14.

21. On avant-garde music and "radical chic," see Taruskin, The *Oxford History of Western Music,* vol. 5, 342–50.

22. Hansjörg Pauli, Für *wen komponieren Sie eigentlich?* (Frankfurt: Fischer, 1971), 7. Pauli's interviews originated in a series of radio broadcasts from the preceding two years.

23. Hans Werner Henze, "Does Music Have to Be Political?" [1969], in *Music and Politics: Collected Writings 1953–81,* trans. Peter Labanyi (London: Faber, 1982), 167–71. Henze recounts his extensive involvement with student and Cuban politics during the late 1960s and early 1970s—which resulted in a notable radicalization of his musical style—in a number of essays in *Music and Politics,* and in *Bohemian Fifths: An Autobiography,* trans Stewart Spencer (London: Faber, 1998). For a recent perspective on the notion of "musica impura," which Henze developed in response to these experiences, see Arnold Jacobshagen, "Musica impura. *Der langwierige Weg in die Wohnung der Natascha*

Ungeheuer von Hans Werner Henze und die Berliner Studentenbewegung," in *Rebellische Musik*, ed. Jacobshagen and Leniger, 109–24.

24. Luigi Nono, "Musik und Revolution," in *Luigi Nono: Text—Studien zu seiner Musik*, ed. Jürg Stenzl (Zürich: Atlantis, 1975), 107–15. A wide-ranging interview with Nono regarding his political engagement, which had its origins in Italian Marxism of the immediate postwar years, is included in Pauli, *Für wen komponieren Sie eigentlich?* 106–27. For a recent investigation of the impact of Nono's evolving political outlook upon his often esoteric compositional preoccupations, see Bruce Durazzi, "Musical Poetics and Political Ideology in the Work of Luigi Nono" (PhD. diss, Yale University, 2005).

25. Cornelius Cardew, cited in Coriún Aharonián, "Cardew as a Basis for a Discussion on Ethical Options," *Leonardo Music Journal* 11 (2001): 13–15, esp. 14. For more on Cardew's evolving outlook on music and politics, see *Cornelius Cardew: A Reader*, ed. Edwin Prévost (Matching Tye: Copula, 2006); Virginia Anderson, "British Experimental Music: Cornelius Cardew and His Contemporaries" (master's diss., University of Redlands, 1983); Timothy D. Taylor, "Moving in Decency: The Music and Radical Politics of Cornelius Cardew," *Music and Letters* 79, no. 4 (1998): 555–76. Similar problems confronted African American free jazz musicians; see Eric Porter, *What Is This Thing Called Jazz? African American Musicians as Artists, Critics and Activists* (Berkeley and Los Angeles: University of California Press, 2002), 191–239.

26. Translated as "Art and the Revolution," in *Music and Politics*, 178–83, esp. 182.

27. See, notably, Bürger, *Theory of the Avant-Garde;* and Huyssen, *After the Great Divide.*

28. This distinction was already being promulgated in Germany during the 1950s; see Beal, *New Music, New Allies,* 63–64. A later, influential version of this binarism may be found in Michael Nyman, *Experimental Music: Cage and Beyond* (London: Studio Vista, 1974; second edition, Cambridge: Cambridge University Press, 1999). For a stimulating study that throws light upon the complex relationship between experimental and avant-garde tendencies during the 1960s, see Eric Drott, "Ligeti in Fluxus," *Journal of Musicology* 21, no. 2 (2004): 201–40.

29. Other prominent figures of relevance to this volume to visit Cuba during the sixties included Luc Ferrari, Luigi Nono, Hans Werner Henze, and Amiri Baraka. Castro's famous dictum "Inside the revolution, everything; outside the revolution, nothing" first permitted and then (from the end of the sixties) suppressed musical avant-garde experimentation. See Paul Century, "Leo Brouwer: A Portrait of the Artist in Socialist Cuba," *Latin American Music Review* 8, no. 2 (1987): 151–71; and Neil Leonard, "Juan Blanco: Cuba's Pioneer of Electroacoustic Music," *Computer Music Journal* 21, no. 2 (1997): 10–20.

30. Larry Neal, cited by Bernard Gendron in this volume, p. 225.

31. Roger Kimball, *The Long March: How the Cultural Revolution of the 1960s Changed America* (San Francisco: Encounter, 2000), 41.

32. See for instance Geoff Andrews, ed., *New Left, New Right: Taking the Sixties Seriously* (Houndmills: Palgrave, 1999); Stephen Macedo, ed., *Reassessing the Sixties: Debating the Political and Cultural Legacy* (London: Norton, 1997); Arthur Marwick, *The Sixties: Cultural Revolution in Britain, France, Italy and the United States* (Oxford: Oxford University Press, 1999).

1

Avant-garde

Some Introductory Notes on the Politics of a Label

Hubert F. van den Berg

1

Since the 1970s the term "avant-garde" has served in certain sections of the historiography of the European arts as a common designation—a more or less fixed name—for a set of divergent, heterogeneous phenomena that together form some sort of a single entity, a historical ensemble or configuration. In other words, "avant-garde" is treated not just as a theoretical construction or interpretative model *ex posteriori*, but as a historical, once real, now past entity, also regarded in its historical time as—to some extent—a historical unity.[1] The term "avant-garde" itself is far older and was already introduced in the cultural field somewhere in the first quarter of the nineteenth century. It first developed into a regularly utilized denomination only in the late 1930s and 1940s, and became a more fashionable designation for innovative and experimental movements in the arts even later, in the 1950s and 1960s. It was later still that the label "avant-garde" became a common term in historiography. It is remarkable that, on the one hand, the existence of "the avant-garde" (sometimes plural: "avant-gardes") as such a unity is claimed or supposed by many authors, not least as a presupposition for all kind of reflections on "the avant-garde(s)," but, on the other hand, very little consensus seems to exist concerning the question of who or what has to be regarded as "avant-garde(s)," even in a double or triple way.

First, one can notice that quite decisive disagreement exists on the historical extension of the avant-garde. In the historiography of the European arts of the past centuries a number of different sets of phenomena, isms, artists, etc., have been labeled as avant-garde by different authors. One might begin by distinguishing a configuration of isms, which has been labeled by scholars like Peter Bürger and Matei Călinescu not just as avant-garde, but as "historical" avantgarde(s), comprising such movements as futurism, cubism, expressionism, Dada, surrealism, constructivism, poetism, zenitism, and many more.[2] These are not just historical because they are regarded as the true historical kernel of the avant-garde (as they often are) but also because they received the label "avant-garde" at a point when they were already history and when new avant-garde movements had meanwhile emerged (after the Second World War). Some simply confine the avant-garde to this historical configuration. Others also include later formations, described by Peter Bürger and others as "neo-avant-garde" or "latest" avant-garde,[3] including such movements as Cobra, Fluxus, Pop Art, the Situationist International, minimalism, concrete art, and land art. Still other authors, for example the British art historian Francis Frascina and the German historian Corona Hepp, use "avant-garde" rather as a label for developments in the second half of the nineteenth century, with a peak around the previous *fin de siècle*, and the "historical avant-garde" as their tail end.[4] Whereas Bürger or Wolfgang Asholt and Walter Fähnders[5] see a clear-cut rupture between the avant-garde and preceding symbolism and *fin-de-siècle* aestheticism, Frascina and Hepp regard symbolism and aestheticism as core elements of the avant-garde. But even wider notions of the avant-garde (or maybe "avant-gardism" instead of "avant-garde") can be found, in which "avant-garde" serves as an umbrella term for phenomena or concepts accompanying modernity from the Age of Enlightenment right up to the present, as, for example, in publications by Renato Poggioli, Charles Russell, and John Weightman.[6]

There are not only considerable diachronic differences but also many differences in opinion concerning the sets of isms, movements, and groups that should be regarded as part of the avant-garde in a certain period of time. Bürger by and large excludes cubism and expressionism from his historical avant-garde, whereas others, like Dietrich Scheunemann saw these as major movements of the early avant-garde.[7] The same holds true for fauvism and rayonism, which many regard as precursors rather than formations in the avant-garde complex. Constructivism, which is remarkably absent in both Bürger's *Theorie der Avantgarde* and in Scheunemann's opposing views, appears as a core element of the Central European historical avant-garde, according to the panorama presented by Timothy Benson (and what to think of Mondrian or Malevich?).[8] In a similar way, for the period after the Second World War one can observe that in some accounts Cobra and the Situationist International are virtually absent, with the so-called neo-avant-garde being confined—for example, in Bürger's *Theorie der Avantgarde*—to abstract expressionism, minimalism, Pop Art, and Fluxus. In this last case the difference might reflect not just a focus on different movements but also a focus on the United States rather than on Europe, rather as Bürger's predilection for Dada and surrealism can be put down to his background in French literary studies.

Nevertheless, both the preference for and neglect of certain movements is mostly related to some theoretical rationale as well. And here, once again, quite profound disagreement can be observed. Much has been written about the aims, the program, intentions, aesthetics, and practice of the avant-garde, but only very little consensus seems to exist regarding its common properties and features. Whereas—to take one of the oldest theoretical reflections on the avant-garde—Clement Greenberg stresses in his essay "Avant-garde and Kitsch," the elitist character of the avant-garde, its self-chosen isolation and detachment from the rest of society, Peter Bürger claims the opposite, namely the pursuit of a return of art in the practice of everyday life.[9] Whereas some, like Bürger, regard the attempted reunification of "art and life"—the escape from or even demolition of the ivory tower of autonomous high art—as the main purport of the early avant-garde, others, like Scheunemann, neglect this revolutionary intention and focus solely on the aesthetic response to technological innovations, new forms of production, and the development of new media like film and photography as the quintessence of the avant-garde.[10] Whereas some stress the totalitarian purport of "the avant-garde,"[11] others stress the antiauthoritarian, libertarian dimension of the avant-garde as a whole.[12] Many other disagreements over the purport of the avant-garde could be added.

2

Observing these different ways of understanding the term "avant-garde," one might ask: are all these different scholars actually referring to the same phenomenon? Probably not. The label "avant-garde" might be used nowadays as a fixed historiographic denomination, be it for different formations and configurations, but one should notice as well that it also serves as a metaphor, not just to situate certain phenomena historically, but also to qualify them. Unlike many other terms in the history of the arts, which are originally metaphors as well—for example, "movement," "current," or "school"—the term "avant-garde" is accompanied or even introduced in most historiographic accounts and theoretical assessments by often quite extensive detours reminding the reader that it was originally a military term: specifically, that part of an army that marches in front of the main army corps, explores the battlefield, and engages as first army unit in battles with the enemy. Aspects of this original military meaning are then frequently mobilized in the description of the aesthetic avant-garde, used as a parameter for the qualification of certain artistic groups, movements, individual artists, and currents as "avant-garde." The forward position of the "avant-garde" in a military context, the fact that this avant-garde is in the forefront, preceding the main sections of the army, operating rather isolated as the annunciation of something larger still to come, its operations in enemy territory, its function as a reconnaissance unit—all these and other aspects are then related to the emergence of new movements, new currents, new schools heading toward a new art, a new literature, new cultural practices. As well as exploring new territory, these movements and practices have to tackle the resistance of existing, traditional forces in the cultural field, before, when successful, establishing themselves as a new order or paradigm, as part of a linear understanding of history ruled by progress, constant innovation, the continuous replacement of the old by the new and, one might add, by an understanding of cultural history as a theater of war. The question, raised by Charles Baudelaire in the early 1860s, of whether such analogies are appropriate, might be left open. It is important, though, to see that the label "avant-garde" is often used as a rather arbitrary qualification, and not so much as a quasi-neutral historiographic denomination.

There is another important aspect in the common usage of the term "avant-garde." As mentioned already, one should keep in mind that the label only became fashionable—both as a self-denomination and as a historiographic term—after the Second World War. The term was introduced in the cultural field much earlier by the Saint-Simonist Olinde Rodrigues, who, in an imaginary conversation in 1825, offered artistic support to Saint-Simon with the remark: "It is we, artists, that will serve as your avant-garde...."[13] Thereafter the term was used (initially only in French and other Romance languages) in the sense of the common military concept of *"servir d'avant-garde"*—serving as avant-garde. It took, however, until the middle of the twentieth century before "avant-garde" became a more common, frequently used term. Even among those groups and individual artists, who are nowadays often referred to as historical avant-garde, the term was anything but fashionable. Occasions where those belonging to the historical avant-garde refer to themselves as "avant-garde" are quite rare. Some of these avant-garde movements certainly had a self-understanding in which they defined themselves in spatial metaphors suggesting that they were holding a position more forward, more advanced then other sections of the artistic and literary field. It was quite common to refer to oneself as creators of a "new art" or "newest art," or "modern" or "ultra-modern" or "young" or "youngest" art, but seldom as "avant-garde." There can be no doubt that the spokesmen of these movements preferred as a rule their own labels and brand names, like futurism, expressionism, Dada, constructivism, surrealism, *Zenit* or *De Stijl*. When Clement Greenberg published his essay "Avant-garde and Kitsch" in

1939 in the *Partisan Review*, he was, in fact, one of the first to use the label as a fixed denomination.

3

One should note here, moreover, that the term "avant-garde" has functioned differently in different languages and in different cultural configurations. Notably, in French the word *avant-garde* was more frequently utilized than in other languages; logical, one might think, since it is a French word, but the compatible words in other languages, like *Vorhut* or *Vortrab* or *Vortrupp* in German, did not have the same frequency in cultural discourse. In Spanish or in Polish avant-garde publications, one finds the words *vanguardia* and *awangardny* more often, used by artists and congenial critics as self-denominations or, frequently, as ostentatious (self-) designation—and as such, one might argue, as a fixed designation.[14] In most European languages and cultural configurations, however, the term "avant-garde" is—at least as a fixed term, as colloquial common denominator—virtually absent until the 1940s and 1950s. There are some older examples, which are often quoted, like the series of articles "Revue der Avant-garde" by the editor of *De Stijl*, Theo van Doesburg, published in the Dutch modernist review *Het Getij* in the early 1920s. The fact that this series is often mentioned is no accident. There are not many more examples. Kurt Schwitters, who was a good friend of van Doesburg and is nowadays seen as one of the major representatives of the historical avant-garde,[15] never used the term. He probably did not even avoid it. It was simply not a common category in his reflection on art or in his self-understanding as an artist. Indeed, in Germany, the label "avant-garde" was virtually absent in an aesthetic context before 1945, and this is not only due to the rise of the Nazis, who disabled any proper discussion of aesthetic avant-gardism after 1933. Even before this year the label "avant-garde" was quite rare.[16] Hence, the German art historian Richard Hamann's *Geschichte der Kunst* (1933), which shows a profound knowledge of what we now tend to call "historical avant-garde," does not use the term "avant-garde," but, instead, "expressionism."[17] In fact, the first German book to address in its title something called "avant-garde" in a cultural context is a collection of essays, *Europäische Avantgarde*, edited by Alfred Andersch in 1948–49,[18] with contributions by among others Sartre, De Beauvoir, Silone, Spender, and Koestler—so not directly "avant-garde" in the sense we use it today. The first book title addressing the "historical avant-garde" in German stems from no earlier than 1961: an exhibition catalog on the review and gallery *Der Sturm* with the subtitle *Herwarth Walden und die europäische Avantgarde*.[19] In the case of the Russian avant-garde, the label was also only attributed at a later stage: in the 1910s and 1920s other umbrella terms were used.[20] In an English-speaking context, finally, one finds the same constellation, as Paul Wood pointed out recently:

"Avant-garde" became pervasive as a synonym for "modern art" during the boom in culture after World War II. But many of the movements it is loosely used to refer to predate World War II by several decades, and at the time when they first flourished, the term "avant-garde" was not nearly so often used to describe them.... The concept achieved a kind of dominance or "hegemony" [only] in the period from about 1940 to about 1970.... In artistic terms, these were the decades in which a conception of artistic "modernism" was consolidated, whose most important centre was New York. Modernism, as a specialized critical discourse in art, declined in influence after about 1970, but in wider and less specialized thinking about art during the years since, the term "avant-garde" carried on bearing the meanings it assumed then, and to an extent it continues to do so. "Avant-garde", then, became not just a synonym for modern art in the all-inclusive sense of the term, but was more particularly identified with artistic "modernism", and hence shorthand for the values associated with that term.[21]

At least four reasons can be identified for the virtual absence of the label "avant-garde" in what we now tend to call the "historical avant-garde." In the first place, however much a Filippo Tommaso Marinetti, a Herwarth Walden, or a Theo van Doesburg may be regarded nowadays as prominent representatives of the avant-garde, they saw themselves primarily as representatives of their own avant-garde projects, as futurist, as expressionist, as constructivist, and so on. Marinetti, for example, not only referred to his own circle as "futurism" but also subsumed more or less the whole contemporary avant-garde under this label.[22] Yet, where Marinetti calls every avant-garde artist a futurist, the same artists are labeled by Herwarth Walden as expressionists, whereas Tristan Tzara calls them Dada and Van Doesburg presents at least some of them, whom we now tend to see as futurists, Dadaists, or expressionists, as exemplary collaborators of *De Stijl*; in other words, as constructivists.[23]

In the second place, as we have seen, in the early 1860s Charles Baudelaire had already rejected "the Frenchman's passionate predilection for military metaphors" and not least for the term *littérateurs d'avant-garde*.[24] This military connotation of the term "avant-garde" might be another reason that at least some sections of the configuration of isms we now tend to call "historical avant-garde" consciously abstained from using the term. Schwitters, who frequently spoke out against militarism, might be an example here.

In the third place, one can observe in contemporary publications by and on the historical avant-garde that a whole range of other colloquial umbrella terms existed: other fixed denominations such as "new art," "modern art," or "isms of art." Only when these terms became timeworn and began to lose their distinctive quality did it become necessary to replace them by another term, which could distinguish certain trends in the wider field of modern and new art.

In the fourth place, the fact that many movements from the previous decades, like expressionism, cubism, futurism, surrealism, and constructivism had become historical phenomena in the course of time obviously created the desire for an umbrella term of these somehow interrelated movements. And here the label "avant-garde" made its debut as an increasingly colloquial label—only after the demise of the early avant-garde of the twentieth century. As Hans Magnus Enzensberger pointed out in his essay "Die Aporien der Avantgarde" (1962), the label is marked by a curious contradiction that might well have hindered its popularity in previous decades: "The *avant* of the avant-garde ... can only be marked *a posteriori*."[25] Although the notion of "avant-garde" was not completely absent before the period, there is much to support Enzensberger's thesis that, at least as far as the historical avant-garde is concerned, the label functioned as a posthumously applied category.

<h2 style="text-align:center">4</h2>

The fact that—as a rule—the historical avant-garde did not refer to itself as avant-garde has several interesting implications. To begin with, this fact makes any reflection on the metaphorical purport of the label as an indication for the true nature of the labeled phenomena obsolete, at least as far as the early twentieth century is concerned. Such reflections, as in the preface of Richard Kostelanetz's *Dictionary of the Avant-Garde*,[26] say, rather, something about the properties attributable to these phenomena according to the author applying the label, rather than those labeled as such.

This fact also raises an important historiographic question. If the historical avant-garde, at least as a whole, did *not* see itself as avant-garde, to what extent was this avant-garde then a historical unity, or is this unity only a historiographic fiction? One important distinguishing feature of the historical avant-garde, according to avant-garde historiography, was the assumed self-understanding and self-definition as avant-garde.[27] What remains, if this historical avant-garde saw its art as new, young, modern, ultra-modern, and sometimes not even that— abstract artists in particular were aware of the proximity of their art to prehistoric artifacts—but only to a very little extent as avant-garde? Some avant-garde art was undoubtedly new; other art was—as the Dadaist Hans Arp noted in 1916—as old as the oldest human artifacts, in a way a return to the minimalism of pebble culture.[28]

Yet the representatives of the historical avant-garde indeed understood themselves as some form of a unity. While a demarcation of the contours of the avant-garde may be permitted neither in terms of a self-understanding as avant-garde, nor even in terms of the novelty or modernity of avant-garde art, a solution might be offered by the characterization (proposed by Asholt and Fähnders[29]) of the avant-garde as a project, one that, like Habermas's *Projekt der Moderne*, is conceived not as a completed unity, but rather as something that still has (or still *had*) to be completed—that is to say, a project that consists of a number of fragments, which are partially still isolated, yet indicate a future unity to come. One might think, following Gilles Deleuze and Félix Guattari, of a rhizome-like entity or multiplicity,[30] or, following Michael Hardt and Antonio Negri, of a multitude with some degree of cohesion, but at the same time marked by an obvious heterogeneity, diversity, or some extent of incoherence.[31]

Since the form and content of the artifacts, as well as the aesthetics and program of the groups involved, are marked by much heterogeneity and many incompatibilities and contradictions, the cohesion and collective dimension of the avant-garde are best conceived as the lines and nodes of a rhizome-like network, which can be regarded as the nomadic, deterritorialized *locus communis* constituting what we now tend to call "the historical avant-garde." The fact is, that in the configuration of isms, groups and movements nowadays often summarized as "historical avant-garde," a mutual feeling, understanding, or spirit of collectivity can be discerned. This internal, mutual understanding was documented in a book like *Isms of Art*, edited by Hans Arp and El Lissitzky in 1925,[32] or the earlier mentioned series of essays "Revue der Avant-garde" by Van Doesburg, as well as by the simple fact that many avant-garde reviews of the 1910s and 1920s, like *Der Sturm*, *De Stijl*, *The Little Review*, and *MA* not only served as a platform for the ism(s) and projects represented by the editors themselves but also for other isms.[33] In the first decades of the past century, the avant-garde network is more or less identical with the configuration of isms that is distinguished in studies that use "historical avant-garde" in a more restrictive sense, such as Peter Bürger's *Theorie der Avantgarde*.[34]

Now, in the present volume, it is the so-called neo-avant-garde, rather than the historical avant-garde, that is at stake. Here, the understanding of the avant-garde as a network also offers a new perspective, in particular when combined with the observation that the label "avant-garde" became a productive, active label only after the Second World War. The conception of the avant-garde as a fluctuating rhizomatic network allows for moments of crisis, like the First World War, the fascist and Stalinist repression in the thirties, the Second World War, and the cold war thereafter, in which many lines and nodes were endangered and extinguished, but others indeed continued, sometimes in exile, sometimes in some underground. To keep to the image of the rhizome, these are moments in which parts of the network are cut off and killed, parts of the root system migrate, new sprouts emerge in different places, superficially as completely new plants, yet stemming actually from the same root complex. Whereas often an almost complete rupture between "historical" and "neo-avant-garde" is assumed, one can observe that there are significant links and continuities between the early and later avant-garde. A clear example is the artistic movement Cobra, which had its roots in prewar movements, but which also served in later years as the starting point for developments like the Situationist International.

5

In many reflections on the twentieth-century avant-garde(s), the avant-garde movements after the Second World War have a slightly dubious or at least problematic character, which is already reflected in the label "neo-avant-garde." Certainly, from a current-day perspective, at a point where the neo-avant-garde is no less historical than the historical avant-garde, the label has some strange side effects.

Enzensberger notes that "avant-garde" is already marked by a strange contradiction, and the same holds even more true for the label "neo-avant-garde." Although the prefix "neo-" may seem perfectly in line with the belief in progress, innovation, and the new, typical for Western modernity, the discernment of "neo-" movements, currents, and styles—at least in the arts—has another dimension. It implies that the movement, current, or style involved is not simply new, but rather a new edition, a new appearance of something old, of something previous. As a consequence, "neo-" styles always possess an aura of the retrograde, the repetition, the epigone, of the *Ewiggestrige*, of living in the past, of trying to revive a past style. As such, something "neo-" is from the outset—at least nominally—at odds with the core avant-garde business of being original, of conquering new territories, of presenting something unprecedented. And it is certainly no accident in this context that many if not all commonly distinguished "neo-" movements, currents, and styles can be qualified as conservative, or as expressions of a conservative or a retrograde aesthetic stand (e.g., neo-Gothic, neo-romanticism and neoclassicism).

As Pierre Bourdieu has pointed out, in the modern European cultural field the (self-) presentation as avant-garde has an obvious strategic character in relation to the attempts of new artists and writers to conquer and consolidate a position of their own in the artistic and literary domains. One of the key aspects of this (self-) positioning as avant-garde is self-evidently the claim to be new, to be the first. In short, the avant-garde claims to be "vanguard," "completely new," "modern," "ultra-modern," or, put differently, to be original. As Rosalind Krauss outlined in her book *The Originality of the Avant-Garde and Other Modernist Myths*, this claim to be original is essential to the (self-) understanding of avant-garde movements:

> The avant-garde artist has worn many guises over the first hundred years of his existence: revolutionary, dandy, anarchist, aesthete, technologist, mystic. He has also preached a variety of creeds. One thing only seems

to hold fairly constant in the vanguardist discourse and that is the theme of originality.[35]

Krauss goes even a step further, arguing that "the very notion of the avant-garde can be seen as a function of the discourse of originality."[36] In the light of the apparent necessity of the avant-garde to be original, the "neo-" predicate is, of course, fatal. The term "historical avant-garde" may cause some unease on this front too. But is an avant-garde of yesterday still not to be preferred over a re-edition of yesterday's avant-garde, above an avant-garde, which is *not* original, as the label "neo-avant-garde" as *contradictio in terminis* is implying?[37] In the case of Bürger's *Theorie der Avantgarde* one should observe that the assessment of the historical avant-garde is quite negative as well. Whereas the neo-avant-garde is dismissed as an inauthentic copycat project, Bürger stresses from the outset that the historical avant-garde failed to meet its (or maybe more precisely Bürger's) objectives. And what is better? What is preferable? To be an authentic failure or an inauthentic success? In order to skip these questions, it seems better to skip the labels, which provoke them in an unnecessary and actually rather outmoded way, since the neo-avant-garde has now become a historical phenomenon itself, a historical avant-garde from a previous century.

Aside from the matter of the terminological adequacy of certain labels, one may ask, Were the implied postwar movements indeed the shallow repetitions that Bürger claimed? They might have repeated some previous experiments and sometimes in a way that did not meet the old standards, which were—as in the case of Dada—not seldom exaggerating mystifications.[38] There can be no doubt either, though, that in many respects the artistic practice of the avant-garde after the Second World War produced a completely different art—in all artistic disciplines. As Hal Foster suggested in his article, "What's Neo about the Neo-Avant-Garde?" one could argue that the avant-garde after the Second World War was in many ways creating, realizing, and developing what the previous avant-garde only started to think about.[39] The fact that the self-understanding as avant-garde only became common sense in the neo-avant-garde seems to confirm Foster's argument.

As for the labeling, the historical avant-garde may in fact be viewed as a retrograde projection by a neo-avant-garde trying to construct a history of its own, which is then turned by critical observers like Bürger against its inventors. The properties attributed by Bürger to the historical avant-garde—an anti-mimetic tendency; the rejection of an organic conception of art; the rejection of art as such or as institution; the ambition to take art out of the holy vicinities of the museum, the academy, the classical theater, the concert hall and opera house into everyday life; the elaboration of a new art practice in line with reflections of the Frankfurt School and Walter Benjamin—all that was rather typical of developments in the arts in the late 1960s and early 1970s, perfectly in tune with the programmatic of the politically engaged (or at least politically conscious) parts of the contemporary avant-garde.[40]

Given the fact that the label "avant-garde" only became fashionable after the Second World War, it seems more adequate, thus, to skip the additional predicate "neo-" and call the movements concerned simply avant-garde, as they themselves did in this period. In the 1960s and 1970s the predicate "historical" may have had a certain additional surplus value, insofar as it referred to the historical roots and predecessors of the contemporary configuration of movements and groups that indeed understood themselves as avant-garde. Noteworthy here is the fact that many representatives of postwar avant-garde formations and sympathetic critics could be found among the chroniclers and historians of the historical avant-garde. In line with Enzensberger, one might argue that only their effort turned the historical avant-garde into an avant-garde.

In short, in the 1960s and 1970s there was indeed an avant-garde that understood itself as avant-garde, to a much stronger degree than that configuration of isms in the first half of the twentieth century, which was only *a posteriori* labeled avant-garde. Representatives of the later configuration of artistic movements defined themselves as avant-garde, yet in a tradition of aesthetic renewal and artistic revolt, elaborating on previous experiments and enterprises from the first decades of the twentieth century. And it is certainly no accident that only since the 1970s has the term "avant-garde" served as a common, more or less fixed denomination in the historiography of and theoretical reflection on the arts. As should now be clear, this was a product of contemporary artistic movements that started to write a history of the arts in their own terms, using a label that was fashionable in the period when the history was written, not when it occurred.

6

Several factors have been mentioned, which probably contributed to the emergence of the notion "avant-garde" as a fashionable label in the second half of the twentieth century. One more needs to be added. "Avant-garde" might signal novelty or a claim to be the first, to be modern, to be at the forefront, and so on. It also signals, however, something else: political engagement and commitment. It is certainly no accident that those artistic movements that we tend to call "avant-garde" had their heydays in two periods of extreme political instability, change, revolt, and revolution—periods in which peaks can be observed not only in the activities of these artistic movements that, in broad terms, combined radical aesthetic experiments and innovations with the ambition to revolutionize both artistic practice and society as a whole, but also in political movements pursuing fundamental change and likewise claiming avant-garde status. Several aesthetic avant-garde movements participated in the revolutionary periods in the wake of the First World War and the protest movements of 1968, and not only aesthetically.

As mentioned before, resonances of the military origin of the term "avant-garde" continue to be heard in its more recent usage in an aesthetic context. It is indeed striking that almost every reflection on the avant-garde explores the military background of the term. This cannot be said for the political background of the term. Often—as in Krauss's or Poggioli's reflections, for example—only the metaphorical aspects of the original military notion are discussed. The fact that the political arena served as an intermediary between the theater of war and the cultural field is frequently ignored. Whereas the notion "avant-garde" may stem originally from the battlefield, the term entered the cultural sphere through politics, where it was already in common use during the French Revolution.

When Olinde Rodrigues described the mission of the artist in relation to the political philosophy of Saint-Simon, for whom the artist had to "serve as avant-garde," he ordained the artist with a political mission: as artistic avant-garde of a political movement, serving the realization of the ultimate goals of this movement. Also in later decades, one can observe (notably in France) that the label "avant-garde" implied simply "political," albeit in a progressive sense. So, when Baudelaire speaks out against *littérateurs d'avant-garde*, he is actually not criticizing aesthetically innovative writers, but rather politically engaged writers of left-wing provenance. The accompanying understanding of the notion "avant-garde" is obviously still very close to the original military meaning of the term and the actual role of the avant-garde on the battlefield: it fulfills the orders of some general command, which directs the army as a whole and is—to use Carl von Clausewitz's dictum—actually continuing politics with other means. In this context, as von Clausewitz elaborated in his famous *Vom Kriege*, the avant-garde only serves and obeys.[41]

It is not until the turn of the twentieth century that a new avant-garde concept emerges, again initially in the political, then in the artistic sphere. In 1902 Lenin publishes the pamphlet *What Is to Be Done?* as a contribution to discussions concerning the course of the Russian social-democrat party.[42] In this pamphlet he not only defines the proletariat as the vanguard of the coming revolution but also defines the Communist Party as the vanguard of the proletariat—the vanguard of the vanguard, as it were. The change is obvious: the avant-garde is no longer receiving orders, but giving them; it is no longer a few units serving as a battle force in the forefront, but identical with or supplanting general command.

This new, Leninist version of the avant-garde—as political leadership at the forefront, giving direction to the following revolutionary forces—is soon joined by an artistic version following the same rationale, one that draws upon an idealist aesthetic perspective. Within idealist aesthetics, as formulated initially by philosophers like Shaftesbury, Schiller, Schelling, and Hegel, art functions as a utopian representation of a better future life, and is ordained with the special mission of giving direction to human progress.[43] The missionary role of the artist in idealist aesthetics could easily be merged with the new Leninist understanding of an avant-garde, which likewise fulfilled the role of precursor, albeit in the political field.

This new conception, shaped by a primarily aesthetic perspective, is first articulated in the context of what later would be called "the historical avant-garde" by the Italian futurists in 1909, and repeated in many of their later manifestos as well.[44] The futurists' aesthetic orientation was—of course—completely at odds with the primacy of the political in Lenin's conception of the world. There can be no doubt, though, that in the following century artists who used the term "avant-garde" were often well informed about the Leninist concept, not least after the Russian Revolution, when Communist parties acted as a rallying point for the European and American critical intelligentsia until as late as the 1970s.

One artist to adopt the Leninist avant-garde concept and give it an aesthetic turn was Theo van Doesburg. In the first essay in "Revue der Avant-garde," van Doesburg opens with the claim that "all modern and ultra-modern groups of the whole world march" under the slogan "avant-garde"

> in the direction of a completely new way of expression in all forms of art. Avant-garde already expresses the notion of an *International of the spirit*. This international possesses no other rules and regulations than the inner urge to give life an ideal-realistic expression and interpret life in art purely aesthetically.[45]

Van Doesburg then continues: "At present, 'Avant-garde' is the *collective denomination for all revolutionary groups of artists*. And not just in the field of modern aesthetics, but likewise in the field of modern politics, the word is a general slogan and battle cry."[46] This last claim was undoubtedly an overstatement, as the label was actually quite uncommon, at least in the cultural field.

In the rest of the essay van Doesburg discusses only the aesthetic avant-garde. He apologizes that there is no place for the social avant-garde in the limited space he has in *Het Getij*.[47] Was this the real reason for excluding the social avant-garde, as he called it? Probably not entirely. In 1922, van Doesburg was also involved in an attempt to found a Constructivist International, already alluded to in *Het Getij* as an "International of the spirit." In debates around this International, the question of the two avant-gardes became a hot issue that finally led to a conflict between van Doesburg and some Hungarian constructivists with a communist inclination (including Ernö Kallai, László Péri, László Moholy-Nagy, and Alfréd Kemény). Were they two equal wings, as van Doesburg suggests in *Het Getij*? Was the aesthetic avant-garde actually superior? Or had the aesthetic wing to submit itself to the seemingly more general avant-garde in the sociopolitical sphere? In brief, the Hungarians demanded that "artists fight together with the proletariat for a communist society," and pleaded for the creation of a new "Proletkult-organisation" under the leadership of the Communist Party.[48] Van Doesburg answered with a manifesto, titled "Anti-tendenzkunst" in Dutch and "Manifest Proletkunst" in German, asserting that art has to follow its own rules, without any obedience to alien objectives, be it communist, religious, or nationalist:

> Art . . . as envisaged by the whole avant-garde, is neither proletarian nor bourgeois. It develops forces, that are strong enough to influence culture as a whole, instead of being solely influenced by social relations. . . . What we, modern artists, prepare instead, is the monumental work of art, superior at large to all placards, whether made for champagne, Dada or communist dictatorship.[49]

7

This disagreement evidently put an end to any attempt to bring about a Constructivist International. It is very instructive, though, for a double conflict that marks discussions throughout the twentieth century both *within* avant-garde sections of the cultural field, and among artistic and political groupings that understood themselves as the ultimate avant-garde. As far as the aesthetic avant-garde was concerned, one might argue that the conflict in fact concerned two opposed avant-garde concepts, of which one—the Leninist version—gave the self-assigned avant-garde a considerable degree of aesthetic sovereignty, while the other one—the Saint-Simonist version—ordained the avant-garde to political servitude.

Both concepts stemmed from the nineteenth century—the Leninist one from the end, the Saint-Simonist from the beginning. In this respect, it is quite remarkable that the notion "avant-garde," which was, hence, a product of the nineteenth century, could still become as fashionable and popular as it did after the Second World War, not least due to its political connotations, which are most evident in the debates in and around the avant-garde in the post-1945 period. Simultaneously, this long (pre-) history might explain in part why the label "avant-garde" soon came into disrepute: it was simply a concept of another age. Enzensberger had in 1962 already foreseen the short shelf life of the label "avant-garde" as a popular self-denomination in the artistic field. As he suggested, the "avant" of an avant-garde can only be distinguished in hindsight, thus posthumously, and so is quasi-automatically associated with the death of the phenomena labeled as such. In other words, the emergence of the category "avant-garde" as a common denomination in artistic discourse triggered straightaway rumors about the supposed death of the avant-garde. But another cause of the demise of the avant-garde concept was most certainly its tight relation to the political sphere, and within this political sphere to a certain type of left-wing radicalism that landed in a terminal crisis in the 1980s, and received its lethal blow when the Soviet empire collapsed in 1989. Much criticism in the late eighties and nineties, often from a postmodern perspective, targeted in particular the apparently totalitarian tendency of much aesthetic avant-gardism, not least on the basis of affiliations with political avant-gardism with undeniable totalitarian traits.[50]

At the same time—despite all suggestions about the death of the avant-garde, or the impossibility of presenting oneself still as avant-garde in the context of the high arts[51]—a Google search on October 19, 2007, shows that the term "avant-garde" could be found on 11.2 million Web pages on that day. If one adds the same term in other languages, for example, "vanguardia" in Spanish, the number rises considerably—to 15.6 million hits in total on the same day. Many Google hits do not involve any form of aesthetic avant-garde, but even if one reduces the 11.2 million hits for "avant-garde" by the additional search terms "art," "kunst," and "konst," some 2.39 million hits remain. And that is quite some more than the 21,200 hits that one finds if one searches for the exact formulation "death of the avant-garde." Some may believe that the avant-garde is dead, but they still have to convince the rest of the world, it seems. Automobile factories like Mercedes or Renault, lingerie producers, glossy magazines, and many other commercial enterprises aiming for maximum turnovers happily use the label. One other completely arbitrary example to conclude: in October 2004, the culture section of the Dutch newspaper *NRC Handelsblad* contained an article titled "Mona Lisa with Camel's Head: Chinese Avant-garde Flourishes in Shanghai."[52] The article is not hinting in any way at the popularity of the term "avant-garde" in Maoist discourse some three decades earlier, but is devoted exclusively to current developments in twenty-first-century China—in an exclusively positive, jubilant way. This and many other similar articles in art reviews in the printed press, as well as on the Internet, indicate that the notion "avant-garde" obviously has a vivid afterlife, despite its apparent demise in aesthetic debates in the late twentieth century. This resurgence of the label could be taken as further indication of its rhizomatic character, which reflects not only the heterogeneous configuration of movements to which it has been applied, but also its hybrid multitude of meanings.

Notes

1. This chapter elaborates and revises reflections on the historical phenomenon of the avant-garde in the European arts in Hubert van den Berg, "Kortlægning af det nyes gamle spor. Bidrag til en historisk topografi over det 20. århundredes

avant-garde(r) i europæisk kultur," in *En tradition af opbrud. Avantgardernes tradition og politik*, ed. Tania Ørum, Marianne Ping Huang, and Charlotte Engberg (Hellerup: Spring, 2005), 19–43; Hubert van den Berg, "On the Historiographic Distinction between Historical and Neo-avant-garde, " in *Avant-garde/Neo-Avant-garde*, ed. Dietrich Scheunemann (Amsterdam: Rodopi, 2005), 63–74; Hubert van den Berg, "Life and Death of the Avant-garde on the Battlefield of Rhetoric— and Beyond," in *Forum: The University of Edinburgh Postgraduate Journal of the Arts* 1 (Autumn 2005), http://forum.llc.ed.ac.uk/issue1/Berg_Avant.html; Hubert van den Berg, "Mapping Old Traces of the New: For a Historical Topography of 20th-Century Avant-garde(s) in the European Cultural Field(s)," *Arcadia* 41 (2006): 331–51; Hubert van den Berg, "'A World-wide Network of Periodicals Has Appeared...' Some Notes on the Inter- and Supranationality of European Constructivism between the Two World Wars," in *Nation, Style, and Modernism: CIHA Conference Papers 1*, ed. Jacek Purchla and Wolf Tegethoff (Kraków: International Cultural Centre, 2006), 143–55.

2. Peter Bürger, *Theorie der Avantgarde* (Frankfurt: Suhrkamp, 1974), 44; Matei Călinescu, *Faces of Modernity: Modernism, Avant-Garde, Decadence, Kitsch, Postmodernism* (Bloomington: Indiana University Press, 1977), 140.

3. Bürger, *Theorie der Avantgarde*, 79; Cathérine Franclin et al., *L'ABCdaire de l'Art Contemporain* (Paris: Flammarion, 2003), 33.

4. Francis Frascina, ed., *Modernity and Modernism: French Painting in the Nineteenth Century* (New Haven, Conn.: Yale University Press, 1993); Corona Hepp, *Avantgarde. Moderne Kunst, Kulturkritik und Reformbewegungen nach der Jahrhundertwende* (Munich: dtv, 1987).

5. Wolfgang Asholt and Walter Fähnders, eds., *Manifeste und Proklamationen der europäischen Avantgarde (1909–1938)* (Stuttgart: Metzler, 1995); Wolfgang Asholt and Walter Fähnders, eds., *Der Blick vom Wolkenkratzer: Avantgarde-Avantgardekritik—Avantgardeforschung* (Amsterdam: Rodopi, 2000).

6. Renato Poggioli, *The Theory of the Avant-garde* (Cambridge, Mass.: Belknap, 1968); Charles Russell, ed., *The Avant-Garde Today: An International Anthology* (Urbana, Chicago: University of Illinois Press, 1981); Charles Russell, *Poets, Prophets, and Revolutionaries: The Literary Avant-Garde from Rimbaud through Postmodernism* (New York: Oxford University Press, 1985); John Weightman, *The Concept of the Avant-Garde: Explorations in Modernism* (London: Alcove, 1973).

7. Dietrich Scheunemann, ed., *European Avant-Garde: New Perspectives* (Amsterdam: Rodopi, 2000), 7.

8. Timothy O. Benson, ed., *Central European Avant-Gardes: Exchange and Transformation 1910–1930* (Cambridge, Mass.: MIT Press, 2002).

9. Clement Greenberg, "Avant-garde and Kitsch," *Partisan Review* 6 (1939): 34–49; Bürger, *Theorie der Avantgarde*, 42–44.

10. Scheunemann, *European Avant-Garde*, 15–48.

11. Boris Groys, *Gesamtkunstwerk Stalin: Die gespaltene Kultur in der Sowjetunion* (München: Hanser, 1988); Dirk von Petersdorff, "Das Verlachen der Avantgarde: Rückblick auf eine ästhetische Prügeley," *Neue Rundschau* 106 (1995): 69–73.

12. Michael Scrivener, "An Introduction to an Anarchist Aesthetic," *Freedom* 40 (1977) 23:[I–IV].

13. Quoted in Călinescu, *Faces of Modernity*, 103.

14. In the 1920s one of the spokesmen of the Spanish avant-garde movement *ultraismo* published a survey of the early European avant-garde using the label "avant-garde": Guillermo de Torre, *Literaturas europeas de vanguardia* (Madrid: Edición Caro Raggio, 1925). In Poland, the futurist and constructivist art journal *Blok* (1924–27) presented itself explicitly as an "avant-garde" journal in its subtitle, *Czasopismo awangardy artystycznej*, meaning "Review of the Artistic Avant-garde."

15. This is seen in a recent exhibition in the Sprengel Museum in Hannover and Museum Boymans-Van Beuningen in Rotterdam; cf. Karin Orchard and Isabel Schulz, eds., *Merzgebiete: Kurt Schwitters und seine Freunde* (Cologne: DuMont Literatur- und Kunstverlag, 2006).

16. As pointed out by Ulrich Weisstein, "Le terme et le concept d'avant-garde en Allemagne," *Revue de l'Université de Bruxelles* 1 (1975): 10–37.

17. Richard Hamann, *Geschichte der Kunst von der altchristlichen Zeit bis zur Gegenwart* (Berlin: Verlag von Th. Knaur Nachf., 1933), 873–92.

18. Alfred Andersch, ed., *Europäische Avantgarde* (Frankfurt: Verlag der Frankfurter Hefte, 1949).

19. Leopold Reidemeister, ed., *Der Sturm: Herwarth Walden und die Europäische Avantgarde. Berlin 1912–1932* (Berlin: Nationalgalerie in der Orangerie des Schlosses Charlottenburg, 1961).

20. Gérard Conio, *Les Avant-gardes entre métaphysique et histoire: Entretiens avec Philippe Sers* (Lausanne: L'Age de l'homme, 2002), 9–14.

21. Paul Wood, ed., *The Challenge of the Avant-Garde* (New Haven, Conn.: Yale University Press, 1999), 10.

22. Cf. unpaginated reprint of the 1924 manifesto *Le Futurisme mondial* in Giovanni Lista, ed., *Marinetti et le Futurisme": Études, documents, iconographie* (Lausanne: L'Age d'homme, 1977). Although Marinetti claims the whole contemporay avant-garde and environs to be futurist in this manifesto, the Italian futurists, due to their obsessive predilection for the military, actually used the term "avant-garde" quite frequently.

23. Herwarth Walden, *Expressionismus: Die Kunstwende* (Berlin: Verlag Der Sturm, 1918); Tristan Tzara, "Quelques Présidents et Présidentes," *Dada* 6 (1920): n.p.; Theo van Doesburg, "Principieele medewerkers aan De Stijl," *De Stijl* 8 (1927): 59–62.

24. Quoted in Călinescu, *Faces of Modernity*, 110–11.

25. Hans Magnus Enzensberger, *Einzelheiten II* (Frankfurt: Suhrkamp, 1984), 63.

26. Richard Kostelanetz, ed., *A Dictionary of the Avant-Gardes* (New York: Schirmer, 2000): ix–xii.

27. Walter Fähnders, *Avantgarde und Moderne 1890–1933* (Stuttgart: Metzler, 1998), 199–200.

28. Cf. a programmatic note by Hans Arp from 1915 in Alfons Backes-Haase, *Kunst und Wirklichkeit: Zur Typologie des DADA-Manifests* (Frankfurt: Hain-Athenäum, 1992), 35; Ben Nicholson, Naum Gabo, and J. L. Martin, eds., *Circle: An International Survey of Constructive Art* (London: Thames and Hudson, 1937); Lucy R. Lippard, *Overlay: Contemporary Art and the Art of Prehistory* (New York: New Press, 1983).

29. Wolfgang Asholt and Walter Fähnders, eds., *'Die ganze Welt ist eine Manifestation'. Die Avantgarde und ihre Manifeste (1909–1938)* (Darmstadt: Wissenschaftliche Buchgesellschaft, 1997), 1–9.

30. Gilles Deleuze and Félix Guattari, *Rhizome: Introduction* (Paris: Éditions de Minuit, 1976); Gilles Deleuze and Félix Guattari, *Mille Plateaux: Capitalisme et schizophrénie* (Paris: Éditions de Minuit, 1980).

31. Michael Hardt and Antonio Negri, *Multitude: War and Democracy in the Age of Empire* (London: Hamish Hamilton, 2005).

32. Hans Arp and El Lissitzky, eds., *Die Kunstismen: Les Ismes de l'art. The Isms of Art* (Erlenbach/Munich/Leipzig: E. Rentsch Verlag, 1925). Although the book offers a survey of the avant-garde, the label "avant-garde" is not used by Arp and Lissitzky. It is only introduced in an inserted leaflet in the 1990 reprint. See Alois Martin Müller,"Letzte Truppenschau, Dernière Revue des Troupes, The Last Parade," in *Die Kunstismen: Les Ismes de l'art. The Isms of Art*, ed. Hans Arp and El Lissitzky (Baden: Müller Verlag, 1990), n.p.

33. These reviews often directed the attention of their respective readerships toward other avant-garde magazines. See also van den Berg, "A Worldwide Network of Periodicals."

34. In Bürger's case, though, with the essential difference that several movements that he denies the status of "historical avant-garde movements" (see *Theorie der Avantgarde*, 44) also belonged to the historical configuration.

35. Rosalind Krauss, *The Originality of the Avant-Garde and Other Modernist Myths* (Cambridge, Mass.: MIT Press, 1986), 157.

36. Ibid.

37. One can observe that the "neo-" label was used by former Dadaists like Raoul Hausmann and Hans Richter to discredit avant-garde developments after the Second World War. As the references in Peter Bürger's *Theorie der Avantgarde* indicate, Bürger based his own judgment on the "neo-avant-garde" partially on their polemical assessments, which aimed at securing credit for the role they claimed in the historical Dada movement. See van den Berg, "On the Historiographic Distinction."

38. Cf. Hubert van den Berg, *From a New Art to a New Life: Avant-Garde Utopianism in Dada* (Aalborg: Center for Modernismeforskning, Aalborg Universitet, 2006).

39. Hal Foster, "What's Neo about the Neo-Avant-Garde?" *October* 70 (1994): 5–32.

40. Benedikt Hjartarson, "At historisere den historiske avantgarde," in *En tradition af opbrud: Avantgardernes tradition og politik*, ed. Tania Ørum, Marianne Ping Huang, and Charlotte Engberg (Hellerup: Spring, 2005), 44–60.

41. Carl von Clausewitz, *Vom Kriege* (Berlin/Leipzig: Behr's Verlag, 1915), 274–81.

42. Vladimir I. Lenin, *What Is to Be Done? Burning Questions of Our Movement* (Moscow: Progress, 1969).

43. Cf. Terry Eagleton, *The Ideology of the Aesthetic* (Oxford: Blackwell, 1990).

44. Cf. Asholt and Fähnders, *Manifeste und Proklamationen*, 3–120.

45. Theo van Doesburg, "Revue der Avant-garde," *Het Getij* 6 (1921): 109.

46. Ibid.

47. Ibid.

48. Quoted in Hubert van den Berg, *The Import of Nothing: How Dada Came, Saw and Vanished in the Low Countries (1915–1929)* (New Haven, Conn.: G. K. Hall, 2002), 169.

49. Ibid., 167.

50. Cf. Groys, *Gesamtkunstwerk Stalin*; Von Petersdorff, "Das Verlachen der Avantgarde."

51. Cf. Paul Mann, *The Theory-Death of the Avant-garde* (Bloomington, Indianapolis: Indiana University Press, 1991).

52. "Mona Lisa met kamelenkop. Chinese avant-garde bloeit in Shanghai," *NRC Handelsblad* (October 15, 2004), *Cultureel Supplement*: CS3.

Part I

IDEOLOGIES

2

"Demolish Serious Culture!"

Henry Flynt and Workers World Party
Benjamin Piekut

On the evening of April 29, 1964, a group calling themselves "Action Against Cultural Imperialism" mounted a picket line in front of Town Hall on West 43rd Street in New York (see figure 2.1). Inside the hall was a "gala concert" sponsored by the West German government, with music by Karlheinz Stockhausen, Hans Werner Henze, Paul Hindemith, and others. The performers included Stockhausen himself, pianist David Tudor, and percussionist Max Neuhaus.[1] On the sidewalk in front of the hall were the demonstrators: philosopher and composer Henry Flynt; the artists Ben Vautier, Ay-O, and Takako Saito; Fluxus impresario George Maciunas; and the violinist and filmmaker Tony Conrad. (Amiri Baraka observed from across the street.[2]) They bore signs reading "Fight Racist Laws of Music!" and "Fight the Rich Man's Snob Art," and, according to *Die Welt*, made quite a racket by chanting "Death to all fascist musical ideas!"[3] The group's leaflet attacked the composer as a "lackey for the West German bosses," and claimed that his "repeated decrees about the lowness of plebian music and the racial inferiority of non-European music, are an integral, essential part of his art and its 'appreciation.'"[4]

On September 8, the group staged another demonstration outside Judson Hall on West 57th Street.[5] In Vautier's place was the poet and activist Marc Schleifer, later known as Abdallah Schleifer. The occasion was a performance of Stockhausen's *Originale*, a wild theater piece directed by Allan Kaprow, which featured such avant-garde and Fluxus luminaries as Allen Ginsberg, Charlotte Moorman, Dick Higgins,

Figure 2.1 Action Against Cultural Imperialism demonstration at Town Hall in New York City, April 29, 1964. Left to right: Henry Flynt, Ben Vautier, George Maciunas, Ay-O, and Takako Saito. Photo by Peter Moore © Estate of Peter Moore/VAGA, New York, NY.

Nam June Paik, James Tenney, Alvin Lucier, Max Neuhaus, and Jackson Mac Low.[6] The circus like atmosphere inside the hall carried over to the demonstration going on outside, with some performers reportedly trying to join the picket.[7] Even though the language on the group's leaflet seems quite clear—"Stockhausen—Patrician 'Theorist' of White Supremacy: Go To Hell!"—many commentators thought the demonstration was a staged part of the performance. In his *New York Times* review of the concert, for example, Harold Schonberg reported, "Some said they were part of the show. Others said no, including the picketers, but nobody believed them. . . . [T]hey looked like the participants in 'Originale,' they acted like the participants in 'Originale,' and they were dressed like the participants in 'Originale.'"[8] Jill Johnston, dance critic for the *Village Voice* and also a participant in the performance, wrote, "I don't know why the Fluxus people were picketing the concert . . . , but it might have been interesting if the director had invited the picket line to participate as 'guests.'"[9] In 2004 Flynt, who organized the demonstrations with Maciunas, recalled, "[T]he issue became . . . very confused. . . . I mean, people did not understand even the point that I was making. I would have to say they were disasters, actually. They were disasters."[10]

The confusion about the origin and meaning of these demonstrations has not subsided, because the story is often told from the perspective of Maciunas and Fluxus, the loosely organized performance art movement of the mid-1960s. In that version of the story, Flynt is cast as Maciunas's sidekick, the outside influence who pulled him to the left and set off the internal feuds of Fluxus.[11] Although he enjoyed a close friendship with Maciunas, and his writings appeared in some Fluxus and proto-Fluxus publications, Flynt's association with Fluxus was one of convenience and necessity; desperately seeking a forum for his ideas, Flynt took any publication opportunities he could find. Nonetheless, Stockhausen biographer Michael Kurtz attributes the *Originale* protest to Maciunas alone and makes no mention of Flynt.[12] The art historians Michel Oren and Hannah Higgins also frame these protests within the boundaries of Fluxus history, arguing, respectively, that Flynt and Maciunas's political program was a major factor holding the Fluxus movement together, and that it reflected a major rift within the movement.[13] Yet Flynt's demonstrations were about more than mere squabbles among members of the European and Euro-American avant-garde, and any critical account of his work that cannot widen the scope of its inquiry beyond the experimental art world is woefully incomplete.

In this chapter I hope to correct some of these misunderstandings and to introduce into an account of Flynt's developing attitude toward the avant-garde a set of references that rarely make it into conversations about American experimentalism and performance in the 1960s. This requires a trip outside of the somewhat parochial narratives of experimentalism into histories of the Left, the civil rights movement, and popular music styles. Drawing on new interviews with Flynt, I will concentrate in particular on his experiences in the sectarian Left between 1962 and 1967. By 1964 Flynt was a committed member of the Marxist-Leninist Workers World Party (WWP), and that organization was a major force leading him to the complicated position articulated in the 1964 demonstration. Flynt's engagement with certain tendencies in downtown experimentalism, his commitment to non-European musics, and his involvement in Workers World were interrelated moments in a more general movement away from European and Euro-American high culture, culminating in his abandonment of the downtown avant-garde in favor of a roots music-based populism. The year 1964 was key in this transition, and the following account treats the anti-Stockhausen demonstrations as a significant moment in Flynt's developing interest in joining African American popular music with Marxism-Leninism, a move that eventually led to his 1966 political rock recordings. Flynt produced these recordings to demonstrate how a communist cultural policy ought to sound, and did not regard them as "avant-garde," per se. Nonetheless, his theoretical treatments of African American vernacular music reveal a continuing interest in such avant-garde predilections as formal innovation, newness, engagement with new sonic technologies, and sonic complexity. Connecting these qualities to the black liberation movement and the wider fight against imperialism, Flynt sought to reframe these concerns of the avant-garde within the context of group identity and collective struggles for self-determination.[14]

"No More Art!"

Born in 1940 to middle-class parents in Greensboro, North Carolina, Flynt majored in mathematics at Harvard in the late 1950s. He was also a classically trained violinist and composer, whose close friend and classmate Tony Conrad (later a well-known violinist and filmmaker) introduced him to the latest music and ideas of the European and American avant-garde, particularly those of Californian composer La Monte Young, who moved to New York in late 1960. After withdrawing from the university in the spring of 1960, Flynt devoted himself to private philosophical and musical pursuits, frequently visiting New York until he relocated there permanently in 1963. In February 1961, Young had introduced Flynt to the New York avant-garde at his well-known concert series held in Yoko Ono's loft. Young's word pieces of 1960 inspired Flynt to theorize an aesthetic practice that could dematerialize the conventions and ordainments of traditional high culture; moving "beyond art" was certainly in the air, and Flynt was eager to contribute to the project. An important step in this regard was his "Essay: Concept Art" (1961), in which he wrote, "'Concept art' is first of all an art of which the material is 'concepts,' as the material of for ex[ample] music is sound. Since 'concepts' are closely bound up with language, concept art is a kind of art of which the material is language."[15] Concept Art held the possibility for Flynt of being an entirely new, unprecedented activity that could ultimately supersede "art" itself. Always a reactive thinker, his aesthetic projects at this time were specific responses to the concerns of John Cage and Young; as he later put it, "I thought I was explaining to them what their own professed goals meant. That was my purpose."[16] That his works and ideas were met with indifference and (at times) ridicule led Flynt to suspect that other experimentalists were not truly committed to discovering new aesthetic practices for which there was no mold. His loss of confidence in the avant-garde became more exaggerated in 1962 and 1963, when he developed an explicit anti-art position, grounded both in Concept Art and in a new theory of aesthetic experience that he first called "acognitive culture," then "Veramusement," before finally settling on the term "Brend."[17] The new theory dismissed institutionalized activities of serious culture (composition, painting, theater) on the grounds that they exist only because of social expectations and pretensions. Brend describes a purely inward-directed aesthetic experience, undertaken only because it is liked by an individual, and guaranteed to be "new" because it does not rely on someone else's artistic production. He later wrote, "[M]y anti-art theory was a philosophical argument that if taste is subjective, then nobody is more able than me to create an experience to my taste....I was serious enough about this to have destroyed my early artworks in 1962; and thereafter I did not produce art."[18] In early 1963, Flynt led anti-art demonstrations at the Museum of Modern Art, the Metropolitan Museum of Art, and Philharmonic Hall at Lincoln Center, and delivered lectures on the subject in the spring and summer. Photographs taken at the time reveal a variety of strident, agitprop slogans: "Demolish Serious Culture!" "Destroy Art!" "No More Art!" "Demolish Concert Halls!" and "Demolish Lincoln Center!"[19]

Young, who had been an accomplished jazz saxophonist in the 1950s, was also instrumental in Flynt's growing love of jazz. As Flynt later recalled, "Young's episode as a jazz pianist-composer was little celebrated, but it provided me with a permanent inspiration."[20] Both admired the recordings of John Coltrane, but unlike Young, Flynt also thought highly of Ornette Coleman (most of Flynt's music between 1961 and 1965, in fact, was an attempt to translate Coleman's style to piano, violin, and other instruments). Flynt was also interested in other U.S. vernacular musics, and hearing country blues for the first time had a huge impact: "I heard that, and it *completely* turned me *all* the way around. Totally. From that moment on...I've been...a conscious, dedicated enemy of...the European vision."[21] When Flynt and Young recorded a series of improvised duets in January 1962 (Flynt on violin, song flute, and saxophone; Young on piano), Flynt directed him to alter his usual swinging triplet subdivision to a faster duple subdivision characteristic of early rock 'n' roll players like Little Richard.[22] This signified a shift from Young's predilection for jazz to Flynt's interest in other more commercial styles, a transition in musical vocabulary that itself symbolized emerging social and cultural differences between the two. Young was not a populist, and was not responsive to Flynt's desire to take their act into the clubs. In a 1968 interview, Young stated, "The reason I discontinued my work in jazz was to progress into more serious composition."[23] Such a statement would have been unthinkable to Flynt, who was already beginning to view both jazz and vernacular musics as being far *more* "serious" than "serious composition."[24] The ideological gulf between Young and Flynt would never close, and with the exception of one encounter in 1969 or 1970, the 1962 sessions would be the final time they played together. Flynt went on to develop a personal style on the violin and guitar, combining Young's pedal-point harmony and static repetition, Coleman's free playing, and the riffs and licks of U.S. vernacular music traditions.[25] Flynt's first recorded example of this idiosyncratic style, "Acoustic Hillbilly Jive" (1963), features abstract noise explorations, Young-influenced riff repetitions, and the hillbilly sound that would gain his lasting interest.[26]

Concurrent with Flynt's education in jazz and black popular music and his involvement in downtown experimentalism was his growing commitment to the far left. The poet and anarchist Jackson Mac Low had given Flynt's name to the Marxist-Leninist WWP sometime in early 1962, and soon Flynt began receiving and reading their news-paper, *Workers World*.[27] A secretive and hierarchical organization, the WWP split off from the Trotskyite Socialist Workers Party (SWP) some years after the Soviet invasion of Hungary in 1956—WWP supported the invasion, while the SWP viewed the incident as an unsuccessful workers' rebellion against Stalinist control. The WWP's internal orga-nization and leadership style could be described as Stalinist—there was an exclusive central committee and party members were expected to accept the committee's direction without discussion. The party favored action over critical discourse and theory. Having organized one of the earliest demonstrations against the Vietnam War, WWP displayed the kind of commitment to anti-imperialism and Third World Marxism that is usually associated with the second half of the 1960s.[28] Worker's World should not, however, be considered a part of the New Left movement. Though it was constituted only a few years before the Port Huron Statement (1962) and the founding of Students for a Democratic Society, WWP was much more dogmatic than the students, antiwar protesters, Free Speech advocates, and militant civil rights activists in the New Left. The party's leadership, particularly founders Sam Marcy and Vincent Copeland, emerged from the industrial labor base in Buffalo, New York, even though its membership was no longer drawn from this sector of the working class.

In the pages of *Workers World*, Flynt read articles about anticolonial struggles in Africa, Southeast Asia, South America, Cuba, and the Caribbean. He also would have learned about a particular Marxist interpretation of the civil rights struggle. In 1928, over the protesta-tions of the Communist Party USA (CPUSA), the Moscow-based Com-intern (also known as the Third International) officially recognized the "black belt" counties in the American South as an oppressed nation, and thus cast the civil rights movement as one of nationalist libera-tion.[29] Though the Communist leadership withdrew the "nation-within-a-nation" thesis in 1958, it remained a crucial principle for black radicalism outside the CPUSA in the 1960s, when it received new support and theoretical force from Mao Tse-tung.[30] It was also of critical impor-tance to the majority-white membership of Workers World, who framed the global class struggle in terms of imperialism and the fight against capitalist European-U.S. colonial expansion. As a 1965 *Workers World* headline declared, "In Selma, Bronxville, and Vietnam: The Enemy Is the Same!"[31] The WWP claimed to "support the right of the Black nation to choose whatever form of relationship to the United States will best advance their struggle for liberation from oppression: that is, the right to integrate, separate, federate, or any other political path."[32] Before the slogan "Black Power" emerged in the summer of 1966, sectarian groups like Workers World consistently supported militant black radicalism; indeed, WWP's split from the SWP had been connected to their advocacy for Robert F. Williams, president in the late 1950s of the Monroe, North Carolina, branch of the NAACP.[33] Williams advocated armed defense of African Americans in the face of terror attacks from the Ku Klux Klan, and gained notoriety in 1959 when, after a Monroe jury acquitted a white man of assault and attempted rape of an African American woman, he declared, "This demonstration today shows that the Negro in the South cannot expect justice in the courts.... He must meet violence with violence, lynching with lynching."[34] When Williams became a national story, the SWP set up a front organization to raise funds and provide legal assistance.[35] Although the details of internal disagreements in the party may never be known, it appears that a faction that would later become WWP was the most vocal on this imperative. As WWP leaders wrote in 1959, "It is our tendency that has taken the initiative to build a revolutionary group *in the South*. And we are the first tendency to have *done it* .... The Negro movement of the South ... is most probably the torch which will light the whole powder barrel of the American working class."[36]

In the spring of 1963, a few months after the publication of Williams's autobiographical *Negroes with Guns* (which Flynt avidly read),[37] Flynt visited his parents in Greensboro, and observed a civil rights demonstration.[38] He sent a letter about the experience to *Workers World*, a letter they subsequently printed as an article.[39] Witnessing this event profoundly affected him; he wrote, "It was one of the great experiences of my life." The young correspondent had asked some protesters their opinion of Williams's advocacy of self-defense; he reported that "[t]hey didn't seem to think it was necessary .... But as one youth said cagily—'Not yet, anyway.'"[40]

It was his commitment to Workers World that brought Flynt to New York permanently in May 1963, when he began taking part in such party activities as demonstrations, marches, and meetings, including a trip to Washington, D.C., for the March on Washington in August 1963. The leaflet for the April 1964 Stockhausen demonstration reveals that Flynt had assimilated the language and concepts of orthodox Marxism. "[Stockhausen's] patronage comes mainly from the government-owned Cologne Radio," he wrote. "Like all court music, Stockhausen's Music is of course a decoration for the West German bosses."[41] While Flynt's rhetoric is clearly informed by the terms of class struggle, he also makes a more subtle point about the modality of Stockhausen's musical-theoretical domination. The leaflet begins by referring to a lecture that Stockhausen had given at Harvard in 1958, a talk attended by Flynt and Conrad. Although Flynt was only beginning to be interested in jazz at the time of the lecture, by 1964 he had, retrospectively, become enraged by what he remembered as the composer's patronizing remarks on jazz: "Stockhausen contemptuously dismissed 'jazz' as 'primitive ... barbaric ... beat and a few single chords ...,' and in effect said it was garbage."[42] In Flynt's eyes, Stockhausen did not even consider jazz to be music, or at least music of any significance. Through his lectures and the journal *Die Reihe*, Flynt argued, Stockhausen articulated a vision of music that only includes his own in dialogue with that of other avant-garde European composers. The music of the rest of the world does not even exist—or, in the words of *Die Reihe* contributor Wolf-Eberhard Von Lewinski, it "can be summed up by adding a question-mark after 'music.'"[43] By calling attention to the gaps and silences in Stockhausen's musical discourse, Flynt was attempting to reinsert subaltern musical traditions into the discussion, and thus to place Stockhausen and his colleagues into the context of a global hierarchy of cultures.

This motivation became more pronounced in the extraordinary September 1964 leaflet, "Picket Stockhausen Concert!"—one of the most audacious documents on politics and the avant-garde to come out of the 1960s. Here, the emphasis is on imperialism, and specifically the way that art music has supported European claims to global supremacy by "develop[ing] the most elaborate body of 'Laws of Music' ever known: Common-Practice Harmony, 12-Tone, and all the rest, not to mention Concert etiquette." Flynt points to Alfred Einstein's statements on jazz ("the most abominable treason") as just one example of a powerful apparatus that produces the grounds upon which musical value is assessed. Stockhausen is singled out as a target of Flynt's critique because, unlike his fellow "rich U.S. cretins Leonard Bernstein and Benny Goodman," the German composer is "a fountainhead of *'ideas' to shore up the doctrine of white plutocratic European Art's supremacy*, enunciated in his theoretical organ *The Series* [*Die Reihe*] and elsewhere." In 1962 or 1963, Flynt might have attacked this music because it made false claims to originality, or because it was pretentious. Now, however, he viewed the social pretensions of high culture as playing a crucial role in European global domination.[44]

The final two sections of the document bundle together Flynt's experiences in the avant-garde and the radical left with his passion for black popular music.[45] With himself obviously in mind, Flynt writes, "There are other intellectuals who are restless with the domination of white plutocratic European Art. Maybe they happen to like Bo Diddley or the Everly Brothers. At any rate, they are restless with the Art maintained by the imperialist governments." Even these intellectuals, he continues, are held in bondage by the arbitrary myths supporting the supremacy of European art, "surrounded by the stifling cultural mentality of the social-climbing snobs." Flynt's directions on how to break these bonds of snob culture make direct reference to his anti-art crusades of the previous year or two: "The first cultural task of radical intellectuals, especially whites, today, is . . . not to produce more Art (there is too much already)." Finally, naming his enemy along the intersection of race, nation, and class that was common in the rhetoric of the WWP, he proclaimed, "The first cultural task is publicly to expose and fight the domination of white, European-U.S. ruling-class art!"

Although the 1964 demonstrations have been somewhat clouded by the partial and incomplete understanding of critics and historians, they make complete sense in light of the three primary aspects of Flynt's work in the early 1960s. His avant-garde aesthetics—Brend and Concept Art—contributed to the 1964 protests as much as to the anti-art projects of 1962. If the avant-garde was truly interested in new aesthetic modalities—as Young declared in his "Lecture 1960," "I am not interested in good; I am interested in new"[46]—Flynt argued that they should "throw away the crutch of the label 'Art,' and . . . crystallize unprecedented, richly elaborated activities around unprecedented purposes."[47] Though Stockhausen's *Originale* appeared to be a transgressive work of avant-garde music theater, it nonetheless relied on old conventions to achieve this aura of transgression. Moreover, Flynt reasoned, Brend had rendered traditional aesthetic experience obsolete, so if Cage and his associates in the downtown experimental scene were serious about dissolving the boundary between art and life, then works like *Originale* were to be dismissed as reactionary, not supported and celebrated. Along with this dialectical relationship to the avant-garde, Flynt's musical allegiances were shifting to black popular traditions, which he had begun to see as an alternative to the solipsistic aesthetics of Brend. The fact that these non-European musics were ignored by Stockhausen in his writings on music was in turn given added significance for Flynt by the anti-racist, anti-imperialist ideology of Workers World Party. These impulses combined to motivate Flynt's public intervention against European music—each was interconnected with the others. As he told a radio interviewer in 2004:

> Here I'm deciding that the best musicians in the U.S., perhaps doing some of the all-time best records are . . . on the bottom rung of the status ladder. What conclusion do you draw from that? . . . One had to become socially involved, I thought . . . . You had the civil rights movement, the Cuban revolution, the Vietnam War, you had . . . an African political awakening, the so-called "year of freedom," 1960, in which many colonies gained their formal independence. At that time, all of this was the same thing to me.[48]

Indeed, in the same manner that WWP was making global connections in its class analysis ("In Selma, Bronxville, and Vietnam: The Enemy Is the Same!"), Flynt was combining insights and conclusions from each of these separate discourses, using Brend, Concept Art, and the race/class analysis of the left to critique the avant-garde. His skill as a polemicist would be honed in the years following the 1964 demonstrations; but his growing appreciation for the revolutionary nature of black vernacular musics meant that the target of his critique began to shift—toward the cultural Eurocentrism of the left itself.

"Communists Must Give Revolutionary Leadership in Culture"

Flynt spent the next few years as a party worker—attending meetings and demonstrations and occasionally speaking for them in forums on the race and colonial question. He also wrote for *Workers World* from 1964 to 1966, and even edited the newspaper for a few weeks in 1965.[49] His numerous articles, written under the pseudonym "Henry Stone," fall into three general categories: reporting on civil rights demonstrations and crimes throughout the United States; breathless accounts of decolonization and nationalization in Africa (Zanzibar, the Congo, Southwest Africa); and longer background pieces on imperialist aggression in Laos, Vietnam, and Indonesia. In July 1966, he interviewed three black civil rights leaders (Ivanhoe Donaldson, Jim Haughton, and Mae Mallory) on the subject of Black Power and what it meant to them.[50] In one of his last stories for the paper, he reviewed a benefit concert for the Student Nonviolent Coordinating Committee at the Village Gate, where Stokely Carmichael shared the stage with groups led by Marion Brown, Jackie McLean, and Archie Shepp. "The juxtaposition of Carmichael's high political awareness with a score of the black community's musicians was a logical, timely, and refreshing development," he wrote.[51] The review was the first time music—or any of the arts—was mentioned in *Workers World*.

The support that Workers World gave to the civil rights movement and to black radicalism in general should be understood in the context of a long history of white involvement with African American freedom struggles. The relationship between the two was often tense, and by the 1960s many black radicals were deeply suspicious of having their cause co-opted and superseded by the imperatives of white Marxism. Harold Cruse, for example, questioned the collaboration between the Trotskyists and the civil rights movement when he wrote, "This 'alliance' is meant to build the Marxist party, *not* the Negro movement, in order to rescue the Marxists from their own crisis."[52] Williams was also outspoken on this subject. Living with his family in Cuba after fleeing a trumped-up kidnapping charge in 1961, he eventually overstayed his welcome by repeatedly criticizing the Communist Party of Cuba for its implicit defense of racial hierarchy.[53] But unlike most white radicals who endeavored to direct African American freedom struggles from afar, Flynt tried to extend the movement by launching a postcolonial critique of his own immediate circle, the composers and artists of the white avant-garde. As he wrote in the September leaflet, "Whatever path of development the non-European, non-white peoples choose for their cultures, we will fight to break out of the stifling bondage of white, plutocratic European Art's domination." He was more specific in a 1964 *Village Voice* interview, explaining that he thought black jazz musicians and writers should be encouraged to go their own way, while their white counterparts "should devote themselves solely to the propagation of Afro-American art forms in white intellectual circles."[54]

It was becoming apparent, however, that Flynt's enemy was not only European serious culture but also the cultural Eurocentrism of the left. In WWP, cultural matters did not rank as a priority for the party, evidenced by the complete lack of coverage in *Workers World*, while the official organ of Soviet communism in the U.S., *Soviet Life*, only reported on festivals of heroic folk art and the occasional performance of a great Russian symphony. Flynt insisted that the Left's love of Woodie Guthrie-style folk music had to be brought up to date:

> I just found it absolutely shocking, because Workers World had deliberately latched on to the black issue . . . . Here they were, pounding on that in their newspaper, and yet the fact that there was an entire form of music which was created in the United States by these people that they were advocating for just completely bypassed them . . . . I found that just outrageous. I kept nagging them. I said, "You cannot go on like this, with Beethoven and Pete Seeger . . . . [T]he cultural revolution is right under your nose, right here at Atlantic Records. That's the culture of revolution."[55]

In fact, following the 1964 demonstrations, the head of Workers World advised Flynt that he shouldn't introduce a new theory through the flimsy medium of a leaflet. His project lacked political clarity, and if he wanted to make a complex theoretical statement, he would have to do so in a longer document. This resulted in Flynt's pamphlet *Communists Must Give Revolutionary Leadership in Culture*. The publication was designed by Maciunas and made a striking impression: the bold text treatment sprawled out over five wide columns of body copy, and the whole thing was folded four times and banded to a one-inch-thick slab of styrofoam, included to illustrate Maciunas's ambitious idea for mass-produced housing. It was published by World View, the imprint of Workers World, whom Flynt had persuaded to lend their logo to the project; but otherwise, Workers World offered no support.

Flynt's most developed statement on culture and politics during the 1960s, *Communists Must Give Revolutionary Leadership in Culture* shows evidence of his wholesale estrangement from the Left on the cultural question even while his suggestions for cultural policy were steeped in communist rhetoric and the Stalinist cult of efficiency. Explaining his motivation, the author writes, "*For clarity, somewhere, sometime, the best possibility* in culture for the present period has to be defined."[56] Flynt provides three conditions that must be met by a properly revolutionary culture: first, it must increase the productivity of labor; second, it must promote the equality of all workers and reduce the stratification of labor by nationality or other categories of false consciousness; and third, it must bring workers to grips with reality, and must "be done with escapism in culture." Flynt then investigates these three conditions in a range of cultural practices: the "applied arts" (industrial design), music (together with dancing and poetry), film, theater, visual arts, and fiction.

The section on music, by far the longest in the pamphlet, presents Flynt's case for the radical nature of popular musics. Although he lists styles from Jamaica, Africa, Brazil, India, and Cuba, his focus is on African American popular music, which he refers to in the language of the times as "street-Negro music." Flynt does not conceive of this as a narrow category, however, for it "includes every authentic popular music in the world today, except the European or Anglo-American, which is simply washed up."[57] Important for Flynt was that this music could not be reconciled with European bourgeois art. In an apparent swipe at folk heritage festivals and the like, he writes, *"Further, it must be absolutely clear that street-Negro music is not 'folk art.'"* Because the implicit judgment of "folk art" was that it was something antiquated, humble, and pathetic, Flynt was motivated to argue that the music of Buddy Guy, Bo Diddley, John D. Laudermilk, and the Trashmen was clearly none of these things, and thus not "folk." Crucial to Flynt's argument about the modernity of black popular music was the technological basis for its many innovations. Not only does the music use "advanced instruments" like the many types of electric guitars and electric organs, but it also engages with such cutting-edge electronic recording techniques as reverberation and over-dubbing, and relies on radio stations for distribution. For Flynt, all of these technological investments positioned "street-Negro music" in the vanguard of musical evolution.

Flynt's advocacy for "street-Negro music" was based not only on aesthetic and technological grounds but also on its subversion of the racial hierarchy that European music—both elite and popular—supported. Economic stratification had fractured the global workforce, Flynt explained, and a white labor aristocracy was now situated "at the top of the world proletariat." This upper layer of the proletariat "seeks to consolidate its privileges, and uses methods pioneered by the aristocracies of earlier eras," including the use of art to differentiate and consolidate the upper class. For this reason, European popular music now performed a reactionary role, in that it was understood to be higher and purer than low, "racial" "street-Negro music." In order to eliminate the stratification of labor and resist the formation of a labor aristocracy (his second condition for a revolutionary culture), Flynt demanded that all "folk music" and "folk ballet" be replaced by "street-Negro music." Because they were understood by Flynt to be projects of legitimization and purification, these folk genres betray just as much deference to "the mysteries of snob culture" as do forms like opera, Western art music, the "legitimate Theatre," bourgeois modern art, and poetry, and thus are equally responsible for the persistence of white supremacy.

Flynt then turns his attention to the internal dynamics of communist cultural policy. "Now there is no nonsense about bringing this music-dancing to the masses, because they created it," he writes. "The almost insuperable problem is to bring street-Negro music to the Communists." The problem, he maintains, is that Communists retain significant sympathies for European court musics. To address this unacceptable situation, Flynt offered several suggestions: Communists should begin listening to R & B and rock 'n' roll radio programs; they should replace their classical record collections; they should only play "street-Negro music" at parties, which ideally would take the form of dances. Only after the Communists have integrated "street-Negro music" into their lives will it be time to address their frequent complaint that this music is decadent and manipulated by the bourgeoisie. In particular, the hedonism of most of the song texts in these genres would have to be corrected: "Somebody will have to encourage an open call to rebellion in the lyrics."

That "somebody," it turned out, would be Flynt himself. By late 1965, he was not only theorizing and writing about the relationship between Marxist anti-imperialism and black popular music, he was also beginning to put his ideas into practice. After learning the rudiments of guitar playing from Lou Reed, Flynt began writing explicitly political rock 'n' roll songs, cobbling together a pickup band, the Insurrections, which consisted of sculptor Walter De Maria on drums, Art Murphy (who would later appear on Steve Reich's classic *Four Organs* album)[58] on keyboards, and jazz bassist Paul Breslin. Flynt played guitar and sang. The band recorded about ten songs in three sessions during the first half of 1966, a collection of material that Flynt hoped would show Workers World exactly how the movement's music should sound. For Flynt, this necessitated his reinvention as a Gramscian organic intellectual—that is, an intellectual who recognizes his position in the social hierarchy, and uses it to help communities gain revolutionary consciousness. In his 1980 essay "The Meaning of My Avant-garde Hillbilly and Blues Music" (revised in 2002), he writes:

> For me, innovation does not consist in composing European and academic music with inserted "folk" references. It consists in appropriating academic or technical devices and subordinating them to my purposes as a "folk creature." An outstanding prototype of this approach was Bo Diddley's use of the electric devices of pop music to project the Afro-American sound.[59]

Noting that "these repertoires are the voice of the unsubjugated autochthon," Flynt admired the iconoclasm and inherent rebelliousness of U.S. popular musics. His avant-gardist allegiance to progressivism persisted, however, and Flynt aimed to extend these traditions, as Coleman and Coltrane had extended the language of jazz. "Of course the musical languages of the autochthonous communities need to be renewed—to absorb new techniques and to respond to changing social conditions—and they also need to be refracted through an iconoclastic sensibility, an ennobling taste."[60] In his own music, Flynt's "new techniques" included the opening up of blues and country to extended melodic improvisation, the elimination of chord progressions, the incorporation of extreme glissando and ornamentation, and the complex, swinging beat characteristic of African American music—all of which make this music *more* complex than "serious composition."[61]

The songs were not exactly radio friendly; Flynt was no Chuck Berry. Nonetheless, the combination of Flynt's splintered guitar style and De Maria's rollicking approach to the beat created an unusual sound, perhaps more at home in histories of garage, punk, or no-wave than in R & B and electric blues. The influence of Young can be detected in the extended static harmonies of many of the tracks, and Flynt's lyrics made up in clarity what they lacked in poetry. In "Uncle Sam Do," he sings,

> Nobody talk peace like Uncle Sam do
> Nobody talk peace like Uncle Sam do
> Uncle Sam talk peace, and drop napalm on you.
>
> Nobody hate Africa like Uncle Sam do
> Nobody hate Africa like Uncle Sam do
> He send d' C.I.A. to make uh rightist coup.
>
> Uncle Sam stores his H-bomb in your town
> Uncle Sam stores his H-bomb in your town
> If it chance to go off, you'll never be found.
>
> Set uh fire under Uncle Sam's feet
> Set uh fire under Uncle Sam's feet
> Burn baby burn till he feel uh heat.

In other songs, Flynt celebrates the riots in Watts, criticizes the draft board's targeting of the poor, and fantasizes about the capture and cooking of a European missionary in Africa. He was initially inspired by Bob Dylan's "Subterranean Homesick Blues," which was released in the spring of 1965 and contained elliptical references to the counterculture and police surveillance, but Flynt's lyrics were obviously much more explicit and to the point.

Flynt was not entirely alone in calling for R & B and other black popular styles to be used in spreading revolutionary messages to the workers, but no one had offered such a developed justification. Roland Snellings (later Mohammed Askia Toure) wrote in October 1965 of "Rhythm & Blues as a Weapon," but his impressionistic celebration of the music as a political force presented nothing like the doctrinal rigor of Flynt's formulation.[62] Although it was common for soul musicians in the late 1960s to play benefits, donate to civil rights organizations, and speak out for the cause, historian Brian Ward notes that in the music of the early and middle 1960s there was little more than "sympathy and synchronicity" with the movement. Amiri Baraka observed that such songs from the first half of the decade as "Keep on Pushin'" and "Dancing in the Street," "provided a core legitimate social feeling, though mainly metaphorical and allegorical for Black people."[63] As Ward concludes in his magisterial study of race consciousness in black popular music, "[T]he claims that Rhythm and Blues provided some sort of explicitly running commentary on the Movement, with the men and women of soul emerging as notable participants, even leaders, tacticians and philosophers of the black struggle, have usually depended more on partisan assertion than hard evidence."[64] (The single notable exception is Nina Simone, who wrote the seething "Mississippi Goddamn" in 1963. Her refined cabaret style, however, was a far cry from the electric sound that had so captivated Flynt.) Indeed, it appears that Flynt's attempted integration of radical messages with the latest popular styles had no precedent. Although Flynt cannot be considered a "real part" of 1960s black popular music (*I Don't Wanna*, an album of the Insurrections material, wasn't released until 2004, and Flynt's music is unlikely to have been enjoyed by most R & B audiences at the time), it wasn't for lack of trying—he sent demo recordings of his duets with Young to Atlantic in 1962, and pitched the Insurrections material to Folkways and ESP-Disk in 1966.[65]

In 1967, Flynt left Workers World. He had grown dissatisfied with the party's unwavering support for the Soviet Union, and his friend Ben Morea, leader of the anarchist group Black Mask, influenced him to question the organization's rigid hierarchy and its stifling of open debate. His misgivings were reinforced by a lecture he heard Herbert Marcuse deliver in 1967, in which the Frankfurt school philosopher offered an immanent critique of Soviet policy. In the end, Flynt no longer wanted to be a foot soldier in such a party, and gradually dissociated himself from the group. Yet the ideology of Workers World had clearly been important in the development of his anti-art critique in general, and of his attacks on Stockhausen in particular. Flynt's involvement in anti-imperialist activism encouraged him away from the abstraction of the downtown avant-garde in favor of vernacular styles; he thought of his 1966 rock recordings as an entirely new project. Nonetheless, the Insurrections material shows the continuing influence of Young's pedal-point harmony and Coleman's adventurous approach to improvisation, and these influences would remain active in Flynt's music for years to come.

In 1980 Flynt wrote, "The utopia in human relationships to which my philosophy is directed is unattainable in the foreseeable future. Activities are worthy, then, whose contribution is to keep the dream alive. To ennoble the cultural media of a non-privileged, autochthonous community is a way of ennobling the community itself."[66] Flynt's avant-gardism consisted of embracing the sound language of his home community—that is, roots music of the rural South—and then extending it through technological innovation and compositional invention. This is a rather different view of the artistic vanguard than is usual—we don't tend to think of Cage or Stockhausen as linked to the traditions of a local community. Flynt looked to black performers such as Bo Diddley, Jackie Wilson, and Memphis Slim for inspiration, modeling his own extensions of U.S. vernacular musics on these earlier artists who successfully updated their tradition with new sounds, new technologies, and new kinds of virtuosity. In this regard, Flynt was more in line with theorists of the Black Arts Movement than he was with those of the white experimental scene. For example, Baraka's important essay, "The Changing Same (R&B and New Black Music)" attempted to chart a mutable African American essence as it appeared in both rhythm and blues and avant-garde jazz. The goal was to illuminate the role that free jazz played in the black liberation struggle, and thereby to connect this avant-garde form with more popular (and, perhaps, more "populist") genres. Like Baraka and other Black Arts writers, Flynt was concerned with repositioning the ideas of innovation, advancement, and technical "progress" into the context of group identity. As one of the very few 1960s experimentalists to tackle questions of race, imperialism, collective struggle, and the role of expressive culture in these discussions, Flynt's campaign to demolish serious culture was bewildering to many observers. Enlarging the frame through which we view this campaign not only dispels this bewilderment but also pushes conversations about experimentalism into productive circulation with other trends in 1960s culture.

Notes

1. See Raymond Ericson, "Showcase Offers Music of Germany," *The New York Times*, April 30, 1964, 29.

2. Henry Flynt, interview with the author, New York City, Dec. 8, 2004.

3. R. B., "'Stockhausen, Go Home!' Zeitgenössische deutsche Musik in New York," *Die Welt*, May 12, 1964, 11.

4. Henry Flynt, "Fight Musical Decoration of Fascism!" (New York: Action Against Cultural Imperialism, 1964), http://www.artnotart.com/fluxus/hflynt-fightmusicaldecor.html.

5. See Susan Goodman, "Anti-Art Pickets Pick on Stockhausen," *The Village Voice*, Sept. 10, 1964, 3, 8. A photo essay on the cover of the *Village Voice* from Sept. 17, 1964, also included an image of the protesters.

6. The performance is documented in Peter Moore's film *Stockhausen's Originale: Doubletakes* (New York: Electronic Arts Intermix, 2004).

7. In a 1980 interview with Fred Stern, Charlotte Moorman recalls that she and Allen Ginsberg joined the picket. The interview can be seen at http://www.youtube.com/watch?v=wiEJdOlgcDE.

8. Harold C. Schonberg, "Music: Stockhausen's 'Originale' Given at Judson," *The New York Times*, Sept. 9, 1964, 46.

9. Jill Johnston, "Inside 'Originale,'" *Village Voice*, Oct. 1, 1964, 6, 16.

10. Flynt, interview with the author, Dec. 8, 2004.

11. Michel Oren refers to Flynt as "Maciunas's sidekick"; see his "Anti-Art as the End of Cultural History, " *Performing Arts Journal* 44 (1993): 1–30. In the second edition of *Music in the Western World: A History in Documents* (Belmont, Calif.: Thomson Schirmer, 2008), Piero Weiss and Richard Taruskin include Flynt's leaflet for this demonstration, but misattribute it to Maciunas and the Fluxus movement (463–65).

12. Michael Kurtz, *Stockhausen: A Biography* (London: Faber and Faber, 1992), 132.

13. Michel Oren, "Anti-Art as the End of Cultural History" and Hannah Higgins, *Fluxus Experience* (Berkeley and Los Angeles: University of California Press, 2002).

14. For a fuller discussion of two significant subjects—Flynt's place in the avant-garde circle around La Monte Young, and his growing enthusiasm in these years for the blues, R & B, early rock 'n' roll, and world folk musics—see Henry Flynt, "Mutations of the Vanguard: Pre-Fluxus, During Fluxus, Late Fluxus," in *Ubi Fluxus Ibi Motus: 1990–1962*, ed. A. Bonio Oliva (Venice: Ex Granai della Repubblica Alle Zitelle, 1990), 99–128; Flynt, "La Monte Young in New York, 1960–62," in *Sound and Light: La Monte Young and Marian Zazeela*, ed. William Duckworth and Richard Fleming (Lewisburg, Pa.: Bucknell University Press, 1996), 44–97; Branden W. Joseph, "Concept Art," in *Beyond the Dream Syndicate: Tony Conrad and the Arts after Cage*, 153–212 (New York: Zone Books, 2008); Benjamin Piekut, "Taking Henry Flynt Seriously," *Institute for Studies in American Music Newsletter* 34, no. 2 (Spring 2005): 6–7, 14, http://depthome. brooklyn.cuny.edu/isam/NewsletS05/Piekut.htm.; and Piekut, "Testing, Testing . . . : Networks of Experimentalism, New York 1964" (PhD diss., Columbia University, 2008). See also Alan Licht, "The Raga n' Roll Years," *The Wire* (October 2004): 26–29; and Ian Nagoski, "That High, Dronesome Sound," *Signal to Noise* (Winter 2002): 50–53.

15. Henry Flynt, "Essay: Concept Art," in *AN ANTHOLOGY of Chance Operations . . .*, ed. La Monte Young (Bronx, N.Y.: L. Young & J. Mac Low, 1963), n.p.

16. Henry Flynt, interview with the author, New York City, Nov. 2, 2004.

17. Henry Flynt, "My New Concept of General Acognitive Culture," *décollage* 3 (1962): n.p. On Veramusement see "Against Participation: A Total Critique of Culture," at http://www.henryflynt.org. On Brend, see "Down with Art," in *Blueprint for a Higher Civilization* (Milan: Multhipla Edizioni, 1975), 63–66.

18. Flynt, "Mutations of the Vanguard," 121.

19. These events are described in Flynt, *Blueprint for a Higher Civilization*, 69–70.

20. Flynt, "La Monte Young in New York," 72.

21. Flynt, interview with the author, Nov. 2, 2004.

22. These tapes have not been published.

23. Richard Kostelanetz, *The Theatre of Mixed Means* (New York: Dial, 1968), 187.

24. In a 1974 essay, he argued that "ethnic sound elements" are "far more complex than the elements of classical music," pointing to the developed use of continuous pitch change (glissando), non-arithmetic durations, and a raga-like approach to mode. See Flynt, "The Politics of 'Native' or Ethnic Music," *Zweitschrift* 2 (1976): 27–28.

25. Recordings are commercially available on the Locus Music, Recorded, and Ampersand labels.

26. Henry Flynt, "Acoustic Hillbilly Jive," on *Back Porch Hillbilly Blues, Vol. 1*, Locust Music (2002).

27. Flynt, interview with the author, Nov. 2, 2004.

28. On this subject, see Max Elbaum, *Revolution in the Air: Sixties Radicals Turn to Lenin, Mao and Che* (London and New York: Verso, 2002).

29. See Robin D. G. Kelley, "Reds, Whites, and Blues People," in *Everything but the Burden: What White People are Taking from Black Culture*, ed. Greg Tate (New York: Harlem Moon Broadway Books), 44–67; and Cedric Robinson, *Black Marxism: The Making of the Black Radical Tradition* (Chapel Hill: University of North Carolina Press, 1983).

30. Robin D. G. Kelley, *Freedom Dreams: The Black Radical Imagination* (Boston: Beacon, 2002), 60–109.

31. "In Selma, Bronxville, and Vietnam: The Enemy Is the Same!" *Workers World*, March 11, 1965, 1.

32. Dierdre Griswold, "A Brief Resume of the Ideology of Workers World Party," reprinted in the House Committee on Internal Security, *The Workers World Party and Its Front Organizations*, 93rd Cong., 1974, 27.

33. On Williams, see Robert F. Williams, *Negroes with Guns* (1962; Detroit: Wayne State University Press, 1998); Harold Cruse, *The Crisis of the Negro Intellectual* (1967; New York: New York Review Books, 2005); and Timothy B. Tyson, *Radio Free Dixie: Robert F. Williams and the Roots of Black Power* (Chapel Hill: University of North Carolina Press, 2001).

34. Williams, *Negroes with Guns*, 26.

35. See Tyson, *Radio Free Dixie*, 111–15. On the SWP and their uneasy relationship with the black radical tradition, see Cedric Robinson, *Black Marxism*, 278–85. For an excellent assessment of the SWP's overtures to black radicals written in the early 1960s, see Harold Cruse, "Marxism and the Negro," *Liberator* (May 1964): 8–11 (part 1); (June 1964): 17–19 (part 2).

36. "Proletarian Left Wing of SWP Splits, and Calls for Return to Road of Lenin and Trotsky," *Workers World*, March 1959, 7.

37. *Negroes with Guns* was an edited collection of interviews between Williams and Marc Schleifer, who participated in Flynt's September 1964 demonstration.

38. Flynt, interview with the author, Dec. 8, 2004.

39. Henry Flynt [Charles Henry, pseud.], "I Saw the Birth of Freedom in Greensboro, N.C.," *Workers World*, May 25, 1963, 1–2.

40. Ibid., 2.

41. Henry Flynt, "Fight Musical Decoration of Fascism!"

42. Ibid.; ellipses in original. Though he was clearly paraphrasing from memory, Flynt was not too far off the mark. In the written version of Stockhausen's lecture, he refers to jazz as "melodic inventions within a given basic rhythmic and harmonic scheme," in the course of distinguishing it from more "serious" experiments in "directed chance" by Cage and others. See Karlheinz Stockhausen, "Electronic and Instrumental Music," in *Audio Culture: Readings in Modern Music*, ed. Christoph Cox and Dan Warner (New York: Continuum, 2004), 378.

43. Wolf-Eberhard Von Lewinski, "Young Composers," *Die Reihe* 4 ([1958] 1960): 1.

44. In his 1964 interview with Susan Goodman, Flynt mentioned that he was next turning his attention to sites of the social reproduction of

Eurocentrism by planning demonstrations at Juilliard and Art High School to protest the fact that they only taught European music. See Goodman,"Anti-Art Pickets Pick on Stockhausen," 8.

45. He even sent a copy of the leaflet to Robert Williams in Cuba. See Henry Flynt, "George Maciunas and My Work with Him," *Flash Art* 84/85 (1985): 49.

46. La Monte Young, "Lecture 1960," *The Tulane Drama Review* 10, no. 2 (Winter 1965): 75.

47. Flynt, "Mutations of the Vanguard," 109.

48. Henry Flynt, interview by Kenneth Goldsmith, WFMU, East Orange, N.J., Feb. 26, 2004.

49. Flynt, interview with the author, Dec. 8, 2004.

50. Flynt [Henry Stone, pseud.], "Black Leaders on 'Black Power,'" *Workers World*, July 22, 1966.

51. [Henry Flynt], "Black Music at SNCC Benefit Linked to Liberation Struggle," *Workers World*, Jan. 20, 1967, 4.

52. See Harold Cruse, "Marxism and the Negro," *Liberator* (May 1964): 9. See also C. E. Wilson, "Black People and The New Left," *Liberator* (June 1965): 8–10.

53. See Tyson, *Radio Free Dixie*, 292–96.

54. Goodman, "Anti-Art Pickets Pick on Stockhausen," 8.

55. Flynt, interview with the author, Nov. 2, 2004.

56. Henry Flynt, *Communists Must Give Revolutionary Leadership in Culture* (New York: World View, 1965), n.p.

57. Flynt's terminology is reminiscent of Herman Gray's recent reflections on "the road and the street, . . . places where musicians borrowed and mixed styles and experimented with new possibilities. In the process, they created music that was dynamic, dialogic, and fashioned out of the experiences and needs of everyday life." Herman Gray, *Cultural Moves: African Americans and the Politics of Representation* (Berkeley and Los Angeles: University of California Press, 2005), 49. My thanks to George Lewis for pointing out this similarity.

58. Steve Reich, *Four Organs; Phase Patterns* (Shandar SR 83 511).

59. Henry Flynt, "The Meaning of My Avant-garde Hillbilly and Blues Music" (1980; revised 2002), n.p., http://www.henryflynt.org/aesthetics/meaning_of_my_music.htm.

60. Ibid.

61. Flynt's essay was focused on his longer, instrumental compositions from the late 1960s through the early 1980s, but the Insurrections' songs belong in this lineage, for they were an early attempt to assimilate popular music traditions into Flynt's larger political and aesthetic program.

62. Roland Snellings, "Keep on Pushin': Rhythm & Blues as a Weapon," *Liberator* (October 1965): 6–9.

63. Amiri Baraka, "The Changing Same (R&B and New Black Music)," in *Black Music* (New York: Morrow, 1967), 208, quoted in Brian Ward, *Just My Soul Responding: Rhythm and Blues, Black Consciousness, and Race Relations* (Berkeley and Los Angeles: University of California Press, 1998), 204.

64. Ward, ibid., 290.

65. Flynt, interview with the author, New York City, April 1, 2005; Bernard Stollman, interview with the author, New York City, Dec. 5, 2006.

66. Flynt, "The Meaning of My Avant-garde Hillbilly and Blues Music."

3

Forms of Opposition at the "Politiek-Demonstratief Experimenteel" Concert

Robert Adlington

On May 30, 1968, the front pages of Dutch newspapers were dominated by news from the French capital. Headlines read "Paris in Confusion" and "Resignation Expected";[1] following weeks of anti-government strikes and protests in Paris, the overthrow of President Charles de Gaulle was widely predicted. That evening, a large audience assembled at the Carré Theatre in Amsterdam for an event that became a landmark in the musical life of the city. The "politiek-demonstratief experimenteel concert" brought together a remarkable roster of musical talent. Leading young composers Peter Schat, Louis Andriessen, and Misha Mengelberg were each represented by a new work. Schat and Andriessen had already gained a reputation as foremost carriers of the avant-garde flame following their studies with (respectively) Pierre Boulez and Luciano Berio. Mengelberg held parallel careers as composer and jazz pianist: in the early sixties he took part in Fluxus performances in the Netherlands, and at the end of 1967 he had founded the pioneering improvisation collective, the Instant Composers Pool (ICP). Mengelberg's collaborator in the ICP, the saxophonist and composer Willem Breuker—later to become perhaps the best-known figure in Dutch jazz—played in the ad hoc "mobiel ensemble" assembled specially for the concert. Also among the performers were Reinbert de Leeuw, later internationally known as a concert pianist and conductor of the Schönberg and Asko Ensembles; Jan van Vlijmen, since 1967 co-principal at the Hague Conservatoire, and later to become director of both the Netherlands Opera (1985–87) and the

56

Holland Festival (1991–97); the playwright, theater director, and Concertgebouw violist Lodewijk de Boer; and instrumentalists who subsequently went on to develop influential solo careers, including Stanley Hoogland, Paul Verhey, Werner Herbers, and Geert van Keulen. The conductor was Edo de Waart, today well known overseas from his work as Principal Conductor of the San Francisco and Sydney Symphony Orchestras (1977–85 and 1993–2003, respectively). The concert additionally included spoken contributions from Harry Mulisch, then as now one of the foremost living Dutch novelists, and Jan Kassies, former director of the Federation of Artists' Associations and secretary of the Dutch Arts Council, and since 1966 director of the Amsterdam Theatre School. Luminaries in the audience included Bruno Maderna, chess grand master and writer Jan Hein Donner, and numerous younger composers soon to gain prominence in the Netherlands, including Paul Termos, Guus Janssen, and Gilius van Bergeijk.[2]

The concert—which was subsequently toured to three other Dutch cities—formed part of a series of events mounted by young Dutch musicians in the late 1960s, in which hostility to the established musical world, identification with radical protest movements, and a conviction in the value of avant-garde musical experimentation intermingled in productive and sometimes contradictory ways.[3] The title of the event could not have demonstrated more clearly the belief that political demonstration and aesthetic experiment were natural bedfellows. Yet in statements made at the time, the composers repeatedly insisted that music itself could not be considered political. As we will see, the apparently exclusive focus of the new works upon purely musical concerns was one of a number of facets of the event that caused bemusement among the large audience, and that lent an air of rowdy uncertainty to the evening. More than one commentator was led to remark on a "discrepancy between theory and practice."[4]

I begin with a description of the concert itself, of which there exists no sustained documentary account. As with many of the political manifestations in 1960s Amsterdam, the concert was a boisterous affair, one that fully merits being retold in its own right. The second section briefly examines aspects of the concert that appeared inconsistent with its ideological goals: these include the organizers' attitude to the performers; their reliance on institutional subsidy; and their hostility to popular music and ideas of comprehensibility. More detailed attention is then given to the pieces by Andriessen and Schat. These were presented as purely musical experiments; but earlier statements by the composers point to a close relationship between their compositional preoccupations and the anarchism that dominated Dutch street protest in the middle of the decade. In conclusion, this affinity with anarchism is placed in the context of 1968 Amsterdam, when a growing interest in communism led to sharp differences amongst the politically engaged—differences that clearly manifested themselves during the concert, and that set the music at odds with the composers' own evolving political goals.

A "Madurodam Revolution"

The "politiek-demonstratief experimenteel" (PDE) concert was planned as a statement of resistance to existing models of concert giving. Two years previously, Schat, Andriessen, and Mengelberg, together with fellow composers Reinbert de Leeuw and Jan van Vlijmen, had gained public notoriety with a vigorously worded open letter to the *Algemeen Handelsblad*, attacking the programming policy of the Concertgebouw Orchestra and particularly its "amateuristic" approach to contemporary music. Their proposed solution was that Bruno Maderna should be installed as principal conductor alongside Bernard Haitink.[5] The letter was strategically timed. It appeared five days after a violent protest, engineered by the anarchistic Provo movement, during the controversial royal wedding between Princess Beatrix and the German Claus von Amsberg, who had belonged to the Nazi Youth during the Second World War. Smoke bombs were thrown during the procession; the aggressive police response that followed sparked an escalation of Provo protests and police clampdowns over the next few months.[6] For many young musicians, orchestral practice was redolent of the stagnant social order of the postwar era in the Netherlands, which the lively street demonstrations of Provo had sought to unsettle since 1965. The composers' letter was followed by a public meeting, a TV broadcast, and a pamphlet documenting the affair, the latter published by the literary journal *De Gids*.[7]

The campaign was unsuccessful, but dissatisfaction with the institution of the symphony orchestra continued to grow. The PDE concert sought to present an alternative to the predominating formats for "serious music" performance. The choice of the Carré Theatre as venue was significant: a former circus theater, it was and remains principally associated with cabaret, musicals, and revues (although in 1966 it had also been the venue for Peter Schat's ambitious music-theater work *Labyrint*). The concert's "mobiel ensemble," assembled principally from members of the Netherlands Wind Ensemble, the Amsterdam Percussion Group, and the Amsterdam String Quartet, was intended as a direct riposte to established symphony orchestras. Much was made of the fact that musicians were chosen to suit the idiosyncratic scoring of the music, rather than vice versa. Equally, the performers were chosen specifically for their commitment to contemporary repertoire—in critical contrast to the symphony orchestra, which was deemed "neither technically nor mentally able" to perform contemporary music.[8] The concert also showcased the potential of the Studio voor Electro-Instrumentale Muziek (STEIM), recently founded by Schat, Andriessen, and a number of other composers: all three pieces on the program involved some form of amplification or live sound diffusion. Details of presentation were rethought: the musicians dressed informally, and the start time was set back to a fashionably relaxed 9:30.[9] Above all, in contrast to the tokenistic practice of inserting a new work in a predominantly traditional program, the concert focused exclusively on music's "current language":[10] each of the three pieces on the program was receiving its first performance.

From its initial conception the concert was thus intended as a critical gesture toward the symphony orchestra. However, events in the first months of 1968 were to lead to a significant magnification of this political element. In January, Peter Schat traveled to Cuba to attend the historic Cultural Congress in Havana. He returned to the Netherlands convinced that Castro's Cuba, in sharp contrast to Soviet Russia, managed both to realize the basic tenets of communism *and* to cherish artistic experimentation: "In Cuba you can hear advanced electronic music played [from loudspeakers] on the street. Their attention, their spirit is directed towards it. The musical revolution goes in tandem with their own revolution."[11] This was not a case of sudden politicization for Schat, the basement of whose Amsterdam house had served as a meeting place for the Provos a couple of years earlier.[12] However, the trip to Cuba clinched an ideological shift for Schat, from the anarchism of Provo to a broadly communist outlook;[13] his work for the PDE concert, *On Escalation*, now received a dedication to Che Guevara, who had died the previous October. Schat had been accompanied on his trip by his friend Harry Mulisch, who had established a reputation in the Netherlands as literary spokesman for Amsterdam's radical political movements through a book-length account of the Provo years, *Bericht aan de rattenkoning* ["Message to the Rat King"].[14] Mulisch was to become an important collaborator for the composers as the concert neared. In May he was in Paris, witnessing with pleasure the development of the most iconic of the year's protest movements: "The pumps had no petrol, the banks were closed, factories and institutions were occupied, everyone hoarded what they could, now and then in the evenings the lights suddenly went out, and I was filled with a great satisfaction."[15] Schat and Andriessen briefly joined Mulisch in Paris, where they saw Sartre speak at the occupied Odéon Theatre.[16]

At a press conference on May 15—the day the Odéon was occupied—Peter Schat revealed the newly political emphasis of the concert, declaring that the event was intended to take a demonstrative position "against our late-capitalist social system."[17] The thirty-six-page program book for the concert, launched during the press conference, juxtaposed analyses of the three musical works with excerpts from the writings of Lenin, Mao, Guevara, Trotsky, Marcuse, and Adorno. In subsequent interviews, Schat elaborated upon his commitment to "undermining the capitalist system," and Andriessen confirmed that the intention of the concert was to "clearly underline our political conviction and to declare our solidarity with the world-revolution."[18] (As we will see, Misha Mengelberg was less convinced of the new turn taken by the event.) As the concert approached, added tension was lent by a growing public controversy around the much-loved Carré Theatre itself. At the time, its future lay in the hands of the wealthy businessman Reinder Zwolsman, who had plans to demolish the hall in order to build a hotel on its valuable riverside location. This, alongside news that Andriessen and Schat had just returned from Paris, stoked rumors that Carré, like the Odéon in Paris, was to be occupied following the concert.[19]

On the night of the concert itself, both "Sjiek Links" and "ultra-links" ("chic left" and "ultra-left") were represented in force.[20] According to one press reporter, the hall was packed with "revolutionaries, counter-revolutionaries, hippies, career-agitators, Vietnam demonstrators and a good many ordinary music-loving bourgeois."[21] Agitational literature, and posters of Castro, Guevara, and Ho Chi Minh were sold at stalls in the intervals, and red flags and banners were draped around the hall as the evening progressed (see figure 3.1). Between the musical performances, passionate political speeches were delivered by Jan Kassies, who predicted that the evening marked the inauguration of a newly democratic relationship between art and the public, and by Harry Mulisch, who addressed issues ranging from sexual liberation to poverty in Latin America, and declared Carré to be "the property of the people."[22] Outside, 200 policemen reportedly surrounded the building, fearful of insurrection.[23]

Figure 3.1 Red flags and posters of Castro, Guevara, and Ho Chi Minh are displayed by the audience at the "politiek-demonstratief experimenteel" concert, Carré Theatre, Amsterdam, May 30, 1968. Photo © Pieter Boersma.

Yet the attendees formed no united oppositional front. Before the concert, Mulisch had been fearful of the influence of "provocateurs," intent on disrupting the serious purpose of the evening by agitating for an occupation that would only leave the impression that the Left was "vandalistic" and "semi-fascistic."[24] His attitude was revealing of the uncertainty of direction of Dutch oppositional culture at this particular historical juncture. As the historian Hans Righart observed, "[I]n the Netherlands, 'May '68' had already taken place in 'June 1966'," when the Provo demonstrations had reached their height.[25] Provo had disbanded, however, in May 1967; and the focus of Amsterdam's counterculture subsequently shifted to the city's growing and conspicuously apolitical hippie scene. The Netherlands' radical student movement, meanwhile, followed the developments in France and Germany with interest; but Dutch student activism and widespread industrial unrest were only to become significant forces a full year after the Paris *evénéments*. Mulisch's and Schat's recent conversion to Marxism, and their distancing from the anarchistic Provo with which they had been so closely identified, were indicative of the transitional quality of 1968 for many Dutch radicals. A number of ex-Provos remained prominent in Amsterdam's political life, and the clash between their playful activism and the more earnest revolutionary endeavor of those now flirting with communism could be uncomfortable. This was played out in a very public way during the PDE concert by the "absurdist" interventions of the ex-Provo Jacob Jutte.[26] A week earlier Jutte had caused a disturbance at the conclusion of a meeting of Amsterdam's Kritiese Universiteit—formed by the students in imitation of the Kritische Universität at Berlin's Freie Universität—by addressing the meeting in an SS officer's cap, seized from an exhibition display case. Now, in the Carré Theatre, he noisily heckled the spoken contributions of both Jan Kassies and Misha Mengleberg, and twice made his way onto the stage, where (to a lively reception from the audience) he tested out some of the percussion instruments (see figure 3.2). Schat was furious at the disruption, and angrily castigated "these people who . . . think that revolution means undisciplined behaviour."[27]

A general disorderliness prevailed throughout the concert. The musical part of the evening was clearly of secondary concern to many in the audience, and the unapologetically avant-garde idiom of the new pieces prompted restlessness and then noisy disturbances, including choruses of hand-clapping, shouted slogans, and whistling. Folded paper planes drifted around the hall, and the rhetorical peroration of Jan Kassies' introductory speech was met with a streamer of toilet paper lobbed from the balcony. The motives of the concert organizers were unhelpfully clouded by Misha Mengelberg, who in his program note baldly disclaimed involvement in "this political diatribe disguised as a programme book." The heady atmosphere was further enhanced, as Mulisch later recalled, by "the metaphysical sweetness of wafting hemp fumes."[28]

Figure 3.2 Peter Schat (right) remonstrates with Jacob Jutte (center) during the "politiek-demonstratief experimenteel" concert. Misha Mengelberg can also be seen (left), as can the inflatable plastic chamber used for Mengelberg's piece *Hello Windyboys* (rear right). Photo © Pieter Boersma.

Following the end of Schat's piece—the last on the program—the differences among the assembled crowd came fully into the open. Permission to conclude the evening with a public discussion involving the country's most prominent student leader, Ton Regtien, had been withdrawn by the manager of the theater, who was fearful that this might ignite a more serious conflagration. Nonetheless, a substantial proportion of the audience remained in the auditorium and, with the help of a megaphone, a chaotic debate started up. Amid chants of "Viva Dutschke!" and impromptu renditions of the *Internationale*, opinions were exchanged about the desirability of occupying the building. For many in the press, it seemed clear that "the revolutionaries in fact did not know where they wanted to go with their revolution."[29] One contributor proposed a vote to establish the majority view. Harry Mulisch, meanwhile, attempted to persuade people to disperse, with the reassurance that the city authorities were about to buy Carré back for "the people." Peter Schat was preoccupied with carrying the percussion instruments—loaned from the Concertgebouw Orchestra on the condition that Schat himself took financial responsibility for them—to safety.[30] Schat's and Mulisch's subsequent departure—"not to the barricades," as one press reporter sarcastically noted, "but to somewhere more comfortable"[31]—was met with angry accusations in the next day's press that they were "pseudo-revolutionaries and salon-communists."[32] But the number of remaining occupiers gradually dwindled, until the last left peaceably at 3 a.m. In the words of one reporter, "music was made, but history was not."[33]

Musicians, Money, and Misha Mengelberg

Many of those present at the concert would have sensed that events in Paris had themselves taken a decisive turn: a few hours before the concert, Mulisch, for one, heard De Gaulle's famous radio broadcast announcing new elections, followed by reports of huge pro-Gaullist rallies in the capital.[34] This undoubtedly contributed to the evening's lack of revolutionary conviction. But so did a number of aspects of the concert that appeared to be at odds with the organizers' own ideological goals. For instance, the newly politicized tone of the concert had been decided without consulting the musicians, for some of whom it came as a nasty surprise. Many of them played for the Concertgebouw Orchestra, and their noses had been put seriously out of joint by a draft of the program booklet that, not content with declaring that "the symphony orchestra symbolises nothing less than the glory of our capitalist system,"[35] had linked the Orchestra to I. G. Farben, the German manufacturer of the Auschwitz gas Zyklon B. Some hasty diplomacy was necessary in order to prevent the musicians withdrawing a matter of days before the concert.[36] However, a number of them insisted on a statement at the front of the program book distancing them from the concert's political goals. Thus while Andriessen was busy reminding readers of the *Algemeen Dagblad* that "the workers are alienated from their production,"[37] the composers' own attitude to their musicians revealed some of the same high-handedness that they enthusiastically criticized elsewhere.

The underpinning of the event by various forms of public subsidy was the cause of further critical attention. The program book for this vigorously antiestablishment event identified no fewer than seven public funding bodies, including the Ministry of Culture, Recreation and Welfare; the City of Amsterdam; and (most piquantly) the Prins Bernhard Fonds, a cultural fund established by the husband of the reigning head of state, Queen Juliana. During the press conference two weeks before the concert, members of the press were not slow to point to the apparent contradiction of accepting financial support from the system the organizers sought to overthrow.[38] Schat argued in response that there was no alternative, and attempted to characterize the dependency as a decoy: "under cover of the subsidy-foliage we prepare for a revolution."[39] In his introduction to the program book, however, he acknowledged the difficulty of resisting "falling into the hands of the established order and thereby getting used as an ideal symbol of . . . 'the progressiveness of our social system,' or of a false pluralism that beats itself on the chest and declares that 'even so, we permit it,' without anything essentially being altered." The chances of this were increased, he conceded, "by breathing the (subsidy-) oxygen of the social system."[40]

Such difficulties might have been avoided had the requirements for the musical side of the evening been less costly, and had the music itself held a broader popular appeal. But such "commercial" considerations were very far from the composers' minds. Indeed, they went out of their way to distance themselves from the popular music that in the Netherlands, just as elsewhere, was fueling the counterculture.[41] Speaking shortly before the PDE concert, Schat argued that rock music was essentially anachronistic:

> The Beatles make exclusive use of the harmonic and melodic character-
> istics of the French court music of Rameau and the like: the aesthetic
> colour is pastoral, innocent, for which semi-castrato voices are very appro-
> priate. I enjoy listening to it, but it is not the musical expression of this
> time.... What's important is that ... which is done for the first time.[42]

The hostility to popular music was expressed in more uncompromising terms by Konrad Boehmer, whose article in the program book mounted an attack upon the idea of "comprehensibility," arguing that it was "by no means the expression of the ideal relationship between work and listener."[43]

Nowhere was this ambivalence about comprehensibility more evi- dent than in the one piece on the program that (paradoxically) actively encouraged audience participation. Misha Mengelberg's *Hello Windy- boys* comprises, in the words of Kevin Whitehead, "a friendly competi- tion between two wind quintets, who variously try to trip each other up or persuade their rivals to co-operate."[44] The competition is made more intriguing by the confinement of one of the groups to a soundproof plastic chamber, with communication made possible by an electronic sound system that is turned on and off at random. In his short program note, Mengelberg suggested that "you, as listener, can perhaps uncover the playing rules"; and in a spoken introduction before the performance he invited anyone able to do so to join in. However, the interaction between the instrumentalists is not fixed in advance; rather, it is deter- mined by six pages of written instructions that lay down a set of complex rules for navigating a number of rudimentary musical ideas. It is, in other words, a "game piece": entertaining for the musicians, but quite unpredictable and opaque for a listener. In this light, it is difficult not to see Mengelberg's apparently benign romancing of the audience as, in fact, an additional provocation, not least given the prominence of the politicized attendees from whom he preferred to keep himself well removed. Flagging up the existence of the work's obscure proce- dures—its status as a particularly recondite kind of *musica reservata*— was hardly in keeping with the socially committed spirit of the event. Unsurprisingly, the audience's contribution quickly degenerated into a welter of catcalls, booing, and premature applause, and the perfor- mance ground to a halt after eight minutes.[45]

On *Escalation* and *Contra Tempus*:
Autonomy and Anarchy

Mengelberg was, however, not alone in conceiving his music as being entirely detached from the concert's political ends: this view was shared by all three composers. In a 1967 interview with a Marxist student magazine, Peter Schat argued that: "[m]usic can never be intrinsically engaged: it is a disinterested game with high stakes, never serving particular interests. Understand me well: a composer can certainly be engaged as a person with what's happening. That's an entirely different matter."[46] In spite of the ideological reorientation he had undergone in the meantime, Schat appeared to adhere to this stance at the time of the PDE concert. In his introduction to the program book, he declared,

> Music is not able to express anything, let alone transmit political messages. On that point every musician spontaneously and rightly agrees. . . . [Music is not] able to alter society, or even to represent or feed the growing loathing of late capitalism with its inherent economic and fascistic might. Once again, music can express nothing other than music.[47]

The point was reiterated in interviews with the press, with Schat describing the idea that political messages can be translated into music as "infantile" and pointing to the necessity of a verbal element "in order to communicate our intentions more clearly."[48] This was seconded by Andriessen, who cited his compositional guru: "Music can, according to Stravinsky, express nothing, certainly not political convictions."[49] The composers' pronouncements on the link between music and politics placed the emphasis instead upon the framework within which music is presented—in other words, the trappings of performance. Harry Mulisch summarized the prevailing view: "Just like mathematics, music can only have 'meaning' in its application: through conjunction with words and pictures, or by making an opera for example. But it has *political* significance only through its performance practice."[50] When presented as part of a standard symphony orchestra concert, for instance, a composer's inherently apolitical endeavors were placed at the service of an event that acted "as an ideal confirmation of our social system."[51] The PDE concert aimed first and foremost to resist this absorption into the capitalist system:

> Music can certainly get used for political ends. It can just as readily be used as a status-symbol for a right-wing regime as for a left-wing regime, that is, if I remain silent about it . . . if I'm not careful that the framework in which it takes place is unambiguous.[52]

The composers' repeated insistence on the apolitical nature of their music, confirmed by their program notes' focus on abstract questions of musical organization, doubtless provided further cause for perplexity amongst the audience. In spite of their active involvement in the political movements of the time, the composers appeared to adhere wholeheartedly to the formalist ideology that had risen to dominance among the European avant-garde during the 1950s, and which many critics have since viewed as signaling modernist music's fundamental neglect of worldly matters.[53] Audience members at the PDE concert could certainly be forgiven for finding the music irrelevant to the pressing imperatives of the time. Moreover, subsequent commentators have argued that formalism, far from maintaining a position of political neutrality, carries its own reactionary freight by virtue of the assumptions it makes about listeners' competence to decode it. Pierre Bourdieu, notably, has argued that the ability to assume the "aesthetic attitude" necessary to the decoding of modern art's "games of form" is entirely dependent on social privilege.[54]

The composers' view of the relation of music and politics was not, however, untouched by equivocation. The program booklet for the concert, for instance, presented a range of views on the relationship between music and politics, some of them mutually contradictory. On the one hand, Trotsky was quoted (from his "Literature and Revolution") as arguing that art must be allowed to pursue its own path and had no responsibility to the Party. An excerpt from Marcuse's *One-Dimensional Man* similarly warned of the danger of allowing art to be absorbed into administered society and the consequent loss of its "oppositional, alien and transcendent elements." On the other hand, Mao was quoted as insisting that both formal *and* political considerations must be highly developed in art; and an extended extract from Guevara's essay "Socialism and Man in Cuba," while scorning socialist realism, also leveled harsh criticism at any concept of artistic "freedom" that disguised an underlying impulse to escape the problems of society, and the "decadence" that tends to spread "in the fertilised soil of state subsidies." For Guevara, experimental art too readily "becomes a convenient safety valve for human anxiety," and thereby defeats "the idea of using art as a weapon of protest"—an idea that both Schat and Andriessen had nonetheless explicitly discounted, Guevara's advocacy notwithstanding.[55]

The composers themselves, on occasion, also contradicted their assertion that music is of itself apolitical. Schat's observation, quoted earlier, that in Cuba, "the musical revolution runs parallel with their own revolution," signaled a faith in the congruity of artistic novelty with "progressive" social ideas—that, as Konrad Boehmer expressed it in the program book, the "fundamental alteration" of society should go hand in hand with the fundamental alteration of music.[56] Andriessen found similar progressive resonances in the innovative instrumentation of the pieces in the concert, with the prominent role given to electronic manipulation: the concert presented "a revolutionary symphony orchestra, revolutionary in its line-up and revolutionary in its foundation."[57]

Both composers had in fact ventured more specific parallels between musical and political ideas, albeit a couple of years before the

PDE concert. In an article written in 1966 at the height of Provo, Schat examined the relation of tonality and serialism, the principles of the latter having dominated his music since his studies with Boulez at the beginning of the decade.[58] The tonal system had rightly been rejected, he contended, as it represented a "hierarchy of tones" intended to ensure that "the society of sounds, which it controls, should be once and for all unalterable." But he now believed that serial thought, too, "cannot transcend the tonal thought-principle" because of the centripetal force exerted by the basic form of the series. Both tonality and serialism are "hierarchical-deterministic approaches to sound"—"reflections of each other," rather than opposites. A real opposition to the "mono-central tonality idea," Schat argues, can only be found in "anarchy, a world of fragments and ad hoc solutions, chaos." In compositional terms this meant opening oneself to the widest range of compositional resources, including tonal and serial material, "note constellations," noise, "time structures," and chance. At the same time, Schat's choice of terminology here established a clear (if tacit) connection between his purely compositional manifesto and the political ideology with which he was at the time intimately associated—that of Provo, which, as its founding statement had declared, "considered *anarchism* as the source of inspiration for opposition."[59]

Andriessen had enjoyed no comparable involvement with Provo, but he was not left untouched by the politicization of these years, and, writing in 1966, he also made a connection between his compositional practice and the period's social unrest. For Andriessen, the key principle was what he termed "stylessness," a principle that he was currently exploring in a series of works revolving around quotation and stylistic allusion: "Scores are now being created which are collages of other scores. . . . I would call this phenomenon a kind of democratisation: there is no idolising of individuals, nor any subjectivity, and in that sense society, or rather the awareness of society, has had influence."[60] A year later, he focused the analogy further: "If tonal music is a form of feudalism, then twelve-tone music is democracy, anarchy is the future, and so stylelessness will also increase in significance."[61] Andriessen's comments have in common with Schat's the implication of the admission of a broader range of types of material to the composer's palette—an admission that characterized much avant-garde music in the later 1960s, in no small part as a symbol of the cultural democratizing of the era. But whereas Schat focuses on the abstract properties of compositional material, Andriessen shifts the emphasis toward the agency of the composer in his or her social context: for him, the analogy hangs on the ousting of the monologic (and in Andriessen's eyes, autocratic) voice of the artist by a neutral handling of the received forms thrown up by contemporary culture. As his 1966 article spelled out, pop art's celebration of the commonplace—a phenomenon that represents "the socialization of art on a scale unequalled in history"—provided a model for musical stylelessness.[62]

In light of comments such as these, it is not surprising to discover that, on closer inspection, both composers' pieces for the PDE concert, far from remaining wholly detached from the politicized context in which they were presented, take up positions in the political debate. The works' "purely musical," essentially formalist concerns—the "disinterested games" with which both composers professed to be wholly preoccupied—need, in other words, to be understood as significantly shaped by their ideological commitments, and indeed comprise one of the principal means through which this engagement is handled.[63] This is particularly evident in Peter Schat's piece *On Escalation*. The score eschews all extra-musical reference, beyond the Guevara dedication; and Schat's programme note explained that the concept of "escalation" refers to various musical processes, a connotation reinforced by the piece's periodic quotations from Ravel's *Bolero*. However, the work's title is in fact borrowed from a study published in 1965 by the cold war military strategist Herman Kahn, which evaluates the likely stages of international conflict in the nuclear age. Kahn had gained notoriety among leftist circles for his advocacy of the feasibility of nuclear warfare; excerpts from his book also make an appearance in Luigi Nono's Vietnam piece *A floresta è jovem e cheja de vida* ("The Forest Is Young and Full of Life," 1966). Schat, like Nono, appropriated Kahn's ideas for contrary ideological ends. His piece stages a gradually "escalating" symbolic revolution, in which the "dictatorial" conductor is overthrown by six guerrilla practitioners playing a vast array of percussion instruments. As Schat explained in his program note, the music is split into two halves: that which occurs "inside the score," by which Schat means fully notated music under the control of the conductor; and that which occurs "outside the score," meaning more improvisatory material triggered by musical and gestural cues from the percussionists. The stage layout positions the percussionists in a large circle, with the other instrumentalists arranged between each percussionist. In the course of the piece, all of the instrumentalists shift from an initial loyalty to the beat of the conductor to join the percussionists in a "led improvisation." Shortly before the conclusion, the score announces "Conductor dismissed."

On Escalation makes full use of the range of ad hoc compositional materials envisaged in Schat's 1966 article; and its fundamental process—the decentralization of authority—underscores the anarchist connection. The liberatory ethos of the piece is further symbolized by the aleatoricism associated with the percussionists' "led improvisation." *On Escalation* makes use of a notational device previously deployed in Schat's theater work *Labyrint*, whereby short notated cues arranged around a geometric shape may be played by the percussionist in any order; these then trigger musical fragments positioned at the same place on the shape in the parts of the instruments following that percussionist (example 3.1). The instrumentalists' fragments in turn

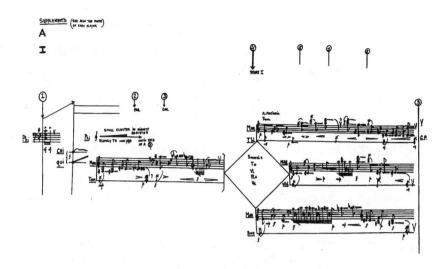

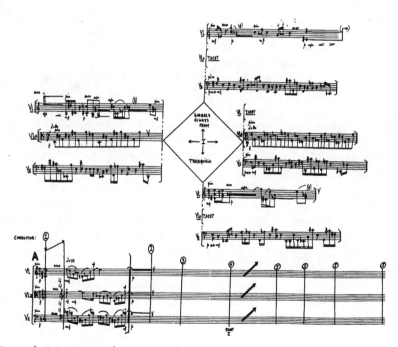

Example 3.1 Peter Schat, *On Escalation*, p. 18 of full score, showing percussion cues for string players at start of piece. Reproduced by kind permission of Donemus, publishing house and information center of Dutch contemporary music.

become less fixed as the piece progresses: first, precise rhythmic values are jettisoned; later, the instrumentalists are presented simply with a collection of pitches and rhythms on which to improvise. The piece accordingly culminates in a collective jam session.

Andriessen's piece *Contra Tempus* does not emulate *On Escalation*'s concrete enaction of the overthrow of power; instead, it extends his exploration of the idea of stylelessness, whose political ramifications he had laid out two years previously. The work's title—"Against Time"—can, like "On Escalation," be understood to refer to purely musical processes, and Andriessen's program note lists a number of these: the proportional structure of the score (6:4:5:8:7), which gives the sense of certain sections "stealing" time from other sections; simultaneous processes of acceleration and deceleration; the use of two or more different tempi simultaneously. But additionally, it is intended polemically, as a statement of intent to admit musical materials drawn from diverse historical periods. This is most obviously reflected in the use of quotation in the piece's third section, where phrases from Machaut's Mass are juxtaposed with fragments from Andriessen's own *Ittrospezione III* (1965)—a direct expression of Andriessen's conviction that musical citation "needs to be conceived of as an engagement, an identification, a recognition of oneself in something different."[64] In fact, *Contra Tempus* makes less use of quotation and style citation than earlier works such as *Souvenirs d'Enfance* (1966) and *Anachronie I* (1967). But the anarchistic disavowal of a prevailing unitary discourse is expressed through other means, notably a sense of abrupt formal dissociation. This is particularly marked at the start of the fourth section, which suddenly embarks on a rasping timbral experimentation, in the form of scraped piano strings, oboe multiphonics, and muted brass and string glissandi. Elsewhere, sharply etched instrumental contrasts underline the music's unpredictable and apparently arbitrary successions.[65]

Above all, in *Contra Tempus* stylelessness manifests itself in terms of what Andriessen calls the "dissolution of style" ("stijlverval")[66]—and specifically, the atrophy of the proprieties of serial technique, in which he had gained a rigorous training during his studies with Berio. The twelve-note series that forms the basic material for the first part of the piece, for instance, contains (as he explains in his program note) both a major and minor triad, by virtue of an interchangeable B flat and B natural in the middle of the row (example 3.2). This facilitates the emergence of harmonies that clearly allude to functional tonality—and which thereby point decisively forward to Andriessen's later music. The work's scoring is also intended as an "anachronistic" reaction "to the heterogeneous forces used in strict atonal music":[67] in place of pointillism and orchestrational fragmentation, block scoring is preferred, with families of instruments typically combined homophonically or even in unison.

Example 3.2 Twelve-note series for Louis Andriessen, *Contra Tempus*.

But the most pointed form of resistance to serial orthodoxy is indicated at the start of Andriessen's program note, where he recalls the "despair" aroused by the exacting compositional demands of his intricate serial score *Ittrospezione II*, written for Berio in 1963. To let off steam, he indulged in "wild piano improvisations," subsequently notated in the graphic score *Registers*; and he came to the conclusion that "it makes no difference whether you do or don't write notes" (while conceding that musicians usually feel happier with them).[68] The continuing importance of improvisation for Andriessen appears to be born out in *Contra Tempus* by the trenchant opening section for four keyboards, where the twelve-note series is clearly spelled out at the start (see example 3.3), but thereafter appears to act as a point of reference rather than determining the fine detail. (The first four notes of the series recur particularly prominently, but otherwise both the complete note-row and recognizable segments of it frequently disappear from view.) In these ways, the piece makes clear that "the exceptional and the dangerous"—which Andriessen claimed in the program book to be "the most important qualities of a composition"—are to be sought in the avoidance of all authority, including that which had come to dominate the mainstream of European avant-garde music.

Example 3.3 Louis Andriessen, *Contra Tempus*, opening page (reduced score; original scoring: vibraphone, glockenspiel, and four amplified keyboards). © Boosey & Hawkes Music Publishers Ltd. Reproduced by permission.

The Politiek-Demonstratief
Experimenteel Concert in Context

In both *On Escalation* and *Contra Tempus*, the composers' "purely musical" preoccupations can be directly connected to elements of the politicized milieu in which they worked—in particular, the anarchism of Provo. To what extent others at the concert were able or prepared to read this symbolism from the inner workings of the scores remained a moot point. But a more general level of affinity between the composers' endeavors and Provo was beyond question. In their publications and pronouncements Provo had laid great emphasis upon "self-development, self-realisation, the development of personal, individual creativity," impulses inhibited by repressive governments and consumer culture.[69] Prompted by the Situationist ideas of the painter Constant Nieuwenhuys, Provo argued that "you are your own creativity," and urged people to "play in all forms and fantasies." For the leading Provo Roel van Duyn, the absurdity and antiauthoritarianism of Dada made it the "artistic pendant of anarchism"; Dada "has realised in art what anarchism advocates for society." The three pieces at the PDE concert could hardly be considered Dadaist, but they are certainly examples of the imaginative creativity "in all forms and fantasies" that Provo sought to promote. Since the nineteenth century anarchist thinkers had defended artistic individualism from the constraints imposed by official institutions, and Provo's attitude merely represented an extension of the historical connection between anarchism and the avant-garde.[70]

At the same time, though, those aspects of Provo's anarchism that made it receptive to avant-garde art—and which had made Provo appealing to progressive artists in equal measure—were also those that raised the greatest friction with Marxist communism. Provo was suspicious of communist dogma and its centralizing and bureaucratic character; but it was also unapologetically disdainful of the desires of the masses. Provo's analysis of contemporary society placed the "provotariat" minority—the politicized students, artists, and street dropouts who creatively resisted authority—in opposition to the conformist majority, the mass of "acquisitive, hard-working, oppressed, boring, unimaginative" people who had sold out to the superficial products of commerce.[71] The latter included both bourgeois and working classes, who were termed the "klootjesvolk"—literally, the "testicles-people," or perhaps more idiomatically, the "jerks." Unsurprisingly, the Dutch Communist Party viewed Provo's derision of the tastes of ordinary people as elitist, and was damning of its focus upon imagination and individualism at the expense of the economic questions underlying social injustice.[72] In this way, the values embodied at different levels in the composers' pieces were out of step with the communist elements conspicuously present at the PDE concert, for whom the claims of complex art were decidedly less compelling, and even cause for suspicion, not least when it offered little for the nonspecialist to enjoy.

A corresponding tension naturally also arose between the pieces and the composers' own recent ideological reorientation toward communism. Their claim that their music expressed nothing can be seen as a strategy to defuse this perception: the insistence that this was the case carried the implication that the music embodied no ideological difference to which anyone, including themselves, might object. It was to prove less easy to disguise the contradiction with the project on which Andriessen, Schat, Mengelberg, and Mulisch set to work shortly after the PDE concert, an ambitious theatrical homage to Che Guevara titled *Reconstructie*. For G. Barendrecht, writing on *Reconstructie* in the pages of *De Internationale*—the journal of "the Dutch section of the Fourth International (Revolutionary-Marxist wing)"—the complexity and self-conscious cleverness of the work was a manifestation of the "professional wizardry, the exclusivity" endemic to bourgeois art, which presented an obstacle to artistic "collectivising in the deepest sense."[73] Similarly, at the PDE concert, while Schat had bemoaned the lingering and disruptive influence of anarchistic provocateurs during the concert, for others, the musical part of the evening, far from being threatened by the evening's absurdist manifestations, had to be counted among them.

The progressive model of performance laid out by the PDE concert gave an indication of things to come: in its use of a bespoke ensemble, its novel venue, and its informal atmosphere, it set down a template for the distinctive ensemble culture that was to thrive in the Netherlands during the 1970s. But the concert also manifested a remarkably traditional view of composition, one that completely eschewed the participatory thrust of radical musicians elsewhere in Europe and beyond.[74] Such an abandonment of the composers' customary control of proceedings would have been all too redolent of the free-for-all hippie counterculture that by 1968 had largely supplanted Provo in Amsterdam, and which was regarded on the Left as politically uncommitted. This attitude accounted for the sharp contrast of atmosphere between the Odéon and Carré theaters in May 1968: the first, "a sort of revolutionary forum, club and doss house," with "sunbathing on the roof" and (it was reported) a "permanent orgy-room" in the cellar;[75] the second, home to an evening of didactic musical and spoken presentations, with the organizers overwhelmingly concerned to maintain the decorum necessary for the appreciation of their new creations. Yet the composers' insistence on musical autonomy underplayed the new works' active, integral role in the proceedings. By adopting formal approaches indebted to anarchism, by making a stand for creative experiment, and by rejecting the wider participation of those present, the music performed at the concert made its own unmistakable, if discordant, contribution to the concert's "political demonstrative" character.

74 Sound Commitments

Some of the archive work for this study was undertaken by my research assistant Jochem Valkenburg (Katholieke Universiteit Leuven). I am also grateful to Louis Andriessen, Konrad Boehmer, and Frits van der Waa for invaluable ideas, assistance, and feedback. This research was made possible by generous grants from the Arts and Humanities Research Council and the British Academy.

Notes

1. *De Telegraaf* and *Algemeen Handelsblad,* May 30, 1968. Page numbers for newspaper sources are given where known.

2. Harry Mulisch, *De toekomst van gisteren* (Amsterdam: De Bezige Bij, 1972), 220; Kevin Whitehead, " 'U kunt meehoppen. Hop, Hop, Hop. Hop ze!' " *De Volkskrant,* Nov. 15, 1996.

3. For a short but reliable account see Leo Samama, "Muziek en het onbehagen in de cultuur in de jaren zestig," in *Een muziekgeschiedenis der Nederlanden,* ed. Louis Peter Grijp (Amsterdam: Amsterdam University Press, 2001), 743–49. The best English account is Rudy Koopmans, "On Music and Politics: Activism of Five Dutch Composers," *Key Notes* 4 (1976): 19–36.

4. These are the words of the experimental writer Bert Schierbeek, speaking following the concert to *Het Parool,* June 1, 1968.

5. For an English-language account of this campaign, see Kasper Jansen, "Bruno Maderna and Dutch Concert Life," *Key Notes* 11 (1980): 31–36.

6. James C. Kennedy, *Nieuw Babylon in aanbouw: Nederland in de jaren zestig* (Amsterdam: Boom, 1995), 132–36.

7. *Achter de muziek aan: het Concertgebouworkest ter discussie* (Amsterdam: Bezige Bij, 1967).

8. See Louis Andriessen, "Het symphonie-orkest achter de muziek aan," in *Muzikale en politieke commentaren en analyses bij een programma van een politiek-demonstratief experimenteel concert* (Amsterdam: Polak en Van Gennep, 1968), 24–26. An English translation appears as "The Symphony Orchestra Marching behind the Music," in Louis Andriessen, *The Art of Stealing Time,* ed. Mirjam Zegers, trans. Clare Yates (Todmorden: Arc Music, 2002), 124–27.

9. These and other details in the following account of the concert are drawn from newspaper reports: *Vrije Volk, Algemeen Handelsblad, Brabants Dagblad, Nieuwe Rotterdamse Courant, Het Parool, De Telegraaf, Tubantia,* and *De Volkskrant* (all June 1, 1968); *Groene Amsterdammer* and *Haagse Post* (both June 8, 1968).

10. Andriessen, "Het symphonie-orkest" 25–26.

11. Peter Schat, cited in K. L. Poll, "Hofnarren van de bourgeoisie," *Algemeen Handelsblad,* May 25, 1968, 1–2, esp. 2.

12. Niek Pas, *Imaazje! de verbeelding van Provo (1965–1967)* (Amsterdam: Wereldbibliotheek, 2003), 208–9.

13. Lidy van Marissing, "Kunstenaars spelen de rol van hofnar in deze maatschappij" [interview with Peter Schat, April 1968], in *28 Interviews* (Amsterdam: Meulenhoff, 1971), 33.

14. Harry Mulisch, *Bericht aan de rattenkoning* (Amsterdam: De Bezige Bij, 1967). Mulisch also wrote a warm memoir of his Cuban visit: *Het woord bij de daad* (Amsterdam: De Bezige Bij, 1968). His later collection of essays *De toekomst van gisteren* contains an account of the PDE concert itself; and the concert is also

evocatively fictionalized in his later magnum opus *De ontdekking van de hemel* (Amsterdam: De Bezige Bij, 1992); translated in English as *The Discovery of Heaven*, trans. Paul Vincent (Middlesex: Penguin, 1998).

15. Mulisch, *De toekomst van gisteren*, 229.

16. Poll, "Hofnarren van de bourgeoisie," 2.

17. "Mobiele groep voor nieuwe muziek in kunstmaand," *Parool*, May 16, 1968.

18. Poll, "Hofnarren van de bourgeoisie," 2; "Omroepwereld verzet zich tegen politieke concerten," *Algemeen Dagblad* (Rotterdam), May 29, 1968.

19. Mulisch, *De toekomst van gisteren*, 236–37.

20. "Carré: een actie die geen actie mocht zijn," unattributed newspaper article in Peter Schat archive, Nederlands Muziek Instituut.

21. "Revolutionairen en muziekminnaars 'bezetten' Carré," *Algemeen Handelsblad*, June 1, 1968.

22. Ibid.

23. Leo Samama, *Zeventig jaar Nederlandse muziek, 1915–1985* (Amsterdam: Querido, 1986), 261.

24. Mulisch, *De toekomst van gisteren*, 236–37.

25. Hans Righart, *De eindeloze jaren zestig: Geschiedenis van een generatieconflict*, reprint of 1st ed. (Amsterdam: Amsterdam University Press, 2006), 262.

26. "Na concert Carré 'bezet'," *De Volkskrant*, May 31, 1968.

27. Peter Schat, cited in "Het volk beslist!" *Haagse Post*, June 8, 1968.

28. This is Harry Mulisch's phrase, from the fictionalized account of the PDE concert in *The Discovery of Heaven*, 85.

29. "Het volk beslist!"

30. Peter Schat, *Muziek voor wie niet weg is* (typescript draft of an unpublished autobiography [1974]), 88–89; copy in NMI Peter Schat archive.

31. "Carré: een actie die geen actie mocht zijn."

32. Mulisch, *De toekomst van gisteren*, 240.

33. Han G. Hoekstra, "Madurodam-revolutie in Carré," *Het Parool*, June 1, 1968. Madurodam is a miniature model town near Den Haag. The subsequent performances in other venues were correspondingly more sober affairs.

34. Mulisch, *De toekomst van gisteren*, 238.

35. Schat, "Inleiding," in *Muzikale en politieke commentaren en analyses*, 5–6, esp. 5.

36. This letter, dated May 26, 1968, may be found in the NMI Peter Schat archive. It became a hostage to fortune when, in 1969, the management of the orchestra quoted it in its entirety in a press release intended to defuse the composers' renewed campaign against the orchestra. For a full account of the affair, see Jacqueline Mineur, "Actie notenkraker: componisten tegen het Concertgebouworkest" (PhD diss., Rijksuniversiteit Utrecht, 1989), 41–43.

37. Andriessen, cited in "Omroepwereld verzet zich tegen politieke concerten."

38. See the reports in *Algemeen Handelsblad, Parool*, and *Trouw* (all May 16, 1968).

39. Poll, "Hofnarren van de bourgeoisie," 2.

40. Schat, "Inleiding," 6.

41. The important role played by popular music in Dutch dissident movements throughout the sixties is stressed throughout Righart, *De eindeloze jaren zestig*.

42. Poll, "Hofnarren van de bourgeoisie," 2.

43. Konrad Boehmer, "Repressieve kunstpolitiek," in *Muzikale en politieke commentaren en analyses*, 28–29. Boehmer had assisted in the compilation of the program book.

44. Kevin Whitehead, *New Dutch Swing* (New York: Billboard, 1999), 67.

45. I am grateful to Wim Laman at the Dutch broadcaster VPRO for providing me with an archive recording of the performance. This appears to be the only part of the concert to survive on tape.

46. "Interview met Peter Schat," *Kontrast* 4, no. 3 (1967): 11–13.

47. Schat, "Inleiding," 5–6.

48. Schat, cited in Poll, "Hofnarren van de bourgeoisie," 2; and in "Weerstand tegen politiek concert," *De Telegraaf*, May 28, 1968.

49. Andriessen, cited in "Omroepwereld verzet zich tegen politieke concerten."

50. Mulisch, *De toekomst van gisteren*, 236.

51. Schat, "Inleiding," 5–6.

52. Schat, cited in Betty van Garrel, "Peter Schat, terug uit Cuba," *Haagse Post*, undated cutting contained in NMI Peter Schat archive.

53. See my introduction to this volume.

54. Pierre Bourdieu, *Distinction: A Social Critique of the Judgement of Taste* (London: Routledge, 1984), especially 4–5.

55. See the excerpts from Trotsky, Marcuse, Mao and Guevara in *Muzikale en politieke commentaren en analyses*, 20, 32, 12 and 14 respectively.

56. Boehmer, "Repressieve kunstpolitiek," 28.

57. Andriessen, "Het symphonie-orkest," 24.

58. Peter Schat, "Tooi die danseres na de idioot," *De Gids* 129, no. 1 (1966): 44–50. The version of this article that appears in Schat's *De Toonklok: Essays en gesprekken over muziek* (Amsterdam: Meulenhoff, 1984), 20–24, is shorn of its original second half.

59. *Provo* 1 (July 12, 1965): inside front cover.

60. Andriessen, "Mendelssohn, Fizzy Drinks and the Avant-garde" [1966], in *The Art of Stealing Time*, 52–56.

61. Andriessen, cited in Ernst Vermeulen, "In gesprek met Louis Andriessen," *Ouverture* 2, no. 5 (January 1968): 5–7.

62. Andriessen, "Mendelssohn, Fizzy Drinks and the Avant-garde," 52.

63. A different argument, one associated with Theodor Adorno, proposes that ostensibly autonomous musical works are critically "engaged" by virtue of their very resistance to the everyday meanings of "administered society." Here, however, I am arguing more simply that Andriessen's and Schat's works are less autonomous than they claimed.

64. Andriessen, "De tijd in tegenspraak," *De Gids* 131, no. 8 (1968): 178–81. This article reproduces Andriessen's lengthy note on *Contra Tempus* from the PDE concert program book, but with a new introduction.

65. Further analytical remarks on *Contra Tempus* may be found in Yayoi Uno Everett, *The Music of Louis Andriessen* (Cambridge: Cambridge University Press, 2006), 50–56.

66. The term is used in the new introduction of "De tijd in tegenspraak." The Dutch noun "verval," like the English "dissolution," can carry a moralistic imputation.

67. Andriessen, "De tijd in tegenspraak," 180.

68. Andriessen, "Interieur verslag van de gebeurtenissen sinds Ittrospezione II voor orkest," in *Muzikale en politieke commentaren en analyses*, 8–11, esp. 8.

69. Roel van Duyn, *Het Witte Gevaar* (Amsterdam: Meulenhoff, 1967), 108.

70. See Donald D. Egbert, "The Idea of the "Avant-garde" in Art and Politics," *American Historical Review* 73 (1967): 339–66.

71. Kennedy, *Nieuw Babylon in aanbouw*, 133.

72. See Virginie Mamadouh, *De stad in eigen hand: Provo's, kabouters en krakers als stedelijke sociale bewegingen* (Amsterdam: Uitgeverij Sua, 1992), 63.

73. G. Barendrecht, "Kunst en revolutie," *De Internationale* 12, nos. 6–7 (1969): 7. See Robert Adlington, "'A Sort of Guerrilla': Che at the Opera," *Cambridge Opera Journal* 19, no. 2 (2007): 167–93.

74. See, for instance, the chapters by Amy Beal and Eric Drott in this volume.

75. Patrick Seale and Maureen McConville, *French Revolution 1968* (London: Heinemann, 1968), 108; Keith A. Reader with Khursheed Wadia, *The May 1968 Events in France: Reproductions and Interpretations* (Basingstoke: Macmillan, 1993), 154.

4

Aesthetic Theories and Revolutionary Practice

Nikolaus A. Huber and Clytus Gottwald in Dissent

Beate Kutschke

From the end of 1968, the musicians, composers, and music writers of Germany's New Music scene immersed themselves in the question of how to contribute, through music, to the political upheaval initiated by the student and protest movements of the 1960s. "New Music," according to the program as it was pursued by contemporary musicians, "should actually be music that is adequate for a new society."[1] Yet, while this decision was easily taken, precisely how to carry out this program was by no means clear—and did not become any clearer during the following years. The reason for this situation was obvious: music, a nonverbal sign system, is unable to refer unambiguously to political issues, just as in general terms its relationship to extramusical meaning cannot be verified. However, the West German avant-garde music scene of the early 1970s—the period in which the new leftist spirit manifested itself most intensively in the musical field—was especially notable for its numerous discussions and debates about the nature of political music, its perfection and failures, conducted by musicians and music writers with endless energy and engagement. In turn, this lively discourse on political music helped to promote musical works that, in the opinion of their critics, could be considered as accomplished examples of the genre.

This chapter throws light on one of these debates: the argument between Nikolaus A. Huber and Clytus Gottwald in 1971–72 about Huber's composition *Harakiri*. It investigates the terms of the debate, first with regard to the musical facts—and in particular a comparison made at the time between Huber's *Harakiri* and Hans Otte's contemporary piece *Zero*—and second with regard to the ideas of Theodor W. Adorno, who provided the new leftist avant-gardists with some of their politico-aesthetical ideas, but against whom many were also reacting in the desire to move beyond critical theory toward political practice. *Harakiri*, it will emerge, provides an exemplary case study for the debates surrounding the idea of politically engaged music in West Germany in the early 1970s.

The Suicide of Music

Nicolaus A. Huber (b. 1939) could accurately have titled his 1971 composition for twenty-five musicians, one conductor, one female speaker, tape, and loudspeaker "Presque rien," i.e., "almost nothing"—had Luc Ferrari not used this title the previous year. Huber's composition, which was in fact named *Harakiri*, was indeed almost nothing. Central to the piece is a long crescendo, which builds slowly for a minute and a half.[2] This is preceded by a pedal tone lasting almost ten minutes; and followed by a resounding thunderclap, a pause, a patter of rain on a metallic surface (for almost a minute), and a short spoken declaration (section 3). For the rain noise, Huber suggests a timbre that resembles a "resonating metal roof, light, a somewhat sharp timbre."[3]

The pedal tone—or better, pedal noise—of section 1 is produced by thirteen violins playing on an A string detuned by more than two octaves to G-flat (see figure 4.1). Not surprisingly, the strings are so flabby that they cannot vibrate properly. Instead of a sound with a distinct pitch, the listener hears the rough, coarse, breathy scrubbing of the bow over the string. This section of nonevent and nothingness is interrupted by similarly minimal, but slightly enlivening occurrences: first, a noisy dissonance of tremolos and vibrato sounds, *piano-pianissimo*, performed by the strings; second, a dissonant "snap" on the harp; and third, an agglomeration of sounds and "stimmlos," breathy noise, irregularly increasing and decreasing in intensity between *pianissimo* and *piano-pianissimo*. Two and a half minutes later, section 2 begins. Although it is more or less impossible to produce a reasonable sound on the flabby strings, Huber uses them to perform the long crescendo that finally emerges out of the aspirating, coarse groaning of the first section, and builds to a hissing noise.

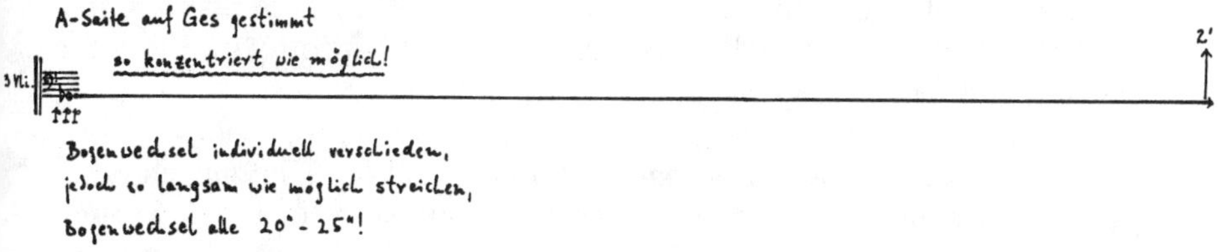

Figure 4.1 Nicolaus F. Huber, *Harakiri*, full score, p. 1. The instruction above the violin stave reads "A string tuned to G flat. As concentrated as possible!" © Bärenreiter Verlag, Kassel. Reproduced by permission.

Let us leave section 3 and its radio-play-like appendix aside for a moment and focus on the first two sections. What do they signify, especially the salient musical elements—pedal tone and crescendo— that dominate these sections? According to traditional ideas of composition, the various acoustical elements that shape a musical work are related to one another. They *refer* to one another on the basis of the gestalt-like similarity epitomized by motives and subjects, for instance, and in this way enable music to signify, i.e., to possess meaning.[4] It is well known that in the course of the twentieth century alternative approaches to composition arose in opposition to this aesthetic-semiotic concept, which focused instead on the qualities of sounds themselves. Huber, however, aligns himself with neither of these two constrasting aesthetic concepts, be it the program of sound qualities or the emphasis on music's meaning that emerges from referentiality (as in traditional music). Rather than attracting the listener's attention through distinctive timbral and articulatory qualities, the scrubbing noise of the pedal tone and the crescendo are conspicuously arid and sterile. These lifeless "anti-sounds"—and this is Huber's purpose—do not invite being listened to and enjoyed.

Just as Huber's composition does not pursue an aesthetics of sound quality, so the thinned out, haggard pool of gestalts—the pedal tone and the crescendo—fails to constitute a meaningful sign system in the traditional sense. Although the crescendo emanates from the pedal noise, the musical elements of the first section—the almost inaudible pedal noise and the similarly inaudible interruptions, which are over before the listener is able to recognize them properly—appear to be essentially isolated. Thus, the pedal tone apparently serves nothing more than to indicate that the piece has started, that "music *is*" at that moment. In light of the emptiness of the pedal-tone, the build up of the crescendo is unmotivated, as if simply annexed to the first section.

However, if Huber's piece neither constitutes musical referentiality nor displays distinctive sound qualities, what is the effect of his composition? To what degree can *Harakiri* be considered meaningful? As I will demonstrate, Huber directs attention to another, third dimension: the pedal tone and the crescendo as they exist in the hands of the composer, namely as formal modules, morphemes of composition. The neutralization of the function of the crescendo that accompanies its isolation becomes especially recognizable in comparison with the role of crescendos in traditional compositions. In Western musical culture, a crescendo that builds up over several measures and is followed by a new musical section is a formal element of revolution, enhancement, and transcendence; it serves to lead from one stage or phase to the next, the latter hierarchically higher positioned and/or different in status. (The open-ended crescendos that occur at the end of musical compositions or phrases similarly signify a transcendental process; they prefigure what is beyond the composition and what cannot be shown.) In Huber's work, in contrast, the crescendo remains teleologically pointless. To what does the crescendo lead? A thunderstorm, i.e., an acoustic event that possesses not musical, but *extra* musical meaning. To put it bluntly: the crescendo leads out of the music; it leaves the realm of art. So, from where to where does it lead? From stasis and nothingness (the pedal tone) to nature.[5]

It is to this negation of musical form and meaning that the title of Huber's composition most obviously refers. The Japanese term "hara-kiri" denotes a specific form of suicide carried out in connection with shame and/or the loss of honor: the individual kills himself by cutting open his stomach or belly. In Germany, the term "harakiri" is often used to "poetically" circumscribe any sort of suicide. Huber has never specified the precise significance of the title of his piece. In light of the constitution of the piece as described above, however, the title could easily be interpreted as indicating the suicide of music in general or, at least, of the piece as a musical work.

How, though, does this analytical finding of "musical suicide" in *Harakiri* relate to the spoken declaration at the end of the piece, which we have not yet mentioned? This closing section does not articulate the abolishment of music, but warns of the dangerousness of specific musical elements. "The practice of crescendo and decrescendo," the speaker declares, "is hidden in war and peace, in work and recreation, in everyday and holiday, in taking a life and sparing one, in sunrise and sunset, in repression, in moods, in pleasure, in destruction.... Crescendi are not free of value/Music conceals their dangerousness,/mystifies their use. One should no longer, under the guise of structure, make a parade with crescendos which are no more than themselves!"[6] In what follows, I will discuss this closing declaration and the musical structure's relationship to extramusical issues, in light of various ideas of political music as they were articulated in the debate between Huber and Gottwald.

Cancellation of the Premiere

In August 1970, Clytus Gottwald, producer for New Music at the Süddeutscher Rundfunk in Stuttgart from 1967 to 1988, commissioned a composition by Huber,[7] at this time thirty-one years of age and toward the start of his career as a composer. The remuneration was to be 3,000 DM, half of which was paid immediately after Huber accepted the commission in December 1970. According to the season prospectus published in June 1971, the premiere of *Harakiri* was scheduled for February 4, 1972. Thus far, everything went according to plan. However, having received Huber's work in summer 1971, Gottwald refused to fulfill the contract, i.e., to premiere the composition in the framework of a public concert.

Gottwald's refusal, and the critique of *Harakiri*, which he developed in order to justify his decision, spurred—not surprisingly—a heated debate between Huber and Gottwald in which further people, "adjutants" of Huber and Gottwald, were also temporarily involved: these included Wolfgang Timaeus, director of the department "Music, stage and orchestra" at the publishing house Bärenreiter[8] and Huber's agent; Willy Gaessler, director of the music program of the Süddeutscher Rundfunk; and Reinhard Oehlschlägel, new music producer at Deutschlandfunk Köln. The initial discussion took place in private, through written correspondence between Huber and Gottwald. In mid-1972, however, the dissent became widely known because of the initiative of two young, exceptionally active music students, Frieder [Friedrich Christian] Reininghaus and [Jürgen] Habakuk Traber.[9] Stimulated by Oehlschlägel, they published excerpts of the letters, as well as their own comments, in the July/August issue of *Melos*, one of the leading journals of contemporary music in Germany.[10] The publication, which clearly took a stand in favor of Huber, initiated the public sequel of the debate, for Gottwald felt pressured to respond to Reininghaus and Traber's presentation with additional arguments supporting his decision, and Gottwald's reply in turn prompted a response from Huber. Only after a further round in the November/December issue was the debate concluded.[11]

What were the arguments exchanged by the opponents? Paying tribute to *Harakiri*'s distinctive constitution, Gottwald diagnosed the suicide—or better, murder—of music in Huber's piece. *Harakiri*, he argued, is not a composition, but directed *against* composition. This observation led him to refuse to consider the piece as an artwork, as he indirectly and dialectically explained in his first letter to Huber, written on November 10, after he had received the score of *Harakiri*: "What you had articulated by musical means in *Informationen* [Huber's composition *Informationen über die Töne e-f* for string quartet (1965/1966)], is degraded to mere compositional relief in *Harakiri*. . . . If composing, in your view, has become impossible, such an impossibility needs to be composed: one should not dodge it."[12] And he added in a schoolmasterly tone: "Such a habit of making-oneself-comfortable indeed has no future."[13]

Gottwald's expressions "compositional relief," "dodging," and "making oneself comfortable" shed light on what irritated him. In his view, *Harakiri* was not the product of "labor." In applying this criterion to music, Gottwald pursued an aesthetics that—in contrast to the aesthetics of the genius, according to which the artwork's value increases if it emerges suddenly, by an unforeseeable and uncontrollable stroke of inspiration, as has been said of Mozart for instance—was inspired by the model of Beethoven, who is well known to have amply elaborated his ideas. Following an aesthetic concept aligned with the criterion of craft, the genius's moment of illumination had to be completed by a considerable amount of intellectual time and energy, by means of which the initial idea was further developed. Gottwald's assessment of *Harakiri* as the product of insufficient labor becomes even more obvious in a report from Huber's agent Timaeus, according to which Gottwald made "remarks [about *Harakiri*] such as 'pulled together in half an hour'."[14] Gottwald clearly considered Huber to have been lazy. In his view, the amount of work and intellectual energy that had gone into *Harakiri* was not worth 3,000 DM, which at this time equalled two months' of an average household's net income.[15]

Why did Gottwald apply an aesthetics of labor to *Harakiri*, instead of an aesthetics of genius for instance? Or—and this would have been even more plausible—why did he not avail himself of Adorno's theories, of whom he was usually a fervent advocate and whose texts belonged to the reading list of any new leftist avant-gardist musician and music writer at this time? If he had done so, he could easily have interpreted the emptiness of *Harakiri*, not as an aesthetic failure ("lack of labor"), but as an aesthetic *necessity*, for according to Adorno's aesthetics of the "availability of musical material," music history determined for the composer the kind of musical material available at a given time. In light of this notion, Gottwald could have argued that Huber did not choose deliberately to compose *presque rien*, i.e., refuse to invest compositional labor, but, governed by the musical material available at this time, had no other choice.

Furthermore, Gottwald's professional activities meant that he was familiar with current compositional techniques and thus knew that Huber's "lack of compositional labor" by no means collided with current compositional aesthetics. Gottwald was a multitalented specialist in avant-garde music, both as a music writer and as a musician. After earning a Ph.D. in musicology in 1961, he subsequently made his living as a cantor in Stuttgart. During this period, he founded the celebrated avant-garde vocal ensemble Schola Cantorum Stuttgart, whose director he was to remain until 1990. In 1967, he additionally became producer for New Music of the Süddeutscher Rundfunk. As director of the Schola Cantorum, he engaged himself for the premiere of numerous avant-garde compositions, among them well-known works such as Dieter Schnebel's . . . *missa est* and *Maulwerke*, György Ligeti's *Lux aeterna*, Mauricio Kagel's *Hallelujah*, Karlheinz Stockhausen's *Aus den sieben Tagen*, and Klaus Huber's *Erniedrigt-geknechtet-verlassen-verachtet*. Moreover, Gottwald's advocacy for avant-garde music sometimes came at a personal cost. In 1970, the production of the film *Hallelujah*, which occupied Stuttgart's Paulus church for a week, as well as the general presence of New Music in this Christian environment, provoked increasing protests by the congregation's council and priests against the "occupation" of the church, and finally pushed Gottwald to resign. This was the very same year in which he commissioned *Harakiri*.

In any case, as a specialist in New Music, the musician, music writer, and radio producer Gottwald could hardly claim to be astonished by excessive aesthetical reductionism as regards either the resulting product or the amount of time and intellectual energy used to create the artwork. After Fluxus and Cage's desire "to let sounds be themselves," not to forget the ready-mades in the field of visual arts (such as Duchamp's *Pissoir/Fountain* of 1917), artworks could no longer shock their percipients on account of the lack of time, work, and energy invested by their creators. The director of the music program at Süddeutscher Rundfunk, Willy Gaessler, although agreeing with the arguments of Gottwald, compared Huber's compositional method with Giacinto Scelsi's method of writing music on only one pitch,[16] and thereby—unintentionally—undermined Gottwald's arguments. Furthermore, Gottwald already knew that Huber pursued a decisively reductionist compositional style. Huber's string quartet *Informationen über die Töne e–f*, which, having been well received at the *Allgemeines Deutsches Musikfest* in Munich 1967, must have inspired Gottwald to the commission was, as the title already says, based on heavily reduced material, the notes E and F. All in all, Gottwald's criticism of the insufficiency of compositional labor lacked consistency. At the same time, as we will see, the lack of labor argument, on the basis of which Gottwald justified his initial refusal to pay the remaining half of the commission fee, was somewhat marginal to the underlying set of arguments around which the debate revolved, which involved the larger question of the "right" concept of politically engaged music.

Even if the lack of labor argument was a rather weak justification when the whole pool of available aesthetic theories is taken into account, Huber himself did little to allay Gottwald's criticisms. He attempted only half-heartedly to rebuff Gottwald's impression that he had aimed to cash in a good salary for no work. Indeed, he encouraged Gottwald's interpretation by creating the impression that *Harakiri* was opposed to music and that he intended to abolish composition in general. "In *Harakiri*, the acoustical event does not establish itself immediately as music. In this respect it is *not* music. By avoiding congruence between what can be heard and music, I made it difficult to mistake what are presented as *elements* of music as music itself" (italics added).[17] This he declared in the program note that he sent Gottwald on November 13, 1971, right after the commissioner had informed him of his doubts as regards the quality of the piece.[18] And in his letter of November 27 he confirmed: "I don't care for composition [...] what matters is not composition [...] please, please, no composition anymore!!!"[19] Such a discourse could easily be interpreted as confirming Gottwald's suspicion of Huber's laziness. What Huber truly intended to convey, however, only becomes visible when viewed in the light of the sociocultural climate at the time of *Harakiri*'s creation.

Music as Sociopolitical Mirror; Negativity and Utopia

As I will demonstrate, Gottwald was mainly bothered not by *Harakiri*'s compositional technique, but by its political message, or more exactly: the political message that he attributed *to* the composition. The late 1960s and early 1970s chronicle a decisive politicization in the German music scene.[20] An avant-garde composer who wanted to be taken seriously had to demonstrate not only a leftist politically engaged attitude but also the *right* leftist attitude by means of his music. That *Harakiri* was a political piece was quite obvious because of the spoken declaration at the end, which (as we have seen) placed the crescendo, i.e., a musical element, in relation to sociopolitical situations and accused music in general of concealing this relationship. However, the two opponents could not agree about whether *Harakiri* as a composition succeeded or failed to articulate this political critique appropriately.

What Gottwald's ideal might have been, in light of which he evaluated *Harakiri*, Reininghaus and Traber attempted to deduce by comparing Huber's composition with another piece programmed in the February 1972 concert: the orchestral work *Zero* by Hans Otte who, like Gottwald and Oehlschlägel, was a radio producer of new music at this time.[21] At the concert, Gottwald had honored Otte's piece—in preference to the other new work on the program, Luciano Berio's *Bewegung* (1971)—with an audience discussion, a decision that also conveniently extended the length of the concert, which had been shortened by the cancellation of *Harakiri*, to a normal duration.[22] *Zero* consists of a single musical event ("klangliches Ereignis"[23]) that is to be repeated 224 times. The *klangereignis* lasts about ten seconds and is contained within a 7/4 bar, beginning suddenly and explosively on the second beat—the first beat is a pause—and then fading out between the fourth and the seventh beat. The main compositional idea, however, is not endless repetition, but the subtle modification of each event, which results from its distinctive notation. For every repetition of the 7/4 bar, the score asks the performers (orchestra and choir) to choose one event out of a pool of possible events of different length, intensity, and timbre: a trill, a diminuendo pedal tone, glissando, various tone cascades and atonal fanfares, as well as diverse modes of cheering or screaming exclamations.[24] Further modifications are implemented by the conductor, who indicates slight changes of speed and, thus, of the recurrence of the *klangereignis*. The result is a kaleidoscope-like series of loud, energetic, and excited tutti clusters, quite similar to techniques in the visual arts developed by Andy Warhol:[25] the repetitive presentation of a motive such as *Campbell's Soup Can* or the *Marilyn* prints (both 1962), which are, in spite of their repetition, always different.

Ignoring the subtle modification of the *klangereignis*, Gottwald suggested that the composition "faces the merciless monotony of working life without major aesthetical rupture and mediation." The "powerlessness" that the musicians most likely feel while producing these 224 repetitions during a performance of *Zero* should stimulate "rage."[26] This interpretation, propagated by Gottwald through the *Melos* debate, was initially developed in a radio program about *Zero* broadcast on July 21, 1972, that is, half a year after the premiere and a few weeks before the publication of the debate's first part. Whereas the first thirty-five minutes of the forty-minute broadcast, presented by the music journalist Wolfram Schwinger, was a harsh critique of the composition (in Schwinger's view *Zero* was "neither traditional, nor modern or even avant-gardist, but simply bad—and very, very boring on top of everything"[27]) Gottwald's commentary underscored the work's strengths: as well as the sociocritical impact mentioned above, its focus on one sound had to be considered alongside earlier canonical works such as the *Vesperae Beatae Mariae Virginis* of Monteverdi and the *Rheingold* prelude of Wagner. In the context of the public debate, Gottwald picked up the analogy with assembly-line types of labor in order to explain what proper politically engaged music might be. He considered the main compositional idea of *Zero*, the uncountable repetitions of a *klangereignis* over thirty-five minutes that (in his view) confronted the merciless monotony of the working life, to be the composition's "social truth."[28]

Gottwald's formulation that "the composition *faces* [sich stellen] the monotony of the working life"—a formulation that suggests that the composition is an acting subject in the philosophical sense and, thus, able to "face" an object—reveals the methodological basis of Gottwald's interpretation. He considered the overall musical structure of *Zero*, the repetitions, as analogies to modes of labor that are similarly repetitive. In this light, the formulation "the composition faces . . . " has to be read as "the composition mirrors (or depicts) . . . ." According to Gottwald, *Zero* mirrored the merciless monotony of working life, i.e., made its *negative* impact on workers palpable to the musicians and audiences.

Gottwald's focus on negative aspects of West German society and their depiction in musical works was by no means an arbitrary one. The concept of negation and negativity played an important role in Adorno's philosophy, which shaped the music aesthetic discourse of the politicized climate of the early 1970s. Soon after the publication in 1966 of Adorno's *Negative Dialectics*, which propagated the term, the monograph became obligatory reading among New Leftists, including many musicians. Not surprisingly, ideas of negativity also played an important role in Gottwald's critique of *Harakiri*. With regard to the thunderclap and the patter of rain, which in Gottwald's view represented nature, he remarked: "Nature can be rescued aesthetically only through *negation*, not through the positivism of a thunder clap" (italics added).[29] What did Gottwald mean by this? The answer becomes clear only in the wider context of Adorno's aesthetic theory. Adorno, like his fellow philosophers and sociologists of the Frankfurt School, especially Max Horkheimer, placed much weight on exposing sociocultural and political forces such as the so-called culture industry, which seduced and soothed their audiences by means of light entertainment. The complement of both this critique and the constant warning—from the early 1950s onward—of the arrival of another totalitarian state following the Third Reich, was the idea of utopia, an idea that also played an important role in the New Leftists' struggle for a better world.[30] Interestingly, the sociopolitical idea of utopia, like the ideas of the culture industry and the menace of the emergence of a totalitarian system possessed a place not only in Adorno's socio-philosophical thinking but also in his music-aesthetical thinking. In his view, exceptionally accomplished works foreshadowed a utopian state. The mechanism of foreshadowing, however, had to be imagined as an *indirect, mediated* process.

Because utopia is unknown—according to the literal translation, utopia is a "no place"—it cannot be depicted. Adorno explained this idea most clearly in his *Aesthetic Theory*, published posthumously in 1970, and read by Gottwald shortly thereafter.[31] Adorno wrote: "Art is not more able than theory to concretize utopia, not even negatively. The cryptogram of the new is the image of collapse; only by virtue of the absolute negativity of collapse does art enunciate the unspeakable: utopia."[32] The reason for the impossibility of depicting utopia intentionally by means of art or theoretical thinking is that fantasy necessarily fails to depict that which does not exist; fantasy usually only repeats or recombines what is already well known. Adorno expressed this idea at another point in *Aesthetic Theory*: "If the effort is made to envision a strictly nonexisting object through what epistemologists dubbed *fantasizing fiction*, nothing is achieved that cannot be reduced—in its parts and even in the elements that constitute its coherence—to what already exists" (italics added).[33] If utopia, notwithstanding, emerges in artworks, it does so—this is Adorno's real insight—only *ex negativo*, "by virtue of the absolute negativity," i.e., when the artwork depicts a *negative* sociopolitical condition. Utopia, i.e., a *positive* social or worldly condition, emerges from the depiction of the negative, just as, in the well-known example of the Danish psychologist and phenomenologist Edgar Rubin, the profiles of two white faces emerge from the profile of a black goblet on a white background.

In the context of this matrix of ideas—sociocultural critique and the emergence of utopia *ex negativo*—the concept of nature that Gottwald found epitomized in *Harakiri*'s thunderclap and patter of rain plays a central role. As an important value that the Frankfurt School opposed to the technical world, nature is equivalent to utopia. Having been increasingly erased by the technical progress, rationality, and instrumental reason that have become our "second nature," *true* nature—so called *first* nature—must be recovered. This conclusion could be drawn from Horkheimer's and Adorno's well-known lament about the "compulsion of nature"[34] in the *Dialectic of Enlightenment*. This rediscovery of first nature also formed one of the key purposes of the rising ecological and alternative movements following the protests' climax in 1967/1968.[35] In light of Adorno's verdict upon the positive depiction of utopia, however, Gottwald could easily criticize Huber's piece for aiming at depicting nature, i.e., utopia, in the form of a thunderclap and rain noise, instead of letting it emerge from the isomorphic representation of negative social conditions, as (in Gottwald's view) Otte's *Zero* had done.

Having reconstructed Gottwald's implicit basis for his critique of *Harakiri*—his reception of Adorno's philosophy—it should be noted that, in fact, he did not apply Adorno's ideas faithfully. For utopia (or nature) does not emerge through its negation, as Gottwald demands, but *ex negativo*, i.e., as a sort of side effect of the process of negation. In brief, it is not nature itself (as a positive value) that has to be negated in an artwork, as Gottwald suggests, but it is the negative *loss* of nature that has to be *depicted* in the artwork. This matter notwithstanding, it remains to be asked: what were the reasons and theoretical ideas that motivated Huber to write a piece that, as he himself claimed, *refused* to be music?

The Drive for Praxis

In his first response to Gottwald's concerns, when the premiere of *Harakiri* had not yet been canceled, Huber explained: "My piece is certainly not a piece of success, of thundering applause or for critics, but it offers considerable material for *practice*" (italics added).[36] In the program note that he sent to Gottwald together with this letter, he wrote:

> The piece is about the presentation of various degrees of *activity*. These must be separated from each other in order not to be misunderstood as the formation of structure. The long-lasting sound receives a new meaning. It is the result of *activity* which makes it break out of the familiar energy framework. [italics added][37]

And in the declaration at the end of *Harakiri*, Huber had announced: "After a long, cumulative concentration, a crescendo indicates the departure, the departure to the exterior, to *activity*" (italics added).[38] These quoted passages are not only informative of Huber's music-poetic program but also represent typical new leftist ideas prevailing in the early 1970s. As the New Music scene in Germany took on board the New Leftists' political program, a discourse that stressed "practice" and "activity" could not be misunderstood. Huber clearly aligned himself with the call for practice, as it had been launched by the engaged students and political activists in the wake of 1968. The importance of the ideas of activity and practice for the New Left—and new leftist musicians—became especially visible in the conflicts that the politicized students had with their teachers and mentors Adorno and Herbert Marcuse. Indeed, this was the issue that finally led to the New Leftists' break with Adorno. As early as the beginning of the 1960s, student groups publicly demanded the transformation of theory, especially critical theory, into practice.[39] This demand was also reflected in the writings of the so-called revolutionary group Subversive Aktion, founded in 1963 and which may be considered as one of the artistic seeds of the New Left, complementing the cognitive orientation provided by the Frankfurt School. The "homo subversivus," as one of the numerous manifestos of Subversive Aktion declared, "have decided to realize all possibilities of the human *hic et nunc* by vital and experimental execution" (italics added) against the repressive world.[40] Similar critique was soon to emerge from Adorno's own students. In the summer of 1969 Hans-Jürgen Krahl accused critical theory of being incapable of "formulating the criteria of a revolutionary *realpolitik*" (italics added).[41] First and foremost, however, the students directed their critique against Adorno himself. From 1967, the students frequently interrupted Adorno's lectures and humiliated the esteemed philosopher. Flyers accused his Critical Theory of "critical powerlessness"[42] and declared that "the old Adorno and his theory . . . disgusts us because it does not tell how we can best set fire to this shitty university and some America-houses in addition—one for each terror attack on Vietnam."[43]

In light of the changing relationship between Adorno and the protesting students, Huber's emphasis upon practice and activity—which, as he claims, manifests itself in *Harakiri*—becomes understandable. For the discrepancy between theory and practice mattered equally in the musical field, where it was connected with a deep crisis in the image of New Music and its sociocultural relevance. In the context of the political upheaval of the sixties, advocates of German avant-garde music had to face a problem that could already be traced back to the late 1940s and 1950s, but was not openly discussed before 1970: namely New Music's lack of acceptance by wider audiences. While, in the framework of Germany's reconstruction, New Music had been actively supported by the allies and, on this basis, had received a solid institutional basis that included specialized broadcast departments, concert series, and festivals, New Music had never gained wide popularity among audiences. On the contrary, it was rejected by the majority of music lovers and even musicians. This discrepancy between institutionalization and popular rejection had already come to light a few months after the establishment of various regular radio programs dedicated to

New Music.[44] At the beginning of the 1970s, numerous articles published in the music periodicals *Melos* and *Neue Zeitschrift für Musik*, as well
as flyers distributed by radical students, reflected the contemporaneous
situation. They welcomed the fact that New Music appeared to be
institutionally anchored and culturally established and integrated.
However, at the same time, they disapproved of the fact that it was
desocialized and isolated because only insiders—a cultural elite—were
willing to enjoy it.[45] In light of this general disregard for New Music, its
ability to contribute to the political upheaval and sociopolitical reform
of German society appeared to be rather limited. How could music that
lacked the appreciation and acceptance of the majority have a political
impact on large numbers of people, the so-called masses, who were
indispensable to changing society from the bottom?

In defiance of this hopeless situation, new leftist musical avant-
gardists were driven to propel sociocultural change by means of their
music. They did this by replacing *cultural* practice (corresponding to
theory) with *political* practice (i.e., action). Musicians founded avant-
garde music ensembles such as Musica Negativa (1969), Hinz & Kunst
(1972), and the Free Music Group (1970), all of which were dedicated
to the performance of sociopolitically critical compositions or improvisations that replaced authoritarian, composer, and conductor-oriented
modes of performance by grassroots democratic ("basisdemokratisch")
ones.[46] Composers articulated their willingness to support the new
leftist striving for revolt and reform by writing politically engaged
compositions; Hans Werner Henze's oratorio *Das Floß der Medusa*
(1968) and his concert composition *El Cimarron* (1969–1970), as well
as his music theater pieces *La Cubana* (1973) and *We Come to the River*
(1976) are conspicuous examples.

For Huber, whose political engagement had been incited by his
teacher Luigi Nono and the activities of the student movement, and
who had read Karl Marx, Marcuse, Georg Lukács, Mao Tse-tung, Leon
Trotsky, and accounts of the Commune de Paris, the transfer of music
from the realm of art to that of political activity was especially urgent.[47]
Correspondingly, Huber dedicated *Harakiri* to the stimulation of praxis
and action and, at the same time, rejected those types of music that
"paralyzed" listeners and prevented them from becoming politically
active. In this light, it becomes easier to see why Huber and Gottwald
fought about the idea of redemption. Whereas Gottwald interpreted
"the Fortissimo-blow" of the thunder as redemption,[48] Huber insisted
that it "should *not* redeem. Otherwise the question regarding the sense
of the effort of the crescendo would not be understandable." And he
indirectly reproached music for "isolating energies, with which it
works, from a significant practice, that is to say: instruments (in this
case) create concealment" (italics added).[49] These sentences express—
if somewhat enigmatically—the problem Huber wished to have recognized regarding music, and avant-garde music especially: its quality of

siphoning—in Huber's words, isolating—"energy" from political activity. It is this quality that Huber called the "weakness of music."[50]

This view was shared by many of Huber's colleagues, including Frank Wolff, a cellist who gave up his formal musical studies in 1966 and subsequently became a federal chairman (Bundesvorsitzende) on the SDS (Sozialistische Deutsche Studentenbund, or Socialist German Student Union), because he felt that, at this time of political change, he could not justify an exclusive focus on bourgeois music performance at the expense of political action.[51] Most musicians, however, pursued a less radical mode of political activity by combining music and politics, but at the same time remaining skeptical toward music and its political potential. Correspondingly, Huber explained to Gottwald:

> Compositional problems are altogether pseudo-problems; they are our problems; that is the reality....The less that *Harakiri* relieves us [and] the more it imposes upon us, the better. Nothing *should* be carried out in *the piece*! Does *The Capital* of Marx carry out the revolution?[52]

Unlike Wolff, Huber did not leave the musical field, but aimed at transforming it in order to make it suit his political purposes. Huber's above-cited claim that he no longer wrote music—a claim that Gottwald could consider confirmation that his "lack of labor" reproach was justified—must be interpreted in this context. While Gottwald, as commissioner, measured the elaboration of the work in relation to the remuneration, Huber was, right from the beginning of his conversation with Gottwald, fully immersed in the political discourse. What counted for him was the political quality of his music, not his obligation as commissioned composer. This he believed to be measured by the transformation of music into political practice that, in his view, implied the negation of musical form and meaning, i.e., *Harakiri*'s suicide. It is in this light that, regardless of Gottwald's critique, Huber could proudly claim that *Harakiri* was marked by creative achievement and that, by avoiding the production of structure, he, Huber, had assigned the "length of a sound a new function" and new significance, namely, to call for political practice.

For the premiere of *Harakiri*, finally given by an ad hoc orchestra during the Darmstadt summer course in July 1972,[53] Huber wrote a new version of the piece's final declaration. It comprised a call to arms against a catalog of perceived social evils: "Fight the intellectual profiteers/fight the uninterested pleasure/fight the subjective expression/fight the exploiters of human underdevelopment/fight empiricism/fight the finished works/dispossess the possessors of music."[54] By asking the musicians to recite the slogans with a lifted fist, *Harakiri*'s finale availed itself of behavior modes typical of political demonstrations. More clearly, Huber transformed the performance of music into a political demonstration that, unlike the latter, however, preserved its aesthetical character by articulating the political ideas only in an enigmatic, diffuse mode.

Conclusion

The dissent between Huber and Gottwald is typical of the situation in the early 1970s, when the avant-garde music scene, inspired by the new leftist climate, strove to contribute to the reform of West German society. Musicians, composers, and music writers struggled to come to terms with the concept of political or politically engaged music. The arguments put forward in discussions and debates could be reckless and imprudent and often did not withstand critical inspection, but they were entered into with engagement and optimism. Most of the key ideas that unfolded during the discussion had been shaped by Adorno. This, however, by no means led to clarification. The complex and multifarious ideas revolving around utopia, negativity, and nature created misunderstandings and contradictions among new leftist musicians and music writers. The exchange was further complicated by the critical attitude that the new leftist students had developed toward Adorno during the late 1960s and which manifested itself most clearly in anti-Adornian notions such as the call for practice. Thus, in the musical field, Adornian and anti-Adornian ideas and imperatives co-existed and competed with each other.

This ambiguity manifested itself in the dissent between Huber and Gottwald. Whereas both shared the belief that current sociopolitical conditions were far from tolerable, and that music had to be considered as being related to these issues, the consequences that they drew from this diagnosis diverged. Gottwald focused on the depiction of negative sociocultural conditions (such as the depiction of assembly line-like work conditions in Otte's *Zero*); Huber, in contrast, aimed at negating traditional musical elements and transforming music into direct political practice. Both, however—though they were apparently not aware of their common ground—concluded that aesthetic reductionism, as exemplified by Otte's *Zero* and Huber's *Harakiri*, provided the appropriate musical conversion of sociocritical and political aspirations. Sympathizing with reductionist and, thus, radical avant-gardism, they by no means advocated "mainstream" political music—unlike many of their colleagues, including members of the above-mentioned ensemble Hinz and Kunst, who drew on the tradition of Hanns Eisler and the workers' song of the 1920s and 1930s and, thus, promulgated agitprop-like modes of music making. This however is another story, to be told in a different context.

Notes

1. Christian Wolff, "Zur Situation," in *Darmstädter Beiträge zur Neuen Musik XIV*, ed. Ernst Thomas (Mainz: Schott, 1975), 9–11, esp. 10.

2. *Harakiri* does not have conventional bars but uses time-span notation.

3. Nicolaus A. Huber, *Harakiri* (score) (Kassel: Bärenreiter, 1971).

4. Nelson Goodman, *Languages of Art* (Indianapolis, Cambridge: Hackett, 1976).

5. The thunderstorm itself, as it is presented in Huber's piece, is certainly an artificially created product. This however can be disregarded for the moment. What counts is the fiction: the piece's narrative, which describes the transformation of an almost nonexistent musical sound into the evocation of nature.

6. "Crescendo- und Decrescendo-Praxis steckt in Krieg und Frieden, in Arbeit und Erholung, in Alltag und Feiertag, im Morden und Schonen, im Sonnenaufgang und Sonnenuntergang, in Unterdrückung, in Stimmungen, in Freude, im Zugrunderichten.... Crescendi sind nicht wertfrei/Musik verheimlicht ihre Gefährlichkeit, /mystifiziert ihren Gebrauch. Unter dem Schutz von Struktur sollte man mit Crescendi, die nur sie selbst sind, keinen Staat mehr machen!"; Huber, *Harakiri.*

7. Today, after various reforms of the German radio landscape, the Süddeutscher Rundfunk is a part of the Südwestdeutscher Rundfunk. Following the reconstruction of Germany's cultural and radio landscape after 1945, most radio stations in West Germany possessed departments promoting New Music, and devoted a fixed amount of broadcasting time to it. They were equipped with a reasonable budget that allowed their editors to organize concerts and commission contemporary composers.

8. Verlagsdirektor für den Bereich "Musik, Bühne und Orchester"; the indication of Timaeus's profession in Nicolaus A. Huber, *Durchleuchtungen: Texte zur Musik 1964–1999*, ed. Josef Häusler (Wiesbaden: Breitkopf & Härtel, 2000), 389 is incorrect.

9. Inspired by the events of 1968, Traber and Reininghaus had in 1969 initiated the Theorieplenum, a student working-group at the Stuttgart conservatory that aimed at addressing music's sociopolitical implications.

10. Habakuk Traber and Friedrich Christian Reininghaus, "Chronologie eines Kompositionsauftrages," in *Melos* 4 (1972): 252–58.

11. Traber and Reininghaus, "Chronologie eines Kompositionsauftrages," 252–58; Clytus Gottwald, "Viel Lärm um nichts," in *Melos* 4 (1972): 253–58; Clytus Gottwald, "'Harakiri'—zum letzten Mal," in *Melos* 6 (1972): 388–89; Nicolaus A. Huber, "Apropos, Viel Lärm um Nichts'," in *Melos* 6 (1972): 388–89; Nicolaus A. Huber, "Harakiri—Nachwort des Komponisten," (1998) in Huber, *Durch-leuchtungen*, 400–401. All the *Melos* articles are reprinted in *Durchleuchtungen*, 387–400.

12. "Was in Ihren Informationen auskomponiert wurde, ist in Harakiri zur bloßen kompositorischen Entlastung abgesunken.... Wenn schon Komponieren nach Ihrer Meinung unmöglich geworden ist, dann muß solche Unmöglichkeit komponiert werden: Nicht ist ihr auszuweichen"; letter of Gottwald to Huber, November 10, 1971, in Traber and Reininghaus, "Chronologie eines Kompositionsauftrages," 252.

13. Ibid.

14. He made "Äußerungen wie 'in einer halben Stunde daherkomponiert' und ähnliche"; letter of Timaeus to Gottwald, December 23, 1971, in Traber and Reininghaus, "Chronologie eines Kompositionsauftrages," 254.

15. According to the Federal Statistical Office (Statistisches Bundesamt), the average income of a household (2.7 persons per household) was 1,384 DM (net income) and 1,900 DM (gross income) in 1969. Between 1969 and 1973

the income increased significantly. In 1973, the income of a household (still 2.7 persons per household) was 2,040 DM (net income) and 2,500 DM (gross income).

16. As for instance in Scelsi's *Quattro pezzi per orchestra (ciascuno su una nota sola)*.

17. "In *Hararkiri* etabliert sich das akustische Ereignis nicht selbst unmittelbar als Musik. Insofern ist es *keine* Musik. Dadurch, daß zu Hörendes und Musik sich nicht mehr decken, ist es schwergemacht, das, was Elemente der Musik darstellen soll, selbst als Musik mißzuverstehen."

18. Progam note by Huber, November 13, 1971, in Traber and Reininghaus, "Chronologie eines Kompositionsauftrages," 252.

19. Letter of Huber to Gottwald, November 27, 1971, in Traber and Reininghaus, "Chronologie eines Kompositionsauftrages," 253.

20. The idea that music, especially avant-garde music, should contribute to the revolution and reform of German society manifests itself clearly in the debate around Henze's *Raft of the Medusa* at the time of its premiere on December 9, 1968. All other types of classical music were also subject to politicization; see Martin Elste, "Die Politisierung von Sprache und Kriterien der Musikkritik nach 1968," in *Musikkulturen in der Revolte*, ed. Beate Kutschke (Stuttgart: Franz Steiner, 2008), 65–73.

21. Otte (1926–2007) was the head of the music department of Radio Bremen from 1959 to 1984.

22. The real reason why Otte and not Berio had been invited to participate in an audience discussion on his composition may have been that Berio was in the process of relocating from the United States to Italy and thus was not likely to be available, whereas Otte lived in West Germany.

23. Otte, commenting on his composition during the audience discussion; Wolfram Schwinger and Clytus Gottwald, broadcast on *Zero* (live recording of the world premier, the audience discussion and commentaries) as part of the series *Musik unserer Zeit*, July 21, 1972.

24. The score of *Zero* has never been published and could not be obtained from the composer before his death or, later, from his widow. My description is based on secondary sources (Schwinger and Gottwald, broadcast on *Zero*) and auditory analysis.

25. Otte himself considers his composition to be in the minimalist tradition of Steve Reich, La Monte Young, and Terry Riley (cf. Schwinger and Gottwald, broadcast on *Zero*).

26. Gottwald, "Viel Lärm um nichts," in *Melos* 4 (1972): 253–58, esp. 257.

27. Schwinger and Gottwald, broadcast on *Zero*.

28. "*Zero* hat seine gesellschaftliche Wahrheit . . . darin, daß es sich dem erbarmungslosen Einerlei des Arbeitsalltags ohne größere ästhetische Brechungen und Vermittlungen stellt."

29. "Ästhetisch ist sie [die Natur] zudem nur in ihrer Negation zu retten, nicht durch den Positivismus eines Donnerschlags"; letter of Gottwald to Huber, November 26, 1971, in Traber and Reininghaus, "Chronologie eines Kompositionsauftrages," 253.

30. See, for instance, the lecture series "The end of utopia" (Free University Berlin in 1967) in which philosophers, sociologists, and students discussed "the possibilities of political opposition in the metropolises in connection with the liberation movements in the countries of the Third World"; subtitle of the publication of the lecture series: *Das Ende der Utopie*, ed. Horst Kurnitzky and Hansmartin Kuhn (Berlin: Maikowski, 1967).

31. Clytus Gottwald, e-mail to the author, August 7, 2007.

32. Theodor W. Adorno, *Aesthetic Theory* (1970), trans. Robert Hullot-Kentor (London and New York: Continuum, 2004), 41. "So wenig wie Theorie vermag Kunst Utopie zu konkretisieren; nicht einmal negativ. Das Neue als Kryptogramm ist das Bild des Untergangs; nur durch dessen [des Bildes?] absolute Negativität spricht Kunst das Unaussprechliche aus, die Utopie"; Theodor W. Adorno, *Ästhetische Theorie* (1970) (Frankfurt: Suhrkamp, 1993), 55.

33. Adorno, *Aesthetic Theory*, 227. "Sucht man, wie die Erkenntnistheorie es taufte, in phantasierender Fiktion irgendein schlechterdings nichtseiendes Objekt sich vorzustellen, so wird man nichts zuwege bringen, was nicht in seinen Elementen und selbst in Momenten seines Zusammenhangs reduktibel wäre auf irgendwelches Seiende"; Adorno, *Ästhetische Theorie*, 259.

34. "Any attempt to break the compulsion of nature by breaking nature only succumbs more deeply to that compulsion. . . . In the mastery of nature, without which mind does not exist, enslavement to nature persists. By modestly confessing itself to be power and thus being taken back into nature, mind rids itself of the very claim to mastery which had enslaved it to nature"; Max Horkheimer and Theodor W. Adorno, *Dialectic of Enlightenment* (1944), ed. Gunzelin Schmid Noerr, trans. Edmund Jephcott (Stanford: Stanford University Press, 2002), 9, 31. "Jeder Versuch, den Naturzwang zu brechen, indem Natur gebrochen wird, gerät nur umso tiefer in den Naturzwang hinein. . . . Naturverfallenheit besteht in der Naturbeherrschung, ohne die Geist nicht existiert. Durch die Bescheidung, in der dieser als Herrschaft sich bekennt und in Natur zurücknimmt, zergeht ihm der herrschaftliche Anspruch, der ihn gerade der Natur versklavt"; Max Horkheimer and Theodor W. Adorno, *Dialektik der Aufklärung* (1947) (Frankfurt: Fischer, 1969), 15, 39.

35. Beate Kutschke, *Neue Linke/Neue Musik* (Cologne and Weimar: Böhlau, 2007); Beate Kutschke, "The Scream in Avant-garde Music: The New Left and the Rediscovery of the Body," in *The Modernist Legacy: Essays on New Music*, ed. Björn Heile (Aldershot: Ashgate, 2009).

36. Letter of Huber to Gottwald, November 13, 1971, in Traber and Reininghaus, "Chronologie eines Kompositionsauftrages," 252.

37. Gottwald, program note, November 13, 1971, in ibid.

38. Declaration at the end of score, in Huber, *Harakiri*.

39. Ingrid Gilcher-Holtey, *Phantasie an die Macht* (Frankfurt: Suhrkamp, 1995), 94.

40. The homo subversivus "[hat] sich entschieden . . . , alle Möglichkeiten des Menschlichen Hic et nunc im lebendigen Vollzug experimentell zu realisieren"; "Subversive Aktion," in *Subversive Aktion*, ed. Frank Böckelmann and Herbert Nagel (Frankfurt: Neue Kritik, 1976), 119–21, esp. 121.

41. "Andererseits teilt Marcuse das Elend der kritischen Theorie und das ungeschichtliche Selbstbewusstsein entstehender revolutionärer Bewegungen; er ist unfähig, die Kriterien einer revolutionären Realpolitik, bündnispolitischer Kompromisse, organisationspraktischer Stabilisierungen studentischer Protestbewegungen und klassentheoretischer Analysen zu formulieren"; Hans-Jürgen Krahl, "Fünf Thesen zu 'Herbert Marcuse als kritischer Theoretiker der Emanzipation'," in Hans-Jürgen Krahl, *Konstitution und Klassenkampf* (Frankfurt: Neue Kritik, 1971), 198–302, esp. 301.

42. "Kritische Ohnmacht verbreitet"; quote of flyer, by gaz, "Gutachter," in *Frankfurter Allgemeine Zeitung*, July 8, 1967, 9.

43. "Was soll uns der alte Adorno und seine Theorie, die uns anwidert, weil sie nicht sagt, wie wir diese Scheiß-Uni am besten anzünden und einige Amerikahäuser dazu—für jeden Terrorangriff auf Vietnam eines"; quoted by Alex Demirovic, "Bodenlose Politik—Dialoge über Theorie und Praxis" (1989), in *Frankfurter Schule und Studentenbewegung: von der Flaschenpost zum Molotow-cocktail,* vol. 3, ed. Wolfgang Kraushaar (Hamburg: Rogner & Bernhard bei Zweitausendeins, 1998), 71–98, esp. 84.

44. Cf. Edgar Lersch, *Rundfunk in Stuttgart 1934–49* (=*Südfunk-Hefte* 17), ed. Süddeutscher Rundfunk Stuttgart (Stuttgart: n.p., 1990), 86–91; and Beate Kutschke, "Die Huber-Gottwald-Kontroverse—Die Inszenierung der Neuen Musik als politische Manifestation," in *Die Macht der Töne. Musik als Mittel politischer Identitätsstiftung im 20. Jahrhundert,* ed. Tillmann Bendikowski, Sabine Gillmann, Christian Jansen, Markus Leniger, and Dirk Pöppmann (Münster: Westfälisches Dampfboot, 2003), 147–69.

45. Cf. "Braucht die Neue Musik noch Festivals?," in *Melos* (1972): 2–10; SDS-Projektgruppe Kultur und Revolution and AStA of Hochschule für Musik Berlin, "In Sachen Henze" (flyer), distributed at Planten un Blomen, Hamburg, on December 9, 1968, Carl von Ossietzky Staats- und Universtitätsbibliothek Hamburg, Hinz und Kunst archive; Aktionsgruppe Unkult der Uni ffm, without title (flyer), January 27, 1969, quoted by Dieter Kühn, "Musik und Revolution," in *Melos* 1970: 394–401.

46. Beate Kutschke, "Angry Young Musicians: Gibt es eine Sprache der musikalischen Avantgarde für '1968' ?," in *1968: Ein Handbuch zur Kultur- und Mediengeschichte der Studentenbewegung,* ed. Martin Klimke and Joachim Scharloth (Stuttgart: Metzler, 2007), 175–86; Kutschke, *Neue Linke/Neue Musik.*

47. Nicolaus A. Huber and Frank Zielecki, *Politisches Komponieren: ein Gespräch* (Saarbrücken: Pfau, 2000), 3; Nicolaus A. Huber, e-mail to the author, Aug 4, 2007.

48. Gottwald, "Viel Lärm um nichts," 255.

49. "Der Fortissimo-Schlag 'soll' eben *nicht* erlösen. Wie wäre denn sonst die Frage nach dem Sinn des Crescendo-Aufwandes verständlich! Musik isoliert Energien, mit denen sie arbeitet, von einer *deutlichen* Praxis, das heißt: Instrumente wirken (in diesem Fall) verschleiernd"; Huber, "Apropos 'Viel Lärm um Nichts'," 388.

50. "Schwäche der Musik"; Huber, "Apropos 'Viel Lärm um Nichts'," 388.

51. Frank Wolff, e-mail to the author, May 29, 2007.

52. "Kompositorische Probleme sind allesamt Scheinprobleme, sie sind unsere Probleme, da ist die Wirklichkeit. . . . Je weniger uns *Harakiri* abnimmt, je mehr es uns auferlegt, desto besser ist es. Es *darf* nichts *im Stück* ausgetragen werden! Wird im *Kapital* von Marx die Revolution ausgetragen?"; letter of Huber to Gottwald, November 27, 1971, in Traber and Reininghaus, "Chronologie eines Kompositionsauftrages," 253.

53. Huber, *Durchleuchtungen,* 409.

54. "Kampf den intellektuellen Schiebern/Kampf dem interesselosen Wohlgefallen/Kampf dem subjektiven Ausdruck/Kampf den Ausbeutern menschlicher Rückständigkeit/Kampf dem Empirismus/Kampf den fertigen Werken/Enteignet die Musikbesitzer"; Nicolaus A. Huber, "Harakiri—Nachwort des Komponisten" (1998), in Huber, *Durchleuchtungen,* 400–401, esp. 400.

Part II

RETHINKING THE POPULAR

5

"Music Is a Universal Human Right"

Musica Elettronica Viva

Amy C. Beal

Beyond the rupture of the economic conditions of music, composition is revealed as the demand for a truly different system of organization, a network within which a different kind of music and different social relations can arise. A music produced by each individual for himself, for pleasure outside of meaning, usage, and exchange. . . . But the dangers are immense, for once the repetitive world is left behind, we enter a realm of fantastic insecurity.[1]

An art form which aims for highest efficiency in times of the highest urgency must be based on dialog. It must reject the possibility of the impartial observer, present but not involved in the communication process, as contradictory to the idea of communication itself. . . . Such an art form must be improvised, free to move in the present without burdening itself with the dead weight of the past.[2]

The music is outrageous—inexorable; . . . larger than life.[3]

From the open windows of a Rome apartment across the street from the 1800-year-old Pantheon, in early September 1966, a group improvisation complemented the ambient sounds of the Piazza della Rotonda below. The uninhibited nature of the improvisation—instrumental, electronic, vocal, serene, aggressive, playful, and spontaneous—suggested an attempt to "make music with whatever means are available."[4] This seemingly innocent statement, made by American composer Frederic Rzewski in 1967, strips away the layers of training, technique, and talent

traditionally demanded by Western art music.[5] Taking universality as
a springboard, Rzewski's statement reflected the attitudes of Musica
Elettronica Viva (hereafter: MEV), an improvisatory live-electronic
group born in Rome in mid-1966. The group's founders included Allan
Bryant, Alvin Curran, Jon Phetteplace, Carol Plantamura, Frederic
Rzewski, Richard Teitelbaum, and Ivan Vandor.[6] They joined forces for

Figure 5.1 From left to right: Alvin Curran, Caspar the dog, Edith Schloss,
Richard Teitelbaum, Barbara Mayfield, Nicole Abeloos Rzewski, and Frederic
Rzewski, in front of Bramante's "Four Rivers" Fountain, Piazza Navona, Rome,
Italy, ca. 1968. Photograph by Clyde Steiner. Used with permission of the
photographer.

the purpose of exploring collective music making, and as a means for putting their own works out into the world. Gradually they also came to believe that music's potential as a catalyst for revolutionary action had yet to be tapped. Liberating music making—and thus music itself—could help intensify the struggle against elite institutions and their stronghold on culture. Alvin Curran's 1995 declaration that MEV believed "music is a universal human right" and "a form of property that belongs to everyone" underscores the notion that anyone, anywhere, could be a musician; everything, everywhere, could be a source of music itself.[7] In this reformed musical utopia, all people would collectively own the means for the production of music, and would experience music directly, unmediated by the mainstream cultural apparatus (and "beyond the rupture of the economic conditions of music," as Attali puts it). Emancipated from the constraints of their conservatory training, musicians would enter into a classless musical society where they were indistinguishable from—or at least equal partners with—nonmusicians. These basic challenges to the tenets of Western music, and MEV's eventual (though perhaps only temporary) rejection of the elitism attached to the postwar avant-garde, laid the foundation for the activities, attitudes, and "collective epiphanies" of the MEV protagonists during the late 1960s. Though their experiments in collectivity were far from tension-free, sometimes contradictory in nature, and only partially successful, MEV's ambition reveals much about the role improvisation played in ideologically minded American-European music networks of the late 1960s.

Background and Origins

The main protagonists were all born during the Depression, came of age by the late fifties, and were primarily trained in neoclassical and serial techniques in the most elite and exclusive Ivy League academies of the United States. As beneficiaries of the post-Kennedy-era foundation culture boom, most of them eventually enjoyed generous grants that took them to Europe. Frederic Rzewski (b. 1938) spent his undergraduate years at Harvard University. His colleagues there included David Behrman (b. 1937), with whom Rzewski had attended a private secondary school in New England, and Christian Wolff (b. 1934), whom Rzewski first met in Darmstadt (Germany) in 1956. (At Harvard, Wolff majored in Classics, not music.) Rzewski did his graduate work in composition at Princeton University before moving, more or less permanently, to Europe. Soon he established himself as one of the most talented avant-garde pianists after David Tudor. He lived in Italy on a Fulbright grant from 1960 until 1962, studying composition privately with Luigi Dallapiccola in Florence from 1960–61, and then in Rome. Rzewski played frequently in Italy, premiering Alvin Lucier's *Action Music for Piano, Book I* in Rome in June 1962, and performing Morton Feldman's *Intersection II* in the 25th Music Biennale in Venice that same summer, among other engagements; then from late 1963 until early 1966, he lived in Berlin as a Ford Foundation fellow studying with Elliott Carter. Following his Berlin residency, Rzewski moved back to Rome.

Alvin Curran (b. 1938) and Richard Teitelbaum (b. 1939) did their graduate work in composition at Yale University. Curran, too, came to Berlin as a Ford Foundation fellow chosen by his former Yale teacher Carter, for residency in 1964. That year in Berlin, Rzewski and Curran met the do-it-yourself inventor Gordon Mumma (b. 1935), known for his cheap but effective homemade electronic circuitry (Mumma was passing through Berlin after performing at the Venice Biennale with the ONCE Group). Curran went to Rome directly from Berlin, and still lives there today. Early on he lived in an apartment at Piazza Navona and earned money playing piano in cocktail bars on the Via Veneto. By the time Curran arrived in Rome (in a Volkswagen driven by Joel Chadabe, who had also been in Berlin studying with Carter as a Ford Foundation guest), most of his soon-to-be collaborators were already there. The American singer Carol Plantamura, who had met Rzewski while they were concurrent "Creative Associates" at the State University of New York at Buffalo in the mid-1960s, was in Rome to study with Luigi Ricci of the Rome Opera. Teitelbaum had already been in Italy on a Fulbright grant for two years, studying composition with Goffredo Petrassi in Rome (alongside Cornelius Cardew) and with Luigi Nono in Venice. In 1966, while the others were rehearsing their first improvisations, Teitelbaum was back in New York working in a brainwave research lab at Queens College. He bought a used Moog synthesizer, and David Behrman taught him to solder and how to build simple electronics. Teitelbaum, who had recently published a fifty-five-page, densely analytical article titled "Intervallic Relations in Atonal Music" in the *Journal of Music Theory*, spent much of the summer of 1967 playing with saxophonist Steve Lacy (1934–2004), who would become an important player in MEV history.[8]

Unlike several of his privileged collaborators, the Californian Jon Phetteplace (1940–91) didn't enjoy generous grants or even hold a college degree, let alone an East Coast private school pedigree. After high school, Phetteplace traveled independently to Austria and Italy, studying cello and composition when and where he could. He collaborated with Sylvano Bussotti, putting on concerts of John Cage's work in Florence.[9] By 1965 he was living in the Rome apartment that would soon host MEV's earliest sonic experiments. As we shall see, the intentionally nonhierarchical collaborations between university-educated musicians like Rzewski, Curran, and Teitelbaum, and their autodidactic fellows like Phetteplace did not always proceed smoothly. Though one of MEV's chief aims was to break down typical musical hierarchies based on levels of professional training (or lack thereof), the contrasting educational backgrounds of the central players, and the varying degrees to which they were willing to thrust aside standard notions of artistry, ownership, and virtuosity, would prove to be a source of ongoing conflict in the group.[10]

These young composers entered an ancient foreign city in which the latest American music enjoyed a special place. The American Academy in Rome, poised symbolically on walled Rome's highest hill, was an established institution renowned for upholding rigorous standards of indisputable quality. The coveted Samuel Barber Rome Prize in musical composition, the Paul Fromm Composer-in-Residence prize, and the impressive list of past Fellows—Barber, Carter, Copland, Foss, Hanson, Rochberg, Sessions, and Wuorinen, to name just a few—speak to the Academy's enduring authority in the musical world since the 1920s. Concert series in the Academy served as crucial bridges between new American music and Italian audiences, and they were typically supported by the Italian public radio network (RAI). The network's steady promotion of American music events at the American Academy, especially during the 1960s, helped many American composers get their works heard by an international audience at a time when production and distribution of new music recordings posed sometimes insurmountable challenges in the United States.

The Roman new music ensemble Il Gruppo di Improvvisazione Nuova Consonanza (hereafter Nuova Consonanza), founded by Italian composer Franco Evangelisti (1926–80), maintained close ties to the American Academy in Rome. Evangelisti, who served as something of a local mentor to the MEV composers, had been a key player in Darmstadt's most vital years, attending every year from 1952 until 1961. In 1963 the Accademia Filarmonica Romana (hereafter: AFR) established a festival called Nuova Consonanza, and the following year Evangelisti founded his performing group of the same name. Dedicated to collective, spontaneous music making rather than composition, Nuova Consonanza functioned as an avant-garde improvisatory ensemble—one of the first of its kind in Europe—in which all improvising members were composers.[11] Nuova Consonanza clearly influenced MEV not only in their thinking about composition, improvisation, and collectivity—and their "alternative" status outside the standard practices of the musical establishment—but also in their performance practice and their approach to the production of sound itself. Nuova Consonanza's tendency to handle instruments in unconventional ways, as well as their use of "noise-producing objects," also aligned them with MEV. Nuova Consonanza collaborated with MEV during their early days, and thus provides an intriguing intersection between this particular composers' collective and the American Academy.

International contemporary music festivals provided an important arena within which such groups could flourish during the 1960s, and like other countries in postwar Western Europe, Italy maintained its fair share. Inspired by activities at the Darmstadt Ferienkurse (which many Italian composers attended regularly during the 1950s, including Evangelisti, Nono, Luciano Berio, Bruno Maderna, and others), the annual Rome festival Nuova Consonanza commenced in late May/

early June 1963 with its first event "Manifestazioni di Musica Contemporanea," sponsored by Rome's Deutsche Bibliothek, the AFR,
and the SIMC (the Italian branch of the International Society of
Contemporary Music).[12] Outside Rome, other opportunities for new
music included the ongoing international panorama offered by the
Venice Biennale, the First International Congress of Experimental
Music in Venice, and new music events in Florence, Palermo, and
elsewhere. Such festivals brought many Americans together with
their European colleagues for the first time during the 1960s.

Upon moving to Italy, the MEV founders came under the influence
of artists, writers (especially the figure of Umberto Eco), and composers
entrenched in the Italian tradition of political avant-gardism. Nono
served as an important model, even though he never entirely abandoned the sole-author role of the traditional composer. With his
Communist-leaning *La fabbrica illuminata* for soprano and tape
(1964), which featured words of factory workers and the sounds of
factory machinery, he began to stage performances of his music in
factories themselves, as part of a revolutionary stance that involved
separation from the institutionalization of the avant-garde as it had
evolved in Western Europe since 1945.[13] Nono's forty-minute anti-
Vietnam protest piece *A floresta é jovem e cheja de vida*, which premiered
in 1966 at the Venice Biennale in collaboration with the Living Theatre, made use of found political texts. Many of Nono's tape works from
this period included the sounds of the times: street demonstrations
(*Contrappunto Dialettico alla mente*, 1967–68), for example, or Fidel Castro reading a letter from Che Guevara (*Y entonces comprendió*, 1969–70).

This tradition received sustenance in the late 1960s from a creatively optimistic climate of protest and collective action that was to
explode in the students' and workers' revolts of 1968. The powerful
tradition of revolutionary Marxism in Italy (Cafiero, the Labriolas,
Bordiga, Togliatti, and others), and the strong voice of the Partito
Comunista Italiano (the largest working-class party in Italy, which
won 27 percent of the vote in the May 1968 elections) provided a
backdrop to these developments.[14] The moral, social, economic, and
intellectual upheavals of the time also gave rise to a self-conscious
engagement with the writings of political philosopher Antonio
Gramsci.[15] Gramsci had been incarcerated between 1929 and 1935,
during which time he wrote hundreds of letters and thousands of
pages of notebooks. The Prison Notebooks, in which "Gramsci emphasized the pivotal role of intellectuals in the culture wars," became
profoundly influential on Italian artists during the late 1960s.[16] In the
words of Belgian political theorist and Marxist thinker Chantal Mouffe:
"This phenomenon [of interest in Gramsci's writings], which has developed in the wake of the events of 1968, is certainly linked to a
renewal of interest amongst intellectuals in the possibilities of revolutionary transformations in the countries of advanced capitalism."[17]

Finally, the historical context of the MEV group and their migration to Italy reflects the rapidly expanding "foundation culture" in the United States itself during the 1960s, which included increased distribution of Ford Foundation and Guggenheim grants and Fulbright Commission fellowships for composers traveling abroad, as well as the establishment of the National Endowment for the Arts in 1965. This unprecedented situation led American music historian and critic Peter Yates to ask: "What is [the living American artist] doing in Europe on his Fulbright? Is he being encouraged to sell American music, styles, composers, to the natives?" These crucial questions, coupled with Yates's plea to "discover the native artist, the local artist, and give him a place to work where he lives," suggest that the climate for new American music in western Europe—both for radical experimentalists like the MEV composers and for institutionally honored American Academy in Rome Fellows—offered welcome opportunities mostly unavailable at home.[18] This essay focuses principally upon the activities and agendas of MEV as articulated by the players themselves. The wider implication of new American music on politicized foreign soil during a time of great social upheaval remains an unexplored yet potentially revealing subtext, deserving of further investigation.

Early Performances

Once the young Americans had all met up in Rome and "abandoned their Yale tweeds," as Curran joked, they began playing together regularly.[19] Musical revolution was not their primary agenda at first. Teitelbaum has characterized MEV—somewhat misleadingly—as "Ivy-League dropouts who were denied access to studios" (Curran, Rzewski, and Teitelbaum all, in fact, completed their university degrees).[20] Gaining access to the electronic studios was not easy for these foreign newcomers, and thus in the beginning, as young composers lacking a steady outlet for their new music, they mostly came together to perform their own live electronic works and some by others, much of it multimedia in character (see appendix for a descriptive listing of MEV's core repertoire at this time).[21] Their first public performances took place in September 1966, when the group was featured in several concerts of electronic and instrumental music at the first avant-garde music festival (*Avanguardia Musicale I*) put on by the AFR. The festival consisted of five concerts in the Sala Casella: three featured electronic and live electronic music, one featured instrumental music, and one focused on the music of Giuseppe Chiari. The final evening highlighted Evangelisti's Nuova Consonanza group. An abstract photograph by Phetteplace graced the cover of the festival's program. Publicity for the program listed the first concert simply as "musica elettronica viva"—"live electronic music" in Italian—and legend has it that this arbitrary generic description of the content of their concert provided the group with its enduring moniker. In January 1967 they appeared in a collaboration with a local musical theater company at the Teatro dei Satiri, and soon they were playing regularly in Rome and elsewhere. Musica Elettronica Viva now included a number of occasional additional players, including Michiko Hirayama, Vittorio Gelmetti, and Nicole Rzewski. The group performed again in the second avant-garde music festival put on by the AFR in late March and early April 1967, presenting compositions by themselves and Chiari. The Sonic Arts Union, a live electronic quartet of American composer-performers (Robert Ashley, David Behrman, Alvin Lucier, and Gordon Mumma), played the final concert of the festival. Of the Sonic Arts Union Phetteplace later wrote in his journal: "They are so good, our group might die."[22]

Alongside these first public appearances and the growth of the early disparate forces into a flexible ensemble, MEV embarked on an epic "social journey from self-absorption to group commitment."[23] In early 1967, Rzewski described MEV in a letter to Cage, whom he had met in the mid-1950s through Christian Wolff: "A private, un-official, un-chartered, fly-by-night co-operative venture initiated by serious composers who dedicate themselves to the creation-and/or-performance of live electronic music."[24] Around the same time, Phetteplace expressed the optimism they all felt at the beginning: "Music as a liberating experience. Communication as the way to a possible revolution in human relations. . . . Music may be the archetype for a broad transformation of human relations." In Phetteplace's apartment next to the Pantheon, they went about discovering music for themselves, as if inventing it for the very first time. Their instruments included an early portable synthesizer made from electronic organ parts, percussion, saxophone, trumpet, cello, tape recorders, large olive oil cans, springs, a glass plate, miscellaneous wood and metal objects, rubber bands, and voices. Despite this variety of sound sources, they sometimes joked that their improvisations were simply exercises in feedback. Musica Elettronica Viva put contact microphones on everything, and amplified it all with a homemade PA system. Teitelbaum, who returned to Rome in the fall of 1967 with what is widely acknowledged as the first synthesizer introduced to Europe, described his instrumental technique during this time in this way: "I used to play my synthesizer with my toes, using spring-loaded rocker switches to trigger the envelope generators so I could keep my hands free to twirl knobs."[25] Rzewski later remarked: "By the grace of God, we didn't get electrocuted."[26]

Some of the early improvisations led to conflicts regarding the value of musical training as opposed to found sound, chance, and freedom. In a diary entry in September 1967, Phetteplace wrote of conflicts within the group. Even though he believed that music could contribute to degrees of freedom—emotional, psychological, and physical—he was irritated by some interpretations of the word:

> The subject came up, speaking of freedom, during one of the improv.'s, of
> my resenting the presence of a highly amplified doorbell one person [Alvin

Curran] was playing, while I had only the cello: [the doorbell] covered most other sounds, simply blotting them out, and the player justified it by stating it was something from everyday life, thus useful. I suggested that one leave that chance to everyday life itself: if it must be heard, someone may ring the doorbell at any moment, and yet it wouldn't be amplified: I, on the other hand, had devoted some years to the cello, and didn't wish everyday life to smother out my chances for achieving artistry with it: still, I see I perhaps should not have unplugged my phone before each rehearsal of the improvisation—should be free of that fear by now, and let it ring, perhaps not answering, as many times I fail to: "freedom," not even the least of it, cannot, I believe, become part of a ritual, except as a paradox, of which I personally feel no strong need (at the moment).[27]

This situation demonstrates how, to some degree, the people most invested in the art music tradition were the most willing to toss it aside, whereas someone like Phetteplace, an institutional outsider who had struggled to get where he was musically, wanted to protect the tradition and his "chances for achieving artistry with it." A few months later, he admitted that he still had "grave doubts" about the "fundamental value"of Cage's and Chiari's chance music. Similar power struggles born out of the conflict between control and freedom arose in other groups at the time, as Eddie Prévost recalls in relation to the British free improvising group AMM:

It soon became apparent that music was itself a powerful social mechanism. There were, of course, power struggles within these musical exchanges and collaborations. The freedom to play loudly at the expense of the audibility of another's music is a common arena for dispute. Less common, but as relevant, are issues of hyper- and microactivity, of forbearance, of generosity toward others in letting certain developments occur.[28]

As their interest in the concept of musical freedom developed, Rzewski increasingly believed that "improvisation is the art of the possible."[29] Together they moved from a works-based concept (playing pieces by individual composers) to a socially conscious performance practice (improvising as a means toward collective liberation). Drawing inspiration from the African American avant-garde, including innovators like Ornette Coleman, Cecil Taylor, Albert Ayler, Sun Ra, and musicians associated with the Association for the Advancement of Creative Musicians (AACM), MEV increasingly turned to freedom as a metaphor for a new musical paradigm. Soon, free music—and freeing music and musicians—became an ideological as well as an aesthetic obsession.

"Research": *Spacecraft, Soup, Soundpool*

An early collective improvisation dubbed by Rzewski *Spacecraft*, which MEV used on tours, oscillated, like many MEV works, between "intense violence and meditative peace," as Teitelbaum put it. Rzewski published a "Plan for Spacecraft" in *Source* magazine in January 1968. "Form for a music that has no form," he began cryptically, and continued in a metaphysical manner about the situations the musicians might encounter in the "occupied and created space" of this tight-knit group improvisation, which might last as long as six hours.[30] Teitelbaum later recalled that *Spacecraft*

> combined internal meditative processes with electro-acoustic techniques to create a kind of "space" designed to dissolve barriers between individual egos and merge them into a collective consciousness. By mixing and highly amplifying each musician's signals through a common (and cheap) sound system, the inter-modulation, distortion, inherent unpredictability of analog devices, and the physical displacement and movement of sounds between distantly placed loudspeakers created out-of-body sensations and loss of individuality in the dense noise textures produced.[31]

Rzewski himself admitted that "*Spacecraft* was [still] a composition in the sense that it was based on a particular combination of ideas."[32] Teitelbaum has recalled that "by 1968 we started feeling, especially Frederic, that what we were doing was too hermetic, too elitist. We were playing in these students' venues, and the radical students would come up and confront us with the elitist character of our work, so we just decided that everybody should play."[33] As a result of these concerns, which were directly related to the 1968 conflicts erupting all over Europe, the next step for MEV was audience participation, a move that placed them close to many radical American theater movements.[34] *Zuppa* ("Soup") was inaugurated in October 1968 and performed at L'Attico, an avant-garde gallery space near the Spanish Steps. The published "recipe" for *Soup* calls for several dozen acoustic sound sources and a variety of electronic equipment.[35] Steve Lacy described the piece in this way:

> That was for non musicians, for the folks who had never touched an instrument but who needed to participate in a collective session like that. Before they came, the people didn't know they were going to play. Right away on entering, they saw the musicians completely letting loose, and lots of instruments available there. It's not a proper, conventional sound; it's an utterly unheard of sound. And at the time, that interested us a lot, the unheard of sounds. So for us it was perfect. There was material for us to work with, starting from that sound offered by some guy. So we took that sound and added another sound right after. You had to be really on your toes, in a better than normal state to make music; that is, if a fellow doesn't know how to play an instrument, he can't make a phrase, he can make a sound that might be more interesting than a whole phrase by a musician. But you mustn't lose that sound. You have to seize it immediately, in a way that encourages him to produce another sound. It's a sort of psychological game like that and it was fascinating. Everyone loved that. But it was also a very fragile situation. We discussed lots of notions about musician/nonmusician, public/nonpublic. And we put into question precisely all those categories. It was in the air at

that time, not just for us in Rome, but for lots of people in different places, for example the Living Theatre, Fluxus, Merce Cunningham, Cage.... Lots of people were interested in breaking barriers.[36]

The implications of this "fragile situation" provoked a similar but more radical piece, *Soundpool* (1969), which further explored ways of involving an untrained but eager audience in the collective activity of free music making. Musica Elettronica Viva simply invited everyone to "bring a sound and throw it into the pool." Curran described performances of *Soundpool*:

> On these occasions any one of us could have found themselves making music side by side with many people we had never seen before; professionals from Parma, working class from Bologna, revolutionaries, intellectuals from Paris, university students from Albany, elderly women concert-goers from London, Jazz musicians from Copenhagen, Black Panthers from Antioch College, Bourgeoisie from Tilburg, Holland, Skinheads from north London and Hippies from Amsterdam and New York, and children from Louvain and Bruxelles. In short there were hundreds, and modestly speaking, a few thousand people had played with MEV at that time. There were singing, chanting, droning, drumming on chairs, tables, walls—there were masses of people simply being themselves in the protective and self-evolving community of improvised collective music.[37]

By the summer of 1968 MEV had rented a living/performance space in the Trastevere district of Rome (on the left [or west] bank of the Tevere river), "an old damp soot-covered foundry" in a narrow street.[38] This "floating commune" performed nightly, inviting anyone to join them.[39] Steve Lacy recalls:

> We lived in an old warehouse space that had a good sound. The same group every day, and we'd play for hours. Some amateurs and a few professionals: the music free of all restrictions. The form only as it happens. Nothing forbidden. We would change instruments sometimes and play objects that made sounds (walls, windows, tin cans). There was nothing to say about the music, it was the thing we did, that's all. We wanted to really cook the material among us until it came out nice. Never a question of doing it in public for money. Music like that, completely crazy, most people aren't interested (now a bit more, perhaps). For us that research was a necessary pleasure.[40]

Liner notes for the 1968 Mainstream Records recording of MEV's *Spacecraft* announced that "these studio performances will continue in 1969 on a twice-weekly basis (every Friday and Saturday from 9 to 11 p.m., open to the public and free of charge)." Rzewski explained that "we put up posters in the neighborhood. The idea was that we'd play every night. Anybody could come. We had our collection box, but we were lucky if there was enough in it for a pizza."[41] Alvin Curran recalled that on one occasion the Art Ensemble of Chicago dropped in.[42] But Phetteplace noted in his diary that often no one showed up except the MEV circle, and some nights the neighbors threatened to call the police if they didn't stop playing. Lacy, who lived in this Trastevere space for some time, remarked:

> There were neighbor problems so that we couldn't make noise after ten o'clock at night, or we'd be in trouble. So we put a ceiling on the music. We'd improvise until three o'clock in the morning, but at a very, very, very low level. Nothing louder than this was allowed. And we got away with it for awhile. At least we kept the research going like that. And the neighbors couldn't complain because they couldn't hear it. But it was happening.[43]

Having left behind a works-based tradition of formal concerts for passive audiences, MEV fully disavowed any preconceived expectation of what a "performance" should be. They went beyond found sound and studio synthesis, and created their own sessions of "political therapy"—"therapy" being increasingly necessary in the months following the dramatic escalation of violence in the protest movement in Rome and Milan during March 1968, when police and students clashed in bloody street battles.[44] Sometimes bordering on a cathartic collective ritual without beginning or end, MEV liberated, asserted, and empowered themselves (and anyone willing to join in) by "amplifying junk, banging on junk, scraping on junk and just discovering the natural music that exists in everything all around us."[45] They challenged the audience and themselves to become protagonists in a musical and social revolution. An audience-participation piece like *Soundpool* figured well in this formula, since it was described as "a free improvisation session whose limits are undefined." The concept included a program providing "rudimentary information on the techniques of improvisation."[46] Borrowing a phrase from Cornelius Cardew's Scratch Orchestra "Draft Resolution" (first published in *The Musical Times* in June 1969), Rzewski called these opportunities "improvisation rites."[47] Sharing a ritualized space with the group, free from the constraints of ensemble hierarchies or confines of a score, anyone could express themselves musically while listening to other voices, an idea closely connected to the soul-searching political discussions—sometimes loud, heated, and emotional; sometimes decisively productive—taking place on college campuses and elsewhere all over the Western world. "We became a tribe," recalled Curran, "and we believed that the new directions in music would have a transformative effect on society."[48]

Paradise Now: Protest, Piazzi, Prisons

In July 1968, the exiled American theater troupe the Living Theatre, led by the anarchist-pacifists Julian Beck and Judith Malina, were in residence at the renowned Avignon Festival in France. Musica Elettronica Viva was also there, scheduled to perform a few days after the premiere of the Living Theatre's latest work, *Paradise Now*. The Living Theatre eventually withdrew its performance due to a variety of conflicts with local officials. Many activists present put pressure on MEV to cancel their own performance out of solidarity with the Living Theatre, but Julian Beck himself urged them to play, which they did. Much of the controversy stemmed from *Paradise Now's* revolutionary content. Along with the "actors," the spectators create, and become, the piece itself—leading to a universal liberation of art and mankind ("The Beautiful Non-Violent Anarchist Revolution") depicted in eight three-part sections. Like MEV's *Soundpool, Paradise Now* was created for everyone. In describing their non-ownership of the piece, Beck and Malina renounced copyright and royalties, and explained that *"Paradise Now* is not private property: it is free for any community that wants to play it."[49] In addition to rejecting private property as a move toward true collectivity, the Living Theatre believed that performance should be based on reality and honest expression rather than on fictional works and the "acting" of emotion.[50] Influenced by the Living Theatre's commitment to being "real," Rzewski, who had first met its founders in Berlin in 1963, requested that MEV "not wear masks, [but] rejoice in nakedness."[51] Along with this metaphorical disrobing, MEV made a conscious choice to minimize their link to institutions, and the model provided by their friends in the Living Theatre motivated them toward a greater level of activism and political engagement. Part of this move was inspired by music that occurred spontaneously on the streets during demonstrations in the summer and fall of 1968, an in-the-moment music fitting to the struggles going on around them. In August 1968, MEV initiated a series of informal (and illegal) midnight performances in the public square Piazza Navona, creating electronic soundscapes for the people who happened to be there (not unlike the Living Theatre's events in the streets), which often included plainclothes policemen, tourists, and homeless people. Phetteplace described some of these events in his journal:

> Played feedback pc. with radios with ind. mics, cont. mics, Steve Lacy with mouthpiece only, Rzew and Teitelbaum in Pza Navona. All very high sounds, very loud and good. Rzew. wanted to walk around; I wanted to sit down in circle in piazza. . . . Lots of plainclothesmen in P. Navona heard the piece; no arresting tho we played after 11 p.m. (11:30–12:30). Drunk man (old, decrepit) fascinated, congratulated and embraced me. All good.[52]

That year MEV also participated in a benefit concert at Saint Paul's Church for civilian victims of the war in Vietnam, put on by "Americans in Rome for Immediate Peace in Vietnam." Phetteplace described the Avignon experience and other events in a passionate letter to Cage, and mused about the most effective, engaged method of "protest" for artists in these conflicted times:

> The problem seems to become more and more that of letting everyone who wants to listen listen, while trying to pacify in some other way those who are evidently so troubled by the atmosphere of the concerts that rather

than develop the habit of listening develop the habit of not coming to the concert at all, as a form of "protest." Our protest cannot be made up of only silences, *if* there is anything to contest....I deeply question whether "protest" action does more than to strengthen what it is one is protesting. There are two activity-fields now: one has to do with constraints and power/profit.... The other has to do with facilitating life and its enjoyment by 100% of the people (inanimate "beings" being also honored, air not polluted, etc.). This is what should attract our energy and time, whenever thru circumstances we are still "free to act."[53]

Bringing music to the oppressed classes became central to their agenda. In particular, factory workers and prisoners became subjects of interest to MEV, in keeping with issues of concern to the New Left.[54] In late 1968, Rzewski wrote to Cage: "We have been working in the direction of 'audience participation.' People *do* want to play. Some interesting evenings at our studio with twenty-five to thirty people playing. Some joyful noisemaking. Children too. We call it 'Soup.' Also we've been playing in factories and prisons."[55] In November 1968 MEV performed at Rebibbia Prison on the outskirts of Rome. According to Phetteplace's notes, the ensemble included himself, Lacy, Rzewski, Teitelbaum, Vittorio Gelmetti, and Franco Cataldi. In his diary he observed that "Alvin would be great for prisons; Steve Lacy got the closest to their hunger...then Bach...then Beethoven." The program included Beethoven (Piano Sonata Op. 110), Bach ("Adagio" for cello and piano), a group improvisation, Thelonious Monk ('Round Midnight), a second group improvisation, and "Pf. music—S.L., Fr. R." Phetteplace later described his impressions of the event:

> The improvs. was somewhat like [R. D.] Laing's critique of that 19th cent. German pathologist who stuck needle in forehead of 24-yr old schizophrenic girl: "experimental music." When the glass-plate scratching got going, that's when they cringed: I wished I could stop it all—the electronics, I mean. The audience: Director (late—but just enough), chief guard, priest (mean), 40 young prisoners (ca. 18–30), one of whom had a face and head of Kalinowsky, but more corrupt somehow (how?), all sentences for 10–30 years; and one grey-haired, near catatonic, tall thin old prisoner.[56]

That night Phetteplace wrote in his diary: "No sleep after Rebibbia concert; they were so grateful." Two days later he wrote a letter to a prisoner he had met, named Antonio Risso, who wished for mail. Musica Elettronica Viva's desire to bring music to the bleak spaces of punishment and hard labor continued the Italian-Marxist tradition of engagement with the incarcerated and the oppressed.

Conclusion

In assessing MEV's activism during a period of just under three years, it would appear that their participation in direct action events (protests, prison performances, benefits, etc.) were more effective than the more experimental "research" (as Lacy described it) of pieces like *Soup* and *Soundpool*, which aimed to eradicate social boundaries by allowing all people to become musicians in whatever way they desired. Alvin Curran has written that

> there had never before been a music made on such far reaching principles of individual freedom and democratic consciousness.... What the group MEV (along with AMM) essentially did was to redefine music as a form of property that belonged equally to everyone and hence to encourage its creation freely by and through anyone anywhere.... We believed that the music was the property of no one individual or author, but that of the group, and that music is a universal human right, and any human being, by mere will, can also be a music-maker.[57]

In reality, these admirable beliefs did not guarantee that all people would be capable of productively engaging in the process of music making, any more than the lofty goals of communal living hindered continual arguments about who had to do the dishes or take out the trash. In an interview, Steve Lacy agreed that "we no longer wanted a difference between the public and the musicians." "But for us," he continued,

> it didn't last, and after six weeks we stopped that and started to do the normal concert again. It was like the myth of Prometheus, really. The public will tear you apart if you expose yourself like that. After a while, they no longer appreciate it and they start to destroy everything. We didn't know it would be like that but it was. Why? I don't know. It was very mysterious, a bit frightening too.[58]

Musica Elettronica Viva's founders later recalled that the group was "just a bunch of friends, more or less a chance happening" and "a tribe, driving around in a VW bus."[59] But, in fact, the group represented something more significant than those flippant characterizations, namely, a musically minded attempt to dissolve social hierarchies within the deeply symbolic structures of musical form, ensembles, concert ritual, and performance practice.[60] To what degree MEV succeeded in establishing "music as a universal human right," even for a brief mythical moment, remains to be evaluated. Indeed, around or soon after 1969, a number of events brought permanent changes to MEV's trajectory: some members returned to the United States (Phetteplace, Rzewski, Teitelbaum); the group fractured into various short-lived subspecies (The Contraband; MEV²); and MEV composers began exploring extended solo improvisation (Curran, most notably in his *Canti e Vedute del Giardino Magnetico* [1974]) and more traditional forms of composition (Rzewski's set of thirty-six virtuosic solo piano variations, *The People United Will Never Be Defeated* [1975], for example).[61] A version of MEV first toured the United States at the start of the 1970s, joined by guests Maryanne Amacher, Anthony Braxton, and others. Over the next few years many more improvisers played with MEV, including Karl Berger, Jon Gibson, George

Lewis, and Garrett List. Though MEV lived on, and indeed still exists at the time of this writing, it functioned after its initial period as a more or less fixed ensemble comprising highly skilled composer-performers who gave approximately one public performance per year.[62] Though improvisation remains their primary mode of musical expression, and revolutionary ideology remains prominent in the protagonists' recent writings— "we urgently call for an open revolt against the encroachment of governmental ignorance and corporate speculation in the arts and call in the stead for a program of massive proportions to regenerate dignity and real work places for American artists where unfettered experimentation may take place," Curran and Teitelbaum wrote in 1989—their attempt to help all humans realize their potential as music makers seems to have been abandoned.[63] This is not to imply that MEV's engagement was insincere, that its "research" failed, or that its attempts to "make music with whatever means are available" were made in vain. They were without question made in the creative and rebellious spirit of their time. But perhaps, in the capricious climate of the late 1960s, the optimistic music of Lacy's "fragile situation" was threatened not so much by the burden of ideology, but by simple human behavior—the revolutionary flavor cooked out of the soup by the masses it was meant to feed.

Appendix

An undated, typewritten document held in the Jon Phetteplace Papers, titled "Programs of Musica Elettronica Viva," lists the following:

Program I

David Behrman, *Wave Train* (for two to five performers with stringed instruments, magnetic inductance microphones, amplifiers, sine-wave generator, ring-modulator, loudspeakers, and tape [15'])

John Cage, *Imaginary Landscape No. 5* (live version for two players by Jon Phetteplace, with two tape recorders and phonographs [3'])

Frederic Rzewski, *Impersonation* (for four two-track tape recorders, amplifiers, four-channel photocell-mixer, amplified vocal sounds [15'])

Luc Ferrari, *Und So Weiter* (for amplified piano with accessories and two-track tape [10'])

Jon Phetteplace, "new composition for three players with violoncello, magnetic microphone, and photocell-divider" (13')

Allan Bryant, *Quadruple Play* (for rubber bands with resonators, contact microphones, amplifiers, reverberation, and four loudspeakers, with audio controlled lighting system [12'])

Program II

Frederic Rzewski, *Composition for Two* (for amplified glass plates, metal springs, wood, and accessories, with two two-track tapes, modulators, and mixer [17'])

Jon Phetteplace, *No. 4, 1967* (full-track tape [16'])

Giuseppe Chiari, *Lyndon Johnson*, Text (electronic version by Phetteplace and Rzewski [10'])

Allan Bryant, "new work for electric string and reed instruments with reverberation" (15')

Takehisa Kosugi, *Anima 7* (electronic version with violoncello [7'])

Program III

Allan Bryant, "new work for electric string and percussion instruments, using Sylvania luminescent panels" [15']

Jon Phetteplace, *Gira—Gira* (for soloist with portable record player [10'])

MEV, *Rotonda Combine* (collective work for any four tapes, photocell-mixer, and extras [10'])

Giuseppe Chiari, *Pubblico* (for solo cello, tape recorder, and accessories [20'])

Mauricio Kagel, *Antithese* and *Memetics* (*Metapiece*) (for piano and electronic tape [10'])

Frederic Rzewski, *Piece with Projectors* (for two groups of musicians using electronic sound sources, dancers, and slide projector operators [12'], with photographic material by Jon Phetteplace)

Material for Special Programs, Lectures, Etc.
I. Longer Works; Lecture; Short Programs

Giuseppe Chiari, *Le Corde* (for speaker and piano tuner, with three pianos [at least two grands], projector, amplifiers, loudspeakers, tape, and blackboard [ca. 1 hour])

Chiari, *Teatrino* (for one player, with piano, tape recorder, phonograph, microphone amplifiers, electric drill, and accessories [ca. 45'])

Pietro Grossi and S2FM Studio, "Composition of electronic music from the studio in the Conservatorio L. Cherubini, Florence, 6 to 8 channels" (45'–80')

John Cage, *Where Are We Going? And What Are We Doing?* (Lecture for speaker and three tapes, with electronic operations four simultaneous texts, in a special version with translations in Italian and German by Jon Phetteplace, for two performers [45'])

II. Miscellaneous Tapes

Frederic Rzewski, *Zoologischer Garten* (23')

Vittorio Gelmetti, *Modulazioni per Michelangelo; Treni d'Onda a Modulazione d'Intensita; Prossimamente*

Karlheinz Stockhausen, *Telemusik* (17')

Jon Phetteplace, *No. 1, 1965* (14'); *No. 4, 1967* (16'); *Gira–Gira* (30')

Giuseppe Chiari, *Musica Verita* (10' to 120'); *Il Cielo e la Terra; Quando il Cinema e Lontano*

Michael Sahl, *The Waltz* (8')

Information
Frederic Rzewski, 55 via della Luce, Rome, or Jon Phetteplace, piazza
della Rotonda 2, Rome.

Notes

1. Jacques Attali, *Noise: The Political Economy of Music*, trans. Brian Massumi
(Minneapolis: University of Minnesota Press, 1985), 137, 146.

2. Frederic Rzewski, program notes for Festival Internationale del Teatro
Universitario (Parma, March 23, 1968), reprinted in *Source* 3, no. 2 (July 1969): 91.

3. Steve Lacy, "MEV Notes" (ca. 1968), reprinted in *Steve Lacy: Conversations*, ed. Jacob Weiss (Durham, N.C.: Duke University Press, 2006), 244.

4. The earliest extant recording I have found of an MEV improvisation was
made on September 4, 1966, in Jon Phetteplace's apartment at Piazza della
Rotonda 2. (Jon Phetteplace dates this performance as September 4, 1967, but
all available evidence suggests that this session, labeled "Improvisation 5," was
recorded one year earlier.) The recording is held in the Jon Phetteplace Papers,
Mandeville Special Collections Library, University of California, San Diego.

5. Frederic Rzewski, "Musica Elettronica Viva, Words: For Larry Austin,"
Source 2, no. 1 (January 1968): 25.

6. There are many written anecdotes about the origins of Musica Elettronica Viva, especially by Rzewski, Curran, and Teitelbaum. One of the most
comprehensive is Alvin Curran, "A Guided Tour Through 12 Years of American
Music in Rome," *Soundings* 10 (1976), unpaginated. For other accounts of MEV
and thoughts on improvisation by the primary participants, see Alvin Curran,
"Homemade," *Source* 1, no. 2 (July 1967): 18–41; Alvin Curran, "MEV, Soup,
and History," *Musics* 23 (November 1979): 14–15; Alvin Curran, "Musica Elettronica Viva—Words," *Source* 2, no. 1 (January 1968): 24–27; Alvin Curran,
"Thoughts on Soup—A Recipe," *The Drama Review* 14, no. 1 (Fall 1969): 97;
Frederic Rzewski, "Plan for Spacecraft," *Source* 2, no. 1 (January 1968): 66–68;
Frederic Rzewski, "Little Bangs: Towards a Nihilist Theory of Improvisation"
(lecture delivered on March 31, 2000, in Frankfurt, Germany), reprinted in
German as "Theorie der Improvisation," *MusikTexte* 86/87 (November 2000):
41–45; Frederic Rzewski, "Sound Pool (1969)," *Dissonanz* 6 (September 1970):
13–14; and Richard Teitelbaum, "Live Electronic Music," in *John Cage: An
Anthology*, ed. Richard Kostelanetz (New York: Da Capo, 1991), 139–42. Several
additional, previously unpublished writings and correspondence by Rzewski
regarding MEV history and performance practice can be found in *Nonsequiturs/
Unlogische Folgerungen* (Cologne: MusikTexte, 2007), 252–364.

7. Alvin Curran, "On Spontaneous Music" [1995], accessible at http://
www.alvincurran.com/Curran_writings.html; also published in German in Sabine Feisst, *Der Begriff "Improvisation" in der neuen Musik* (Sinzig: Studio Verlag,
1997); and in Italian as "Della Musica Spontanea" in *Oltre il Silenzio* 2/2 (Rome;
October 1996).

8. See Richard Teitelbaum, "Intervallic Relations in Atonal Music," *Journal of Music Theory* 9, no. 1 (Spring 1965): 72–127.

9. Phetteplace also created Italian translations of Cage's *45' for a Speaker*
and parts of *Silence*, and tape realizations of Cage's indeterminate works. As a

result, he became embattled in a bitter legal dispute with W. Hinrichsen and H. Swarsenski at the C. F. Peters Corporation, Hinrichsen Edition (New York and London), who threatened to sue Phetteplace and Rzewski in 1967 over copyright issues (reproduction rights, fees) regarding translations, realizations, and performance of Cage's works abroad. Copies of this correspondence are housed in the John Cage Correspondence at Northwestern University and in the Phetteplace Papers at the University of California San Diego.

10. Similar tensions affected other like-minded groups of the period. Eddie Prévost, cofounder in 1965 of the British free improvising group AMM, has written: "It is interesting to note how so many advocates of this 'leveling' scuttle back to the protective folds of the musical establishments, leaving their unschooled associates high and dry now that experimentation is (for them) exhausted." Eddie Prévost, "Discourse of a Dysfunctional Drummer: Collaborative Dissonances, Improvisation, and Cultural Theory," in *The Other Side of Nowhere: Jazz, Improvisation, and Communities in Dialogue* (Middletown, Conn.: Wesleyan University Press, 2004), 361. Curran, Rzewski, and Teitelbaum all eventually became college composition teachers. Phetteplace left music almost entirely by the mid-1970s.

11. Gianmario Borio, "Die Improvisationsgruppe Nuova Consonanza," Liner Notes for *Gruppo di Improvvisazione Nuova Consonanza*, Edition RZ 1009 (1992), trans. Laurie Schwartz.

12. Daniela Tortora's book *Nuova Consonanza: Trent' anni di musica contemporanea in Italia (1959–1988)* (Lucca: Libreria Musicale Italiana Editrice, 1990) gives a detailed overview of new music activities in Italy—and Rome in particular—during the 1960s.

13. See Paul Griffiths, *Modern Music and After: Directions Since 1945* (New York: Oxford University Press, 1995), 189.

14. The 1968 election results are found in Robert Lumley, *States of Emergency: Cultures of Revolt in Italy from 1968 to 1978* (London: Verso, 1990), xi.

15. In a 2003 interview with Daniel Varela, Rzewski refers to himself as "a Gramscian"; see "Frederic Rzewski," *Perfect Sound Forever*, http://www.furious.com/perfect/rzewski.html (accessed October 29, 2007). Rzewski, who studied Marxism from a very early age, recalled that his first piano teacher was "a Communist," and would give him political lessons along with the musical; interview with the author, April 2, 1998.

16. Richard Drake, *Apostles and Agitators: Italy's Marxist Revolutionary Tradition* (Cambridge, Mass.: Harvard University Press, 2003), x.

17. Chantal Mouffe, "Introduction: Gramsci Today," in *Gramsci and Marxist Theory*, ed. Chantal Mouffe (London: Routledge and Kegan Paul, 1979), 1.

18. Peter Yates, "An Open Letter to the Foundations," *Arts and Architecture* (August 1963): 9.

19. Rome-based artist (and friend of Alvin Curran) Edith Schloss described MEV's first performances in her "Report from Italy—Dropping Out into Music: The Audience as Orchestra," *The Village Voice*, August 7, 1969.

20. See Joel Chadabe, *Electric Sound: The Past and Promise of Electronic Music* (Upper Saddle River, N.J.: Prentice Hall, 1997), 104.

21. See also Hugh Davies, comp., "International Electronic Music Catalog," *Electronic Music Review* 2, no. 3 (April/July 1967): 108–9.

22. Phetteplace's "1966–67 Notebook" entry; Jon Phetteplace Papers, box 2, folder 6, Mandeville Special Collections, University of California San Diego.

23. Griffiths, *Modern Music and After*, 204.

24. Letter from Rzewski to Cage, March 5, 1967; John Cage Correspondence Collection, Northwestern University.

25. Teitelbaum, in Chadabe, *Electric Sound*, 309–10. See also Randy Raine-Reusch, "Integrating Extremes: The Music of Richard Teitelbaum," *Musicworks* 85 (Spring 2003): 41–53.

26. Rzewski, in Chadabe, *Electric Sound*, 104.

27. Jon Phetteplace, diary entry, September 1967; held in the Jon Phetteplace Papers, Mandeville Special Collections Library, University of California, San Diego.

28. Eddie Prévost, "The Discourse of a Dysfunctional Drummer," 358. It is important to note, however, that unlike MEV, all the original members of AMM—Prévost, Keith Rowe, Lou Gare, and Lawrence Shaeff—had backgrounds in jazz.

29. Rzewski, "The Algebra of Everyday Life," foreword to *Christian Wolff: Cues, Writings, and Conversations* (Cologne: MusikTexte, 1998), 14.

30. See Rzewski, "Plan for Spacecraft," *Source* 2, no. 1 (January 1968): 66–68.

31. Teitelbaum, liner notes to *OHM: The Early Gurus of Electronic Music, 1948–1980* (Ellipsis Arts CD 3670), 44.

32. Rzewski in interview with Monique Verken, *The Drama Review* 14, no. 1 (Fall 1969): 94.

33. Teitelbaum, in Chadabe, *Electric Sound*, 104.

34. See Arthur Sainer, *The Radical Theatre Notebook* (New York: Avon, 1975), 69–79.

35. The sound sources included, among more conventional instruments, glass wind chimes, suspended aerial poles, cowbells, sleigh bells, slide whistles, police whistles, bird calls, harmonicas, bandoneons, metal sheets, glass plates, ping-pong balls, and an empty five-liter Agip lubricant can. See Curran, "Thoughts on Soup—A Recipe," *The Drama Review* 14, no. 1 (Fall 1969): 97.

36. Steve Lacy, interview with Raymond Gervais and Yves Bouliane, in *Steve Lacy: Conversations*, ed. Jason Weiss (Durham, N.C.: Duke University Press, 2006), 70–71.

37. Alvin Curran, "Making Music with People You Have Never Seen Before and Will Likely Never See Again [1985]," accessible on Curran's Web site: http://www.alvincurran.com/writings/music%20with%20people.html.

38. Curran, "A Guided Tour through 12 Years of American Music in Rome," unpaginated.

39. Teitelbaum, in Randy Raine-Reusch, "Integrating Extremes: The Music of Richard Teitelbaum," *Musicworks* 85 (Spring 2003): 43.

40. Steve Lacy, "Roba," in *Steve Lacy: Conversations*, 248.

41. Rzewski, in Chadabe, *Electric Sound*, 105.

42. Curran, interview with the author, March 8, 1999. Though very different in their backgrounds and in their relationships to their inherited traditions, the Art Ensemble of Chicago and MEV have some key factors in common, not least that both were self-exiled American improvisation groups in Europe (the Art Ensemble lived in Paris from 1969 until 1971), where they had better opportunities for performing despite the anti-American sentiments of the period. See Lincoln T. Beauchamp Jr., ed., *Art Ensemble of Chicago: Great Black Music Ancient to the Future* (Chicago: AEC Publishing, 1998), 60.

43. Lacy, interview with Christoph Cox, in *Steve Lacy: Conversations*, 225.

44. Christoph Cox, "The Jerrybuilt Future: The Sonic Arts Union, ONCE Group and MEV's Live Electronics," in *Undercurrents: The Hidden Wiring of Modern Music* (London: Continuum, 2002), 36; see also Lumley, *States of Emergency*, 66–67.

45. Curran, interview with the author, March 8, 1999.

46. Rzewski, "Sound Pool (1969)," 13.

47. Rzewski, "Prose Music," in *Dictionary of Contemporary Music*, ed. John Vinton (New York: Dutton, 1971), 595. By 1969, MEV had collaborated with both AMM and the young Scratch Orchestra.

48. Curran, interview with the author, April 25, 2006.

49. Julian Beck and Judith Malina, *Paradise Now: Collective Creation of The Living Theatre* (New York: Random House, 1971).

50. See Julian Beck, *The Life of the Theatre: The Relation of the Artist to the Struggle of the People* (New York: Limelight Edition, 1986); Pierre Biner, *The Living Theatre* (New York: Horizon, 1972); John Tytell, *The Living Theatre: Art, Exile, and Outrage* (New York: Grove, 1995).

51. Rzewski, in "Musica Elettronica Viva, Words: For Larry Austin," 25.

52. Jon Phetteplace, diary entry, September 1967; held in the Jon Phetteplace Papers, Mandeville Special Collections Library, University of California, San Diego.

53. Letter from Phetteplace to Cage, August 3, 1968; John Cage Correspondence Collection, Northwestern University, file "Phetteplace."

54. See Lumley, *States of Emergency*, 40.

55. Letter from Rzewski to Cage, October 31, 1968; John Cage Correspondence Collection, Northwestern University. In an interview with Raymond Gervais and Yves Bouliane, Steve Lacy describes an MEV concert in an occupied factory (Giuseppe Chiari also participated, primarily with a megaphone). See Weiss, *Steve Lacy: Conversations*, 63–64.

56. Jon Phetteplace, diary entry, September 1967; held in the Jon Phetteplace Papers, Mandeville Special Collections Library, University of California, San Diego.

57. Curran, "On Spontaneous Music," accessible on Curran's Web site: http://www.alvincurran.com/writings/spontaneous.html.

58. See Weiss, *Steve Lacy: Conversations*, 70–71.

59. Rzewski in Chadabe, *Electric Sound*, 104; Curran, interview with the author, April 25, 2006.

60. "We are trying to make art into a real experience," said Rzewski. "Our music is not meant to impress people, but to liberate them." Rzewski, in an interview with Monique Verken, *The Drama Review* 14, no. 1 (Fall 1969): 94.

61. Curran and Rzewski also wrote a number of minimalist, indeterminate process pieces for open ensembles (including nonmusicians) during this time, most notably Rzewski's *Les Moutons de Panurge* (1969), and *Attica* and *Coming Together* (1972); and Curran's large set of monophonic pieces *Music for Every Occasion* (1971–72; first published in Michael Byron's *Pieces 3* in 1977).

62. Most recently, at the time of writing, they performed at the prestigious Tanglewood Festival for Contemporary Music in Lenox, Mass., on August 2, 2007. Judith Tick's three-part essay "Generation of '38" (Part I, "Sounding Together While Sounding Apart" [7–11]; Part II, "Music Is What Happens" [35–37]; and Part III, "Because Time Was in the Air" [53–57]), published in

the Festival program booklet, places the MEV generation in a resonant histori-cal context.

63. See Curran and Teitelbaum (for MEV), Program Notes for the New Music America Festival at the Knitting Factory, New York City, August 1989; available on Curran's Web site: http://www.alvincurran.com/writings/mev.html. On this occasion the trio was joined by Garrett List and Steve Lacy.

6

The Problem of the Political in Steve Reich's *Come Out*

Sumanth Gopinath

Among the many ironies in the legacy of the "long 1960s" within the United States, a relatively minor one can be found within the repertory of American electroacoustic music. Specifically, Steve Reich's well-known composition *Come Out* (1966) has, in retrospect, served as the most prominent historical memorial for the legal and political drama known as the Harlem Six case. During most of the 1960s and early 1970s, the plight of the Harlem Six—six young African American men from Harlem wrongfully accused of and sentenced to life imprisonment for the murder of a Jewish storekeeper—came to symbolize the racism and corruption rampant in the American policing and criminal justice systems. Inseparable from the Harlem Riots of 1963, which number among the earliest of dozens of battles between police officers and impoverished black city dwellers during the decade, the cause of the Harlem Six attracted many distinguished spokesmen and women, including Ossie Davis, James Baldwin, Louis Aragon, Bertrand Russell, Gunter Grass, LeRoi Jones/Amiri Baraka, Allen Ginsberg, Paul Sweezy, John Lennon, and Yoko Ono.[1] And yet, today the measure of aware-ness is strikingly different: few reminders of the case can be found in mainstream English-language print media over the past decade—except, of course, in commentaries on *Come Out*.[2] Although for reasons of differential access and usage the Internet serves as an imperfect gauge of mass familiarity, it is worth noting that while *Come Out* has, as of this writing, a short but informative and mostly accurate *Wikipedia* page mentioning the Harlem Six, the Harlem Six case itself does not.[3]

Come Out thus bears the lion's share of the burden of representation for this particular historical situation. We might be tempted to ask, "How does it fare in this regard?" Although most critical writings on the piece avoid this thorny, troublesome question, two recent contributions attempt to interpret the piece in a contextual way and hence at some level engage it. In Lloyd Whitesell's article "White Noise: Race and Erasure in the Cultural Avant-Garde," the author discusses the piece alongside a number of other nineteenth- and twentieth-century artworks, writings, and compositions that demonstrate a tendency for white racial self-representation through the use of techniques and thematics of *negation*. In the case of *Come Out*, racial issues are heightened not because the piece—which is based on the recorded voice of Daniel Hamm, one of the Harlem Six—uses the vocal utterance of a black man but because its compositional process (to be explained below) ends up erasing the presence of that man, revealing instead an "aural condensation of 'backgroundness' without color."[4] The implication from Whitesell's reading is that the piece at some level *does not* concern itself with the Harlem Six case and in fact is perhaps much more about Reich himself. Mitchell Morris, in his essay "Musical Virtues," takes a different tack. He provisionally attempts to assess the ethical "virtues and vices" of the piece within a longer essay arguing for a kind of "ethical criticism" of music—one ostensibly based on context-specific rather than universal criteria.[5] In Morris's estimation, *Come Out* fares reasonably well, successfully representing a critique of the state, the trauma of violence, and mourning. But the piece also enacts a certain degree of sublimated violence against Hamm himself, exploits his pain for aesthetic gain, and fails to pay Hamm for royalties or damages in any sense.

Both Whitesell and Morris have contributed valuable interpretations of *Come Out*, and my reading of the work resonates in many ways with theirs.[6] But I want to argue for a somewhat different approach, one built upon the following four perspectives.

1. Given the relative lack of analytic specificity characteristic of the arguments described above, I would argue that it is helpful, even necessary, to focus on sonic particularities before we can make more *concrete* observations and thereby emerge with a powerful reading of an aesthetic utterance.[7]
2. The problem of defining historical context, while always difficult in interpretation, is to some extent clarified in studying *Come Out*. That is to say, the Harlem Six case should at least serve as *one*, if not *the* contextual locus that might help provide a perspective on the piece itself. Although, as we shall see, Reich's involvement in the case was limited, the historical particulars resonate in all sorts of ways with the rather inchoate auditory information found in the piece itself.[8] Consideration of details of the case provides a useful historical framework for interpretation that

hitherto has been mostly ignored or oversimplified in previous readings of Reich's piece.

3. If Whitesell and Morris orient their readings around problematics of *self-representation* or *ethics*, respectively, it is my contention that we would do much better to ground a study of *Come Out* in a notion of the *political*. Taking our cue from the fact that Reich has often called this piece a "political piece,"[9] it is a simple matter to acknowledge that the work directly engages a particular political situation and historical moment within a larger social and political movement (the Civil Rights/Black liberation movements). But what might our specific understanding of "politics" be in this case? I propose that it is fruitful to invoke Fredric Jameson's now-established notion of the "political unconscious"—in which political positions and ideologies, whether coherent or half-formed, are revealed through the psychoanalytic and ideo-logical analysis of narrative.[10] Indeed, the Freudian unconscious might serve as a powerful model for the ambiguous yet suggestive fragments of sound in Reich's work. Although Reich himself claims that the composition's structuring process intensifies the meaning of Hamm's recorded words (hence implying that the piece becomes more concrete), he also described his works as creating aural "Rorschach test[s]," in which the listener has a great deal of freedom to interpret what is heard.[11] Just as this hermeneutic flexibility makes *Come Out* less a text to decode and more a site of interpretive struggle, one that mimics the political contest itself, so Jameson's variant of the political resists the possible foreclosure of meaning found in notions of representa-tion and ethics, no matter how provisionally or contextually defined. To state the problem as simply as possible, the extreme variability of possible readings means that *Come Out* does not have a single, clearly defined politics. Nor can we unproblematically tally up a balance sheet of positions—progressive, liberal, conser-vative—or ethical merits/demerits, since signifiers in the piece mutate and transform kaleidoscopically, merging oppressor and oppressed, self and other, organic and inorganic. But it may be that the compositional choice to create a work—indeed, an entire aesthetic—that effectively imitates the unconscious itself was in fact a political choice of sorts, one that aligned Reich with both earlier psychological modernisms and the contrarian currents of the New Left and counterculture.[12]

4. Following the insights of Tia DeNora, we might emphasize that artifacts—including artworks—in and of themselves don't have a politics, and that instead they come to be used politically in various ways, such as through acts of interpretation.[13] Contri-buting yet another close reading of an artwork is in many ways against the spirit of what DeNora is herself trying to do in her

ethnographic work, but with this in mind, I hope to argue for a reading of *Come Out* that is both fully aware of its intention to steer the discourse around the piece toward greater historical specificity, and attuned to the work's *political potentialities* that may have some relevance to our present condition.

Keeping these four perspectives in mind, the following essay outlines details of the Harlem Six case and Reich's relationship to it, offers semiotically oriented analytical comments on the work, teases out the various lineaments of an interpretation based on that analysis, and ends with a brief reflection on the composition's political utility today.

The Harlem Six Case

By the mid-1960s, the Civil Rights Movement had begun to splinter. After the achievements of the passing of the Civil Rights Act (1964) and the Voting Rights Act (1965), activists increasingly turned their attention to Northern cities, where *de facto* segregation was entrenched and seemingly impossible to transform through legal change. Protest and civil disobedience campaigns in both the North and South were met with increasingly violent responses by police and white residents, perhaps most famously in the march on Chicago led by Martin Luther King Jr. in the summer of 1966. These hostile conditions encouraged the continuing growth of Black Nationalist politics, particularly in conjunction with the expansion of the Nation of Islam thanks to the rise of an electrifying and politically engaged preacher, Malcolm X. The period also witnessed the related rise of "Black Power," which emphasized to varying degrees notions of black separatism, economic self-reliance, and cultural politics, and of the Black Panther Party, which brought a black Marxist and anti-imperialist agenda to the forefront of the Black liberation movement.[14] Equally significant, conflicts between black city residents and police officers escalated into full-fledged battles in dozens of cities throughout the decade including New York (Harlem and Bedford-Stuyvesant, 1964), Los Angeles (Watts, 1965), Newark (1967), Detroit (1967), Washington, D.C. (1968), and Baltimore (1968).[15]

The case of the Harlem Six began amid the beginnings of this racial turmoil in April 1964. Due to the increasing tensions, the city administration had placed squads of heavily armed riot-control police along 125th St. in Harlem—a decision that would provoke further violence. On the 17th of that month, a young black schoolgirl "brushed against a crate of grapefruit" at a fruit stand, knocking some of the fruit onto the ground. Other schoolchildren picked up the fruit and tossed them about "like baseballs." The proprietor blew his whistle to attract the attention of the beat policeman, but riot-control police appeared and began to attack the children with clubs. A few people intervened, including a number of black teenagers who began to fight back and exhort the surrounding crowd to do the same. Several people, including teenagers Daniel Hamm and Wallace Baker, were taken to the 28th precinct police station and beaten mercilessly. (Baker's injuries resulted in serious brain damage from which he never recovered.)[16] The next day, the youths and the others were released from the station, intending to file charges of police brutality against the cops involved in the beatings.

The incident, later known as the Little Fruit Stand Riot, would surely have been forgotten had it not been for a subsequent event in which the Hungarian Jewish proprietor of a used clothing store on 125th St. and Fifth Ave., Margit Sugar, was attacked and stabbed to death. Looking for a group of suspects upon which to pin the murder charges, officers and detectives identified a group of six friends who had previously successfully resisted arrest on an unconnected charge. Within hours of the murder, Hamm and Baker, and their friends William Craig, Ronald Felder, Walter Thomas, and Robert Rice, soon to be known as the Harlem Six, were rounded up by the police (along with about one hundred other young black men), intimidated and beaten again, and pressured to sign confessions—to which Hamm and Rice acceded.

The media quickly turned against the youths, assuming that they were guilty and that their crimes included a racially motivated anti-white murder. Denied independent representation—the courts having decided (following a law from 1902) that they required state-appointed representation due to their indigence—the six were all found guilty of murder and sentenced to life imprisonment, barely escaping the death penalty, which had been ruled unconstitutional just prior to the conviction. On advice from the progressive black lawyer Conrad Lynn, the mothers of the six requested an appeal on the basis that the law denying them the right to pay for their sons' defense was unconstitutional. They then set about the task of raising funds, collecting money on the streets of Harlem.

A number of intellectuals and activists soon became involved in this effort and began advocating on behalf of the six young men. These included the celebrated novelist and essayist James Baldwin, who would arguably become the most important public spokesperson for the Harlem Six, writing several journalistic pieces about the case and also penning an eloquent petition signed by national and international luminaries. Another crucial figure in this tale is Truman Nelson, a self-educated Marxist novelist and historian who had become known as a radical antiracist in the tradition of the abolitionists.[17] In autumn 1964 he wrote *The Torture of Mothers*, perhaps the best-known treatment of the Harlem Six case. Although the book is certainly flawed—reviewer June Meyer criticized its confusing, unclear presentation of the case's facts and often-bombastic prose[18]—it nonetheless comprises a powerful discussion of the case and plea on behalf of the six. Nelson made use of his own transcriptions of taped testimony from participants in the events surrounding the case.[19] Setting the quotations in bold type and separating sentences and even phrases from each other (as opposed to collecting them in paragraphs), the testimony reads like a kind of postwar American poetry instead of transcribed depositions or interviews. Moreover, the black vernacular English represented in these transcriptions—one whose "Southern" aspects were becoming slowly, but by no means completely, "northernized"—is rendered without the exaggerations of black dialect caricatures or even black cultural nationalist poetry. The result is a somewhat smoothed-out but noncaricatured rendering of the black subjects in the book, a rendering that helps "the defendants tell their stories with a passion that confers a dignity upon them beyond the power of the police to dismiss [such] stories."[20]

In the following years, the case gained increasing notoriety as an example of the unjust state machinery of the New York (and U.S.) justice system, and a growing number of international intellectuals and celebrities began to demonstrate their support for the appeals case and retrials of the six.[21] The appeals case was eventually successful in 1968, but a protracted series of retrials was to follow, lasting until 1973. Toward the end of the retrials it became increasingly clear that the district attorney's case against the six was based entirely on fabricated evidence, and that the prosecution's star witness, Robert Barnes, was probably involved in the murder himself.[22]

Reich's political involvement in the case of the Harlem Six was accidental and took place during the case's early development. Having recently returned to his hometown of New York from San Francisco, where he spent the first half of the 1960s, he moved into a loft on Duane Street in what is now called TriBeCa, and spent time with friends in the art world and downtown music scene. While he was getting settled in the city and waiting for something to "come along,"[23] an interesting opportunity arose sometime in late 1965 or early 1966. As Reich states,

> [A]t that period of time I was continuing musically the ideas that were originated in *It's Gonna Rain*. The first thing was a piece called *Come Out* which was done here in New York and how that came about was that a man by the name of Truman Nelson, who was a civil rights activist and a friend of Malcolm X's wife—'cause Malcolm was dead at that point—asked me would I be a tape editor for a benefit for the re-trial of the Harlem 6. . . . It turned out he had ten reels of reel to reel tape of interviews with the police, mothers of six black kids, the six black kids, all of which concerned the murder of a white woman in I guess it was the Bronx in 1964, which murder happened, but for which six black kids were arrested. It was like a re-run of the Scottsboro case. The point of the benefit was to have a re-trial. The first trial had happened with court-appointed attorneys and all six were serving time for it. What they wanted to do was to have a re-trial with a lawyer of their own choice . . . and so they wanted to do a benefit at Town Hall and as one of the little details on the program, they wanted me to edit these tapes down to some sort of little scenario that Truman Nelson gave me

so that it could be used as a dramatic sound collage. I explained to him that that was not my stock in trade, but that I would do it on one condition, and the condition was that if I found something in all this mass of tape that I wanted to make a piece out of, he would let me do that. He said, "What do you mean, a piece?" I said, "Take a listen to this." I played him *It's Gonna Rain* and good civil rights activist that he was, he really liked it. [*laughter*] I think he felt it had something to do with John Brown, but he didn't know what. In any event, I did do the editing as requested and did find this one little phrase through all this mountain of material where, Daniel Hamm, who was one of the kids who, it turns out did not do it, said, "I had to like open a bruise up and let the blood come out to show them that I was bleeding." And that little phrase, "de dum ba de dum, come out to show them," caught my ear and I again made a tape loop piece.[24]

Although Reich has not described his work on the dramatic sound collage in detail, he has often commented on his experience of making *Come Out* in terms of searching for and finding a brief but powerful fragment that could become the source for a piece of music: "I was combing through this stuff trying to find the juiciest phrase I could get, because I realized that that's where it was at: to get raw speech material that really had musical content, and then go from there."[25] The context of the quotation can be found in the transcriptions of Hamm's words in Nelson's *The Torture of Mothers*. Hamm's recounting of the brutal treatment he and others were subjected to by the police after the fruit stand incident demonstrate that Reich had a wide array of powerful textual images—descriptions of being beaten, spat upon, and otherwise humiliated—from which to make a piece of music. But, as implied in his comments above, Reich found the melodic and rhythmic profile of the segment "come out to show them" compelling in addition to the textual meanings of the phrase. This suggests that it was of utmost importance that the excerpt should be pitched and pulsed and could possibly be used in a pitch-centric and metrical way. Nonetheless, as we shall see, the striking image of Hamm opening a bruise and the semantic ambiguities arising from the words "come out to show them" also add to the contradictory messages and sound images found in the piece.

Reich completed the sound collage and *Come Out*, presenting both as part of a benefit by the Charter Group for the Harlem Six on April 17, 1966, at Town Hall. The program for the benefit included a number of different presentations, including "more familiar and more popular types of 'protest music,'"[26] a speech by actor Ossie Davis—who had given the eulogy at Malcolm X's funeral—and a dramatization of various passages of *The Torture of Mothers* (which probably included the sound collage).[27] *Come Out* itself appears to have been presented during the collection of contributions and, according to Reich, was ignored: in Reich's words, "[*Come Out's*] world premier [*laughs*], which nobody cared about because it was a benefit for the retrial of the Harlem Six . . . , was literally used as pass-the-hat music."[28] While this may be an accurate description of the situation, since no members of the audience of the benefit were questioned about the piece, it is difficult to know what the audience's exact response was. After the benefit, Reich did not appear to continue any significant involvement with the case, though he may have followed its progress in the news. Instead, the piece provided Reich with an opportunity for jump-starting his fledgling compositional career—itself further boosted when *Come Out* appeared on the "New Sounds in Electronic Music" LP on Columbia records.[29] One month after the benefit, Reich held a series of concerts on May 27–29 at the Park Place Gallery that was reviewed favorably by Carman Moore in the *Village Voice* (Moore particularly liked *Come Out*), thereby initiating his institutional relationship with minimalist art and sculpture.[30]

Analyzing *Come Out*

Come Out begins with the recorded voice of Daniel Hamm, from testimony probably taken at the Friendship Baptist Church shortly after the fruit stand incident. Hamm's words, "I had to, like, open the bruise up and let some of the bruise blood come out to show them," describe his actions in the police station, where he and several others had been severely beaten by several police officers. As we have seen, Reich's selection of this opening phrase had as much to do with what he perceived to be its melodic and tonal aspects as its political and social content, and the treatment of the recorded human voice has been one of his recurring compositional interests. Examining the opening statement as a melody, it can be approximately transcribed as shown in example 6.1, which is spelled a quarter-tone flat for notational convenience. As can be seen from the transcription, the fragment sounds quite tonal, fitting within a B-minor scale and embellished with chromatic passing tones (E-flat and C-natural). Thus, in excerpting the

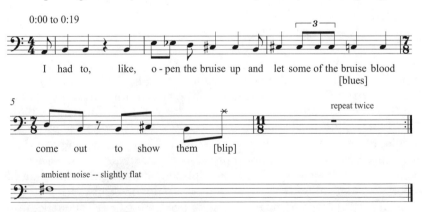

Example 6.1 Steve Reich, *Come Out*, opening sound recording (transcription by Sumanth Gopinath). © 1987 Hendon Music, Inc. Reproduced by permission.

testimony in a particular way according to his aesthetic preferences—
and not due to some "essential" musicality of black voices—Reich
rendered Hamm's recorded voice in an abstracted, "musical" way.
The tonal characteristics of this treatment have significant interpretive
consequences for the remainder of the piece.

The piece presents the recorded fragment in what one might call a
"documentary realist" state. The flat, boxed-in acoustic of the recorded
excerpt, typical of low-tech practical recordings (particularly at the
time), is crucial to the sound world of the piece. The excerpt is repeated
three times, each instance punctuated by one second of silence. In
addition to fixing in the listener's memory the sound of Hamm's
voice, the particular phrase, and the images his words conjure, the
threefold repetition of the excerpt inflects its documentary quality in
an ominous, ritualistic manner. Repeating in such a way so as not to
produce a continuous rhythmic pulse throughout the entire introduction—which would have been possible, since the excerpted statement
can be easily heard as in some kind of 4/4 meter (see the transcription)—the excerpt seems to float in and out of the listener's consciousness. The repetitions of the statement also make evident an interesting
fact about Hamm's enunciation. In stating "bruise" for a second time,
Hamm trips a bit on the phrase "bruise blood,"substituting the allitera-
tive "blues blood" (though the pronunciation sounds somewhere in
between the two possibilities), clearly a highly suggestive malapropism.

After three presentations of Hamm's initial statement, the piece
homes in on the phrase "come out to show them," which is then
subjected to the phase-shifting technique Reich developed in San
Francisco while composing *It's Gonna Rain* (1965). In this "phasing"
process, two different recordings of the same excerpt are played at
slightly different speeds on the left and right channels and slowly
move out of sync. It is significant here that the nature of the repetition
changes from a floating repetition to a groove-oriented one—switching
from what Richard Middleton calls discursive repetition (repetition of
phrases or sections, characteristic of many European-derived musics of
the West) to musematic repetition (immediate repetition of short riffs
or units, particularly common in African-diasporic musics).[31] The
passage can be notated as an approximate 7/8 meter, though example
6.2 shows several ways in which it can be transcribed. All of these
possibilities reveal certain aspects of the excerpt, but the seven-beat feel
of the music, particularly at section beginnings, justifies the use of 7/8.

The experience of listening to the beginning of the phasing process
is startling. Initially, the repetition of "come out to show them" gen-
erates a strange groove of sorts—strange in part due to the odd meter.
Soon enough, however, the phase difference becomes apparent, transforming from something like a slight echo into a pronounced reverberation (around 0:55–1:00) before gradually settling into a new phase
position of a difference of one eighth note at around 1:50, and then a

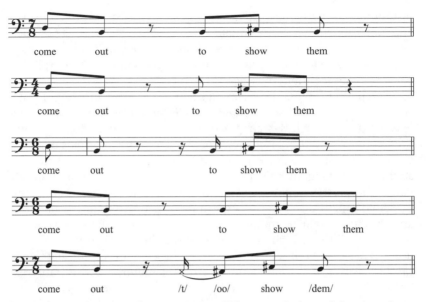

Example 6.2 Steve Reich, *Come Out*, possible transcriptions of the phased fragment opening (transcriptions by Sumanth Gopinath). © 1987 Hendon Music, Inc. Reproduced by permission.

difference of two eighth notes around 2:59. The music thus becomes unfocused and then "locks" into place, like gears that slip and then catch in new locations; example 6.3 shows the "locked in" positions within the section.

The semantic content of the piece shifts radically from the first section into the second and within the second section during the phasing process. In the first case, the textual truncation from the initial excerpt seems to reject the more violent aspects of the original fragment (removing "open the bruise up" and "bruise blood"), perhaps "sanitizing" the text in the process but also abstracting it and thus

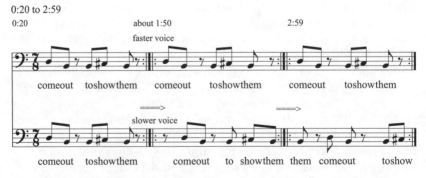

Example 6.3 Steve Reich, *Come Out*, two-voice phasing (transcription by Sumanth Gopinath). © 1987 Hendon Music, Inc. Reproduced by permission.

opening it up to other possible meanings.[32] In the second case, the short phrase is subjected to a further level of abstraction: by the end of this section, due to the phase position, it sounds as if the words "come out" have been separated from "to show them."[33] The sonic aspects of the music—the timbre and acoustical space—also begin to mutate here. In particular, at the outset of the phasing, a form of interference is generated between the left and right channels, which is heard differently depending on the mode of listening. If one listens to the piece with headphones, the effect is one of an eerie panning between the two channels: the signal seems to move quickly from the right channel to the left and back (0:21–0:25) before slowly settling from the right channel to the middle (0:25–0:40). This effect does not occur due to any particular form of conscious sonic manipulation on the part of the composer, but simply due to the signal phase relationships caused by the two waveforms moving out of sync. The net effect is disconcerting and, in conjunction with the flat acoustic environment, creates a strange, claustrophobic listening space.[34]

At 2:59 the two fragments are suddenly doubled and the phasing process begins anew (example 6.4). From this point, the words alternate between states of clarity and obscurity and in the latter case are broken down into their constituent syllables, consonants, and pitched vowels. This results in the emergence of a number of different textural and textual layers. Around 4:20, in addition to the B2 pulse drone, one hears something like "come ma-ma-ma" (or mao-mao-mao?) or an echo-effect in which particular sound layers bounce between the left and right channels.[35] The /sh/ of "to show them," which seems to have separated from the words, also alternates eerily between the channels. At 6:15, the words become clearer due to the thinner texture caused by overlapping, and one hears "come out, come out, come out," "show, show them," and a /sh/ pattern spaced into quarter notes, leading into the downbeat. At 7:30, the three-beat phase difference blurs the texture once more, yielding a blurry "come out, come, come out, come out" and a distinctive /sh/ pattern leading to the downbeat. At the halfway phase point around 8:30, a new set of patterns begins to emerge (see example 6.5), which are reinforced at the beginning of the following section.

With the final section of the piece, beginning around 8:38, the four fragments are doubled—perceived as abrupt because of the stereo-flattening effect—and this is soon accompanied by more disorienting panning or flanging effects that cause the sonic space to whirl around the listener. The "resultant patterns" of this complex texture, shown as an approximation in 2/4 in example 6.6, constitute several different sonic layers that permit different interpretations.[36] The phonemes and pitches of Hamm's voice have here been transformed into:

1. A faint drone or "electrical hum" on B2,
2. An alarm or siren-like figure using all three pitches (D3-C#3-B2),

Example 6.4 Steve Reich, *Come Out*, four-voice phasing (transcription by Sumanth Gopinath). © 1987 Hendon Music, Inc. Reproduced by permission.

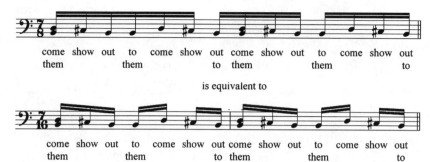

come show out to   come show out come show out to   come show out
them   them   to them   them   to

is equivalent to

come show out to   come show out come show out to   come show out
them   them   to them   them   to

Example 6.5.   Steve Reich, *Come Out*, composite pattern near 8:30
(transcription by Sumanth Gopinath). © 1987 Hendon Music, Inc.
Reproduced by permission.

3. A robotic voice on the offbeats, chanting "ma-ma-ma-ma-
   ma..." on B2 (derived from [c]ome-ou[t]), and
4. Pulses of /sh/ sounds derived from the word *show* that sound
   like some sort of agitated breathing or running, or a shaker-
   instrument.

The eight voices in the textural fabric now render the phasing
process less audible, and the composer does not explore multiple
phase shifts in the section. Around 10:00, the music quakes perceptibly
and by 11:00 the texture settles into a one eighth-note difference,
which has the primary effect of blurring the textural layers described

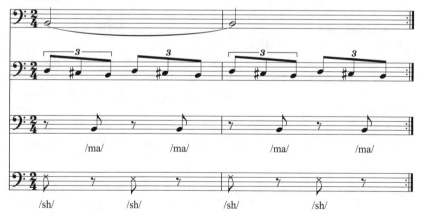

/ma/   /ma/   /ma/   /ma/

/sh/   /sh/   /sh/   /sh/

Example 6.6   Steve Reich, *Come Out*, perceived layers in final section of *Come
Out* (at 8:38) (transcription by Sumanth Gopinath). © 1987 Hendon Music,
Inc. Reproduced by permission.

above. The piece ends with a gradual fade-out, and the music recedes into the distance at its most apocalyptic point.

Interpretive Meanings in *Come Out*

The numerous contradictory sound images, textual references and meanings, and musical signifiers in *Come Out* require a multifaceted interpretation that addresses different aspects of the piece without negating or ignoring their powerful associations. In what follows, I suggest a set of possible readings that loosely follow the temporal development of the piece itself.[37]

The piece begins with a prerecorded sound excerpt. Through its indexicality, the excerpt guarantees the "authenticity" of the source material and therefore bestows a powerful sense of authority upon the composition that is apparent whether or not one knows the excerpt's origins. Reminiscent of Reich's and other writers' comments on his compositions as being akin to photographic representations of sound-objects, the use of taped testimony in Hamm's voice in turn reminds us of the actual field recording used by Reich in *Come Out's* predecessor work, *It's Gonna Rain*, based on the voice of a black Pentecostal street preacher, Brother Walter. *Come Out* may then be documentary only to the "second degree," but the issues of rights and royalties—both raised by Morris, among others[38]—would still seem to apply. And yet, to the extent that documentary artists have long appropriated the "commons" of images and sound waves in order to make work—often in the service of left-progressive causes—an indictment of Reich would have to be evaluated alongside both the many examples of "found sound" recording in both art and popular musics, as well as the new legal regimes of copyright control and intellectual property that greatly favor media conglomerates. Instead of pondering over ethical dilemmas, it may be more fruitful to allow the work's documentarity to encourage us to revisit Hamm's statement. In particular, the suggestive malapropism "blues blood" metaphorically draws the experience of the Harlem Six into the affective and psychological state of "the blues" and, by extension, African American historical oppression and memory in general. As such, the statement illustrates the power of what we might call recorded sound's *auditory unconscious*, which, by analogy with Walter Benjamin's idea of the "optical unconscious" of photography, denotes the ability of the sound recording to register details not easily noticed through ordinary sense perception in real time.[39] Hamm's statement also attests to Reich's quasi-photographic ability to capture poignant, contradictory moments in the sonic equivalent of what Benjamin referred to as the "dialectical image"—a turn of phrase describing the notion that history can be understood most powerfully through constellations of meaning frozen in a single, critical instant, as in a photograph or a quotation.[40] Indeed, *Come Out's* opening functions simultaneously as a sonic documentary photograph *and* a sounding textual quotation.

Once the phasing process begins in earnest, we find that the close "zoom" into the ending of Hamm's statement initiates a process in which the speaker's words are gradually dissolved into apparently incoherent sounds. This moment—which is, incidentally, the moment that concerns the majority of Morris's and Whitesell's interpretations—is one in which the phasing and multiplication processes used by Reich essentially do *violence* to Hamm's voice, and hence, in sublimated form, to Hamm himself and perhaps all of the Harlem Six. However one might assess the relationship between reality and representation at play here, such an interpretation depends on the assumptions that signification in the piece transforms from a concrete sound (Hamm's voice) to abstract noises (sonic chaos = silence/disappearance) and that the various rehearings of the piece enact this violence over and over again in the present. And while I do not entirely subscribe to Morris's trauma-and-mourning memorialization readings of the piece—in part because its affect seems so distant from any sense of mourning[41]—I do agree that the violent concrete-to-abstract trajectory of the piece is compelling and interpretively suggestive.

But it is also illuminating to situate this representation of violence in a broader historical framework, one in which violence is done through and onto speech and text in various ways. In the conjuncture of the mid-1960s—which is, in essence, part of the long historical moment of 1968—we find: (1) the rise of Jacques Derrida's anti-philosophy of "deconstruction," in which speech is seen as doing violence to text while, at the same time, textual certainties are almost violently dissolved to reveal the merciless logic of the supplement; (2) a tendency within 1960s aesthetic utterances—exemplified, for example, by aspects of Baraka's Black Arts aesthetic or Fluxus performances—to express and even simulate violence through texts and discourse; and (3) a broader lineage of postwar electroacoustic works in which human voices become subjected to apparently violent processes of dissolution and transformation—and here, we might think of pieces like Stockhausen's *Gesang der Jünglinge* (1955–56), Berio's *Thema (Omaggio a Joyce)* (1958), or, in a different way, Babbitt's *Philomel* (1964).[42] Reich's work is part of a cultural problematic, then, that exists at the intersection of several lines of development in which violence, voices, texts, and sonic representation commingle, all perhaps in response to the violence of postwar imperialism and the violence against language during the cold war, as well as in anticipation of the powerful state suppressions of the global New Left in the wake of 1968.

The foregoing discussion suggests a specific source of that violence: the State, perceived by many baby boomers as the main enemy during the 1960s and often imagined as the dominant actor within an all-encompassing economic, political, and ideological force field known as

The System. Indeed, from the observations in the preceding discussion alone, we can perceive the relationship between Reich's compositional process and Hamm's voice as figuring the state and the individual, respectively. Morris, in fact, offers just such an interpretation, in which "an actual human being is ground up in an infernal machine that resembles bureaucracy, administration, or any other incarnation of the principle of disengaged instrumental reason."[43] And yet, this interpretation is lacking, in part because it doesn't attempt to address the fragmentary sounds in the later parts of the piece, which are not merely inchoate and abstract. Consider, for example, the sound of the piece from 2:59, when the sonic doubling of the two phase points can be heard as mimicking the sound of police with megaphones calling for someone to "come out, come out," interpellating the listener as a black rioter or "criminal."[44] Conversely, we can hear the voices as being those of protesters, demanding that people *come out* and *show them* (the authorities) that they won't be intimidated.[45] And once we fast-forward to the end of the piece, from 8:38, the layers of sound described earlier—the heavy breathing of someone running away, the sound of muffled police sirens, a mechanized voice saying "ma" or "Mao" (a robotic voice either of resistance or of the State, the latter figured through a mother-child relationship[46]), and the institutional back-ground drone of the piece—paint an image of the aftermath of a riot or protest. Here, then, we see that the dialectic is not only between the state and individual but also between that of the *individual* and *collective*, the latter evoked through the multiplication of voices in the composi-tional process, first organized and later disorganized and scattered. Perhaps the most radical aspect of the piece, then, is the way in which it narrates not only Hamm's oppression but also his putative transformation into an agent-in-battle—a "cop fighter," in the words of the police officers who first arrested and assaulted the six young men. More broadly, it may be these sonic signifiers that moved Edward Strickland to claim that, "*Come Out* reminds us of...contemporary events [like] the Watts riot."[47] Indeed, the historical connection be-tween the case of the Harlem Six and the riots in Harlem is made explicit by the composition's slippage between the voice of Hamm and the sound of an urban uprising.

Despite the power of these political allegories, they cannot exhaust the potential meanings of the underdetermined signifiers that emerge over the duration of *Come Out*. A significant grouping of meanings can additionally be made through the realization that, in various ways, Hamm is treated as an Other. First, we may return to Hamm's voice, and perceive his particular African American accent that presumably locates him in a specific community (black Harlem; African America) at a specific time (mid-1960s). Of course, the brevity of the recorded excerpt might need to be supplemented by Nelson's lengthier quota-tions in *The Torture of Mothers*—and here, formulations like "penny ante" or "billy" (for "billy club") mark Hamm's speech through turns of phrase that have since mostly fallen into disuse.[48] Again, *It's Gonna Rain* provides a useful reference point: in that composition, the particular "grain" of Brother Walter's voice and the recently rural accents of his speech patterns in that case isolated and, thus, depicted one version of African American speech during the 1960s, whereas Hamm's accent, which reflected his own, more (sub)urbanized baby boomer generation, constituted quite another. But in addition to the use of a "black" voice, Reich intersects with at least two other forms of perceptible Otherness. In the first case, we should note Martin Scherzinger's emphasis on the influence of sub-Saharan African musics on Reich's earliest mature compositions such as *It's Gonna Rain*.[49] Indeed, if the /sh/ sounds are perceived as shaker-instruments characteristic of traditional West African group performance, then the stratified rhythmic layers and apparent triplet subdivisions of the ending of *Come Out* are very reminiscent of various types of music from the region, particularly large-group vocal musics.[50] But if Hamm is in some sense depicted as both African American *and* African, he is also inserted into a context that Reich himself has characterized as demonstrating an implicit "sexuality."[51] Taking this comment as a cue, words such as *come* and even *show* can take on sexualized valences, and Hamm's heavy breathing (the same /sh/ sound that can be heard as a shaker instrument) that was earlier interpreted as evoking his running can also be perceived in a sexual context. Here, then, Hamm becomes a physical, sexualized being that resonates with the oversexualization of African American males in the white racial imaginary in the United States. This observation elicits more questions about the racial and sexual dimensions of the case: if the racism of the mostly white police officers was perfectly evident to all, were the group beatings of the six in the precinct jail cell perhaps part of a police culture of brutality that is, in its sweatiness and bald physicality, a sublimation of racialized sexual desire itself?

The final moment under consideration involves a more serious consideration of the work's *affect*. Here, the totality of the acoustic experience of *Come Out* is reinterpreted through the piece's acoustic qualities, sonic textures, and tonal and rhythmic content, all acting in combination with other possible referents such as those described above. How, then, might we characterize the work's affective qualities? Reich has used the term "paranoid" to describe the sound world of his tape pieces.[52] In what ways might the piece actually represent paranoia? Certainly, it is framed in an affectively negative way by the "minor mode" material of the phrase "come out to show them," and the phasing process used by Reich is gradual and methodical, seemingly making the musical textures go steadily out of control. Add to this the repetitive and mechanical nature of the phasing and doubling process, and the panning effect at the beginnings of sections, and the resulting phantasmagorical, mechanical sensibility of the piece might make the term "paranoid" applicable. But the crucial aspect of *Come Out* that makes it seem paranoid is the doubling of voices, which creates a quasi-delay and reverb effect that simulates the sound of multiple voices inside one's head, whirling about in the auditory space.[53] Such techniques resonate powerfully with the uses of reverb and echo techniques in psychedelic musics during the mid-1960s—often as a representation of drug-induced paranoia—and may have originated in representations of paranoia and insanity in postwar Hollywood cinema, especially those of the *film noir* genre. And of course, electroacoustic tape compositions also used similar effects in various ways for some years—Tod Dockstader's *Luna Park* (1961), which is based on the sound of laughter, is one prominent example. The question then remains of the concrete determinant of the particular paranoid ideation being represented in the piece: in other words, whose paranoid experience are we hearing? In a first pass, the experience can be seen as being Hamm's, a psychological portrayal of an individual unfairly facing life imprisonment or even the experience of being trapped with his own thoughts in a prison cell. But when we draw in the signifiers of riots and political conflicts, the broader effect of the piece is one of representing the problematic notion of "black paranoia," both a delegitimizing term and an often real condition inculcated over years of exploitation and manipulation of African Americans by the state and Capital. From a similar perspective, such a condition can be associated with the real paranoia experienced by New Left and Black Power activists as a targeted result of the FBI's counter-intelligence program (COINTELPRO), which infiltrated, spied on, and at times assassinated members of activist and militant groups. On the other hand, the paranoia can be heard as being that of a (white) listener, standing in for Reich himself. In this case, the paranoia is that of white America generally, reacting to the conflagrations in urban areas and the new desegregated order being enforced by the federal government—with white suburban migration being one prominent symptom of this mental state. Moreover, at the heart of any notion of white paranoia in *Come Out* must necessarily reside a species of Jewish American paranoia, in which the memories and awareness of the Holocaust, the dramatic rise of black-Jewish tensions during the heyday of the Black Power movement (particularly in New York after the Ocean Hill-Brownsville conflict in 1968), and the growing investment in and fears associated with the settler-colonial state of Israel constitute a particular post-1960s ethnic sensibility—one that was cynically exploited by prosecutors in the Harlem Six case, with its dramatic instance of black-on-Jewish violence.[54] To the extent that black paranoia, radical paranoia, white paranoia, and Jewish American paranoia are inseparable in the piece, *Come Out* ultimately marks out a "structure of feeling" characteristic of the specific conjuncture beginning in the mid-1960s and extending into the 1970s, hence portraying this historical period as paranoid in much the same way that writer Thomas Pynchon would in novels like *The Crying of Lot 49* (1965) and *Gravity's Rainbow* (1973).

Conclusion

A composition of powerful historical and cultural resonance, Steve Reich's *Come Out* would, from the foregoing interpretations, appear to be inextricably wedded to the historical moment of its creation, however broadly defined. But the realities of incarceration and police brutality that were faced by the Harlem Six are unfortunately still relevant today. Perhaps the greatest crisis presently facing African Americans (and other underprivileged racial/ethnic minorities), particularly urban working-class men and, increasingly, women, is their mass incarceration in for-profit prisons in the past few decades. In a dramatic expansion of the prison system, the number of prisoners in the United States has ballooned over the last thirty years from about 400,000 to more than 2 million, with the imprisoned racial/ethnic population shifting over the last fifty years from 70 percent white to 70 percent nonwhite and with African Americans constituting the majority of these nonwhite prisoners.[55] This system has been described by Angela Davis and others as amounting to a "prison-industrial complex," an interconnected network of private prison corporations, construction companies, multinational investment firms and global trade agreements like NAFTA, food and cleaning service contractors, surveillance and prison equipment producers, law enforcement agencies and legal structures, government lobbyists, correctional officers, and prison-labor contractors.[56] It is this juggernaut that stands behind the individual outrages and scandals of the justice system such as the so-called "Ramparts Scandal" involving the Rampart Division of the Los Angeles Police Department in the late 1990s and, in a more general sense, the brutal logics of racialized, neoliberal-statist neglect and criminalization demonstrated in New Orleans in the aftermath of Hurricane Katrina in 2005.[57]

Although over four decades separate Reich's composition from the present moment, *Come Out* might help to provide a historical understanding of incarceration in the United States today. Specifically, through their direct impact on the prison rebellion movement of the 1970s, the "race riots" of the 1960s served as the initial political impetus for the expansion of the prison system, which became increasingly brutal, privatized, and hidden from public view through the construction of new prisons predominantly in rural America—resulting in a disappearance of "real" imprisonment in the middle-class imaginary that is dialectically linked to the more recent reclamation of older prisons as tourist sites. If we place *Come Out*—a composition inseparable from those 1960s uprisings and based on the voice of an African American man unjustly imprisoned for over a decade[58]—alongside other American minimalist prison compositions, including Frederic Rzewski's works on the 1971 Attica prison rebellion, *Coming Together* and *Attica* (both 1972), and Ingram Marshall's *Alcatraz* (1984), which treats the island and decommissioned prison facility as a sonic space and historical landmark, we might understand these works as collectively tracing out the trajectory from organized rebellion to privatized repression and tourist entertainment. Inaugurating a small "canon" of prison works by American experimental composers, *Come Out* thus serves as a damning reminder of the historical transformation of criminal justice in the United States and a marker of a fundamental political rupture whose impact still reverberates forcefully.

Thanks to Emily Lechner and Sean Nye for their comments on the latest version of this essay, as well as the many others who contributed immeasurably to its earlier incarnations.

Notes

1. Most of these names are found in an advertisement announcing a petition and public call led by Baldwin in support of the six. See the advertisement "Georgia Justice for Harlem Six," *The New York Times*, July 16, 1967, section IV, 4.

2. For an exception, see "Our Century: The Sixties," *The Nation*, January 10, 2000, http://www.thenation.com/doc/20000110/1960s (accessed June 29, 2007). For a recent comment on *Come Out* in the same publication, see David Schiff, "A Rebel in Defense of Tradition," *The Nation*, November 6, 2006, http://www.thenation.com/doc/20061106/schiff/2 (accessed June 29, 2007).

3. See "Come Out (Reich)," *Wikipedia*, http://en.wikipedia.org/wiki/Come _Out_(Reich) (accessed July 9, 2007).

4. Lloyd Whitesell, "White Noise: Race and Erasure in the Cultural Avant-Garde," *American Music* 19, no. 2 (Summer 2001): 177.

5. Mitchell Morris, "Musical Virtues," in *Beyond Structural Listening?: Postmodern Modes of Hearing*, ed. Andrew Dell'Antonio (Berkeley and Los Angeles: University of California Press, 2004), 55, 45, 58–59.

6. Morris's essay, which I encountered only after completing my interpretation of *Come Out*, is in some ways very similar to my interpretation of the piece.

7. Whitesell and Morris offer the most intriguing interpretations of the piece; prior treatments of *Come Out* have been primarily analytic in nature and/or have contributed relatively straightforward, uncomplicated interpretive readings. For the latter, see Michael Nyman, *Experimental Music: Cage and Beyond* (London: Studio Vista, 1974), 130–31; K. Robert Schwarz, "Steve Reich: Music as a Gradual Process, Part I," *Perspectives of New Music* 19, nos. 1–2 (1980–81): 384–88; Edward Strickland, *Minimalism: Origins* (Bloomington: Indiana University Press, 1993), 189–91; David Schwarz, "Listening Subjects: Semiotics, Psychoanalysis, and the Music of John Adams and Steve Reich," *Perspectives of New Music* 31, no. 2 (Summer 1993): 45–46; and Keith Potter, *Four Musical Minimalists: La Monte Young, Terry Riley, Steve Reich, Philip Glass* (Cambridge: Cambridge University Press, 2000), 176–79.

8. I owe the notion of "auditory information" to Jason Stanyek.

9. Here I cite Reich in a personal conversation on June 27, 2005, in New York, though other recent interviews find Reich using the word *political* to describe the piece.

10. A good description can be found in Jameson's eponymous book, *The Political Unconscious: Narrative as a Socially Symbolic Act* (Ithaca, N.Y.: Cornell University Press, 1981), esp. 9–23.

11. For citations and more information on this, see Sumanth Gopinath, "Contraband Children: The Politics of Race and Liberation in the Music of Steve Reich, 1965–1966" (PhD diss., Yale University, 2005), 45–74.

12. Ibid.

13. Tia DeNora, *Music in Everyday Life* (Cambridge: Cambridge University Press, 2000), 34–36.

14. See the fascinating analysis of lumpenist Marxism in the Black Panther Party in Jeffrey O. G. Ogbar, *Black Power: Radical Politics and African American Identity* (Baltimore: Johns Hopkins University Press, 2004), 93–110.

15. For more information on the state of this movement in the mid-1960s, see Howard Brick, *Age of Contradiction: American Thought and Culture in the 1960s* (New York: Twayne, 1998), 104–7, 162–63; Manning Marable, *Race, Reform, and Rebellion: The Second Reconstruction in Black America, 1945–1990*, 2nd ed. (Jackson: University Press of Mississippi, 1991), 86–113; Clayborne Carson, *In Struggle: SNCC and the Black Awakening of the 1960s* (Cambridge, Mass.: Harvard University Press, 1995), 138–45, 162–66, 191–243; C. Vann Woodward, *The Strange Career of Jim Crow*, 3rd rev. ed. (New York: Oxford University Press, 1974), v–viii, 189–220.

16. This account is drawn from the lawyer Conrad Lynn's account of the Harlem Six case in his autobiography *There Is a Fountain: The Autobiography of Conrad Lynn* (New York: Lawrence Hill, 1979), 3–33, esp. 3; Truman Nelson's *The Torture of Mothers* (Boston: Beacon, 1968 [1965]); lawyer William Kunstler's account in his memoir *My Life as a Radical Lawyer* (New York: Birch Lane, 1994), 172–74; Annette T. Rubinstein, "The Not-So-Strange Case of the Harlem Six," *Rights and Review: A Publication of Harlem CORE* (Fall–Winter 1967–68): 21–25; an interview with Annette T. Rubinstein on August 1, 2002; and numerous newspaper articles in the *The New York Times*, the *New York Amsterdam News*, and elsewhere.

17. See Maxwell Geismar, "On Truman Nelson," introduction to *The Torture of Mothers*, v–vi.

18. June Meyer, "Sons and Mothers: The Harlem Six," *The Nation*, April 25, 1966, 496–97.

19. Nelson used preexisting taped testimony recorded at the Friendship Baptist Community Center (on 130th St.), immediately after the fruit stand incident. Meyer claims that Nelson also arranged (and then gathered and edited) taped interviews of the mothers of the six after their sons were apprehended. See Nelson, *The Torture of Mothers*, 21; Meyer, "Sons and Mothers," 497.

20. Nelson, ibid., 3.

21. Baldwin's petition had gained over 3,000 signatures by mid-1967, as mentioned in "Georgia Justice for Harlem Six." During the 1972 retrial, John Lennon and Yoko Ono appeared at one of the sessions. Interested in the "racial overtones" of the trial, Lennon noted, "Racism is a hard thing for whites to understand. It takes a lot to open your eyes, but I see it now because I'm married to a Japanese." See the brief news column by Albin Krebs, *The New York Times*, January 12, 1972, 33.

22. See Lynn, *There Is a Fountain*, 24–31.

23. Potter, *Four Musical Minimalists*, 176.

24. Interview with Ev Grimes, December 15–16, 1987, New York, NY, number 186 a–i OH V, tape and transcript, Oral History of American Music, Yale University, tape 186–b.

25. William Duckworth, *Talking Music: Conversations with John Cage, Philip Glass, Laurie Anderson, and Five Generations of American Experimental Composers* (New York: Schirmer, 1995), 297.

26. Potter, *Four Musical Minimalists*, 177.

27. The benefit was described briefly in *The New York Times*; see "Benefit Aids Appeal of 6 Convicted of Harlem Killing," *The New York Times*, April 18, 1966, 21.

28. Edward Strickland, *American Composers: Dialogues on Contemporary Music* (Bloomington: Indiana University Press, 1991), 40. Reich also takes some credit for the success of the benefit, noting that the piece performed its role "successfully I might add; the kids did have a retrial"; Gabrielle Zuckerman, "An Interview with Steve Reich," Minnesota Public Radio, July 2002, http://www.musicmavericks.org/features/interview_reich.html (accessed December 16, 2003). But whereas his work for the benefit, including the sound collage, was not insignificant, the claim that *Come Out* performed its ostensible political function successfully despite being ignored seems odd, acting as an appropriation of the case for his own uses. Also, it is worth comparing Nelson's approach to the income from his efforts, which went to the cause of the six, whereas Reich made no such arrangement. Finally, Reich appears to have misrepresented the case in various interviews—assuming that one of the six was in fact guilty of the murder despite the evidence to the contrary. See, for example, Reich's comment in the interview with Zuckerman, "Now, there was a murder committed, but one of them did it—not all six."

29. Kyle Gann notes that this piece, along with Terry Riley's *In C*, was very significant for a generation of composers; see Gann's *American Music in the Twentieth Century* (New York: Schirmer, 1997), 325.

30. Carman Moore, "Park Place Electronics," *Village Voice*, June 9, 1966, 17.

31. Richard Middleton, *Studying Popular Music* (Milton Keynes: Open University Press, 1990), 269–84. Middleton sees these categories as both acting on a continuum and in combination with one another, such that their characteristics are not essentialized as European or African.

32. As Eric Drott has pointed out (private conversation, March 2001) the initial text of the piece is already a somewhat sanitized selection of the violent descriptions in the original transcript. For example, in *The Torture of Mothers*, Daniel Hamm is quoted as saying, "They got so tired beating us they just came in/And start spitting on us./And we trying to duck the spit,/But they get on me, all on my face and my hands and my clothes./They even bring phlegm up and spit on me,/Walk all over the top of us,/Make us get on the floor and all that crap./We were actually treated like animals, so to say" (15). I would also argue that Reich's choice of text depicts Hamm during a moment of strength, invention, and resistance—a "trickster" who relies on improvisation to get out of a tough situation.

33. David Schwarz, "Listening Subjects," 44.

34. The idea of the listening space as being claustrophobic and inducing paranoia is based on Michael Veal's comments to me on the piece.

35. Potter includes a similar analysis of the piece; *Four Musical Minimalists*, 177–78.

36. The description "resultant pattern" was originally A. M. Jones's technical term for the composite ensemble rhythm in an African musical texture. Having borrowed the term from Jones, Reich inverted its meaning and used it to refer to perceived lines or patterns emerging from a complex musical texture—a meaning strongly reminiscent of Gerhard Kubik's notion of "inherent rhythms." See A. M. Jones, *Studies in African Music*, vol. 1 (London: Oxford University Press, 1959), 26, 53–54, 76, 191–92; Sumanth Gopinath, "A Composer Looks East: Steve Reich and Discourse on Non-Western Music," *Glendora Review: African Quarterly on the Arts 3*, nos. 3–4 (2004): 136–37; and Martin Scherzinger, "Curious Intersections, Uncommon Magic: Steve Reich's 'It's Gonna Rain' (1965)," *Current Musicology* 79–80 (2005): 32, 42.

37. The following interpretation is based on Gopinath, "Contraband Children," 251–306.

38. See Morris, "Musical Virtues," 63.

39. Walter Benjamin, "Little History of Photography," in *Selected Writings*, vol. 2, ed. Michael W. Jennings et al. (Cambridge, Mass.: Belknap, 1999), 510–12.

40. See Walter Benjamin, "Konvolute N [On the Theory of Knowledge, Theory of Progress]," in *The Arcades Project*, trans. Howard Eiland and Kevin McLaughlin (Cambridge, Mass.: Belknap, 1999), 456–88. For an excellent interpretation of Benjamin's cryptic concept, see Anselm Haverkamp, "Notes on the 'Dialectical Image' (How Deconstructive Is It?)," *Diacritics* 22, nos. 3–4 (Autumn—Winter 1992): 69–80.

41. In contrast, a (politically more conservative) work by Reich such as *Different Trains* (1988) does in fact engage explicitly in such memorialization and powerful, sentimental dwelling upon lost and ruined lives—in this case, Holocaust victims.

42. Thanks to Michael Cherlin for reminding me of the relevance of Babbitt's composition here.

43. Morris, "Musical Virtues," 63. Indeed, judging from his essay, Morris would appear to share the kind of antistatist politics characteristic of the New Left generation.

44. David Schwarz notes more generally that "come out" transforms into an imperative; "Steve Reich," 46.

45. Thanks to Lisabeth Pimentel for this interpretation.

46. The figuring of the State as matriarchal robot is made explicit in Laurie Anderson's "O Superman" (1981).

47. Strickland, *Minimalism*, 190.

48. Nelson, *The Torture of Mothers*, 13, 63.

49. Martin Scherzinger, "Curious Intersections, Uncommon Magic."

50. Elsewhere, I have argued that on account of an abstraction of structural principles of sub-Saharan African musics, Reich's *Come Out* ended up sounding similar to African musics that he had likely never encountered—in this case, vocal musics of the Fulbe in Burkina Faso, for example. See Gopinath, "Contraband Children," 287–89.

51. Steve Reich, *Writings on Music, 1965–2000* (Oxford: Oxford University Press, 2002), 214.

52. Duckworth, *Talking Music*, 297.

53. David Schwarz uses Freud's notion of the "uncanny" to describe this effect ("Steve Reich," 45), but I believe that "paranoid" is more apt here.

54. Lynn (*There Is a Fountain*, 20) notes that prosecutor Robert Lehner provocatively mentioned the Koran while questioning one of the Harlem Six in order to sway the jury (five members of which were Jewish) and Judge Frederick Backer (who was also Jewish). Reflecting on the problematic subject of Jewish American paranoia, one might note that such paranoia is itself gently satirized in the films of Woody Allen.

55. Loïc Wacquant, "From Slavery to Mass Incarceration: Rethinking the 'Race Question' in the US," *New Left Review* 2, no. 13 (January–February 2002): 50, 43.

56. See Avery F. Gordon, "Globalism and the Prison Industrial Complex: An Interview with Angela Davis," *Race and Class* 40, nos. 2–3 (1998–99): 147–57. Also see the Web site of the organization founded by Davis to combat the prison-industrial complex, Critical Resistance (www.criticalresistance.org). Also see Gopinath, "Contraband Children," 306–11.

57. The Rampart scandal is also mentioned by Morris ("Musical Virtues," 64). See the extensive study of the scandal done in tandem with the Public Broadcasting Service's television show *Frontline*, "L.A.P.D. Blues," http://www.pbs.org/wgbh/pages/frontline/shows/lapd/scandal/ (viewed July 30, 2007). During the Hurricane Katrina crisis, the media and police department's emphasis on looting and criminality by a small number of desperate New Orleanians was inseparable from decades of depicting and treating working-class African Americans as criminals, partly for the purpose of legitimizing greater incarceration rates. For more on Hurricane Katrina's impact on New Orleans, see Spike Lee's powerful documentary film *When the Levees Broke: A Requiem in Four Acts* (2006).

58. Hamm was finally released from prison in the summer of 1974 (Lynn, *There Is a Fountain*, 33).

7

The Politics of
Presque rien
Eric Drott

Critical reception of Luc Ferrari's *Presque rien ou le lever du jour au bord de la mer* ("Almost nothing, or daybreak at the seashore") (1967–70) has been consistent in the three and a half decades since its composition. The piece, which presents an apparently unretouched recording of morning in a fishing village by the Black Sea, is generally characterized as a gesture of aesthetic transgression—though there is some disagreement as to what particular principle the work transgresses. For some commentators the minimal intervention in the source recordings that make up *Presque rien* represents a tacit repudiation of the work concept central to Western art since the late eighteenth century. Some of Ferrari's comments support such a reading; he has described the work as "a sort of anti-music," through which he expresses his opposition to "the bourgeois myth of the composer."[1] By this account, the use of magnetic tape to capture a slice of life, and thereby transform it into an object of aesthetic contemplation, places *Presque rien* within a tradition of avant-garde works that stretches from Marcel Duchamp to John Cage and beyond, a tradition that calls into question the boundary separating art and everyday life. But in the case of *Presque rien* it is not the museum's four walls or the concert ritual that frames the quotidian object or event; rather, it is the medium of tape that divorces everyday sounds from their context and, in the process, transforms them into purely musical material.

Alternatively, *Presque rien* has been read as a rupture with the then-dominant aesthetic in French electroacoustic music. Pierre Schaeffer's notion of the acousmatic—which held that the identity of the recorded sound material used in electroacoustic music should be disguised, so that the listener might better attend to its innate morphology—had guided much of the work done in the *musique concrète* studio at the Office de Radiodiffusion-Télévision Française (ORTF) in Paris since its inception in the 1940s. Although Ferrari himself had worked alongside Schaeffer from 1958 to 1966, and is generally identified as a central figure in the history of French *musique concrète, Presque rien's* aesthetic is diametrically opposed to Schaeffer's acousmatic conception. By presenting clearly recognizable sounds, which have undergone little if any overt alteration, the piece marks what Michel Chion and Guy Reibel describe as a "return of the repressed."[2] Audible traces of reality, hitherto barred from *musique concrète*, are encountered at every turn in *Presque rien*.

While there is much to recommend such interpretations, the present essay offers another approach to *Presque rien*. More precisely, I reconsider a way of thinking about the piece that the composer himself first proposed in the years following its composition. In interviews from this period, Ferrari would remark that the use of familiar, recognizable sounds helped dispose of some of the barriers that prevented the comprehension—and thus the widespread public appreciation—of experimental music. At the same time, Ferrari saw in this and other such tape works a model for a new kind of amateur artistic activity, one that would draw upon the ease and affordability of the portable tape recorder in order to open up the domain of experimental music to nonspecialists. To make sense of the ambitions Ferrari held for this work, it is necessary to situate his endeavors within a range of movements and initiatives undertaken in France during the 1960s in order to promote cultural democratization. While there was a growing consensus that access to and participation in culture was a right to which all were entitled, what this *droit à la culture* entailed and how it was to be realized were the objects of fierce debate. In this regard, the approach to tape music that Ferrari hoped *Presque rien* would inaugurate may be understood as furnishing one particular solution to the problem of cultural democratization: a solution that expressed the optimism of a historical moment when the fusion of the avant-garde and the popular seemed tantalizingly near, but one that no less reflected the aporias that constrained the French artistic and intellectual Left's conception of the "popular" during the late 1960s and early 1970s.

In a short autobiographical statement written in 1979, Ferrari provides a color-coded periodization of his career. He calls his early years as a composer, lasting from the 1950s to the mid-1960s, his "black period," the color chosen to reflect the "anarchistic" attitude exhibited by his music during this phase of his career. Conversely, the increasing interest in intimacy, sensuality, and memory that his music was beginning to evince in the late 1970s leads him to identify it as marking the onset

of his "blue period" ("blue like the Mediterranean"). Sandwiched between these two moments lies the period that concerns us in the
present essay, his so-called "red period." During this phase of his career
there is "a certain convergence of the social and the political with
musical intentions"; but there is above all "the demystification of the
work, of art and the artist."[3] Although the first rumblings of Ferrari's
political turn date from 1965 (the year in which he composed the text
piece *Société I*), the events of 1968 seem particularly decisive in solidify-
ing the new direction his work was taking. At the beginning of the year
Ferrari traveled to Havana at the behest of the Cuban cultural ministry,
which had commissioned him to write an orchestral piece to celebrate
the city's bicentennial. This sojourn to a socialist state left a strong
impression: "The encounter with a country that had undergone a
revolution, that was a shock. There was also a confrontation with
musics that had come from Africa, of Spanish influence, popular musics." No less shocking was what Ferrari encountered upon his return to
France: "We came back to Paris in April, and then there was May 68."[4]

There is little doubt that the student uprising and general strike of
May-June 1968 impressed itself upon Ferrari. He had been present in
the occupied Odéon, where the "prise de la parole" by ordinary citizens
found its most acute expression, and he had participated in an abortive
attempt to form a composer's union.[5] And throughout the months of
May and June he would take his microphone and portable tape recorder along with him into the streets to capture the protests (the recordings
of which he would trade with other composers).[6] But beyond such
incidental involvement in the events themselves, the profound social
upheaval that they unleashed seems to have significantly altered his
conception of the composer's role in society. Indeed, Ferrari's comments from the time—like those of many engaged composers and
artists—reflect a widely held belief in the necessity of changing the
audience's relationship to art, of rendering it more active. But unlike
most advocates of "cultural revolution," Ferrari was granted an ideal
platform for putting such beliefs into practice, when later the same year
he assumed a position at the *Maison de la Culture* in Amiens as an
animateur musical.

The history of the *Maison de la Culture* as an institution and cultural
animation as a vocation provides some insight into contemporary perceptions concerning cultural democracy in France, perceptions that (as
I discuss later) played no small part in shaping Ferrari's initial understanding of *Presque rien's* meaning and function. The idea for the *Maison
de la Culture* dates from the early years of the Fifth Republic, and
represents one of the most ambitious undertakings of the newly formed
Ministry of Cultural Affairs. The first minister charged with overseeing
cultural affairs was the author André Malraux, who saw in the *Maisons*
a means for overcoming long-standing disparities in the distribution of
cultural goods in France—with culture understood to be more or less

coterminous with the fine arts. The *Maisons* would provide a forum for the display and performance of work in a range of media (the plastic arts, music, drama, film, and dance), which would thereby be made accessible to the populace. Furthermore, the *Maisons* were seen as instruments that could combat cultural inequality on two fronts simultaneously: geographically, they would help close the gap between culture-rich Paris and the "deprived" provinces; socially, they would ensure that art would no longer be inaccessible to large swaths of the populace, but would henceforth be available to all, regardless of social background. These two objectives, decentralization and democratization, provided the *Maisons* with their *raison d'être*.

Apart from providing spaces for exhibitions and performances, the practical question of how the *Maisons* would go about addressing cultural inequality remained somewhat vague. This was due in part to Malraux's conception of the aesthetic experience, which bled over into the ministry's early policies. According to Malraux, every person possessed the capacity to understand art in an immediate and intuitive fashion.[7] One need not have any prior exposure to the fine arts, or possess any particular education in order to comprehend them. This emphasis on a quasi-mystical meeting of subject and aesthetic object was echoed in early ministry statements. A sketch of the *Maisons'* objectives published in 1961 described the "confrontation" Malraux sought to facilitate: "Out of this [aesthetic] encounter can be born a familiarity, a shock, a passion, another way for each to envisage his own condition.... The confrontation that it [the *Maisons*] enables is direct, [and] it avoids the pitfall and the impoverishment of a simplifying vulgarization."[8]

Such remarks point to another significant element at play in the ministry's conception of the *Maisons*. The ministry would brook no compromise in terms of quality, for offering anything less than the best would mark the failure of cultural enfranchisement.[9] There would be no "vulgarization" of difficult or challenging works; what was presented in the *Maisons* had to rise to international standards, which more often than not meant Parisian standards. Thus at the opening of the Maison in Grenoble, Malraux stated that "the primary *raison d'être* for this *Maison de la Culture*, is that everything essential that transpires in Paris should also transpire in Grenoble."[10] Comments like these helped fuel suspicion that the *Maisons* were instruments of cultural *dirigisme*, vehicles for importing Parisian values to the provinces.[11]

Within the *Maisons* it fell to the so-called *animateurs* to facilitate the encounter between audience and work. What *animation* entailed, precisely, was open to debate, the term being the object of struggle over the years. The prototype for *animation* as a vocation originated in the mid-century "popular culture" and "popular education" movements in France, which had long agitated at a grass-roots level for people's "right to culture."[12] Although the movements exhibited some sympathy to the value of existing working-class cultures, and had striven to raise workers' consciousness of the aesthetic dimensions of their everyday lives, more often than not they devoted the preponderance of their energies to bringing high culture to the people. At the same time, *animation* was invested with a sense of high-minded civic duty, since the cultural militants saw their work as necessary for the formation of a socially aware citizenry. In short, the "popular culture" movement saw culture in general (and high culture in particular) to be the means according to which one's relation to and intervention in the social world might be better managed.

Many of these traits continued to define the cultural *animateur* throughout the 1960s. Far from serving as a neutral conduit, the *animateur* worked to engage audiences actively with art. Ferrari, for instance, notes that individuals' failure to participate in artistic creation was not due to a lack of resources: "At first I worked together with a number of youth groups, who were mostly well equipped, possessing tape recorders, photo and film cameras, and who also had some understanding of how to handle these devices. It was merely that they didn't yet trust themselves to use them."[13] To help people overcome such psychic hurdles Ferrari organized a host of events and activities that would make them more comfortable with artistic practice: open rehearsals, public debates, and the like. As for the youth groups, he encouraged them to come to events at the *Maison* armed with their equipment, "to interview the public and performers, in order that they might become active during the performances and might afterwards assemble the recordings they had made."[14] Although Ferrari's activities as an *animateur* reflected his background as a composer of tape music, his description gives a good idea of how the ideals of *animation* worked in practice. Above all, Ferrari's work as an *animateur* exemplified the vocation's long-standing proclivity for linking artistic and social concerns: "I almost exclusively presented modern music, and in doing so always stressed that it is no longer acceptable to view music as a thing-in-itself, but rather that it must be discussed in the context of modern science, politics—in short all of that which forms society."[15]

However, the desire to connect cultural democracy with social and political concerns was not met with universal approbation. Contentious from their inception, controversies surrounding the *Maisons de la Culture* culminated during and after the events of May 1968. Although the *animateurs'* tendency to push avant-garde works on provincial audiences had been a long-standing source of resentment, it was their perceived role in disseminating subversive ideas that generated the greatest hostility. Gérard Marcus, a Gaullist deputy in the *Assemblée Nationale,* voiced such sentiments in a speech given on the floor of the assembly in November 1968:

One can say, without exaggeration, that they have ... carried their own stones to the barricades of May, as much during the events as beforehand.

To agitate, over the years, before a public of young students, revolutionary myths ceaselessly glorifying the October Revolution, Castroism or Lumumba, to praise anti-militarism, to idealize every kind of rebellion, doesn't this create little by little a psychological terrain favorable to the development of events similar to those that we experienced in the month of May?[16]

The *Maisons* were equally suspect for many on the Left. This is hardly surprising, given that the value ascribed to art was itself increasingly contested, alternately seen as an ideological weapon, a means of evasion, a commodity, or an elitist pursuit. By May 1968 the hostility that had been building toward legitimate culture reached a peak, finding expression in the situationist-inspired graffiti that covered the walls of Paris: "Culture is the inversion of life," "Art is dead, let us free our daily life," or, more pointedly still, "Art is shit."[17]

But even for those on the Left who did not reject culture outright, the *Maisons'* status as state-run institutions made them ripe targets for critique. *Gauchistes* and party communists alike identified the *Maisons* as an "ideological state apparatus," and following Louis Althusser's definition of the concept, contended that they served as an instrument for winning the consent of the masses, and thus contributed to the continued reproduction of existing social relations.[18] Others on the Left saw the policy of cultural democratization as a diversion from the more fundamental issue of class domination. This was a position characteristic of the *Parti communiste*, who argued that animation—no matter how well intentioned—placed "superstructural" concerns above those of the "base." Instead of working to change economic relations, *animateurs* operated at the level of individual attitudes, thereby falling into the idealist trap.[19] No less damning than such critiques were sociological studies that revealed the extent to which the *Maisons* had failed in their task of bringing art to the people. Surveys indicated that most visitors to the *Maisons* came from social groups with high levels of educational attainment (teachers, university students, young professionals), while those seen as "culturally deprived" (the working class and farmworkers)—the very groups that the *Maisons* sought to serve—made up a miniscule fraction of their users. The statistics for the 1969–70 season at Amiens indicated that a scant 2 percent of the attendees identified themselves as workers, with 1 percent as shopkeepers, and 0.4 percent as farmworkers.[20] One explanation for this failure lay in the fact that Malraux and his ministry, in envisaging the *Maisons,* had not accounted for the degree to which differences in social background both prepare and condition one's attitudes toward high culture. This point was made most strongly by Pierre Bourdieu in a series of articles and books critiquing Malraux's policies published in the 1960s. He argued that the kind of "cultural needs" (*besoins culturels*) that the *Maisons* sought to satisfy were not innate—as Malraux would contend—but something inculcated in only those classes for whom the acquisition of cultural knowledge has real benefits: namely, those having access to the educational opportunities, careers, and social networks where cultivation may pay dividends in the long run. As a result, large swaths of the population had no use for the *Maisons*. Bourdieu's assessment of Malraux's grand project is unflattering:

> [T]he *Maison de la Culture* has attracted and gathered together...those whose educational formation and social milieu have prepared them for cultural practice.... [T]he members of the cultivated class feel that it is their right and duty to frequent these lofty places of culture, from which others, lacking sufficient culture, feel excluded. Far from fulfilling the function that a certain mystique of "popular culture" assigns to it, the *Maison de la Culture* remains the *Maison* of cultivated men [*la Maison des hommes cultivés*].[21]

Toward the end of May 1968 the directors of a number of the *Maisons de la Culture*, along with the directors of various "popular theaters" from across France, gathered in Villeurbanne to address the questions raised by critics of cultural democratization. On May 25 they issued a statement in which they expressed their dismay with the direction the *Maisons* had taken, and in which they called for a renewed effort to reach out to the vast "nonpublic" that was still excluded from French cultural life. The declaration began by crediting the events of May for revealing the shortcomings of their efforts, which appeared to many as promoting "a hereditary, exclusionary culture, which is quite simply to say, a bourgeois culture."[22] In order to address the "nonpublic" for whom "bourgeois" culture held little interest, it was necessary for *action culturelle* to furnish the individual with "a means of breaking out of his current isolation, of leaving the ghetto, of situating himself more and more consciously in a social and historic context."[23] This not only redoubles the *animateurs'* concern with linking cultural production to social affairs but also de-emphasizes their role in prose-lytizing on behalf of high culture: "This is why we deliberately refuse any conception which would make it [culture] the object of a simple transmission."[24] Instead, culture must be active: "To speak of *active culture* is to speak of *permanent creation*, it is to invoke...an art which is ceaselessly in the process of being made."[25] Culture was no longer to be conceived as a static patrimony, a collection of objects to be enjoyed by as many people as possible, but as a medium of social action.

Whether he was aware of it or not, when Ferrari assumed the position of *animateur musical* at Amiens, he was injecting himself into this fray. (In fact the *Maison*'s biweekly newsletter published excerpts from the Villeurbanne declaration the same month that Ferrari began his residence there.[26]) It is against this backdrop that Ferrari's ideas concerning his role as both composer and *animateur*, and the possibilities of public participation in the creative process, come into focus. In a series of interviews with Hansjörg Pauli conducted at the time of his tenure in Amiens, Ferrari expresses in strong terms his desire to reach out to and animate the sort of (non-) public described by the Villeurbanne statement. Discounting the idea that contemporary music's failure to appeal to mass audiences has to do with either this music's difficulty or the (non-) public's lack of aesthetic aspiration, he instead indicts the establishment for failing to attend to the "claims" of the people:

> I'm not so sure that the public would rebel if we valued its claims somewhat higher in general. Who can say, then, that a worker or a farmer can't be as open to cultural matters as an arts manager, a program director, or a culture minister? My contact with the public has shown me on many occasions that an immense respect is present in so-called simple people for any kind of work, even for artistic work, even for that which is expressed in seemingly the most eccentric forms.[27]

While he conveniently places a good deal of blame for the lack of interest in contemporary music on corporate and state control of the mass media, Ferrari does not exempt composers from his critique, acknowledging that the language they habitually employ in explaining new music has played no small role in alienating audiences: "We should wean ourselves from discussing technical compositional questions in public. That doesn't help anyone."[28] Rejecting formalism, Ferrari suggests that a more fruitful approach to the problem of public engagement may reside less in "explaining" music than in connecting it to the quotidian world. It is here that his aforementioned concern with discussing music "in the context of modern science, politics—in short all of that which forms society" assumes a strategic function, as a way of imbuing contemporary music with a sense of relevance. But rather than settle for making new music more comprehensible or pertinent—an approach that still treats culture as a fixed thing to be transmitted to the public—Ferrari suggests that the more pressing need is that of promoting participation, of providing individuals with the means for their own self-expression. In granting equal recognition to amateur creativity, Ferrari's undertaking seems to accord with the program outlined in the Villeurbanne declaration, in its promotion of an "active culture." Along similar lines, Ferrari denounces the professionalization of art, casting it as a pernicious impediment to a generalized, collective creativity. Indeed, certain of his remarks go so far as to suggest that society as a whole might be better off without music as a separate sphere of activity: "The concept of music will need to disappear in any case. It has a long past; as a consequence it has engendered conventions; that has imposed limitations on it; now it stands in our way. . . . It is too specialized, and I believe that our thinking is evolving away from specialization."[29]

In making such arguments Ferrari placed himself in a curious predicament, one shared by a number of other radical artists at the time. For in renouncing professionalism, Ferrari apparently renounced whatever authority he had as a composer. A host of questions followed from this:

how does an artist continue to work within the cultural sphere when the logic of one's position leads to a repudiation of that very sphere? How does one give up composing without *really* giving up composing? A way out of this quandary was to produce pieces that were more akin to games or loosely organized musical scenarios than works. In the mid-60s Ferrari had begun writing text scores (he called them "realizables"), which provided groups of amateurs and professionals with outlines for collective activity. What is more, the abandonment of the work concept allowed Ferrari to rid himself of the now problematic title of "composer," trading it in for the more attractive designation of "*réalisateur.*" He explains to Pauli that "composers should become game leaders, who draw up rules according to which amateurs might be able to meaningfully engage themselves." But the term was all the more attractive to Ferrari because of its other connotations: "Am I a musician, a composer? Some days I answer by saying that I am a *réalisateur.* That doesn't mean a lot, except that within the word realization there is the word reality and the word realism."[30] It is within this confluence of impulses, at this juncture where animation, audience participation, and realism meet, that we begin to discern the various aspirations that came to be lodged in *Presque rien.*

The recordings for *Presque rien no. 1* were made during the summer of 1968, in the town of Vela Luka on the isle of Korcula, in what was then Yugoslavia (now Croatia). Ferrari had traveled there that August to participate in an arts festival, and was particularly impressed by the stillness that fell over the village at night: "It was very quiet. At night the silence woke me up—that silence we forget when we live in a city. I heard this silence which, little by little, began to be embellished. . . . It was amazing."[31] Inspired, Ferrari began making recordings of the hours just before dawn. After accumulating a number of these tapes, he noticed certain events that would recur from morning to morning— "the first fisherman passing by same time every day with his bicycle, the first hen, the first donkey, and then the lorry which left at 6 a.m. to the port to pick up people arriving on the boat. Events determined by society."[32] From the material he had collected, Ferrari pieced together over the next few years a sonic representation of a typical morning in Vela Luka, completing it in 1970.[33] In his interviews with Pauli, Ferrari describes *Presque rien* as inaugurating a new genre, although he is quick to deny its status as a "work"; rather, Ferrari explains that

> these things, which I call "The Presque Riens" because they are lacking development and completely static, because really almost nothing happens musically, are more reproductions than productions: electroacoustic nature photographs—a beach landscape in the morning mists, a winter day in the mountaintops.[34]

He continues by stating that one can play these recordings in one's apartment or house, "just as one might hang photos or pictures on the wall."[35] Uncannily prefiguring the ambient nature recordings that would meet with commercial success in the 1990s, Ferrari's comments suggest that *Presque rien no. 1* was not to be listened to as much as heard, used to color or to decorate an interior space.

In many respects *Presque rien* appears to be little more than an intensification of the impulses that originally motivated his first essay in "anecdotal music," *Hétérozygote* (1963–64) in which extracts from field recordings made by Ferrari alternate with electronically synthesized sounds. By the time of *Presque rien*'s realization some six years later, the nonreferential sounds have vanished, leaving nothing but an uninterrupted flow of recognizable, everyday noises. A sense of the changing import ascribed to the use of anecdotal sound can be seen in the liner notes Ferrari wrote for the 1969 recording of *Hétérozygote*, in which he notes that the piece required little technical know-how to be completed. The result is a kind of "poor man's *musique concrète*" since "practically no manipulations were involved and the tape could have been made in a non-professional studio." Ferrari explains that his renunciation of sophisticated studio manipulation arose from extra-aesthetic considerations: "My intention was to pave the way for amateur concrete music much as people take snapshots during vacations."[36] In a review of the recording from the same year, Jean-Michel Damian elaborates on Ferrari's comments, observing that the work calls for "a kind of listening that the musician himself calls 'pop' listening."[37] He notes that this represents a "popular music in the best sense of the term," and that the use of the word *pop* reflects Ferrari's hope that "there isn't a need for any intellectual baggage to appreciate this music." "Pop" listening is, in this sense, an "anti-cultural" form of listening, which according to Damian means that "to enjoy it one need not situate oneself with reference to learned concepts or knowledge. The only culture required is that which each person possesses: the capacity to recall his own memories."[38]

A better understanding of the logic underpinning Ferrari's conception of the "popular" potential of anecdotal or referential sounds can be gained by reading it through the lens of Bourdieu's roughly contemporaneous "Éléments d'une théorie sociologique de la perception artistique" (1968).[39] Bourdieu distinguishes two basic forms of aesthetic pleasure, "the *enjoyment* which accompanies aesthetic perception reduced to simple *aisthesis*, and the delight procured by scholarly savouring, presupposing, as a necessary but insufficient condition, adequate deciphering."[40] Whereas the first of these, "simple *aisthesis*," designates a kind of perception which responds to the sensory stimulus provided by the artwork (for instance, if a painting is colorful or monochromatic), without ascribing to it any particular stylistic or symbolic significance, the second, "scholarly savouring," designates a kind of perception in which the viewer situates the work within a stylistic and/or historic framework and on that basis deciphers the work. However, it is another, even more basic approach to the artwork that Bourdieu sees as the most common alternative to both "aisthesis" and "scholarly savouring":

> Those for whom the works of scholarly culture speak a foreign language are condemned to take into their perception and their appreciation of the work of art some extrinsic categories and values—those which organize their day-to-day perception and guide their practical judgment.[41]

That is to say, those for whom the proper artistic code is lacking will by necessity draw upon everyday experience to interpret the work. When confronted with a representational painting, the "learned" viewer will attend to *how* the object is represented in order to locate the work stylistically (as in "scholarly savouring"), or in order to appreciate its formal or sensual properties (as in "aisthesis"), whereas the "naïve" viewer, having recourse only to the codes that organize "day-to-day perception," will instead attend to *what* is represented.

According to Bourdieu, the various modes of perception are not accorded equal value within aesthetic discourse. Interpreting an artwork according to the schemata of everyday experience has been seen (at least since Kant) as a vulgar form of aesthetic understanding, one that supposes "that every image shall fulfill a function, if only that of a sign."[42] Recast in light of Bourdieu's observations, we might say that Ferrari's objective for *Presque rien* was to invert this hierarchy, to revalue "uncultivated" perception as not only valid but as a privileged mode of hearing, precisely by virtue of its vulgarity. Ferrari's aim, it would seem, was to create a kind of music where the identification of *what* is represented would suffice for an adequate perception of the work. Unlike music that derives its meaning from the play of abstract forms, anecdotal music has the advantage of not requiring any specialized knowledge of musical syntax or style to be deciphered. And insofar as anecdotal music fashions messages out of the quasi-universal code of everyday sonic experience, it is within the grasp of any potential listener, from the most naive to the most educated. Ferrari thus describes his anecdotal works as "an attempt to find a music that is at the same time simple and unfamiliar, and thereby suitable for mass dissemination."[43]

But just because a piece like *Presque rien* need not be interpreted with reference to aesthetic, historic or stylistic contexts does not prohibit a listener possessing knowledge of such contexts from bringing them to bear on the work. Even if the use of clearly identifiable sounds positively encourages "uncultivated" perception, there is no interdiction against somebody adopting a "cultivated" strategy in listening to *Presque rien*. One can therefore imagine two broad approaches to understanding the piece—really, two ideal types—distilled from Bourdieu's modes of artistic perception. A first-order perception would presumably take the sounds comprising the piece at face value, their meaning more or less coextensive with the physical actions or objects that produced them. Or rather, their meaning would be a function of the total context they help create: far from simply presenting a jumble of unrelated signifiers, the various sounds form a proliferating web of physical, social, and affective associations. By contrast, a second-order perception of the work would be bound more to the ways in which it relates to the listener's inculcated expectations. One kind of interpretation that this type of perception enables was mentioned at the beginning of this essay, that which treats the piece as transgressive. In what way it is deemed transgressive depends on the particular stylistic or generic context invoked: it may be the acousmatic tradition within *musique concrète,* or the work-concept inherited from nineteenth-century bourgeois culture. Another alternative is to hear the arrangement of individual sonic events not as transgressing established norms, but as embodying them. For instance, a listener steeped in the Western art music tradition might hear the work as instantiating a standard formal contour, moving from the sparse pacing of events at the outset to the denser activity of the middle section, before tapering off at the end. From this perspective, the sound of a woman's voice singing, which comes about three-quarters of the way through the piece, might be construed as a climax, an eruption of the "purely" musical into the soundscape. Similarly, the foregrounding of the cicadas at the very end of the piece may be interpreted as a purely textural event, an inversion of the figure/ground relationship operative in the work to that point.

Obviously there is nothing that absolutely determines the stance a given listener will adopt when confronted with *Presque rien,* there being some element of choice that one can exercise in acts of aesthetic perception. Yet this volition is, in Bourdieu's analysis, curtailed by social background—not just in terms of educational attainment, but by the instincts and habits acquired from early childhood onward. Given this constraint it is not surprising that much of the critical reception of *Presque rien* has assumed a "cultivated" stance. Originally released on record as part of Deutsche Grammophon's Avantgarde series, a prestige label with a relatively small circulation, the work's audience was limited to a narrow demographic of new music connoisseurs; the upshot of this situation has been that most commentators on the piece have been professional music critics, academics, or other composers. As a result, the populist dimension Ferrari originally imputed to the work has largely been eclipsed, strengthening the impression that whatever meaning *Presque rien* might have is solely a function of its position within the various currents of twentieth-century music. Ferrari himself played no small part in bolstering this interpretive bias; his remarks in later years tended to situate *Presque rien* in relation to contemporaneous artistic movements, such as minimalism and photorealism.[44] Other commentators have promoted formalist readings of the work. Symptomatic is Daniel Teruggi's analysis of the piece: after making some initial observations about its source material, he moves on to a more detailed consideration of the work's formal properties.

However, rather than treat these two approaches as equivalent, Teruggi subtly endorses the latter. He describes how an initial impression of the work as a slice of the sonic landscape is thrown into question by a more attentive listening: "We suspect [Ferrari's] hand, organizing the rhythm of events and thus creating a dramaturgy which would bring this work closer to the musical than to the landscape."[45] By presenting the two approaches to the piece as following a logical progression, moving from a superficial to a refined hearing, Teruggi makes it seem as though any listener who is attentive will hear the work in formal, rather than referential, terms. "Scholarly savouring" becomes the telos of an adequate hearing of the work.

That *Presque rien* readily accommodates "scholarly savouring" may be explained in part by the largely negative definition of the popular that underlies Ferrari's conception of anecdotal music. Like many Left intellectuals of the period, Ferrari appears (at least at this point in his career) to have adhered to a fairly restricted notion of the popular. On account of their commercialism, forms of musical expression like rock, *variétés,* or *yéyé* were discounted as potential representatives of an authentic popular culture, regardless of whether or not large segments of the population derived meaning or pleasure from them. Having dispatched what was conventionally understood as being popular, and with no alternatives to fill the resulting void, popular culture became in the eyes of many Left intellectuals an empty concept, lacking positive content. It was precisely this idea—that the working class inhabited a cultural vacuum—that fueled the initiatives for cultural democratization described above. It was this same idea that Jean-Paul Sartre gave voice to when he asserted that "[t]he proletariat does not have its own culture: It either borrows elements from bourgeois culture, or it expresses a total rejection of any culture—which is tantamount to admitting the nonexistence of its own culture."[46] As a consequence, the "popular" mode of listening that *Presque rien* calls upon is defined in strictly negative terms, not by its embrace of a particular popular style, but by its refusal of any form of acculturation whatsoever as a necessary precondition of the piece's enjoyment. For this reason one may very well doubt whether Ferrari's project would have succeeded even had *Presque rien* received wider distribution. For the audiences it would have encountered beyond the rarefied sphere of new music aficionados were not the blank slates imagined by the French Left, but individuals in possession of their own, distinctive forms of cultural knowledge. And judged according to the standards of then-contemporary popular music, the piece would have undoubtedly proved unsatisfying, lacking a clear beat, chord changes, melodic hooks, and the like. Ferrari's works after 1970 would fare better in this regard, as he moved progressively toward a more affirmative conception of the popular, one that acknowledged and incorporated a wide range of vernacular styles. In the late 1960s, however, embracing styles identified as "commercial" appears to have been largely unthinkable for a "serious" composer in France. Hence *Presque rien,* rather than striving to formulate a positive notion of popular culture, instead chased after a degree zero of culture. To the extent that it succeeded in this goal, the piece acted as a mirror, reflecting the values and expectations that listeners brought to it. With its audience effectively limited to a tiny sliver of the population, the piece became the rarefied aesthetic object that its (mainly cultivated) audience presumed it to be.

As the foregoing indicates, the engaged composer in the late 1960s was confronted with a dilemma. Having rejected "bourgeois" music on account of its elitism, there appeared to be few viable alternatives, commercial music being too tainted by its perceived complicity with the culture industry to be recognized as a genuinely popular form of expression. Elitism and commercialization thus formed the Scylla and Charybdis that a composer like Ferrari had to navigate. An article titled "Pour une culture populaire" that appeared in the newspaper *L'Étudiant de France,* the organ of the French student union UNEF (Union Nationale des Etudiants de France), lays out the terms of this dichotomy in a particularly clear fashion.[47] The author observes that the May events not only represented a crisis of social and political institutions, but cultural ones as well. To begin with, so-called serious art has been delegitimized, its claim to the status of the universal revealed as false: "Bourgeois culture is the desire to show off more than it is the satisfaction of experience. Comprehension, being based on erudition, [is] for the same reason reserved for a minority."[48] Yet the alternative fares no better: "Mass culture is nothing more than a vast commercial enterprise destined to make profits and to snuff out any impulse that resists the dominant ideology."[49] This Manichaean opposition leads the author to call for the creation of a "real popular culture," that is to say, a culture that is not only enjoyed by the masses but is also produced directly by them:

> To recognize creation as a fundamental need of man is to desire that the popular classes be freed from the alienation of commercialized pleasure. It is an objectively revolutionary ferment since the desire for freedom of expression and of creation demolishes the cultural privilege of the dominant classes and calls into question their other privileges.[50]

Ferrari was by no means exempt from the lure of such calls to generalize creative activity. As critical as it was for an *animateur* such as Ferrari to render art accessible to the largest possible public, no less important was the inculcation of an active, participatory sensibility in individuals. Ferrari, like the author of "Pour une culture populaire," maintained that people had to be given the opportunity to realize their untapped aesthetic impulses: "Each person is in possession of certain creative capacities. Thus everyone should have the chance to pursue these capacities, to develop them, to live them fully."[51] As far as his own music was concerned, Ferrari advocated that it should serve less as an object of veneration and more as a stimulus: "I myself wish that people who listen to my anecdotal works will not be paralyzed with respect and adoration, but should rather say to themselves: I too can do this."[52] Such statements suggest that Ferrari saw in tape music the potential of becoming a new medium for amateur artistic practice. Made possible by the increasing affordability of portable tape recorders, the realization of this ambition would further require that tape music be demystified, stripped of its aura of technical complexity. In this regard, *Presque rien*, with its minimal editing, offered an ideal prototype for such a practice. More than simply an object of mass contemplation, the piece seems to have been conceived as an incitement to mass creation.

To clarify his aspirations for anecdotal music Ferrari pointed to amateur photography as a possible precedent. Asked whether he really believed that people might go out and record their own tape pieces, Ferrari responded,

> Why not? After all, people take holiday photos and make vacation films; they could just as well record their impressions in sound-pictures [Hörbildern]. The electroacoustic music that I make nowadays may be produced without any equipment beyond that available to every amateur.[53]

The analogy he draws appears straightforward enough; yet Ferrari's reference to the particular practice of amateur photography seems to have been driven in part by the connotations that surrounded it, especially in terms of its perceived social status. The spread of cheap and easy-to-use cameras in the 1950s and 1960s had placed them alongside automobiles and refrigerators as a potent token of postwar mass culture. At the same time, the rapid expansion of the field of photographic activity condemned it to the ignominious designation as a "middlebrow art," as the title of Bourdieu's 1965 study of photography's social uses would bluntly put it.[54] Particularly vilified by French intellectuals and cultural elites was the burgeoning pastime of tourist photography. As one of Bourdieu's informants, a lawyer, would say: "I bring aesthetic concepts to photography. My judgment constantly intervenes to prevent me from taking simple tourist photographs."[55]

That Ferrari chose an activity denigrated as "middlebrow" to be the prototype for the kind of musical practice he hoped to inspire is telling. The analogy was not merely descriptive, but performative as well: invoking the position of one practice (i.e., amateur photography) positioned the other in turn, helping to fix Ferrari's endeavors within a field of social and artistic possibilities. The efficacy of the metaphor lay in the train of associations it brings to mind, especially regarding matters of specialization and social class: for this reason the "vulgar" connotations of amateur photography made it a doubly attractive model for Ferrari. For at the same time as it helped certify his populist leanings, the valorization of a mass-cultural practice can be seen as serving his professional interests, insofar as the embrace of the vulgar in defiance of good taste is a tried and true strategy (that of "épater le bourgeois") for those seeking to take up a vanguard position in the artistic field. Indeed, Ferrari's reference not just to amateur photography but specifically to tourist photography was particularly effective, since it fused two distinct emblems of middlebrow, mass culture in a single activity: mass tourism and amateur photography.

Such self-positioning could only succeed so long as one was aware of the status accorded to photography within the constellation of cultural practices. Yet the class coding of amateur photography does not wholly explain the disdain it generated in certain quarters. Equally important was the belief that the camera—like all other recording devices, including the tape recorder—served to degrade people's experience of reality. The camera gained a political charge, becoming a compact symbol of the reifying forces at play under capitalism. Such readings of photography were part of a broader critique of the image, which found its most pointed expression at the time in Guy Debord's situationist manifesto *La société du spectacle* (1967): "The whole life of those societies in which modern conditions of production prevail presents itself as an immense accumulation of *spectacles*. All that once was directly lived has become mere reprcsentation."[56] As the image encroaches on the real, as fixed representations replace the spontaneity of experience, the individual's perceptive, affective, and cognitive faculties erode. A sclerosis of the senses sets in. Visual experience becomes nothing more than the capacity to recognize something already seen. The landmark sought by the tourist "will be photographed; going further, it will not even be looked at; the cliché will be seen instead. The world comes to resemble the image that has been presented of it."[57] Nostalgia for a lost perceptual innocence lay at the heart of such critiques. The growing cognizance that unmediated perception was under threat, that every sight taken in by the viewer replicated that which is already familiar from books and advertisements, fueled this discourse. And while a more or less neutral instrument like the camera could hardly be deemed responsible by itself for the impoverishment of experience that critics ascribed to it, it nonetheless marked a privileged site where the "domination of the spectacle over life" appeared to assume concrete, material form (see figure 7.1).

Even though the critique of the image undertaken by the situationists and others had no precise analogue in contemporaneous musical debates in France, concerns about the reifying capacity of recording technology find a curious echo in an early critique of *Presque rien*, a critique that would buttress the sense that a "second-order," cultivated perception was the most fitting way of apprehending the work. In 1972, shortly after the release of *Presque rien* on record, Ferrari was

INTERNATIONALE SITUATIONNISTE

j'aime ma caméra
parce que
j'aime
vivre

j'enregistre les
meilleurs moments
de l'existence

je les ressuscite
à ma volonté
dans tout leur éclat

LA DOMINATION DU SPECTACLE SUR LA VIE

Cette publicité de la caméra Eumig (été 1967) évoque très justement la glaciation de la vie indi-
viduelle qui s'est renversée dans la perspective spectaculaire : le présent se donne à vivre immé-
diatement **comme souvenir.** Par cette spatialisation du temps, qui se trouve soumis à l'ordre
illusoire d'un présent accessible en permanence, le temps et la vie ont été perdus ensemble.

Figure 7.1   An illustration from the *Internationale situationniste*, no. 11
(October 1967). Advertisement: "I like my camera because I like to live. I record
the best moments of existence. I bring them back to life in all their brilliance."
"THE DOMINATION OF THE SPECTACLE OVER LIFE. This advertisement for
the Eumig camera (summer 1967) evokes quite exactly the freezing of
individual life, which is itself inverted in the spectacular perspective: the
present is given to be lived immediately *as a memory*. By means of this
spatialization of time, which finds itself subject to the illusory order of a
permanently accessible present, both time and life together have been lost."

interviewed in the *Nouvelle revue française* by François-Bernard Mâche,
another composer concerned with the question of realism in music.
During the course of the interview Mâche assumes an antagonistic
posture, rejecting not so much *Presque rien* itself, but rather its claim
to realism. In Mâche's estimation any intervention on the composer's
part in the unfolding soundscape undermines its authenticity. Since
Ferrari's piece is an idealized representation of daybreak in Vela Luka,

cobbled together from a number of source recordings, it fails to pass muster: "If there is montage, there is composition. You have chosen for example to cleanly cut off the cicadas at the end, after twenty minutes of 'music'—whereas real cicadas chirp for hours. You have thus intervened actively in the acoustic event. You are still a composer, figurative rather than realist."[58]

While much of the dispute revolves around seemingly trivial terminological questions—"réalisme" vs. "surréalisme" vs. "sous-réalisme"—it soon becomes clear that Mâche's difficulty with Ferrari's work stems from what he sees as the fundamentally misrepresentative character of magnetic tape. If the aim of a piece like *Presque rien* is to provide listeners with an accurate image of a particular acoustic environment, its reliance on sound recording—no matter how high the fidelity—will always render the piece inadequate, a pale reflection of reality. Rather than engage in the practice of "sound photography," which by necessity entails the isolation and extraction of sounds from their natural context, Mâche asks if it wouldn't be better to organize "a travel agency where listeners would go to witness in person this sonic spectacle."[59] Such an agency would return sounds to their surroundings, but might also provide the listener with a sense of immediacy and vividness, qualities necessarily lost in a recording: "There are surely places where every day the sunrise is accompanied by marvelous noises at this time of year. Let's go, the stereo will be better."[60] What for Ferrari is a model of a popular artistic practice—the middlebrow form of photography—represents instead for Mâche a distortion, perhaps even a corruption, of our experience of the acoustic environment: "it is necessary to admit that when one transforms the sunrise into music that one listens to in one's apartment, there is already artifice, and thus art."[61] If Ferrari's reference to photography seeks to insert his practice into the realm of the popular, then Mâche's criticism of *Presque rien* reinscribes the piece in the sphere of cultivated apprehension from which it had sought to free itself. Noting that the audience for the work is not the proletariat but "a fraction of the bourgeoisie," Mâche adds that "*Presque rien* is only possible here, in the capitalist West,"[62] thereby rebuffing in an unceremonious fashion Ferrari's ambitious aspirations for the work.

How, then, are we to evaluate the import of *Presque rien*? At first blush, it seems clear that Ferrari's aspirations for anecdotal music—that it might open the door to a form of amateur sound recording practice— went unrealized. There appears to be little evidence that others took up his proposal to go out with portable tape machines in hand and create their own *musique concrète*. On the other hand, if we consider *Presque rien* strictly as an object of aesthetic apprehension, and not as an incitement to creative activity, it seems incontestable that the "cultivated" mode of listening—as noted above—has won out over all other contenders. At least this is the impression given by the critical literature on the piece (what little of it exists). Most critics have thus followed Mâche's lead and placed the piece decidedly on the near side of the art/reality divide. For some, such as Chion and Reibel, the status of anecdotal music as a cultural artifact marks Ferrari's socio-aesthetic project as a failure, inadequate to the composer's intentions: "He's a little bit like our own Cage, less of a philosopher and more easy-going. While proclaiming near and far his disdain for all aesthetic constraints, he has yet to cease playing hide-and-seek with a notion that he pretends to scorn: that of the *work*."[63] For others, most notably Jacqueline Caux, the affirmation of *Presque rien*'s status as a work of art is plain and simply a question of valorization: "If the word masterpiece means anything, then it may surely be applied to *Presque rien no 1, le lever du jour au bord de la mer.*"[64] But if we accept her claim that *Presque rien* is nothing less than a masterpiece, then by the same token we must accept that it will never be anything more than that either.

Nonetheless, one should not be overhasty in drawing conclusions about *Presque rien*'s legacy—either its consignment to the aesthetic realm, or its failure as an impetus to popular creative activity. Ultimately the piece's value resides in the uses individuals derive from it, and we should be mindful of the fact that information about how *Presque rien* has been put to work is scattered and partial. If it appears that a cultivated, aestheticizing approach to the piece has trumped all others, this is perhaps due to the form and nature of the documentation that is available to us: music reviews, journals, and magazines, which all tend to be written by and tailored to a cultivated and aesthetically astute segment of the population. Who knows what others outside this narrow orbit might have made of the piece? Who knows if one of the students that Ferrari worked with in Amiens continued to make tape pieces after his departure in 1969? Every now and then it is possible to catch a glimpse of a different response to *Presque rien,* an alternative history of its impact that stands in sharp contrast to that provided in the musicological literature. Consider, for instance, that during a visit to the United States in 1970, Ferrari participated in an interview with Charles Amirkhanian and Richard Friedman on KPFA radio in Berkeley, California, during the course of which he discussed the recently composed *Presque rien* no. 1. Shortly after the broadcast of this interview, Amirkhanian and Friedman began a radio program called the "World Ear Project," which invited listeners to send in their own tape pieces—their own, homemade versions of "electroacoustic nature photography."[65] While Ferrari's work was but one small piece in a much larger jigsaw puzzle of inspirations that lay behind the initiative (inspirations that include Cage, R. Murray Schafer, and the nascent environmental movement), there is no doubt that his work played some role, however indirect, in the creation of this platform for amateur tape music. Beyond whatever enduring aesthetic value the piece may possess, it is as much here—outside the pale of documented music history, in the practical uses that individuals have drawn from the work—that the ultimate significance of *Presque rien* may very well reside.

I am especially grateful to Brunhild Meyer-Ferrari, for having answered so many of my questions about Luc Ferrari's life and work during the 1960s and 1970s; and to Richard Friedman and Charles Amirkhanian, who not only provided information concerning the origins of the World Ear Project, but in addition located and made available to me a recording of Amirkhanian's 1973 radio program devoted to Ferrari's music.

Notes

1. Ferrari, in François-Bernard Mâche, "Entretien avec Luc Ferrari," *Nouvelle revue française* 232 (April 1972): 115. Reprinted in *La revue musicale* 214–15 (1977): 63–69.

2. Michel Chion and Guy Reibel, *Les musiques electroacoustiques* (Aix-en-Provence: Édisud, 1976), 67.

3. Ferrari, in Jacqeline Caux, *Presque rien avec Luc Ferrari* (Paris: Éditions Main d'œuvre, 2002), 171. In an interview with Charles Amirkhanian he cites the militarization of France under President Charles De Gaulle as being one catalyst for his politicization; Luc Ferrari, interviewed by Charles Amirkhanian, *Ode to Gravity*, KPFA (Berkeley, Calif.), April 11, 1973. A further catalyst was the Algerian War of Independence; Brunhild Meyer-Ferrari, interview with the author, June 7, 2006.

4. Ferrari, in Caux, ibid., 56.

5. Although there were a number of local and national musicians' unions active at the time of May 68, no body existed to protect the interests of composers as a distinct group. The composers' union that was founded on May 22, 1968 (and which included Henri Dutilleux, Gilbert Amy, André Jolivet, Maurice Ohana, Francis Miroglio, Jean Weiner, Jean Barraqué, Claude Ballif, Jean Martinet, and André Boucourechliev) sought to fill this vacuum, and provide a vehicle for the advancement of their political goals.

6. Interview with Brunhild Meyer-Ferrari, June 7, 2006.

7. David Looseley summarizes Malraux's beliefs by saying that "great art . . . does not need to be explained or taught but can be appreciated spontaneously if encountered directly." David Looseley, *The Politics of Fun: Cultural Policy and Debate in Contemporary France* (Oxford: Berg, 1995), 36.

8. From Pierre Moinot, "Les Maisons de la Culture" (1961), reprinted in *Les Affaires culturelles au temps d'André Malraux 1959–1969* (Paris: La Documentation Française, 1996), 384.

9. Brian Rigby, *Popular Culture in Modern France: A Study of Cultural Discourse* (London: Routledge, 1991), 133–34.

10. Malraux, cited in J.-C. Bécane, *L' Expérience des maisons de la culture* (Paris: La Documentation Française, 1973), 54.

11. The phrase "dirigisme culturel" is Becane's, in *L'Expérience des maisons de la culture*, 6. It should be noted that the *Maisons de la Culture* were conceived as a means of countering the fragmentation of the French polity in the wake of decolonization, and that many of its early administrators were former colonial functionaries.

12. For a discussion of these movements, see Rigby, *Popular Culture in Modern France*, 39–67.

13. Ferrari, in Hansjörg Pauli, *Für wen komponieren Sie eigentlich?* (Frankfurt: S. Fischer Verlag, 1971), 56.

14. Ibid., 57.

15. Ibid., 55.

16. Cited in Bécane, *L'Expérience des maisons de la culture*, 32.

17. These and other graffiti from May are recorded in *Les Murs ont la parole: Journal mural mai 68*, ed. Julien Besançon (Paris: Tchou, 1968), 154, 174 and 113, respectively.

18. The notion of the "ideological state apparatus" is introduced in Althusser's essay "Ideology and Ideological State Apparatuses (Notes towards an Investigation)," (1970), in his *Lenin and Philosophy*, trans. Benjamin Brewster (New York: Monthly Review, 1972).

19. The communists' suspicion toward "action culturelle" is discussed in Jean Caune, *La Culture en action: De Vilar à Lang, le sens perdu* (Grenoble: Presses Universitaires de Grenoble, 1999), 198–201.

20. The statistics for Amiens are given in Bécane, *L'Expérience des maisons de la culture*, 23.

21. Pierre Bourdieu, "L' école conservatrice. Les inégalités devant l'école et devant la culture," *Revue française de sociologie* 7, no. 3 (July/September 1966): 344.

22. "Déclaration de Villeurbanne, 25/5/68, " reprinted in Francis Jeanson, *L'Action culturelle dans la cité* (Paris: Editions du Seuil, 1973), 119. English translations of the declaration can be found in Alain Schnapp and Pierre Vidal-Nacquet, *The French Student Uprising, November 1967–June 1968: An Analytical Record*, trans. Maria Jolas (Boston: Beacon, 1971), 579–82; and in Jeremy Ahearne, *French Cultural Policy Debates: A Reader* (New York: Routledge, 2002), 70–75. (All translations of the declaration given here are mine.)

23. "Déclaration de Villeurbanne," in Jeanson, *L'Action culturelle dans la cité*, 120.

24. Ibid., 121.

25. Ibid.

26. "Déclaration de Villeurbanne," *Maison de la Culture d'Amiens* 9 (October 15, 1968): 1.

27. Ferrari, in Pauli, *Für wen komponieren Sie eigentlich?*, 44.

28. Ibid., 48.

29. Ibid., 50.

30. Ferrari, cited in Denys Lemery, "Luc Ferrari: Entretien avec un jeune compositeur non-conformiste . . . ," *Actuel* 12 (1970): 15.

31. "Luc Ferrari: Interview by Dan Warburton, July 22, 1998," http://www.paristransatlantic.com/magazine/interviews/ferrari.html (accessed July 20, 2005).

32. Ibid.

33. Ferrari states in an interview with François-Bernard Mâche that the piece was the product of splicing together numerous recordings in order to provide a representation of a "typical" morning: "[I]n *Presque rien* I chose from all the sounds that accompany the sunrise each morning those which always came back, which were truly typical for me." Ferrari, in Mâche, "Entretien avec Luc Ferrari," 113.

34. Ferrari, in Pauli, *Für wen komponieren Sie eigentlich?*, 58.

35. Ibid.

36. Luc Ferrari, liner notes to *Hétérozygote/J'ai été coupé* (Philips, Prospective 21ᵉ siécle 836 885 DSY).

37. Jean-Michel Damian, "Luc Ferrari: Hétérozygote; J'ai été coupé,"*Harmonie* 52 (December 1969): 68.

38. Ibid.

39. Translated as "Outline for a Sociological Theory of Artistic Perception," in *The Field of Cultural Production*, ed. Randal Johnson (New York: Columbia University Press, 1993), 215–37.

40. Ibid., 220.

41. Ibid.

42. Ibid., 222.

43. Ferrari, in Pauli, *Für wen komponieren Sie eigentlich?*, 46.

44. In interviews Ferrari has described *Presque rien* as instantiating both minimalist and hyperrealist aesthetics. See Caux, *Presque rien avec Luc Ferrari*, 51. See also Jacqueline Caux's introduction to the same volume, 10–11.

45. Daniel Teruggi, "Les Presque rien de Luc Ferrari, " in *Portraits Polychrome: Luc Ferrari* (Paris: CDMC/INA Groupe Edition–Documentation, 2001), 38.

46. Jean-Paul Sartre, "The Risk of Spontaneity and the Logic of the Institution," in *"All We Are Saying..." The Philosophy of the New Left*, ed. Arthur Lothstein (New York: Capricorn, 1971), 294.

47. In "Pour une culture populaire," *L'Étudiant de France* 2 (July–August 1968): 6.

48. Ibid.

49. Ibid.

50. Ibid.

51. Ferrari in Pauli, *Für wen komponieren Sie eigentlich?*, 50.

52. Ibid., 49.

53. Ibid.

54. Pierre Bourdieu et al., *Un art moyen* (Paris: Editions de Minuit, 1965); translated as *Photography: A Middle–brow Art*, trans. Shaun Whiteside (Stanford: Stanford University Press, 1990).

55. Bourdieu, *Photography*, 65.

56. Guy Debord, *La Société du spectacle* (Paris: Buchet–Chastel, 1967). Translated as *The Society of the Spectacle*, trans. Donald Nicholson–Smith (New York: Zone, 1994), 12. It should be noted that the first sentence is a rewriting (or "détournement") of the opening of Marx's *Das Kapital*, with the word *spectacles* replacing that of *commodities*.

57. Jean Keim, *La Photographie et l'homme: sociologie et psychologie de la photographie* (Paris: Casterman, 1971), 43.

58. Mâche, "Entretien avec Luc Ferrari," 114.

59. Ibid.

60. Ibid.

61. Ibid.

62. Ibid.

63. Chion and Reibel, *Les musiques electroacoustiques*, 143.

64. Jacqueline Caux, "Les «Presque rien» de Luc Ferrari," liner notes to Luc Ferrari, *Presque rien* (INA c 2008), n.p.

65. Personal communication from Richard Friedman, September 12, 2005.

Part III

POLITICIZING PERFORMANCE

8

ONCE and the Sixties
Ralf Dietrich

ONCE was an avant-garde art venture that lived and died with the
sixties. Started by a group of young composers, it took shape as an
independent new music festival in the college town of Ann Arbor,
Michigan, in the American Midwest. From 1961 to 1965, the festival
premiered original contemporary concert music, electronic music, theatrical performance pieces, and dance. It became an unexpected success and an important hub of a fledgling, nationwide network of young
performing artists from various disciplines. In due course it attracted
international attention and outgrew its local sponsor, a nonprofit organization supporting theatrical arts. When the sponsor withdrew funding in 1965, calling an end to the festival, ONCE activities were
continued by the so-called ONCE Group, artist friends from various
disciplines who had been participating in the festival and who, under
the direction of composer Robert Ashley, went on to perform original
musical theater pieces across the country until 1970.

ONCE was not the only collective art movement that started
around 1960, involved music, had a strong inclination toward innovation in the performing arts and toward stretching the boundaries of
artistic categories, and struggled for a venue within its own community.[1] But ONCE was perhaps the only one whose existence coincided so
closely with the 1960s as a whole. It is thus particularly suited to an
examination of the intersections and correlations between what its
chief protagonists were doing and the decade in which they were
doing it. Such an examination touches on both historic and aesthetic

issues, without attempting to present a complete history of ONCE or (for instance) a discussion of stylistic emancipation from serialism in ONCE compositions.[2]

The ONCE artists belong to what has been referred to as the "Silent Generation."[3] Mostly born between 1925 and 1935, their formative years were marked by the Great Depression and the Second World War. Some of the ONCE men were drafted during the Korean War and, together with veterans from two wars, went to college with the help of the GI Bill during the McCarthy era. They got married early and their drug of choice was alcohol. They were not the standard-bearers of the social movements with which the sixties have come to be most identified.

The core group of later ONCE members formed in the late fifties, when visual artist Milton Cohen recruited them one by one for his performances of light projections with live electronic music, first in his downtown studio, Ann Arbor's first loft, and later also out of town. Architects Harold Borkin and Joseph Wehrer and composers Gordon Mumma and Robert Ashley were the first to work with Cohen, and were joined in 1962 by visual artist and filmmaker George Manupelli. In 1963 the friends and their wives or girlfriends started performing sculptural theater pieces by Mary Ashley in public places. Soon Robert Ashley was recruiting the same people as performers for his own pieces. Following the 1964 Music Biennial in Venice, Italy, where Cohen's group represented the United States, Ashley seized the initiative to organize the group activities as Cohen gradually withdrew. Among the women performers, Mary Ashley, Cynthia Liddell, and Anne Wehrer would become the most prominent.

That Cohen made Ashley and Mumma his regular collaborators reveals his good instincts. Ashley and Mumma shared a mobile electronic music studio and would become the most proactive ONCE musicians: forming an instrumental duo, giving lecture-recitals, traveling, commissioning, performing, and spreading ONCE repertore—all for little or no money. They were, however, not the only composers in town who had been frustrated composition students of Ross Lee Finney at the University of Michigan, and who had been stimulated by a seminar on the evolution and applications of twelve-tone technique given by Roberto Gerhard during a sabbatical of Finney in early 1960. To create a one-time venue for their own music, Ashley and Mumma teamed up with Roger Reynolds, Donald Scavarda, George Cacioppo, and others, and initiated "A Festival of Musical Premieres"—as the first ONCE Festival, held in February and March 1961, was officially subtitled.

The Festival

For support they turned to a small, local nonprofit organization called the Dramatic Arts Center (DAC). A beneficiary of the postwar university environment, the DAC had been founded (and funded) in 1954 by local business leaders, politicians, law professors, and their theater-loving wives with the intention of establishing a professional repertory theater company in Ann Arbor. When the composers approached the Center in the fall of 1960, the DAC had already produced a play for which Cohen contributed light and Mumma contributed his "first large-scale electronic music" (1959). It had also presented films by Manupelli featuring electronic soundtracks by Ashley (1960), and had sponsored a local "Concert of New Music" with John Cage and David Tudor (1960). More significantly, the DAC had just lost its mission to the University when it was decided that the speech department would launch its own professional repertory theater program.[4] In order not to fold completely, the Center went back to subsidizing other local cultural activities with small grants. Only the recent assertion of the University's local cultural hegemony enabled the DAC to underwrite the ONCE Festival. Following the surprise success of the first festival, the group of ONCE organizers secured further funding by gradually infiltrating the DAC's directorial board, over which Wilfred Kaplan, a faculty member of the mathematics department and the Center's main financial backer, presided. Between 1961 and 1964 Anne Wehrer, Ashley, Manupelli, and Borkin joined the board and Mumma became a staff member.[5] Although Manupelli started the Ann Arbor Film Festival in 1963, of which the DAC remained one of two mainstays into the late 1980s, the ONCE members on the DAC board did not just act as ONCE lobbyists but supported many different events. They could not prevent Kaplan from cutting off funding for ONCE, nor did they quit the DAC board when it happened. In 1967 Anne Wehrer even took over the DAC presidency for two seasons. They simply held on to the only chance of funding they were offered for as long as they could. "Foundation patronage was out of the question," Mumma wrote, "because we were not an institution, but merely a diverse group of artists."[6]

ONCE was never particularly concerned with labeling, nor did ONCE ever position itself explicitly as "avant-garde." The ONCE artists preferred neutral, descriptive terms, such as the already mentioned "musical premieres" or "new music," and they preferred the scientific connotations of "experimental" over the ideological and historical ballast of "avant-garde," without ever explicitly objecting to the latter. However, works premiered (or U.S. premiered) at ONCE concerts between 1961 and 1968 show a clear commitment to the music of the avant-garde: these included music by David Behrman, Luciano Berio, André Boucourechliev, George Brecht, Cage, Barney Childs, Eric Dolphy, Morton Feldman, Gerhard, Gordon Gidley, Toshi Ichiyanagi, Bob James, Udo Kasemets, Alvin Lucier, Pauline Oliveros, Ralph Shapey, Karlheinz Stockhausen, Michael von Biel, and Christian Wolff. At the first ONCE Festival (1961) Boulez's Domaine Musicale performed under Berio's direction in one concert, and the group's former associate Paul Jacobs gave a piano recital; concerts with European music were programmed on equal terms with music by the local composers. However, the only concert officially labeled as avant-garde in the ONCE context opened the second festival (1962); its title, "The New York Avant-Garde," announced a shift from European repertoire to American experimentalism, which the festival would continue over the years. The concert's line-up consisted of La Monte Young and Terry Jennings, and their program proved controversial. Young's performance of his own *Arabic numeral (any integer) (To Henry Flynt)*, consisting of 923 strokes on a large cooking pot resting in his lap, divided not only the audience but even the host composers. With its first two festivals alone, ONCE put the American Midwest on the map of the artist network of the time and situated it somewhere between the scenes in Europe and New York.

ONCE artists were committed to technology as a major agent of innovation, a faith shared at this critical juncture of the cold war by American society at large.[7] When military surplus gadgetry such as transistors and magnetic tapes became available on a massive scale, Cohen, Ashley, and Mumma were able to explore new paths. And once technology made practicing art in new ways a model for social interaction—for the ONCE artists this started with Cohen's collaborative group performances—technology became socially charged. (Electronics even encouraged performers to become composers, as the cases of Tudor and Max Neuhaus illustrate, both of whom performed at ONCE festivals.) Two strands of the ONCE Festival are especially relevant in their relation to the sixties; both involve electronics and can be traced back to ONCE's first all-electronic music program. This, the final concert of the 1962 festival, was advertised—correctly, as far as I can tell—as the "first major electronic music concert in the United States outside of New York City and Los Angeles."[8] On February 18, local composers Mumma and Ashley self-confidently presented pieces of their own alongside works by Milton Babbitt, Boucourechliev, Gerhard, Gottfried Michael Koenig, Bruno Maderna, and Conlon Nancarrow. They turned an economic disadvantage into a technical advantage: as mentioned above, they shared some of their electronic hardware with one another. Unable to afford expensive equipment and lacking access to an institutional studio, they had devised a way to combine two two-channel tape machines in order to be able to work with quadraphonic sound. Since their technical solution was custom made and incompatible with standard four-channel tape machines and tapes (as used by most other composers), their pieces ended up sounding more powerful than the other pieces on the program.[9] They also established key facets of the ONCE agenda, both with regard to aesthetic inheritance and to ideological orientation.

Electronics and Aesthetics—Robert Ashley

Closing the concert was Ashley's composition *Public Opinion Descends upon the Demonstrators* (1961). This piece used electronic music to tackle the disconnection between avant-garde sounds and audience as a problem intrinsic to the concert situation in general. At Cage's and

Tudor's 1960 Ann Arbor concert, Ashley had witnessed a walk-out of the local professorial music establishment.[10] With *Public Opinion* he now focused on the role that an audience plays in a concert (and the impact it has on the music) and staged it for, or rather in, the audience. Using the Fibonacci series, he mapped out six different possible realizations of the piece according to quantitative elements, including audience size. In Size III, which was performed, a human sound-controller (Ashley) operated a highly amplified sound source (a montage of randomly arranged everyday sounds on a prepared tape) according to scored rules and in response to audience activities such as loud speaking, laughing, walking around, or leaving.[11] Every audience member became a potential demonstrator faced with the sonic consequences of the opinion that he or she may have fancied to express or manifest. No matter how they decided to react to this unusual situation, they could not "out-behave" (disturb or break up) the performance. This effectively inverted the customary roles of audience and performers.[12] Without being provocative or "political," the sounds heightened listeners' consciousness of their own reactions. *Public Opinion Descends upon the Demonstrators* was thus a concert piece about the concert situation. The conceptualism of such a meta-piece aesthetic and the theatricality that it implies were a characteristic of avant-garde performance practice in the early sixties.

At the same time as *Public Opinion* Ashley conceived *Something for Clarinet, Pianos and Tape* (1961–62) as a solo piece for his friend, jazz musician Richard Waters. The soloist played three tunes of his own choice, sparsely accompanied by a jazz pianist (Bob James). A tape operator posing as a second pianist (Ashley) bridged the silences between the tunes with applause-like sounds, and the whole was performed in complete darkness in order to heighten the audience's attention. As in *Public Opinion* the main concern of the piece was not the sounds themselves, but that the audience "will *hear* ideas coming out of those sounds—directly out."[13] Again, Ashley employed theatrical artifice to achieve an immediacy of perception intended to ensure that the work was still perceived as *music*.

Two and a half months before the 1962 ONCE Festival, at which both pieces were premiered, Ashley went on record with a radical definition of

> a music that wouldn't necessarily involve anything but the presence of people. . . . We might have a piece from which one participant would come, and, upon being questioned, would say that the occasion was marked by certain sounds. Another person might say that he didn't remember any sounds. There was something else. But they would both agree that a performance of music had taken place.[14]

In March 1963, Ashley expressed further thoughts on the subject during an interview that he conducted with Morton Feldman.[15] The two composers talked about the aftermath of the revolution in the arts that had taken place in New York around 1950, a revolution in which "avant-garde" became an American endeavor and whose musical elements were codified in the graphic scores of the so-called New York School. Those compositions were meant to liberate sound, but the scores worked to liberate performers. For Feldman, who had participated in the revolution, the liberation of the performer was "its most important flaw."[16] Ashley, on the other hand, welcomed the implied shift in focus from *compositions* to theatrical *performances* by flamboyant personalities, including composers themselves (La Monte Young, for example). The mid-century revolution, he argued, amounted to a liberation of the composer as performer. Defining composer-performers by what they were doing and standing for, rather than by what their music sounded like, he saw the ONCE Festival, at least by tendency, as a venue for this new type of composer-performer, a "Festival of Personalities."[17] The festival's character as a *music* festival was then guaranteed by the presence of people like Cage and Feldman (who attended several ONCE festivals as composer-performers) almost more than by the music itself.[18]

Ashley's diagnosis positioned ONCE in relation to the New York School not unlike American Pop Art had positioned itself in relation to Abstract Expressionism: reverent toward the integrity and the personalitics of the older artists, but veering off into new directions in other respects. Acknowledging the debt, Ashley nevertheless recognized the theatricality that marked the new music of the sixties in general—and of the ONCE festivals in particular—and evaluated it more positively than Feldman. ONCE pieces like *Public Opinion Descends upon the Demonstrators* share more with the conceptual pieces of the Fluxus circle than with the New York School, but were developed independently of both.

Electronics and Politics—Gordon Mumma

Another ONCE path focused less on the concert situation and instead opened performance venues up to the world outside. The first half of the closing concert of the 1962 ONCE Festival ended with the premiere of Mumma's tape composition *Soundblock 8: Epoxy*, whose sound distribution over four separate channels was supposed to achieve a sonic analogue to wide-screen cinematography. As a film buff, Mumma knew how important "skillful editing" and "referential cross-cutting" was to creating meaning.[19] The piece's title referred both to a building block of sound material (as used for performances in Cohen's studio), and to how the various sound units were glued together. What the title did not reveal was that the resulting piece was, in fact, a political collage, consisting of multilingual sound bites from newscasts, statements from political speeches (among others, by German Nazis, Charles De Gaulle, segregationist Arkansas governor Orval Faubus, and John F. Kennedy), McCarthy hearings and those of the House Committee on Un-American Activities, and racist remarks by radio preachers, juxtaposed and connected with recordings of audience reactions to both modern music and reactionary politics.[20] Rather untypically for his electronic music, Mumma used only natural, acoustic (i.e., nonelectronic) sound sources and kept them almost unmodified and therefore highly identifiable. The kaleidoscopic, yet panoramic way in which the piece colligated real-life sound fragments and connected social and musical practices suggested an ideological continuity (of "fascism") from the Second World War through the cold war to the opposition to the Civil Rights Movement.

Politically, Mumma was the most outspoken of the ONCE artists. He had experienced denominational segregation as a child, retribution in high school for playing Stan Kenton arrangements, racial discrimination (against "non-whites") in Michigan housing laws, complicity in racial discrimination in the University of Michigan Concert Band when it toured Southern states (without his participation), political hysteria in the mid-fifties when the Berlin Philharmonic Orchestra first came to Ann Arbor, and when the Red Scare hit its peak.[21] Mumma's most significant, and most elaborate, piece in this regard was *Megaton for William Burroughs* (1962–65), in which he equipped nonmusician performers (ONCE members) with contact microphones and utilized the performance space and lighting to highly dramatic effect. With an emphasis that alternated from section to section, *Megaton* combined tapes (prepared and replayed) with (amplified) live action to create something like a live electronic, musical IMAX theater of its time. A performance of *Megaton* would take the audience along on a theatrical trip to drop a bomb, a trip that lasted twenty-five minutes at the premiere (on February 28 at the 1964 ONCE Festival) and could be extended to nearly forty minutes in later performances (of which there were six or seven over the course of three years; *Megaton* was Mumma's major contribution to the ONCE Group's original repertory). From a beginning cloaked in darkness and surrounded by what has since been canonized as early drone and/or noise music, the bombing raid situation (with Mumma as pilot/commander) would slowly emerge visually and sonically in the first half of the piece. The second half used the sound-track of the British film *The Dam Busters* (1954) to clarify the situation, which was then abruptly suspended, leaving the audience to reorient themselves to the lonely timekeeping of a trap drummer, coming from a remote and previously unused part of the performance space.

In *Megaton*, Mumma complemented the frequently cinematic qualities of his electronic music (as in *Epoxy*) with techniques he drew from the work's titular dedicatee, William S. Burroughs. In the first half of the piece Mumma used technology (especially the electronic treatment and spatial distribution of sounds in combination with the lighting) in an attempt to manipulate the sensory perception of the audience, almost to the point of creating acoustic illusions.[22] Technically, he was exercising what Burroughs critically termed "mind control," but in a manner that sided with the nonconformity of Burroughs's writing: "[I]n the introductory sound to *Megaton* (half of which exists only in the head of the listener)," for instance, he experimented with resultant cluster pitches in a manner akin to resultant melodic patterns that are perceived differently from the way they are actually played.[23] In the later half of the piece Mumma submitted the soundtrack of a mainstream movie to an avant-garde treatment. Cutting it up and overlaying the fragments, he reapplied the cut-up technique that Burroughs had applied to literature.[24] *Megaton for William Burroughs* is a rare example of a tribute to and a mature reception of Burroughs at the time, in any discipline. Very much like Burroughs's artistic experiments, the bomb of Mumma's *Megaton* was aimed not just at the conventions of musical performance but also at the mindset of postwar American society, in which, for Burroughs as for Mumma, the ghost of the Second World War still loomed large.[25]

Mumma's conception of *Megaton* began in the spring of 1962, not long after the premiere of *Epoxy*, when he started working as a technical research associate in a laboratory of the University's Institute of Science and Technology. There he became involved in military-sponsored geophysical work, studying and comparing classified tape recordings of earthquakes and underground nuclear explosions. This certainly informed his choice of *The Dam Busters* (for *Megaton*). The film dramatized an experimental project from its mathematical conception over various testing stages to its collaborative team realization.[26] The historical project's goal was the deployment of a "bouncing" bomb in such a way that it would have an earthquake effect. Mumma's laboratory job linked the episode from the Second World War that is depicted in the film with tests of nuclear weapons, the destructive energy output of which was measured in megatons. At the dynamic climax in his edit of the movie soundtrack, the last words Mumma quoted from the film dialogue were: "It's still there!" In the film this referred to the target; in *Megaton* it referred to the bomb. However, it is significant that there were no audible explosions in *Megaton*. If a bomb was indeed dropped during the performance, it was into the minds of the audience. The drummer's lonely timekeeping at the end of *Megaton* now served as a reminder that time might be running out.

After Mumma learned of another experimental project embedded in warfare in the lab, he treated the same subject with increased technical sophistication in *The Dresden Interleaf* (1963–65)—again a sonic montage with a cinematic dramatic curve. This piece, too, uses technology in order to say something about technology. It was premiered at a ONCE Festival, on February 13, 1965, twenty years to the day after the bombing that the piece commemorated, and two and a half weeks before the first U.S. aerial bombardment of Vietnam.

Gaps and Changes

By 1965, the ONCE Festival had firmly established itself within a grow-ing nationwide network of artists. Locally, however, it faced two new challenges. The first came from the University's School of Music. In the spring of 1965, while mass protests against the Vietnam War were gaining momentum across the country, four graduate composition students at the University formed a new music group and called it, with a homonymous pun on a catchphrase that President Johnson had introduced in the University's football stadium during his com-mencement speech in May 1964, the Grate Society.[27] Its members, William Albright, David Andrew, Robert D. Morris, and Russell Peck, had attended ONCE concerts—in the audience, as critics, or as perfor-mers; Peck even as a featured composer-performer—and detected the school's air of rivalry with the ONCE festivals. After they unsuccessfully tried to obtain funding from the school for exchange concerts with other music groups, they followed ONCE's lead and went out into the com-munity. On October 23, 1965, supported by a $50 DAC grant and supplemented by electronic gadgets that Mumma was producing and trying to market at the time, they staged a "birthday concert" at the Ann Arbor Public Library, with pieces for which there was no place in the music school. But as it turned out, they challenged the local status quo on two fronts. For their *Birthday Music (Tombeau)* they projected a picture of the ONCE composers onto a screen and bombarded it with seasonal apple mash they had collected in cider mills outside Ann Arbor. Apparently, the Grate Society's self-dramatized birth was supposed to be a musical tombstone for ONCE—a classic staging of a modernist patricide.

Their "birthday concert" was also a self-assured proclamation of the baby boomer generation. Born between 1943 and 1945, the four students averaged ten to fifteen years younger than the ONCE artists. Unlike the ONCE musicians, they belonged to a generation (maybe the first) whose academic education's exclusive focus on European Ameri-can concert music was significantly counterbalanced by interests in current popular (Peck), Indian (Morris), and earlier African American music (Albright). The Grate Society pieces employed various media (usually magnetic tapes and/or films accompanying actions) and were theatrical, even provocative with a tendency toward the drastic, often funny and/or caustic (parodistic, satirical). They wrapped sex, drugs, and Vietnam in humor (especially bathroom humor), and incorporated many popular culture references, without producing popular music. With the Grate Society, in a taste of things to come, the generation most identified with the sixties started confronting ONCE.

As surprising and drastic as the Grate Society's debut performance may have looked, their relationship to ONCE was actually ambivalent, and so was their "symbolic (as well as actual) castigation. . . . The ONCE people, who, of course, have been the trail-blazers in Ann Arbor, responded favorably . . . , which made us all feel good," Andrew noted afterward.[28] The Grate Society rejected musical processes that unfolded slowly over long durations and required prolonged attention—an interest ONCE shared with the New York School. As Peck recalls, "The ONCE aesthetic was very much based on 'sustained tedium'—with *slow motion* events. They were into concentration. The groups that rebelled, so to speak, wanted action. To ONCE, I think, we . . . looked like cheap sensationalists."[29] The Grate Society's effort to surpass ONCE's theatricality with unsparing means and a heightened focus on effect confirmed Ashley's diagnosis of 1963: "They're not trying to gun you down on sound terms . . . but on personality terms."[30] In fact, all Grate Society members performed pieces by ONCE composers, even inside the music school. Mumma continued to support them with technical aid, and the DAC continued to support them financially. Within a year, ONCE composer George Cacioppo, while remaining involved in ONCE, joined the Grate Society, where he would bring in some of "the ONCE aesthetic."[31] The complex attitude of the young composer-performers toward ONCE echoed the way that Ashley had positioned ONCE in relation to the New York School. Even in America, ambiguous self-alignment with one's predecessors was apparently part of the avant-garde tradition.

More important than the Grate Society's aesthetic challenge, however, was the economic challenge that the DAC posed when it withdrew funding in 1965. The official reason for the withdrawal was that ONCE had become too big for the small nonprofit organization, devouring too much of the seasonal budget. The unofficial reason, claimed or confirmed by practically all ONCE members who were involved in the DAC, was that Kaplan, who also played in an amateur string quartet, had reportedly been under increasing political pressure from selected members of the University's music faculty.[32] The problem was that ONCE could not support itself on its own. The ONCE festivals preceded the art-supporting infrastructures that could have saved them; the implementation of the National Endowment and the State Councils for the arts came too late.

Tellingly, the closest ONCE ever came to government support was in connection with the cultural cold war. For the U.S. government, that conflict's two most prestigious international battlefields were the alternating art biennials in Venice, Italy, and in São Paulo, Brazil. In 1964, the ONCE artists, upon Luigi Nono's invitation, had presented the latest version of Cohen's project at the International Festival of Contemporary Music in Venice, which ran alongside the art exposition. For their first trip to Europe, some of the ONCE artists ended up going into debt. The State Department, by way of its Information Agency (USIA), supplied unprecedented amounts of funding to present American paintings and painters at the Biennale—but nothing for the music festival.[33] When the ONCE Group was invited to the 1965 São Paulo

Biennial, the situation was similar. This time, the USIA and the Smithsonian Institution negotiated a project called "Musical Theater in America Today" but the project got cut because it was "not an exhibit."[34] The ONCE Group's genre-crossing use of several media was still ahead of administrative categories. Again, no travel costs were provided, and this time the ONCE artists were not able to raise them (over $10,000 was needed).[35] Manupelli sent a few of his films, but otherwise ONCE was unrepresented.[36]

The ONCE Group

In order to survive, ONCE had to change both focus and strategy. When universities across the country started slowly to open their doors to more adventurous artistic performances in the mid-sixties, new opportunities arose.[37] ONCE adjusted and mutated into a touring company called the ONCE Group that performed mostly outside of regular concert venues, on campuses and outside of Ann Arbor. (A revived, three-night "ONCE Festival," held in 1968 under the aegis of the University of Michigan's annual spring arts festival, was the nominal exception to this rule and the first ONCE performance in Ann Arbor in almost two years.) Two peculiarities of the group can be traced back to the 1964 ONCE Festival, when Ashley recruited available nonmusician performers instead of trained instrumentalists and staged the premiere of his graphically notated *in memoriam . . . Kit Carson (opera)* (1963) with eight married couples. First, the ONCE Group adopted the festival's theatricality, and developed it further. Input from the artist members and their different backgrounds made the crossing of genres and mixing of media a natural result. A collective rehearsal process and collective realizations of the pieces took priority over working with written scores. The ONCE Group's unique personnel and personality situation made it an American and vocal counterpart to the "instrumental theater" that Mauricio Kagel was developing independently and more or less contemporaneously in Germany.[38] Both Kagel's instrumental theater pieces of the time and ONCE Group pieces continued to use elements of concert music conventions (music, gestures, imagery, and speech) but stopped being pure concert music. And both were, in Ashley's words, *"about* something."[39] Kagel's pieces, like some ONCE Festival pieces, were more about music and its social existence (*Metapiece* was a telling subtitle of a piano work from 1961).[40] The ONCE Group pieces tended to be about extramusical phenomena and social situations, and involved a lot of role-playing.[41] Some of them took their cues from the quasi-communal group dynamic itself.

Second, since the ONCE Group consisted mostly of couples, most of their pieces dealt with gender roles in heterosexual relationships. Despite their ambiguous nature—in this context both sexist *and* proto-feminist—these pieces anticipated approaches of feminist criticism or those of later gender studies by years, if not decades. *Kittyhawk* (1964), for instance, combined the topic of taking off and flying with sexual politics: in up to six simultaneous, parallel subplots—all of which involved physical risk, evoked danger, and had quasi-dramatic climaxes—women were elevated in ways that they alone would not be able to achieve.[42] The connotations of the episodes ranged from oblique sexual symbolism (a pinsetter joining up with bowling balls) to violent assault (a pedestrian being duct-taped to a wall), from the acrobatic (a balancing act) to the psychological (involving self-immobilization).[43] In Ashley's *Combination Wedding and Funeral* (1964), the bride character was not only presented as the object of the combined ceremonies (wedding and funeral) but also, disturbingly, as a monkey.

New Audiences

With the shift from festival to group performances, ONCE audiences changed, too. Young students increasingly brought their claim to involvement in society and politics into performance spaces, and ONCE was not spared. Interestingly, the more polarized and volatile American society in general and the more antagonistic ONCE audiences in particular became, the more communal and generous—literally giving— ONCE Group pieces turned out. In the only performance of *Combination Wedding and Funeral* on May 9, 1965, a New York audience in the Judson Memorial Church was treated to a wedding cake that the ONCE Group had made and that was served from the pelvis of a nude woman who functioned as a double of the bride. In the premiere of *Night Train* (1966) on January 7, 1967, at Brandeis University's Spingold Theater, the ONCE Group distributed small electric light and sound sources and food to the audience. Smell and taste were part of the sensory overload with which the piece attempted to stage collective situations of communication with aliens. The audience reciprocated by bombarding the stage with the gifts, which ensured that the piece was not performed again. The experience also prevented a realization of the group's next piece, *The Place Where the Earth Stands Still* (1966–67), which would have filled an interior space large enough for several hundred people with art pieces and performances lasting seventy-two hours.[44] The audience would have entered the empty space in the morning, free to do anything they wanted but expected not to leave. Everything, including the necessities of life, would have been provided for. Here, within the framework of a utopian community, the element of giving would have reached potlatch dimensions.[45] The piece was to offer an artificial "closed world," a weekend-long glimpse into an alternative society, with perceptions altered by art, a magical or, in anthropological terms, a liminoid experience.[46]

Ashley's *The Wolfman Motor-City Revue* (1967–68) was the only ONCE Group piece that reflected society's darker potential. The piece combined three of Ashley's earlier ONCE pieces into four long "songs" that he scored with various musical background textures. In terms of content, the songs followed a dramatic curve. Covering personal and public extremes and touching on subjects ranging from sexuality as an assertion of social power to daily politics, the first three songs laid out a disturbing social context for the fourth, Ashley's *The Wolfman* from 1964, a wordless, "amplified improvisation on four components of vocal sound" to a prerecorded tape.[47] *The Wolfman* was already notorious for its high volume, enhanced by Ashley's own theatrical rendition "as a sinister nightclub vocalist, spotlight and all," which usually caused the misperception that Ashley was merely screaming into a microphone.[48] The vocal parts and the prerecorded accompaniments of all four songs were amplified and processed separately. This electronic treatment provided another curve, parallel to the dramatic one. As Ashley later put it, "The idea was to get the audience to think of loudness as equals 'dirty.'"[49] At the *Revue*'s climactic finale, *The Wolfman*, aiming at an audible interplay between the two separate amplification systems, gradually reached acoustic feedback.

With the *Revue*, Ashley obviously wanted to arouse more than just the musical establishment. (For that, *The Wolfman* alone would have sufficed.) Unlike *Public Opinion*, which had preempted audience utterances during a performance and made them part of itself, the *Revue* reflected the rise to open violence that U.S. society at large was facing, and displayed it in a sonic distorting mirror. Like Mumma's *Megaton*, it confronted a threat to society. But where *Megaton* addressed a heritage of the past (the threat of a nuclear holocaust), the *Revue* addressed a peril for the future, triggered by the impending armament of the counterculture. In so doing, it sided with those who had the most future: the young—the same young who were the ONCE Group's main audience and whose increasing rowdiness, sometimes putting the performers in physical danger, was a symptom of this peril. Where *Megaton* alluded to subculture (avant-garde art and a "foreign" film), the *Revue* played on popular culture (Motown Records' prepackaged "Motortown Revues" and a classic Hollywood B-picture). This lightweight appearance stood in stark contrast to the drastic semantic and sonic onslaught with which the piece gradually escalated toward the monstrous.

In performance, the ONCE Group refused to stop being provocative and inadvertently upset the tastes of the student generation just as it had upset the tastes of the old guard before. Mostly performing at college and university arts festivals and usually billed as "theater," ONCE found itself still an odd bird sitting on a fence between the recital format it had previously expanded and successfully left behind and the rock festival format that captured baby boomer audiences in the late sixties. By now, the ONCE artists were well over thirty, and some even had teenage children themselves. The relationship of the ONCE artists to the baby boomers became almost parental: supportive, especially of cultural causes, and even when the goals behind those were no longer their own. When, for instance, the city stopped the effort of the "Trans-Love Energies Unlimited" commune to stage free rock concerts in Ann Arbor's West Park, the ONCE artists helped the commune secure permission from the city to continue.[50] On the other hand, their support did not keep them from distancing themselves from what they were supporting. The last ONCE Group piece, Manupelli's film *Cry, Dr. Chicago* (1970–71), contained salty comments on rock festival audiences' lack of discrimination. The cultural and societal energies that ONCE had helped unleash had gone in a different direction and created a gap between them and their late, young audience. But both shared a rebellious spirit, the same spirit that united them in speaking out against the war in Vietnam. The crushing of that spirit in the excessively violent clashes between young mass protesters and various police forces in early 1970 at the University of California, Santa Barbara, at Kent State University in Ohio, and at Jackson State College in Mississippi signaled the beginning of political restoration, and the end of ONCE.

Conclusion

Even a cursory look at ONCE illuminates a course of events that had two equally long halves, each with very different conditions for avant-garde composer-performers. The ONCE Festival was an overdue outgrowth from the fifties. It featured new music from all over the Western world, yet was essentially a communal phenomenon intimately related to the college town of Ann Arbor: it benefited from the local availability of performers and interested audiences, and challenged the hegemony of the University at the same time. Dedicated to expanding and innovating formats of musical presentation, the ONCE musicians created an opportunity for themselves to take and formulate positions toward their immediate (postwar) past, criticizing their ideological continuity and orientation (Mumma) or radicalizing their own aesthetic inheritance from the New York School (Ashley).

Things changed dramatically for ONCE when the festival lost its funding. This significantly reduced ONCE's opportunities to show its ongoing community orientation in Ann Arbor and caused it to morph into a performance group. The ONCE Group toured the college circuit, benefiting from a gradual opening of academic institutions to experimental performances. Where the festival had focused on art, the group now faced society. At the same time, their attention-demanding performances increasingly fell subject to criticism from baby-boomer audiences. Consequently, the ONCE artists found themselves caught in the middle of the decade's defining generation gap, and confronted moreover by an increasingly antagonistic political climate. ONCE ended, just before political reaction set in.

Notes

1. Examples of such collective performance movements within the United States include art gallery "happenings" (since 1957) and "events" (since 1959), the Judson Dance Theater and Fluxus (both since 1962), all in, or originating from, New York City; and the San Francisco Tape Music Center (also since 1962) in California. The most significant (and enduring) example originating in the Midwest was the Association for the Advancement of Creative Musicians (AACM) in Chicago, although this was not founded until 1965 (see George E. Lewis, *A Power Stronger than Itself: The AACM and American Experimental Music* [Chicago: University of Chicago Press, 2008]). Whether the so-called Newport Rebel Festival that Charles Mingus, Max Roach, Ornette Coleman, and others organized in 1960 marked the beginning of a movement is debatable but the similarity of the case with ONCE—American composer-performers frustrated with the lack of an outlet for their music within the established venues taking matters into their own hands—is striking. Cf. Michael C. Heller, "So We Did It Ourselves: A Social and Musical History of Musician-organized Jazz-Festivals from 1960 to 1973" (master's thesis, Rutgers University, 2005).

2. The first scholarly attempt to appraise ONCE in retrospect was an article by Richard James, which emphasized the group's intermedial aspects; see Richard S. James, "ONCE: Microcosm of the 1960s Musical and Multimedia Avant-Garde," *American Music* 5 (Winter 1987): 359–90. More recently, Mumma's former colleague Leta Miller contributed extensive liner notes to the expanded reissue of historic ONCE recordings on CD; see Leta E. Miller, "ONCE and Again: The Evolution of a Legendary Festival," *Music from the ONCE Festivals 1961–1966* (New York: New World Records CD 80567–2 [2003]), 13–95. Other recent appraisals include Thom Holmes, "ONCE and Future Innovators: Robert Ashley and Gordon Mumma," *Electronic and Experimental Music*, 2nd ed. (London: Routledge, 2002), 187–210; and Christoph Cox, "The Jerrybuilt Future: The Sonic Arts Union, ONCE Group and MEV's Live Electronics," ed. Rob Young, *Undercurrents: The Hidden Wiring of Modern Music* (London: Continuum, 2002), 36–44.

3. Neil Howe and William Strauss, *Generations: The History of America's Future, 1584 to 2069* (New York: Morrow, 1991), 279–95.

4. Robert Clyde Chapel, "The University of Michigan Professional Theatre Program, 1961–1973" (PhD diss., University of Michigan, 1974).

5. ONCE Archives, Music Library, Northwestern University, Evanston, Ill. Cacioppo was on the 1963 ballot for new board members but didn't get elected.

6. Gordon Mumma, "The ONCE Festival and How It Happened," *Arts in Society* 4, no. 2 (Summer 1967): 387.

7. See, for instance, Gary Cross and Rick Szostak, *Technology and American Society: A History*, 2nd ed. (Upper Saddle River, N.J.: Prentice Hall, 2004).

8. The only contender for the claim was the San Francisco Tape Music Center, which was established in the fall of that year. See *The San Francisco Tape Music Center: 1960s Counterculture and the Avant-Garde*, ed. David W. Bernstein (Berkeley: University of California Press, 2008)

9. Anne Aitchison recalled the tape sounds of Maderna's *Musica su due dimensioni* as seeming "very subdued after hearing Mumma & Co." Letter from Anne Aitchison to Udo Kasemets, August 29, 1964; Udo Kasemets Papers, Rare Book Collection, Faculty of Music Library, University of Toronto.

10. Robert Ashley, interview with the author, February 19, 1999.

11. Robert Ashley, *"Public Opinion Descends upon the Demonstrators,"* *asterisk 1, no. 1 (December 1974): 51–59. Size VI—a singular, unspeakably loud sound that is capable of killing many millions within thirty seconds—has fortunately not yet been realized; it appears to recognize the threat of a nuclear event, a threat looming large following the U.S. invasion of the Bay of Pigs in Cuba in April 1961.

12. "The 'theater' is in the audience"; see Robert Ashley, "Notes for *Public Opinion Descends upon the Demonstrators,"* *asterisk 1, no. 1 (December 1974): 50.

13. Letter from Ashley to Richard Waters, December 17, 1961, in possession of the recipient (emphasis in original).

14. Ashley made these remarks in his living room in December 1961. See Roger Reynolds, "An Interview with John Cage on the Occasion of the Publication of *Silence,"* *Generation* 13, no. 2 (1962): 49–50.

15. Under the title "Around Morton Feldman," the interview was originally to be included in a book that the ONCE composers planned to compile in order to document new music activities in the United States and in Europe. The book was never finished, and the interview—possibly the earliest surviving document of Feldman's thinking—was never published. The page numbers follow Ashley's transcription, which is archived in the Barney Childs Collection of the University of Redlands, Redlands, California.

16. Morton Feldman, liner notes to the Earle Brown-produced "Feldman-Brown" LP (Time Records S/8007, 1962), reprinted in *Kulchur* 2, no. 6 (Summer 1962): 59.

17. Ashley, "Around Morton Feldman," 24.

18. Ibid., 9–10.

19. Gordon Mumma, "To Portray Man Within His Society: Observations on Certain Achievements in World Cinema," *Generation* 9, no. 1 (Fall 1957): 39, 44.

20. Originally, *Epoxy* featured a recording of the 1959 Berlin Festival, where an apparently organized disruption led to conductor Hermann Scherchen addressing the audience verbally during the performance of Schoenberg's *Moses und Aron*.

21. Letter from Mumma to Peter Yates, April 29, 1965; Peter Yates Papers, Mandeville Special Collections, University of California, San Diego; Mumma, interview with Vincent Plush, May 17, 1982, Oral History American Music, Yale University, New Haven, Conn.; Mumma, interviews and written correspondence with the author, various dates between 1996 and 2006.

22. Mumma's program notes for the premiere credited the influence of filmmakers Stan Brakhage, whose films are about perception itself, and Gregory Markopoulos, whose technical innovations include extremely short ("flashing") visual inserts and superimpositions at the threshold of perceptibility.

23. Letter from Mumma to Udo Kasemets, March 9, 1964; Udo Kasemets Papers, Rare Book Collection, Faculty of Music Library, University of Toronto.

24. Having worked with magnetic tape, Mumma was familiar with the technique. In 1984 Burroughs commented that "the 'cut-up' technique … is merely an application of the montage method (in 1959, already an old hat in painting, as the painter Brion Gysin pointed out at the time) to writing. … Similar quasi-aleatory methods have been used in music by John Cage and Earle Brown, … and in painting by Robert Rauschenberg, to name only a few." William S. Burroughs, "My Purpose Is to Write for the Space Age," *The New York Times Book Review*, February 19, 1984, 9.

25. Cf. Robin Lydenberg, "Sound Identity Fading Out: William Burroughs's Tape Experiments," in *Wireless Imagination—Sound, Radio, and the Avant-Garde*, ed. Douglas Kahn and Gregory Whitehead (Cambridge, Mass.: MIT Press, 1992), 409–37. Mumma conceived other pieces that, among other things, commented with increasing electronic sophistication on the horn literature that he, a freelance horn player, considered outdated: *Hornpieces* (1964), *Horn* and *Second Horn* (1965), and *Third Horn* (1967), which he quickly renamed *Hornpipe*.

26. The project's experimental aspect fascinated Mumma. (His *Mographs* [1962–64] used sponsored research data as material for musical compositions.) From the opening cluster on, a residual ambiguity is built into the piece. It is this, in fact, that saves *Megaton* from being an agitprop piece.

27. The increasing appearance of leading political figures as commencement speakers at American public universities during the early 1960s mirrored the increasing dependence of the universities' research boom on government-sponsored, and often military, research.

28. David Andrew, journal entry, November 5, 1965, in possession of the author [Andrew], unpublished.

29. Letter from Peck to the author, August 18, 2005. Emphasis in original (including the wavy line under "concentration").

30. Ashley, "Around Morton Feldman," 30.

31. Written correspondence Robert Morris to David Snow, November 1, 2001; see also George Cacioppo, "Appendix" to Ernest Herschel, "The Great Society," *Generation* 18, no. 2 (January 1967): 14–15.

32. Interviews and correspondence with the author, various dates between 1996 and 2006. See also letters from Mumma to Kasemets, December 31, 1964, and January 2, 1965; Udo Kasemets Papers, Rare Book Collection, Faculty of Music Library, University of Toronto.

33. The amount of $114,200 paid off; Robert Rauschenberg, represented by twenty-two works that were partly flown in with military aircraft, won the Grand International Prize for Painting. See Folder 9, Box 39, Series 10, Record Unit 321, Smithsonian Institution Archives, Washington, D.C.

34. The project had number 66–062 and a budget of $3,000 for the fiscal year 1966. See Folder 9, Box 7, Series 2, Record Unit 321, Smithsonian Institution Archives, Washington, D.C.

35. "But the newest rejections are more lengthy than the old rejections. That's because asking for money to go to Sao Paulo is more trivial than asking for money to do things in the U.S., to do things in depth, etc. Thus, the foundations are more interested in the Sao Paulo venture, and thus they write longer letters of rejection." Letter from Mumma to Feldman, August 14, 1965; Morton Feldman Collection, Paul Sacher Stiftung, Basel.

36. The U.S. exhibit in São Paulo ended up featuring Larry Bell, Barnett Newman, Larry Poons, Frank Stella et al. Unable to raise travel funds, the ONCE Group also had to abandon plans for a campus tour in California and to decline an invitation to Sweden in 1966.

37. See Sally Banes, "Institutionalizing Avant-Garde Performance: A Hidden History of University Patronage in the United States," *Contours of the Theatrical Avant-Garde*, ed. James M. Harding (Ann Arbor: University of Michigan Press, 2000), 217–38.

38. Kagel introduced the term and his first piece in this vein (*Sur Scène*) in 1960.

39. Robert Ashley, "The ONCE Group," *Source* 3 (January 1968): 21.

40. Ashley and Mumma performed Kagel's *Metapiece (Mimetics)* in a medley-realization of Philip Krumm's graphically notated *May 1962* on February 27, 1963, at the Federation of Women's Clubs in Detroit. The repertory of Ashley's and Mumma's instrumental duo predated the ONCE Group but encompassed many theatrical features that can also be found in Kagel pieces. Ashley's *Details for Two Pianists* (1962) has one performer play at a piano keyboard and another one inside the same piano; Mumma's *Medium Size Mograph 1962* (1962) includes actions that don't necessarily produce sounds; Kagel's *Transición II* (1958) combines both of these elements. Ashley's *To Piano Event* (1963) and Kagel's *Atem* (1970), instead of presenting a traditional performance at an instrument, address the instrument's mechanics.

41. See, for instance, Robert Ashley, "Morton Feldman Says" (1965), *Verbal Anthology* (London: Experimental Music Catalogue, 1972), 6–9; and his "Orange Dessert" (1965), *Diana's BiMonthly* 2, no. 6 (1973): 41–46.

42. The piece was premiered on March 21, 1965, in St. Louis. A score was written for and first published in *Tulane Drama Review* 10, no. 2 (Winter 1965): 192–95.

43. One episode contained elements that were strikingly similar to elements in Yoko Ono's *Cut Piece* from 1964. At the same time (1962–64), Kagel was working on a "scenic Ladies' piece for voices and instruments" called *Die Frauen* (The Women). As far as I can tell, the authors did not know of each other's pieces.

44. According to Mumma, the work was supposed to include "laser holography and spatial projections employing computer graphics"—something Borkin was professionally researching at the time (Gordon Mumma, "Technology in the Modern Arts: Music and Theatre," *Chelsea* 20/21 [May 1967]: 103). According to Ashley, Mary Lucier and Alvin Lucier were supposed to be among the guest artists (Robert Ashley, interview with Lesley Gilmore, April 20, 1991).

45. Over the course of the next nine years, the project mutated first into a continuous nine-day festival (*Music with Roots in the Ether*) that Ashley produced in March 1971 at Mills College and then into a series of nine "video portraits of composers and their music," of which Ashley eventually realized seven (*Music with Roots in the Aether*, 1976).

46. See Victor W. Turner, "Liminal to Liminoid in Play, Flow, and Ritual: An Essay in Comparative Symbology," *Rice University Studies* 60, no. 3 (1974): 53–92. According to Turner, "Liminoid phenomena . . . are often parts of social critiques" (86).

47. Robert Ashley, "*The Wolfman*," *Source* 4 (July 1968): 5; letter from Ashley to Yates, December 23, 1967; Peter Yates Papers, Mandeville Special Collections, University of California, San Diego.

48. Ashley, "*The Wolfman*," ibid., 6. Misperceptions of *The Wolfman* started with the premiere and Feldman's written summary of it (Morton Feldman, "Notes on Contributors," *Kulchur* 5, no. 18 [1965]: 15).

49. Ashley, written correspondence with the author, September 13, 2006. The piece was only once performed in its entirety on May 6, 1969, in York, England, by the Sonic Arts Group (and their partners).

50. ONCE's support of John Sinclair and friends goes back to 1965, when Mumma, Ashley, and Manupelli helped the newly founded interdisciplinary and interracial Detroit Artists' Workshop receive one of the small ($100) grants with which the DAC supported local cultural efforts.

9

"Scream against the Sky"

Japanese Avant-garde Music in the Sixties

Yayoi Uno Everett

In September 1994, the Guggenheim Museum in New York City hosted a retrospective exhibition of Japanese avant-garde art since 1945, titled "Scream against the Sky" after Yoko Ono's conceptual piece of the same name. The catalog of works from this exhibition displays numerous paintings and sculptures that capture the explosive and confrontational spirit of the Anpo Movement in the early 1960s, which was marked by large-scale protests and riots against the renewal of the U.S.-Japan Security Treaty (the "Nichibei Anzenhoshô Jôyaku" or "Anpo" for short). This period gave birth to a rich legacy of artistic and musical avant-garde creativity. This essay examines the interrelation of the discursive trajectories of the postwar avant-garde with the political sphere, focusing on the developments in avant-garde music at the Sôgetsu Center for the Arts in Tokyo during the early sixties, and their ramifications in the following decades.

On September 8, 1951, Japan entered a military partnership with the United States, which spurred political controversy throughout the decade. As the Security Treaty gave the United States the right to station troops in Japan (Article I) and prohibited Japan from giving bases to a third power without U.S. consent, it instilled fear in the minds of many that Japan would soon become a military base in the expanding cold war.[1] Against the conservative Liberal Democratic Party (LDP) which sided with the U.S., the Japan Socialist Party (JSP), Communist Party (JCP), and progressive intellectuals relentlessly opposed these measures through staging protests and demonstrations.[2] Under the umbrella of

187

the JCP, a nationwide student organization called Zengakuren (All-Japan Federation of Students' Self-Governing Associations) gathered force to oppose any compromise to Article IX of the postwar constitution, which prohibited Japan from rearmament; much of their protests revolved around nuclear testing, which proved to be one of the key issues of negotiation when the treaty was revisited in the late fifties.[3]

During the three-year period (1957–60) of Nobusuke Kishi's term as prime minister, the political parties focused on the treaty revision issues, united under the belief that Japan must regain a leading role in world affairs by ceasing its relationship with the dominant U.S. power. In the process, other vital matters such as the JSP's proposal to renounce nuclear weapons, the Vietnam reparations bill, the fisheries agreement with the Soviet Union, and relations with China, became entangled in the controversy over the treaty renewal.[4] In January 1960, despite the continuing disputes among the parties, Kishi announced the renewal of the treaty with certain provisions; this announcement, in turn, ignited massive protests, demonstrations, and strikes and culminated in a national crisis over the course of the next six months. Due to the large-scale revolts led by the socialist parties and Zengakuren in May and June of this year, President Eisenhower's visit to Japan was effectively annulled and Kishi was forced to resign from his post.

The artists and intellectuals who participated in these cultural and political movements were disillusioned with postwar Japanese democratic institutions and demanded a clear break from the "Old Left"—meaning the JCP, which lost popularity with the public after 1952. In challenging the authorities, an artistic revolution also emerged, manifesting itself in junk art, underground theater (Angura), New Wave cinema, Ankoku Butoh,[5] Happenings, and Fluxus. David Goodman describes the state of the "dual alienation" experienced by students and young artists as follows:

> The artists of the sixties generation were educated in the period of extraordinary freedom that the chaos of the immediate post-war period brought, and this accounts in part for a common belief that anarchy is conducive to creativity. Alienated by their own culture, they shared a certain psychological distance from it that empowered them to undertake some of the most trenchant examinations of Japaneseness ever attempted. Greatly influenced by American culture, they were at the same time alienated by the United States, which was occupying their country, testing and stockpiling nuclear weapons, and fighting an unpopular war in Vietnam.[6]

What did it mean to be "Japanese" for the youths who faced the task of rebuilding their cultural identity from the charred ruins of post-atomic history? How did the aesthetic goals and praxis of the postwar musical avant-garde relate to pre-war Japanese and European avant-garde antecedents? In order to answer these questions, this essay explores the developments that took place at the Sôgetsu Center for the Arts in

Tokyo between 1960 and 1964, and the contributions made by John Cage, Toshi Ichiyanagi, Yûji Takahashi, and Yoko Ono to the formation of the radical avant-garde. The first phase of development in avant-garde music in the early 1950s was heavily influenced by European modernist idioms (serialism, musique concrète). The 1960s brought the advent of experimental approaches to performance: moving beyond the formality of concert music, composers and musicians came together to present multimedia events, Happenings, Events, conceptual art, and group improvisations. By focusing on the critical developments that took place at the Sôgetsu Center, I hope to offer an understanding of the musical avant-garde in relation to the changing sociopolitical milieu of postwar Japan.

The Japanese Avant-garde

In concept and praxis, "avant-garde" (*zen-ei* in Japanese) is a term imported from the West, which acquired different forms in the course of the twentieth century. It was initially attributed to the iconoclastic activities and experimentation undertaken by the so-called Mavo group of visual artists during the Taishô period (1912–26), who responded to the social unrest of the 1920s by revolutionizing artistic practice.[7] Influenced by futurist, expressionist, and cubist art forms, the Mavo artists explored anarchistic and constructivist ideologies by disavowing both mimetic reproduction and romantic subjectivity. Depicting events that accorded with a Marxist political agenda, their work contributed to the proletarian movement in the arts, and garnered considerable support from the working class. However, due to increased governmental censorship, the group was forced to disband by 1928.[8] Historically, their activities can be interpreted as a rebellion against the "modernizing" agenda of the post-Meiji era government, which lay emphasis upon rationality, order, and collective conformity. This modernization ushered in not only the rise of mass society and cosmopolitanism but also authoritarianism. Between the early 1930s and the end of the Second World War, political activists were arrested, tortured, and imprisoned, and left-wing artistic and musical associations (such as the Proletarian Musical League) were forced to disband in a period of brutal repression.

After the Second World War, a renewed focus on individual autonomy permitted artists and musicians to break down important barriers, encouraging new aesthetic trends to take root. In 1947, Shûzô Takiguchi and Jirô Yoshihara founded the Japan Avant-Garde Artists Club ("Nihon avangyarudo bijutsuka kurabu"). Critical of market-driven artistic forms of production and formulaic "-isms," Takiguchi envisioned his avant-garde strategy as an exploration of the process or act of creation; for him, "the space of the experimental" connoted the state before artistic languages became conventionalized.[9] The Gutai group (*gutai* meaning concreteness), founded by Yoshihara in the Osaka-Kobe region in 1954, shared a similar ideological basis. The group declared conventional art forms meaningless and aimed instead to "unite the human and material spirits in a cathartic act that simultaneously releases the energy of both."[10] Although averse to political activism, Gutai engaged in its own forms of action events and paintings inspired by Jackson Pollock; as Munroe comments, they pursued art as "an explosive rite to stomp out the dark orthodoxies of pre-war Imperial Japanese culture and usher in the liberal American style democracy which history had unexpectedly granted."[11] The political counterpart of Gutai was to be found in a group of artists with strong Communist Party affiliation who organized Reportage Painting ("Ruporutâju Kaiga") in response to the horrors of war, nuclear holocaust, and social injustices; partly instigated by the JCP, this group sent artists to rural villages and industrial zones to depict instances of imperialism and class struggle.[12] Whether explicitly political or not, such organizations explored art as a form of release and as a means of building new cultural identities that overcame Japan's wartime past.

The aesthetics of the surrealist critic Takiguchi had a profound impact in shaping the first phase of the musical avant-garde. In 1951, he founded the Experimental Workshop (Jikken Kôbo), which brought together figures from a range of fields to collaborate on multimedia projects. The initial members included composers Tôru Takemitsu and Hiroyoshi Suzuki, engineer Hideo Yamazaki, painter Hideko Fukushima, and critic/poet Kuniharu Akiyama. Jôji Yuasa, who joined in 1952, summed up the group's anti-establishment stance as follows: "[I]n liberating music from its own world, we were reacting against the academic conventions, systems, and the establishment."[13] Their artistic visions were unquestioningly modernist in scope and orientation, yet the group sought to incorporate distinctive characteristics of traditional Japanese art forms such as Noh drama and calligraphic paintings.[14] Focusing on the use of new technology, the musical avant-garde sought after new and emerging European trends, such as serialism, dodecaphonic music, and musique concrète, as a way of breaking free from the institutionalized schools of composition based on German or French lineage.[15] Representative works include Takemitsu's *Uninterrupted Rest I* (1952) for solo piano, *Son Calligraphie* (1953); Suzuki's *Metamorphose* (1955) for clarinet and four strings; and Yuasa's *Cosmos Haptic* (1957).

On the political front, the Utagoe ("Singing Voice") movement brought together workers and students in a wide variety of choral activities with leftist and proto-feminist awareness. This movement grew out of the Japanese Association for the Proletarian Arts, founded in 1925, and their meetings included the singing of revolutionary songs to promote the political and social education of the working classes.[16] Although by no means avant-garde with respect to their aesthetic orientation, the mission of the Utagoe movement resonated in the minds of many postwar composers. Hikaru Hayashi, for instance, was a strong advocate of the Utagoe movement, and explored the intersection between and inclusion of folksongs in his original compositions.[17]

In spite of the differences in orientation, many musicians and artists were catapulted into taking concrete political action by the Police Bill controversy of October 1958. The Diet led by Kishi introduced an amendment to the bill that would strengthen police powers to interrogate, search, and arrest people in all public venues. Fearing that this bill was part of Kishi's master plan toward restoring the militarism of the 1930s, the socialists boycotted the Diet and barricaded rooms to prevent deliberations.[18] The earliest written declaration opposing the bill was signed by twenty-seven members of the Seinen Ongakuka ("The Youth Musicians") society of musicians and composers—including Takemitsu, Hayashi, and Toshirô Mayuzumi in November 7, 1958 (a translation of this declaration is provided in figure 9.1). Apparently the public protests against the passing of this bill paid off. After several weeks of uproar and political negotiations, the ruling LDP—which proved to be neither liberal nor democratic—shelved the bill for an indefinite period.[19]

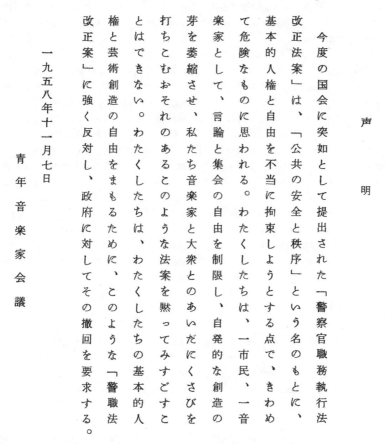

声明

今度の国会に突如として提出された「警察官職務執行法改正法案」は、「公共の安全と秩序」という名のもとに、きわめて危険なものに思われる。わたくしたちは、一市民、一音楽家として、言論と集会の自由を制限し、自発的な創造の芽を萎縮させ、私たち音楽家と大衆とのあいだにくさびを打ちこむおそれのあるこのような法案を黙ってみすごすことはできない。わたくしたちは、わたくしたちの基本的人権と芸術創造の自由をまもるために、このような「警職法改正案」に強く反対し、政府に対してその撤回を要求する。

一九五八年十一月七日

青年音楽家会議

Figure 9.1 Declaration by the Seinen Ongakuka (November 7, 1958).

Declaration

The recent amendment to the bill introduced by the Congress proposes to strengthen police's right to take preventative actions in public venues in promoting public safety and order. We find this to be a great threat to our civil rights and freedom by placing unfair restrictions on our activities. As citizens and musicians, we will not tolerate the passing of this bill, which will severely restrict our freedom to engage in debates, organize meetings, and will place an unnecessary barrier between the musicians and the audience. We strongly oppose the amendment of this bill in order to protect our civil liberties and artistic freedom and ask the government to withdraw the amendment.

November 7, 1958
Seinen Ongakuka Conference

Figure 9.1   Continued.

Despite the ongoing public outcry, the Security Treaty was ratified in January 1960, with additional provisions. This prompted the first Anpo demonstrations, prominent at which were a number of neo-Dadaists, masked and bandaged like mummies. The Neo-Dada Organizers group had been founded the same year, and staged anarchic exhibitions and Happenings. Although they tended to dismiss political ideology altogether, they triggered bloody riots by throwing bricks at police in April 1960.[20] On May 20, prior to Eisenhower's visit, Kishi's party took forceful measures to monopolize the votes on the treaty renewal—bypassing discussion with opposing parties. The public viewed this conduct as anti-democratic and this led the way to the most violent demonstration before the Diet building on June 15 (see figure 9.2).[21] In preparation, numerous musical societies gathered together on June 9 at the Sôgetsu Center for the Arts to plan pro-democratic actions against the renewal of the Treaty. This organization quickly grew to 580 members, and its primary objective was the resignation of Kishi and the dismissal of the Diet. In the event, the demonstration turned into a riot, resulting in hundreds of injured students and police and the death of a twenty-year-old female student.[22] Although forty-seven newspapers published their oppositions to the renewal, the House of Representatives nevertheless passed the bill on June 19.[23]

Participating in a demonstration of this scale was an unprecedented action on the part of Western-trained Japanese composers and musicians, who had mostly occupied a politically neutral position up until this time. While the anarchistic protests ultimately failed to prevent the renewal of the Security Treaty, the artists nonetheless gained a foothold in society by establishing authority and independence against the government. Munroe aptly describes this era in terms of "absolute loss and absolute freedom"; the chaos emanating from the loss or collapse of long-held national

Figure 9.2 Demonstrations before the Diet Building (June 1960). Used by permission of the *Yomiuri* newspaper.

myths (such as the imperialistic configurations of nationhood) ushered in long-awaited freedom for artistic expression without censorship.[24]

Sôgetsu Center for the Arts

Amid the political turmoil and chaos of the early sixties, the Sôgetsu Center for the Arts provided an indispensable venue for artists and musicians to meet, collaborate, and hold performances and exhibitions. Under the directorship of Hiroshi Teshigahara, whose father headed the renowned Sôgetsu Ikebana school, the basement hall of the Center was made available to host a wide range of avant-garde events during its approximately twelve years (October 1958 to April 1971) in existence. In looking back, Teshigahara situates the uniqueness of this period in the unmediated freedom with which artists came together to produce events that included film, dance, music, and Happenings:

> It was a powerful time when artists from different walks of life came together, collided with one another, in pursuit of the unknown. We never had an opportunity like this before and we won't again. Artists could produce what

they want, bring it to the stage and present it. This sort of situation does not happen anymore, now that people count how much it would cost to put together a performance first.[25]

In the initial two years (1958–59), Teshigahara organized viewings of art film and sponsored educational gatherings to promote interest in the traditional arts of Japan.[26] Having established a steady audience base, Teshigahara then launched a series of concerts to promote democratic ideals, which included contemporary music, Happenings, jazz, modern dance, avant-garde film, and underground theater. Within this rich environment of artistic exchange, the musical avant-garde flourished. The different phases of this development can be summarized as follows: concerts by the Sakkyokuka Shûdan (Composers' Group) between 1960 and 1962; *Cage shokku*—a shockwave created by the presence of Cage and David Tudor in 1962; and the emergence of the ensemble New Direction between 1963 and 1964, which contributed further to the era's internationalized outlook. The first of these phases fostered a continuation of the modernist avant-garde idioms established in the fifties, while the second and third phases ushered in the radical branch of the musical avant-garde.

In the first phase, a contemporary music series featured a monthly solo concert of music by nine recognized composers, gathered under the name of Sakkyokuka Shûdan; this included Hayashi, Takemitsu, Mayuzumi, Yasushi Akutagawa, Makoto Moroi, Yoriaki Matsudaira, Akira Miyoshi, and Yoshio Mamiya. Although the pieces typically featured in these concerts were neither political nor unified thematically, they fulfilled the group's mission to promote new works by Japanese composers, which often combined modernist musical idioms with theatrical elements such as pantomime, Noh dance, or projected images. The program notes often conveyed the composer's political or ideological aim. For instance, Hayashi's notes for his solo concert (March 1960) spoke passionately of the importance of foregrounding the human voice—not just by embedding familiar melodies or folk songs in his music, but rather by incorporating the broader mission of the Utagoe movement.[27] Takemitsu's solo concert included an interactive musique concrète piece called *Water Music*, produced with the aid of the engineer Jûnosuke Okuyama. To create the piece, Takemitsu went around Tokyo, recording the sound of dripping water, then cut and spliced the tape for over a month, apparently getting little sleep.[28] The technical skills Takemitsu acquired during these formative years laid the foundation for the musique concrète sounds of urban Tokyo and the electronic manipulation of acoustic instruments in film scores such as *Woman in the Dunes* (1964) and *Double Suicide* (1969).

While the concerts by these "card-carrying" composers received much publicity, the Sôgetsu Center also provided space for less established groups to participate in events. The most significant was the improvisation-based Group Ongaku, headed by Shûkô Mizuno, Yasunao Tone, Takehisa Kosugi, and their colleagues at the Tokyo University of Fine Arts (Geidai). Prompted by Tone, they used forms of intermedia, Happenings, and conceptualism to offer an institutional critique of the arts. Mizuno claims that their performances, which involved engaging in free jam sessions and improvisational activities, echoed much of what Cage was doing around the same time.[29] At the same time, their Fluxus-style events featured gradual processes and disciplined, task-oriented performance to explore the sonic materials of music; for example, Kosugi's *Micro I* (1961) involves wrapping up a microphone in paper and amplifying the crumpled sounds as the paper is gradually removed. After hearing the group's concert at the Sôgetsu Center in 1961, Toshi Ichiyanagi was so impressed by the inventive spirit of the group that he asked them to participate in his first solo concert, which was titled *Happening and Musique Concrète.*[30]

As a further effort to bring international visibility to the Center, Teshigahara invited Edgard Varèse to give a concert in 1961; however, due to illness, the visit had to be canceled. In lieu of Varèse, Ichiyanagi urged Teshigahara to invite John Cage and pianist David Tudor as the first foreign composers to participate in the Contemporary Music Series. In October 1962, the two gave six concerts in Tokyo, Kyoto, and Osaka. In these concerts, Cage and Tudor performed different combinations of music by Cage (*Aria* with *Fontana Mix; Music Walk; Atlas Eclipticalis* with *Winter Music; 0'00"; 26'55.988"*), Christian Wolff (*For six or seven players; For pianist*), Morton Feldman (*Atlantis*), Karlheinz Stockhausen (*Klavierstück X*), Sylvano Bussotti (*Five Piano Pieces for David Tudor*), and graphic scores by Ichiyanagi (*Music for Piano #4*) and Takemitsu (*Corona*). Akiyama recalls how Cage and Tudor's concerts in 1962 shattered every preconceived notion about music, sound, and silence held by Japanese artists and musicians.[31] Utterly fascinated by his experiences in Japan, Cage described his admiration for Tone's work—in particular, the latter's use of maps of the earth's surface to yield directions for the performance of his music. He noted that this technique anticipated a composition he himself had in mind but had not yet written, a sequel to *Atlas Eclipticalis* (1961), which would use maps of the earth rather than of the stars.[32]

The performance of Cage's *Music Walk* (1958) at the Tokyo Bunka Kaikan Hall, with Yoko Ono lying flat across the piano, produced one of the most frequently reproduced images from the Cage/Tudor concerts in 1962.[33] *Music Walk* is an indeterminate piece, consisting of nine sheets of paper with scattered points; a smaller transparent plastic rectangle with parallel lines is placed over the paper, bringing some of the points "out of potentiality into activities." The performers move from one point to another from several playing positions—either at the keyboard, at the back of the piano, or at a radio—and choose one of the lines that refer to five different categories of sounds. Additional small plastic squares with nonparallel lines may or may not be used to make further determinations about the sounds to be produced. By lying across the keyboard, Ono transformed the "music walk" into her own "conceptual walk," and she saw this as her own contribution to the piece; however, the critics dismissed her act as merely eccentric.[34] Her efforts to further "radicalize" the musical avant-garde by pushing the boundaries of performance will be discussed more fully in the following section.

The third phase of development came about through the formation in 1963 of the ensemble New Direction by Ichiyanagi, Takahashi, and Kuniharu Akiyama. The group's statutes emphasized internationalization through the inclusion of composers from abroad, and placed importance upon events that demand the participation of the audience. Although relatively short-lived (1963–64), the group put together six concerts that featured graphic scores by Bussotti, Stockhausen, Feldman, Ichiyanagi, Takahashi, and Kosugi in combination with conventionally notated works by Berg (*Lyric Suite*), Berio (*Sequenza*), Penderecki (String Quartet No. 4), Yuasa (*Interpretation* for Two Flutes I and II), and Boulez (*Improvisations sur Mallarmé* I and II). Most critics welcomed the balancing of repertoire to include a wide range of the contemporary music then in vogue. Akiyama recalls how such events attracted not only composers but also artists, filmmakers, and novelists, who returned week after week to attend the concerts. After Takahashi left Japan to work in Europe, Ichiyanagi organized the concerts by himself until April 1964. The most scandalous event took place when Nam June Paik destroyed the inside of an upright piano with hammer and saw during his solo recital. However, as alternative venues for performances of new music began to open up, composers ceased to gather together at the Sôgetsu Center to work on collaborative projects.[35] After 1965 the Center's focus shifted entirely from music to the promotion of underground theater, film, and animation.

On the Radical Avant-garde

An important breakthrough in the aesthetic orientation of the musical avant-garde took place when the idea of "performance" was opened up, in an effort to break down the traditional barriers that separated audiences from performers, professionals from amateurs, as well as what constitutes music from the noise of daily life. In particular, Happenings played a crucial role in establishing what Michael Kirby has termed a "non-matrixed" model of performance, characterized by the deliberate absence of an information structure containing plot and dialogue.[36] Moreover, "Events," introduced by the Fluxus artist George Brecht, extracted the informational structure of everyday ritual or routine and threw it into high relief for the performer. For example, the performance of Brecht's *Drip Music* required Takahashi to pour water as slowly as possible from a bucket into a fish bowl at the front of the stage, and the audience was completely free to construct whatever meaning they wished.[37] In 1962, the first of Cage and Tudor's visits led many Japanese composers to take radical steps in exploring the emancipatory potential of music making; "Cage's lectures and performances liberated Japanese composers from the rigidities of serialism and notation on a five-line staff."[38] As amateur and professional musicians gathered together at the Sôgetsu Center, their performances often reveled in themes of social alienation and individual autonomy in an attempt to transcend the norms and hierarchies of traditional Japanese society.

Undoubtedly, the difference in aesthetic orientation between the modernist and radical branches of the musical avant-garde pivoted on whether to reject or embrace Cage's experimental views about eliminating the boundary between music and noise. Established composers from the earlier generation (i.e., those associated with Sakkyokuka Shûdan and Jikken Kôbô) were often skeptical: at the time of Cage's first visit in 1962, Mayuzumi openly dismissed Cage's significance as a composer, while Yuasa questioned the premise of abandoning one's will in composing.[39] Even Takemitsu, who shared Cage's interests in Asian philosophy and composed a number of graphic scores, ended up deciding that chance operation was "not structured enough."[40]

Rather than attempting to be comprehensive, I call attention here to the works of three individuals who made distinctive contributions to the Sôgetsu Center in promoting and expanding on Cage's radical aesthetics. In this respect, Ichiyanagi's involvement was critical, along with that of Takahashi and Ono. Having met Cage in New York City in the late 1950s, Ichiyanagi turned his back altogether on traditional conventions of composing (in which he had been trained at the Juilliard School), became involved in Fluxus, and pursued aleatoric and indeterminate procedures in his music throughout the 1960s.[41] In his solo concert at the Sôgetsu Center in November 1961, Ichiyanagi created a sensation by displaying his graphic scores as art in the lobby and offering performances of them on stage. The most striking piece, *IBM: event and music concrète*, called for eight musicians performing different events simultaneously but independently of one another, as the loudspeakers blasted quotidian sounds and noises prepared by Ichiyanagi. The musicians, utterly devoid of expression, performed their individual acts according to the number of repetitions designated by IBM punch cards, and were gradually wrapped up in white paper tape to form a gigantic spider's nest on stage, extending down toward the audience. Although many in the audience questioned the relevance of this work as "music," Kuniharu Akiyama defended its significance in the following manner:

> [T]he disconnected sounds of the electric drill, a falling chair, radio, and piano surrounded us and our eyes simply followed the meaningless

sequence of actions. Yet I was tremendously moved by the experience of utter solitude in the sound and action of each moment that passed by.[42]

In Akiyama's mind, this event clearly stood as a critique of alienation in modern society.

In composing indeterminate scores, Ichiyanagi was very particular about his use of graphic symbols, providing detailed and precise performance instructions. Writing about the significance of graphic notations, he distinguished this form of improvisation from jazz by emphasizing the need to *avoid* preconceived notions for structuring events in time; this was important in order to maximize discontinuity between events and sustain spontaneous interaction between performers.[43] At first glance, his graphic notations do not seem to differ much from those of Morton Feldman, Earle Brown, or Cage from the early fifties. Careful examination of the instructions that accompany Ichiyanagi's graphic scores, however, reveals the extent to which a successful rendering of them depends on the performers' abilities to respond to one another in making decisions on the fly. For Ichiyanagi, liberating sounds through spontaneous musical response signified the liberation of the human spirit. In the program note that accompanied his solo concert at the Sôgetsu Center, he declared that if this new approach to performance represented the extremity of a human cry, "just let out the cry without attaching any kind of meaning to it."[44] Ichiyanagi's emphasis on process and spontaneity curiously echoes Takiguchi's concept of the "space of the experimental" as a state preceding the conventionalization of artistic languages.

As a case in point, the instruction and the first two systems of the score for *Duet for Piano and String Instrument* (1961) are shown in example 9.1. As the instruction states, in addition to interpreting the action corresponding to each symbol, the performer chooses the mode of execution (a or b) based on a choice made by the other performer in the previous event. While the score is read from left to right and there are instructions for how to interpret the different lines that frame the symbols, the time for realizing the events and space in between events is relative and variable. Ichiyanagi's instruction indicates that as a sound comes into being, the performer should follow it with silence or another set of events, without anticipating what comes next. Other notable graphic pieces by Ichiyanagi from this period include *Sapporo* (1962), a piece in which the performers produce sounds associated with different lines in the score while observing other players' signals and the conductor's cues, and *Pratyahara Event* (1963), which calls for the performer to take a specific number of deep breaths in between the execution of successive events.

Even as a student, Yûji Takahashi played an indispensable role in many of the concerts given at the Sôgetsu Center between 1961 and 1963. He quickly became known as a pianist with a niche in contem-

Notations for Piano

a. Should be used when the pianist hears the string player using the bow
b. Should be used when the pianist hear the string player playing without the bow

○	a. Play on the keyboard b. Pizzacato
◇	a. Make harmonics on the keyboard b. keyboard harmonics produced by piano strings.
–○–	a. Armed cluster b. A noise produced with a tool
□	a. Palm cluster b. A noise produced without using a tool
↕	a. Glissando upward or downward b. Vertical glissando on strings
⇕	a. Armed arpeggio b. Horizontal glissando on the strings
•	a. Muted string played on the keyboard b. Muted pizzicato
⊙	a. Unused way of playing on the keyboard b. Unused way of producing noise.

Notations for String Instrument

a. Should be used when the string player hears the pianist using the keyboard
b. Should be used when the string player hears the pianist playing without using the keyboard

○	a. Oridinary bowing b. Pizzicato
◇	a. Harmonic b. Pizzicato harmonic
•	a. Play between bridge and tailpiece b. Snapped pizzicato
○̄	a. Sul tasto b. Make a squeaky sound
⊖	a. Sul poncicello b. Sweep strings with a cloth
⊿	a. Play on tailpiece b. Strike the fingerboard with the fingertips
○̲	a. Reverse the playing position of the bow and fingers b. Strike the body of the instrument
▲	a. Col legno tratto b. Pizzicato by the bridge
▼	a. Col legno battuto b. Pizzicato between bridge and tailpiece
↕	a. Glissando b. Pizzicato glissando
⊙	a. Unused way of playing by using the bow b. Unused way playing without using the bow

Read the score from left to right with either side up in a horizontal position. Four sheets may be played in any order as long as both the pianist and the string player take the same procedure.

Dotted line frame: play with changes such as accel., rit., crescv., dim., etc.
Thin line frame: play without change in tempo or dynamics
Thick line frame: play with extreme change in tempo or dynamics
Without frame: play freely with regard to range, tempo, and loudness

First two systems of the score:

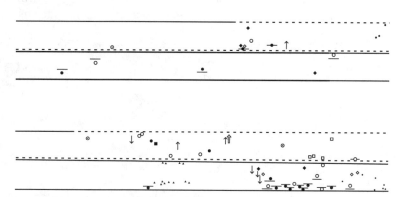

Example 9.1 Ichiyanagi, *Duet for Piano and String Instrument* (1961) (performance instruction, edited by author). Copyright © 1964 by C. F. Peters Corporation. Used by permission.

porary music, acclaimed as a fiercely intelligent virtuoso who could perform Iannis Xenakis's *Eonta* (1963–64)—which was written for him—with complete ease. In the two solo piano recitals he gave at the Sôgetsu Center, he performed Takemitsu's *Piano Distance* (1961), Cage's *Winter Music* (1957), Xenakis's *Herma* (1960–61), as well as indeterminate works by La Monte Young and Keijirô Satoh. When Takahashi organized New Direction with Ichiyanagi, the successful realization of many of the aleatoric and indeterminate scores depended on his unusual versatility and imagination as pianist and composer—Akiyama described his performances as elegant, relentless, and metaphysical.[45] Fellow composer Ikebe Shinichirô praised the ingenuity in Takahashi's simultaneous performances of *L'Ombilic des Limbes* for tape and *Antonin Artaud's Window* for bassoons, contrabass clarinets, and double bass (1963), recalling how the bass was played on its side.[46]

Yet in an essay called "Face the Music" that accompanied the program to his solo recital, Takahashi expressed a viewpoint opposite to Ichiyanagi, insisting that freedom in musical expression is fundamentally unattainable. He was fascinated by Cage's indeterminate scores, which contain multiple possibilities for realization and challenge the audience to contemplate the resulting "vagueness" of sound. Like Cage, he insisted that in order to find new avenues of musical expression, it was necessary to cut oneself off from familiar musical structures and taste. However, he stressed the importance of formulating one's own musical "problem" without following Cage's methods.[47] Takahashi's meandering remarks amounted to a kind of self-declaration, which ultimately led him to pursue formalized mathematical principles as a basis for further compositional studies. Encouraged by Xenakis, Takahashi left Japan to perform and study in Europe and the United States between 1963 and 1972. Most of his compositions, written during this time, derive from stochastic operations and game theory, such as *Chro-*

Example 9.2 Takahashi, *Chromamorphe II* (1964). Copyright © 1969 by C. F. Peters Corporation. Used by permission.

mamorphe II (1964) for solo piano, *Six Stoicheia* (1969) for string quartet, and *Operation Euler* (1969) for three players. *Chromamorphe II* was composed with the aid of Xenakis's program for the IBM7090 computer; two basic motives undergo continual transformation, as the texture alternates between monophonic entries punctuated by silence, and a cacophonic outburst of sounds spread across the registers (see example 9.2).[48]

Finally, Yoko Ono's contribution to the musical avant-garde during the two and a half years she spent in Japan (1962–64) should not be underestimated. For one thing, she is credited for introducing Happenings and Conceptual Art to the Japanese audience. In her conceptual piece *Voice Piece for Soprano* (1961), which ends with a simple instruction to "scream against the sky," she captured the state of angst felt by this generation of artists. In spite of the critics' anticipation of Ono as a promising composer from New York City, her debut performance at the Sôgetsu Center on May 24, 1962 was unfavorably received. Consisting of four multimedia events involving music, poems, and paintings, Ono attempted to break away from the traditional relationship between the audience and performers in the most extreme manner. In an event called *ASO-To David Tudor*, she delivered a nonsensical juxtaposition of declarations taken from Hitler, the Japanese emperor, and French lessons.[49] Her five-hour performance ended at 1:30 a.m. with all the performers standing silently on the stage together with two remaining audience members—the intent behind the *Audience Piece* being that it does not end until the hall is completely vacated. The filmmaker and critic Donald Richie denounced her work as "lacking in originality" and largely "imitative of Cage," and found her passivity on stage and the excruciating length of the events insulting to the audience.[50] Ichiyanagi came to her rescue by explaining the fundamental difference between her aim and Cage's chance operations, emphasizing the point that her artwork invites the audience to actively search for a meaning, and that the piece requires the audience's participation to be complete.[51]

Arguably, the most sensational work Ono produced was *Cut Piece* (1964), in which she invites audience members to get up on stage and cut her clothes with scissors while she maintains a seated pose. This work elicited a wide range of response; when performed as part of her Sayonara concert at the Sôgestu Center, the reception was lukewarm, while in Kyoto a man threatened to stab her with scissors.[52] A video excerpt from the Carnegie Hall performance in 1965 is telling; those who were respectful toward the artist by cutting a small piece of clothing are contrasted by a mocking male subject who "violated" her through aggressive actions that simulated rape.[53] Yoshimoto comments that "[Ono] functioned as a mirror reflecting the feelings of audience members; through watching the performance, the audience discovered voyeurism or violence within itself."[54] This particular work has taken on new politicized meanings in new contexts; as a case in point, Ono performed *Cut Piece* in Paris in 2003 as a form of protest against the Iraq War and in an attempt to promote world peace.[55]

It is deeply ironic that Ono, whose avant-garde art was shunned by the Japanese critics during the early sixties for being too metaphysical, garnered international recognition and flourished as a conceptual artist in New York City. Her mixed reception in Japan reflects the Eurocentric perspective that dominated the reception of the Japanese avant-garde at the time: relying exclusively on Western art-historical discourse to judge Japanese artists, critics were unable to explore critical contexts that departed from this paradigm.[56] Additionally, it seems that the Japanese audience, whose appreciation for art was governed by a high standard of aesthetic refinement and technical mastery, failed to understand the essence of Ono's bold and esoteric approach to art.

In summary, many of the Happenings or Events, be it Ono's *Cut Piece* or Ichiyanagi's *IBM*, may be seen as exterior projections of the collective guilt and fear shared by artists and public at large about Japan's political past and present. Spurred by a common pursuit of liberating one's self from oppressive social conditions, performers engaged in provocative, frivolous, and at times destructive acts as a form of constructive criticism. Regardless of whether such activities would lead to concrete social or political changes, these performances took audiences out of their comfort zone, challenging them to assess the meaning of a work in its social context, rather than simply to marvel at musical or technical refinement as an end in itself. It is precisely in this sense that radical avant-garde musicians ruptured the social norms of artistic performance and laid the aesthetic foundation for creative ventures in theater, dance, and film, filling the void left by the prewar avant-garde.[57]

Conclusion: The Paradox of the Protest Years

In *Radicals and Realists in the Japanese Nonverbal Arts*, Thomas Havens advances the notion that Japanese avant-garde artists from the sixties later turned into realists by articulating a "post-Western" critique of European modernism through global awareness and local engagement.[58] With respect to developments in postwar theater, David Goodman likewise explores the paradox of embracing European traditions as a means for recapturing and rearticulating the "premodern imagination" that was suppressed by the modernizing agenda of the Meiji reform.[59] In the musical domain, however, Havens's position of "post-Western" critique seems difficult to espouse, since European modernism provided the essential aesthetic foundation of the postwar musical avant-garde. Long before the political conditions that spurred the controversy over the treaty renewal, the first generation of avant-garde composers was driven by a common desire to particularize the language of European modernism in order to explore their subjective positions.

Yet there is little evidence to suggest that these or later composers openly resisted or contested European influences, even in the face of the plurality of aesthetic orientations (e.g., minimalism, collage and quotation, cultural fusion) that they have embraced since the 1970s.

Overall, the praxis of the Japanese avant-garde differed from its Western counterparts in several important ways. First, avant-garde art was absorbed into the mainstream during the 1960s; one can go so far as to say that it was a unique movement in postwar Japanese history, when the avant-garde *became* the mainstream. Housewives, students, professionals, and amateurs flocked to see and participate in events hosted at the Sôgetsu Center.[60] Second, the Japanese avant-garde did not emerge as a reaction against bourgeois ideals, but rather as a radical means to free people from decades of political repression dating back to the Taishô era. Last, the Japanese avant-garde differed from social-democratic countries like Germany and the Netherlands in its reliance on privatized sources of funding. Due to Teshigahara's internal connections, the Sôgetsu Center events were principally financed by the Ikebana institution.[61] Ichiyanagi also confided that his concerts would not have taken place without the generous funding from private donors over the years.[62]

This brings us to the key factor that quashed the protest movement: economic prosperity. In revisiting the relationship between the United States and Japan during the period of occupation, it is important to recognize that Japan profited enormously from this partnership. Protests against the renewal of the treaty reflected a desire to escape from the overwhelming political and materialistic influences exerted by the United States. And for this reason, Packard calls the decade of protests a form of "reactionary nationalism"—Japan's way of asserting and protecting its own identity.[63] Paradoxically though, the enactment of the United States' cold war policies abetted Japanese economic growth at home and abroad in unanticipated ways; both the Korean War and the Vietnam War brought great profits and market breakthroughs in Japan.[64] The capacity for long-time economic planning was also made possible by the domination of the conservative Liberal Democratic Party during the formative years of the rebuilding of the Japanese economy. In simple terms, the political infrastructure that had generated resistance in the 1960s contributed to Japan's emergence as a mature bourgeois society by the early 1970s. As the country gained material wealth, the struggle over the subordinacy of Japan's relationship with the United States diminished in intensity.[65] When the treaty's third renewal was issued in 1970, it triggered another wave of anarchistic movements involving free jazz, underground theater, and Woodstock-inspired rock and folk music, but the level of resistance was considerably tamer.

With economic revival in the 1970s, the production and dissemination of art became increasingly commodified—absorbed into what Frederic Jameson calls the "cultural logic of late capitalism," in which

aesthetic production becomes integrated with commodity production.[66] With materialistic wealth and increased opportunities, the
sense of community that united artists and musicians during the sixties
dissolved. And with it came the near extinction of left-wing political
parties. By then, however, the term "avant-garde" ceased to be a
catchword for contemporary music, as any notions of resistance or
rebellion faded away. This is not to say that the Japanese avant-garde
became institutionalized or superseded by postmodern eclecticism—as
Stuart Hobbs argues was the case in North America and Europe.[67]
While the "political thrust" of the musical avant-garde dissolved by
the mid-sixties, its aesthetic principles and techniques continued to
evolve and became amalgamated into newer trends. The next phase
of development in the 1970s and 1980s was marked by pluralism and
the composers' collective desire to embrace a pan-Asian consciousness
by reclaiming Japan's artistic and historical connections with neigh-
boring Asian countries. Following his involvement with Fluxus artists
in New York City, Kosugi returned to Tokyo to form his improvisational band Taj Mahal in 1969, combining elements of North Indian
music with free jazz and live electronic techniques.[68] After his return to
Japan in 1972, Takahashi surprised everyone by abandoning high
modernism in favor of his own brand of "socialist" music, based on folk
songs collected from all over the world. Reacting against institutionalized
forms of performance, Takahashi sought to establish an ensemble where
musicians can participate in creating, rather than simply recreating
music.[69] His travels to Thailand and the Philippines in 1976, and exposure
there to the indigenous protest songs of workers, led him to form his own
ensemble called Suigyû-gakudan ("Water buffalo ensemble"), which
specialized in the singing of folk songs with simple accompaniments of
Taiko drums, harmonium, and toy piano.[70]

Other opportunities were afforded by the National Theatre of
Japan, which commissioned composers to write for traditional ensembles such as gagaku and reigaku.[71] Takemitsu's *November Steps* (1967)
for biwa, shakuhachi, and orchestra ushered in a new trend of composing music for traditional instruments that were imported originally
from China, Korea, Vietnam, and India. Many Western-trained composers (including other members of the Experimental Workshop)
turned to composing for traditional Japanese and historically extinct
Asian instruments with unprecedented fervor. It is in these contexts
that many of the former avant-gardists gravitated once again toward
the use of aleatoric procedures and graphic notations, as exemplified by
the cadenza in Takemitsu's *November Steps*, Ichiyanagi's *Cloud Shore,
Wind Roots* (1984) for reigaku and gagaku, and Takahashi's *Dream of
Heaven* (1989) for reconstructed qin. And it was in the act of embracing
the premodern Japan through the lens of the avant-garde that the
composers came full circle in claiming their multicultural voice in the
"post" postwar years.

In Japan today, the significance of the postwar avant-garde has not entirely faded, as there is renewed interest in reviving music, film, and art through retrospective concerts and exhibitions.[72] Looking back, it would not be far-fetched to claim that radical avant-garde musicians provided the essential steps toward overcoming societal alienation in the postwar era, through their engagement with "the body as the site of sensation and knowledge," an engagement that echoed the Mavo artists' emphasis on direct experience.[73] The concept of corporeality, previously linked to the idea of nationhood (*kokutai*), was transformed by the Happenings and Events into a site of individual and collective exploration of selfhood. It is no wonder that the idea of a primal scream, literally found in Ono's conceptual piece, became the slogan for the Guggenheim's retrospective art exhibition in 1994. "Scream against the Sky"—its cultural resonances sum up the zeitgeist of the postwar Japanese avant-garde.

Notes

1. Because of the military alignment with the United States, to which Japan agreed in order to regain its sovereignty, the Soviet Union refused to sign the Peace Treaty with Japan in 1951.

2. George Packard, *Protest in Tokyo: The Security Treaty Crisis of 1960* (Princeton, N.J.: Princeton University Press, 1966), 23–25.

3. Ibid., 96.

4. Ibid., 153.

5. Ankoku Butoh literally means "Dance of Darkness." Tatsumi Hijikata introduced the dance form in 1959; it evokes images of decay, fear, eroticism, ecstasy, or stillness through combining elements of traditional Japanese dance, improvisation, mime, and German Ausdrucktanz.

6. David G. Goodman, *Angura: Posters of the Japanese Avant-Garde* (New York: Princeton Architectural Press, 1999), 3–4.

7. While there are different views on the origin of the term "Mavo," Gennifer Weisenfeld speculates that the naming has to do with key concepts underlying the movement, for instance, Marxism, anarchism, and the autonomous role of the individual in society. See Gennifer Weisenfeld, *MAVO Japanese Artists and the Avant-garde 1905–31* (Berkeley and Los Angeles: University of California Press, 2002), 4.

8. Ibid., 251.

9. Miwako Tezuka, *Jikken Kôbô: Avant-Garde Experiments in Japanese Art of the 1950s* (PhD diss., Columbia University, 2005), 28.

10. Alexandra Munroe, *Japanese Art after 1945: Scream against the Sky* (New York: Abrams, 2004), 84.

11. Ibid., 84. Munroe explains further that the formation of Gutai was also influenced by the anti-establishment stance established by the Democratic Artists Association, founded in Osaka in 1951 (86).

12. Ibid., 151.

13. Jôji Yuasa, "Jikken Kôbô Concert," liner notes in *Jikken Kôbô no Ongaku* FOCD 3417 (Tokyo: Fontec, 1996), 11.

14. Kôji Sano, *"Jikken Kôbô,"* in *Nihon no Sakkoku-ka: Nijûseiki* [Japanese Composers: Twentieth Century] (Tokyo: Ongakuno Tomo, 2000), 52; Kôji Sano et al., *Nihon Sengo Ongakushi* [History of Postwar Japanese Music] (Tokyo: Heibon-sha, 2007), 307. Sano argues that works composed by elite, Western-trained composers such as Yoritsune Matsudaira's Theme and Variations on *Etenraku* for piano and orchestra (1951) and Toshirô Mayuzumi's *Ectoplasm* (1954) for tape exemplify the first generation of the musical avant-garde, although neither belonged to the Jikken-Kôbô group. Makoto Moroi and Mayuzumi later founded Ars Nova in 1956, which offered avant-garde concerts featuring works by Pierre Schaeffer, Luciano Berio, and Bruno Maderna, alongside those by Moroi, Mayuzumi, Takemitsu, and others.

15. For a comprehensive study of the pre-war schools of composition, see Luciana Galliano, *Yôgaku: Japanese Music in the Twentieth Century* (Lanham, Md.: Scarecrow, 2002).

16. Ibid., 119. The female leader, Akiko Seki, won the Stalin prize in 1955 for her work.

17. According to Takahashi, the JCP led the Utagoe movement up until 1964. Personal communication with Yûji Takahashi, October 6, 2007.

18. Packard, *Protest in Tokyo*, 102.

19. Ibid., 102–3.

20. Munroe, *Japanese Art after 1945*, 151–52.

21. Sano et al., *Nihon Sengo Ongakushi*, 300. Democracy here refers to liberal, American-style democracy, which was rejected by Kishi's LDP.

22. Munroe, *Japanese Art after 1945*, 151.

23. Sano et al., *Nihon Sengo Ongakushi*, 301.

24. Munroe, *Japanese Art after 1945*, 159.

25. Yoshitomo Nara, ed., *Kagayake Rokujûnendai* [Let the 1960s Shine] (Tokyo: Film Art Publisher, 2002), 93.

26. Ibid., 8–9.

27. In the program note for his solo recital at the Sôgetsu Contemporary Series (March 31, 1961), Hayashi states: "Contemporary music should strive to reincorporate the human voice through song. "

28. Kuniharu Akiyama, "Sokowa Rokujûnendai Zeneigeijutsuno Jûdenchi data" [Sôgetsu was the Battery of 1960s Avant-garde], in *Kagayake Rokujûnendai*, 34–66; 38–39.

29. Shûkô Mizuno, "John Cage ga yatteru kotowa mezurashikumo nantomonai" [What John Cage Does Is Nothing New], in *Kagayake Rokujûnendai*, 162–63.

30. Sano et al., *Nihon Sengo Ongakushi*, 332.

31. While Akiyama, among others, thought of Cage as having radically changed the face of the avant-garde in Japan, other composers such as Mayuzumi and Mizuno remained skeptical toward Cage's role as composer (Nara, *Kagayake Rokujûnendai*, 309).

32. Frederic Lieberman, ed., "A Lecture by John Cage," in *Locating East Asia in Western Art Music*, ed. Yayoi U. Everett and Frederick Lau (Middletown, Conn.: Wesleyan University Press, 2004), 196.

33. The photo is widely distributed on the Internet; see for instance http://www.new-york-art.com/YOko-Works-2.htm (accessed November 1, 2007).

34. Midori Yoshimoto, *Into Performance: Japanese Women Artists in New York* (New Brunswick, N.J.: Rutgers University Press, 2005), 95.

35. Sano et al., *Nihon Sengo Ongakushi*, 342.

36. Michael Kirby, "The New Theatre," in *Happenings and Other Acts*, ed. Mariellen R. Sanford (London and New York: Routledge, 1995), 36.

37. Nara, *Kagayake Rokujûnendai*, 57.

38. Thomas R. H. Havens, *Radicals and Realists in the Japanese Nonverbal Arts: The Avant-Garde Rejection of Modernism* (Honolulu: University of Hawaii Press, 2006), 110.

39. In Sôgetsu Art Center's journal (SAC No. 27, 1962), Mayuzumi stated that he thought of Cage as a brilliant philosopher, but not a great composer—arguing that he stopped composing after 4'33." In an essay from 1961, Yuasa expressed his fascination with Cage and chance operation, but questioned whether the act of liberating sound from predetermined structure resulted in the liberation of selfhood (SAC No. 19, 1961).

40. Havens, *Radicals and Realists*, 113.

41. For Ichiyanagi's involvement in Fluxus, see Luciana Galliano, "Toshi Ichiyanagi, Japanese Composer and 'Fluxus,'" *Perspectives of New Music* 44, no. 2 (Summer 2006): 250–61.

42. Kuniharu Akiyama, "Gendai Ongaku no Jiyû to Bôken" [Freedom and Adventure in New Music], *Yomiuri*, December 8, 1961.

43. Toshi Ichiyanagi, *Ongaku o kiku: Ongaku no ashita o kangaeru* [Listening to Music: Thinking about the Future of Music] (Tokyo: Ishikawashoten, 1984), 69–75.

44. Toshi Ichiyanagi, Program notes from Sôgetsu Contemporary Series No. 10. November 30, 1961.

45. Kuniharu Akiyama, "Atarashii Ongaku no hitopaji" [New Music's Page One], *Yomiuri*, March 2, 1962.

46. Shinichirô Ikebe, "New Direction no koro no omoide" [Recalling the New Direction Years], in *Kagayake Rokujûnendai*, 167.

47. Yûji Takahashi, "Facing Music," SAC No. 19, October 1961.

48. For a recording of *Chromamorphe II*, see *Orchestral Space 1966* (Japan Victor Series VX–69), vol.1.

49. Based on a correspondence with Yoshimoto on July 4, 2007.

50. Donald Richie, "Tsumazuita Saizensen: Ono Yoko no zen'ei shou" [Stumbling Front Line: Yoko Ono's Avant-Garde Show], *Geijutsu Shinchô* (July 1962): 60–61.

51. Toshi Ichiyanagi, "Saizenei no koe" [Voice of the Extreme Avant-garde], *Geijutsu Shinchô* (August 1962): 138–39.

52. Kristine Stiles, "*Cut Piece*, 1964," in *Yes Yoko Ono*, ed. Alexandra Munroe and Jon Hendricks (New York: Abrams, 2000), 158.

53. See http://www.youtube.com/watch?v=qqXSjFB08C8 for a video excerpt from the Carnegie Hall recital in 1965.

54. Yoshimoto, *Into Performance*, 100.

55. Ibid., 101.

56. Midori Yoshimoto, "Off Museum! Performance Art that Turned the Street into 'Theatre,' Circa 1964 Tokyo," *Performance Paradigm* 2 (March 2006): 102.

57. See ibid. for an account of the development of performance art in theater and film circa 1964.

58. Havens, *Radicals and Realists*, 220.

59. David G. Goodman, "Japan's Nostalgic Avant-Garde," in *Not the Other Avant-Garde: The Transnational Foundation of Avant-Garde Performance*, ed.

James M. Harding and John Rouse (Ann Arbor: University of Michigan Press, 2006), 250.

60. Conversations with Ichiyanagi, Hayashi, Takahashi, and Yuasa suggest that the affordable price of admission and multimedia aspects of avant-garde performances attracted a host of professional artists, musicians, filmmakers, as well as lay audience.

61. Havens, *Radicals and Realists*, 115.

62. Based on an interview with Ichiyanagi on May 18, 2006.

63. Packard, *Protest in Tokyo*, 341.

64. John Dower, "Peace and Democracy in Two Systems," in *Post-war Japan as History*, ed. Andrew Gordon (Berkeley and Los Angeles: University of California Press, 1993), 12–13.

65. Gordon, ibid., 450.

66. Frederic Jameson, *Postmodernism or the Cultural Logic of Late Capitalism* (Durham, N.C.: Duke University Press, 1991).

67. Stuart D. Hobbs, *The End of the American Avant Garde* (New York and London: New York University Press, 1997).

68. Sano et al., *Nihon Sengo Ongakushi*, 483–84.

69. Yûji Takahashi, *Tatakau Ongaku* [Fighting Music] (Tokyo: Shôbunsha, 1978), 14–15.

70. Some critics were baffled by the radical change in his musical orientation and could not reconcile the stylistic gap between his "highbrow" modernist compositions and the relatively simple arrangements of folk songs. Takahashi's ensemble disbanded after ten years, but to this day, he still adheres to the ideology of using music to bring about social change.

71. Yayoi U. Everett, "Mirrors of West and Mirrors of East: Elements of Gagaku in Post-war Art Music," in *Diasporas and Interculturalism in Asian Performing Arts: Translating Traditions*, ed. Hae-kyung Um (New York: Routledge, 2005), 182. "Reigaku" is a new term assigned to a genre of newly composed works commissioned by the National Theatre of Japan for the purpose of reviving musical practices of historically extinct instruments from the Imperial Court Repository.

72. According to Ichiyanagi, younger musicians engaged in reviving avant-garde music of the sixties include Tomomi Otachi, Osamu Ikebe, and Akiko Samukawa. In July 2007, Ichiyanagi offered a retrospective concert and lecture of music titled "John Cage and Fluxus" at the Asahi Hall in Tokyo.

73. Peter Eckersall, "From Liminality to Ideology: The Politics of Embodiment in Pre-war Avant-garde Theater in Japan," in *Not the Other Avant-Garde*, 227.

Part IV

THE CHALLENGE OF INSTITUTIONALIZATION

10

After the October Revolution

The Jazz Avant-garde in New York, 1964–65

Bernard Gendron

In retrospect, the October Revolution, a festival of new jazz music organized by trumpeter Bill Dixon in 1964 at New York's Cellar Café, was a brilliant publicity stunt, in effect if not in intention. It triggered a resurgence of the jazz avant-garde movement (also known as the "free jazz" and "the new thing") after nearly three years of apparent somnolence and near-absence from the public eye. Ornette Coleman had initiated the first wave of the avant-garde as a movement in late 1959 with his highly publicized extended engagement at the Five Spot in the East Village. This set off a year of acrimonious debate pro and con, dividing the jazz community of musicians and critics. To his proponents, Coleman represented a much-needed new development in jazz, opening a new field of activity, after the great innovations of bebop had turned into cliché. But soon the fanfare subsided, gigs disappeared, Coleman retired, his comrade-in-arms Eric Dolphy passed away, and bossa nova was anointed the next big thing. By 1964, the avant-garde seemed to have been reduced to a minor rivulet meandering far from the mainstream. But, in the wake of the October Revolution, it rebounded dramatically. A new generation of musicians organized, spoke out, and took matters into their own hands. Coleman returned with a flourish and another major star, John Coltrane, joined forces with free jazz. An avant-garde recording industry suddenly appeared, more prolific than ever. Discourses intensified in the jazz press, roiled by increasingly acrimonious debates. Meanwhile, the new African American cultural magazines, associated with the Black Arts Movement,

211

entered the fray to impart a political and racial dimension to the avant-garde aesthetic.

This flurry of events, triggered in part by the October Revolution, took place in less than a year. The ultimate outcome was that, after years of delay and hostility, the jazz press would finally accept (albeit somewhat grudgingly) the avant-garde as a legitimate movement within jazz history, indeed as the central current within the new jazz mainstream. In this chapter, I examine this resurgence of the avant-garde and the many events that contributed to it during this short period (roughly from Fall 1964 to the end of 1965). I am interested especially in the evolving aesthetic of this second wave, as it was declared and perceived by various actors—musicians, critics, promoters. It will become clear that such aesthetic stances and concerns are never pure, but inextricably enmeshed with economic imperatives, political aspirations, and the dynamics of race. Finally, I want to show how the tumultuous events giving rise to the second wave made possible, and perhaps inevitable, the subsequent canonization of the jazz avant-garde as a legitimate extension of the jazz tradition.[1]

The October Revolution

Bill Dixon may have not have foreseen the widespread repercussions of the festival he called "The October Revolution" when he scheduled it for October 1–4, 1964. The small Cellar Café, a coffeehouse located on 91st Street in the Upper West Side, far from the downtown centers of jazz performance, was hardly the kind of site where one would have expected to find a musical revolution. When he accidentally fell upon it in spring of 1964, the Cellar Café was serving up an eclectic and inchoate fare of poetry, film, folk music, and jazz for an audience largely of Columbia University students. Seeking to provide performance opportunities for free jazz musicians otherwise unemployed, Dixon arranged with the owner to produce a weekly Sunday afternoon concert series of new jazz music. In addition to his own combo, Dixon programmed the Paul Bley Quartet, the Free Form Improvisational Ensemble, and the Sun Ra Sextet. A number of emerging avant-garde musicians played in these and later ensembles at the Cellar Café: saxophonists Pharaoh Sanders, Giuseppe Logan, and John Tchicai; trombonist Roswell Rudd; pianists Bley, Sun Ra, and Burton Greene; bassist David Izenson; and percussionists Milford Graves, Sonny Murray, and Rashied Ali.[2]

After four months of these Sunday concerts, Dixon decided on a more dramatic ploy, which was to feature these musicians, and others suffering from the same employment predicament, in a four-day festival at the beginning of October, thus the "October Revolution." Between five and seven groups performed each day in a grueling nine-hour schedule starting in late afternoon and ending with a panel discussion (on "Jim Crow and Crow Jim," "The Economics of

Jazz," "The Rise of Folk Music and the Decline of Jazz," and "Jazz Composition").[3] Dixon's purpose was to demonstrate to jazz critics and others that the new music could draw a significant audience. "The new music is not ahead of the people," he said, "all it needs is a chance to be heard."[4] And indeed he seemed to have proven his point. With advanced advertising in the *Village Voice*, each of the four nights drew capacity crowds with long lines of people waiting their turn in these marathon events.[5] The audience included a number of jazz musicians, some who came without prompting (Ornette Coleman and Gil Evans), and others who came to participate in the panel discussions (Cecil Taylor, Archie Shepp, and Steve Lacy, among others).[6] Though spearheaded by relatively unknown musicians performing in an out-of-the-way place, the October Revolution created enough of a stir to merit two substantial reviews by *Down Beat* writers Martin Williams and Dan Morgenstern, in side by side columns mildly suggesting a debate, which was to erupt in full force a few months later.[7]

The Jazz Composer's Guild

The October Revolution might have soon receded from memory and the process that it had set in motion lost its impetus if it had not been promptly followed up by the formation of the Jazz Composer's Guild, again under Dixon's leadership. A flyer authored by Dixon advertising a weekend of music at the Cellar Café made the following announcement:

> The October Revolution Continues. Cecil Taylor, Archie Shepp, Sun Ra, Mike Mantler, Burton Greene, Roswell Rudd, John Tchicai, and Bill Dixon [Carla and Paul Bley were added later] have united into the JAZZ COM-POSERS GUILD with the idea in mind that music represented by the above-named and others must and will no longer remain part of the "underground" scene.[8]

The Jazz Composers Guild (JCG) followed in a long tradition of avant-garde self-help and self-advertising organizations in the art world, dating at least as far back as Zürich Dada, the Italian Futurists, Bauhaus, and what for Dixon was the most salient model, the artist-run galleries on 10th Street in the East Village.[9] Although there was little precedence for this in jazz—the short-lived Jazz Artists Guild formed by Charles Mingus earlier in the decade was an exception—such organizing activity became a mark of the second wave, sprouting in Chicago (the Association for the Advancement of Creative Musicians), St. Louis (the Black Artist Group), and Los Angeles (the Underground Musicians Asso-ciation).[10] Unlike Dada, Futurism, and other European high-cultural avant-gardes, the JCG did not act like a school, did not publish any aesthetic manifestos, or otherwise try to promote a particular aesthetic agenda. Concerned mainly with economic survival and security, the JCG was a collective whose purpose was to gain recognition and employment from the main players of the jazz industry—the clubs, record companies, and critics—on terms that were nonexploitative. All members were to seek approval of the collective for any employment opportunity, the idea being that any offer to an individual had to benefit the group in some way.[11]

Of course, aesthetics was not altogether irrelevant to these economic concerns, since it was partly because of a shared avant-garde aesthetics, and the supposed lack of a public for it, that the JCG members and their allies had been frozen out of club gigs and recording contracts. Thus, the October Revolution did not signal the creation of a new set of musical ideas—these had been percolating in musical practice since the beginning of the decade—but a forceful attempt to instill these ideas firmly in the jazz marketplace. To quote the JCG flyer, it was an attempt by these musicians to emerge successfully from the "underground scene" into the jazz mainstream. But what was this underground scene that they hoped to leave? And did they ultimately succeed in breaking out?

Jazz Bohemians

The term "underground" has both positive and negative import in the discourses of art. On the negative side, it refers to a lack of access to the key media that would give artists a wide public presence. On the positive side, it refers to artistic communities operating in particular neighborhoods, unrecognized but aesthetically ahead of their times, resisting the dominant styles and values and providing a shelter for the incubation of unfashionable new ideas. Like the term "avant-garde," "underground" has positive political-military connotations, in this case, to the armed resistance movements against the Nazi German occupation in Europe.

In mid-twentieth-century New York, the artistic undergrounds flourished primarily in Greenwich Village and the Lower East Side (the northern part of which had recently been renamed the "East Village"). Jazz musicians did not become an integral part of this bohemia until the early 1960s. Indeed, before 1950, modern jazz, born in Harlem and midtown (on 52nd Street and nearby Broadway), was virtually absent from Greenwich Village venues, where traditional New Orleans and Chicago-style jazz reigned supreme. But by 1957, Greenwich Village and its East Village neighbor had become the New York centers for modern jazz performance, at such thriving venues as the Five Spot, the Half Note, and the Village Vanguard. Modern jazz was by then the music favored by various underground literary groups, such as the Beats and the so-called New York School (e.g., Frank O' Hara), constituting as it were the sound track of their literary lives. Bohemia had become "hip," and jazz, as a cultural commodity, was bohemianized. It was only a short step from this for jazz to become bohemianized also as a cultural practice, as young musicians from the jazz avant-garde integrated with down-town's underground communities. They were drawn initially by cheap rents and, for black musicians, by the growing community of African American writers, painters, and dramatists in the East Village, such as the Umbra Poets and the La Mama Experimental Theater. Already exhibiting a desire to break out of the barriers separating jazz from the rest of the art world, black musicians in particular welcomed alliances with local writers and painters, and in some cases practiced some of these other arts. Some were poets (Cecil Taylor), writers (Marion Brown), and playwrights (Taylor and Shepp); some worked with choreographers (Dixon and Taylor), some with poets (Dolphy), and some (Taylor and Shepp) performed in the Living Theater's production of *The Connection*.[12] For their part, African American poets in the East Village frequently referenced jazz or its practitioners in their work, attesting to a widely held assessment of jazz as the exemplary black art.

Of special strategic importance was the alliance of the black East Village musicians with poet/playwright Amiri Baraka (then LeRoi Jones) and poet A. B. Spellman, who as critics would propagate their own versions of the jazz avant-garde aesthetic. Here perhaps for the first time in jazz history, critics operated not as outsider judges, however sympathetic, but spoke from within the underground music scene itself. Baraka and Spellman conversed frequently with Shepp, Brown, and Sonny Murray at Jones's apartment at Cooper Square or at the Five Spot in the neighborhood. Baraka no doubt picked up important pointers from his jazz confreres while writing his classic *Blues People*, which appeared in 1963 at the peak of the African American bohemian scene and was an intended articulation of its perspective.[13] His work at the same time influenced the self-understanding of these musicians as they sought to give public voice to their aesthetic.

Between 1961 and 1964, this jazz avant-garde, in the tradition of downtown bohemia, performed in coffeehouses (the White Whale, Le Metro, and the Take Three), lofts, churches (St. Mark's, Judson), listener-supported radio stations (WBAI), and political benefits (Women's Strike for Peace, Mobilization for Youth).[14] Such engagements, barely remunerative, were taken up more as a matter of necessity than choice, since by this time, avant-garde jazz was shut out of the club scene and rarely recorded. Significantly, this dearth of opportunities affected even the most established and respected avant-gardists. Despite a growing reputation and small cult following, Taylor, who had appeared frequently in jazz venues and recorded plentifully by the end of 1961, did not issue a recording during the next four years and rarely appeared in jazz clubs, and then only on Sunday afternoons or Monday nights.[15] Understandably, the situation was even more desperate for the second generation.

Thus, from the perspective of the jazz avant-garde, bohemianization was more an exile into a foreign country than the conquest of new territory, despite the beneficial results of loosening the boundaries between jazz and the fine arts and providing avant-garde musicians with the intellectual support lacking in the jazz press. They were caught in the contradiction of being avant-garde (and by definition less accessible to a broad public) and yet belonging, as jazz musicians, to a highly commercialized field of entertainment. Had they been generally welcomed into the venues of classical experimental music and the allied modern dance scene—much of which was also ensconced in the East and West Villages—they might have found a viable home outside the jazz commercial marketplace. But, despite a few inroads here and there, the artificial borders between classical and jazz experimentalism were still being strongly policed by high culture. Here one need only consult John Cage's derogatory remarks about jazz and improvisation, despite his espousal of "indeterminism with respect to performance."[16] In effect, the jazz avant-garde was only a second-class citizen in the downtown musical underground, further underscoring the fact that bohemianization was at best only a short-term palliative for a chronic problem. The only solution appeared to be to leave the underground and to accost the jazz commercial marketplace aggressively and in an organized manner. Thus the October Revolution and the formation of the Jazz Composers Guild.

"The Revolution Continues"

The Jazz Composers Guild lasted less than a year. In terms of its primary objective—to stand as a united front in negotiations with the industry—it was an unqualified failure. The intransigence of the industry was complemented by the weakness of the collective spirit as individual musicians pursued new career opportunities either without permission of the organization or without bringing the organization to bear in their dealings with the industry.[17] But these new career opportunities reflected a signal success of the JCG in its secondary goal: to publicize and showcase its members in various organized concerts.

Immediately after its formation, the JCG began sponsoring concerts for its members, first at the Cellar Café, followed by a Halloween benefit at a Greenwich Village loft whose proceeds were used to finance the next major event, a series of concerts at Judson Hall called "Four Days in December," in the waning days of the month. Using a similar promotional format, this series outdid the October Revolution by extending its media reach beyond the narrow confines of the jazz press. The previously oblivious *New York Times* announced the upcoming series, detailing each of the concerts, two groups playing each night.[18] The first night sold out with a standing room audience—in part due to the growing Cecil Taylor cult—and the other nights saw at least half the seats filled.[19]

It must have been a pleasant surprise that John Wilson, the *New York Times* jazz critic not known to be friendly to the avant-garde, attended the first three concerts and wrote separate and rather sympathetic reviews for each. Perplexed by Taylor's opening Cage-like maneuvers, "weaving an incantation over the innards of the piano" after which he "pummeled, pulled and rubbed the strings," Wilson nonetheless praised him for his occasional "gentle pastoral style" and conceded that even when "beset by furies," Taylor's "playing was clean, his tone full and ringing, and his fingering firm and agile."[20] Not exactly a rave review, but Wilson did dispense with the usual complaints of ugliness, chaos, and mere noise directed at Taylor. His kindest words were reserved for the Jazz Composers Guild Orchestra on the next night, whom he credited for giving the first successful free jazz performance by a large orchestral ensemble (though the Sun Ra Arkestra, whose performance he missed, had been doing this for years). "Eleven jazz musicians took a mad, dizzying dash through the unknown... They produced excitement, suspense, awe and an awful lot of noise. And it was great fun."[21] In the final review, Wilson noted with some surprise that the Archie Shepp Quartet maintained a steady rhythm pattern behind the solos, thus going against the basic tenets of free jazz. This was "just as well," he thought, since Shepp's solos "consisted largely of hoarse, staccato murmurs and mumblings that rose to racking barks at climactic moments."[22] Though it is not clear why such noise effects shouldn't work with free rhythm, Wilson did hit upon an important difference between the first- and second-generation free jazz musicians. In addition to freeing tones from the equal temperament system by operating with microtones (as Coleman did), the second generation, with their squeals, squawks, gurgles, barks, and so forth, were experimenting with timbres that effectively went beyond notes— not merely for the sake of experimentation, but also to expand the expressive power of their music. This should not take away from the fact that both generations were highly diverse in style, aesthetics, and politics, united more by the limits they transgressed than by the new directions they took.

Quite different in tone was A. B. Spellman's review of the Judson Hall concerts for the left-liberal journal *The Nation*, in February 1965.[23] As an active member of the East Village bohemia on familiar terms with the jazz musicians, Spellman could approach the Judson concerts from the inside, warmly and supportively, in contrast to Wilson's bemused Olympian detachment. For Spellman, Taylor was clearly the hero of the series—"[He] penetrates areas of keyboard improvisation that no other pianist approaches"—though he was dubious about Taylor's initial Cagean rituals with the piano strings, which seemed too "academic," a reminder that Taylor is "heavily influenced by European music." In contrast, Shepp, though altogether "committed to the new 'free' improvisation," is, according to Spellman, emphatically rooted in the blues. His "sound is guttural, his inflections are hard but slurred. He wants to move you with every tune." Noting that the audiences were "about two thirds white, and a great many of those Negroes present were jazz musicians"—typical of downtown and midtown avant-garde concerts— he ruefully looked forward to the day when someone would "put on some avant-garde concerts in Harlem and Bedford-Stuyvesant to relieve some of the alienation from black communities the post-bop revolution- ists [were] experiencing."[24] Spellman was giving vent to a discernible shift in the aesthetic stances of the East Village African American intelli- gentsia, reflected in a distancing from the Eurocentric avant-gardes and a growing conviction that the African American arts should speak more directly to African Americans—a shift that would culminate in the Black Arts Movement, barely a month after the publication of Spell- man's essay.

As the Four Days in December series came to a close, the JCG wasted no time in moving to their next promotional gambit. An ad in the *Village Voice*, proclaiming again that "[t]he Jazz Revolution Con- tinues," announced the establishment of the Contemporary Center in Greenwich Village, which was to be the JCG's permanent performance headquarters.[25] They were clearly evoking a narrative of constant transformation, of a flourishing "permanent revolution," whose point of origin was the October Revolution and which continued unabated through the Four Days in December to the events at the Contemporary Center. On this, they got the full support of Spellman and Wilson, who both hewed closely to the story's line—Wilson, writing in a lead Sun- day article about the JCG in *The New York Times*, now seemingly convinced that the October Revolution and its aftermath was a major event in recent jazz history.[26]

The Contemporary Center, located in the loft space of dancer/cho- reographer Edith Stephen above the Village Vanguard, staged weekend concerts, showcasing one member group each night. The audiences do not appear to have been especially large, certainly not as sizable as those at the Village Vanguard downstairs, arguably the most financially viable downtown jazz club at that time. Paul Bley notoriously failed to show for a scheduled performance for fear of facing an empty room when Ornette Coleman was staging his comeback downstairs. The weekend program at the Contemporary Center lasted from mid-January to mid- April, when the JCG, after months of tension, began to fall apart.[27] But other catalysts came into play to assure that the ferment set in motion by the October Revolution would not easily subside.

Catalysts

It took the dramatic intervention of two elder statesmen to give irrevers- ible momentum to the second wave upsurge. Ornette Coleman, after two years of retirement (but not inactivity) suddenly reappeared in early January 1965, a little before the inauguration of the Contemporary Center programs, for a cumulative three-week stand of near sold-out concerts at the Village Vanguard. This was a major media event, with coverage in *Time, Newsweek, The New Yorker,* and the *The New York Times*. It was treated almost as a second coming, waited for with anticipation by critics sympathetic to the avant-garde. "The music needs the return of Ornette Coleman to active playing," proclaimed Martin Williams in his "October Revolution" review. "Hundreds of young players are learning from his records, but his last public appearance—the Town Hall Concert of a couple years ago—had musical elements beyond anything on his records."[28] The reviewers of his concerts were generally welcoming and positive, though puzzled by his unorthodox trumpet and violin playing, instruments that he had just recently taken up.[29] Later in the year, Coleman toured Europe and recorded the classic *The Ornette Coleman Trio at the "Golden Circle" Stockholm*, Volumes I and II.[30] Coleman was now given the role—without his consent—of wise and moderate father of the avant-garde, representing its good side, not given to the excesses of the churlish radical youth.[31]

A few months after Coleman's return, John Coltrane further stoked up the fires of the avant-garde with his recording of *Ascension*, which defines the moment when he crossed over to free jazz after years of hovering on the sidelines.[32] Before this move, Coltrane was the ultimate post-bopper, working within the frame of the steady pulse and improvising over chord changes. No doubt he had pushed these tendencies to their extremes, almost at the point of breakage, with his rapid flurry of notes (the so-called "sheets of sound") and adventurous harmonic explorations. All along he had been sympathetic to the avant-garde, regularly attending Coleman's performances at the Five Spot (followed by long after-hours conversations) and warmly supporting the work of the young avant-gardists, like Albert Ayler. He appeared at their gigs at obscure venues and sometimes helped them get recording contracts. But he did not cross over to free jazz until *Ascension*—a move whose legitimating impact is sometimes compared to Bob Dylan's crossover into rock during the same summer.

The moment could not have been more propitious. At the height of his career, riding on the momentum of the critical and popular triumph of *A Love Supreme*, Coltrane was *the* modern jazz star of the 1960s, with a large following of serious jazz fans and great respect from his musician peers. He was in an ideal position to bring into the orbit of the avant-garde fans and musicians who had previously hesitated, been puzzled or mildly hostile. Still, *Ascension* must have been a shock. Coltrane expanded his quartet to include a bevy of young avant-gardists—a big free jazz band including Shepp, Sanders, Brown, Tchicai on saxophone and Freddy Hubbard and Dewey Johnson on trumpet. The album constituted one swirling forty-minute track, interspersing dense, highly energetic collective improvisation with solos constrained by few parameters other than scalar. Though a latecomer, Coltrane could have claimed with plausibility to have out-outed the most extreme examples of free jazz that preceded him.[33]

Coltrane also deserves credit for having almost single-handedly brought his record label, Impulse, into the avant-garde field. Before-hand, Impulse, in the forefront of jazz recordings along with Blue Note, had developed a broad catalog of diverse jazz styles, but included no free jazz. In the summer of 1964, nearly one year before the *Ascension* sessions, Impulse producer Bob Thiele, under Coltrane's proddings, agreed to record Archie Shepp, on the condition that Shepp play four Coltrane compositions. This resulted in *Four for Trane*, the first of a string of Impulse avant-garde recordings including a regular output from Shepp.[34] What united this catalog was that virtually all the group leaders belonged to Coltrane's circle, either his former or actual sidemen (Shepp, Brown, Sanders) or protégés (Ayler).[35]

Impulse was part of a striking revival of the avant-garde jazz recording industry after a nearly comatose period, a revival that also included ESP-Disk and, to a lesser extent, Blue Note. The result was an unprecedented number of recordings at a rate of production never matched since—by my count, forty by ESP-Disk and twenty by Impulse in a little over two years. Still very much in the hard bop ambit, Blue Note nonetheless produced work by avant-garde elders Coleman, Taylor, and Don Cherry. In addition to the obvious advantages of reaching audiences beyond live venues, this spate of recordings was greeted with a corresponding flurry of reviews in the jazz press, thus extending and deepening the discourses and disputations on the avant-garde. As a further bonus, *Jazz* magazine, owned by Impulse producer Bob Thiele and the lone significant competitor to *Down Beat*, suddenly shifted its coverage policy in early 1965 to become a major promoter of the avant-garde, especially those musicians on the Impulse label.

Though not as expansive in its market reach, ESP-Disk was more committed to avant-garde jazz than was Impulse, and more intimately connected with the scene. Its founder, Bernard Stollman, created the company specifically to record the avant-garde, which it did exclusively over an eighteen-month period. Previously an agent for musicians with little previous knowledge or appreciation of the music, Stollman had his epiphany when listening to Ayler in Harlem: "I was blown away—I'd never heard anything like it." He recruited Ayler as the first artist on his label, resulting in the classic *Spiritual Unity* (ESP 1002), recorded in July 1964, not long after Ayler's first performance at the Cellar Café.[36] At some point, Stollman began to attend performances at the Cellar Café, not far from his home on Riverside Drive. He was there for the October Revolution and enthusiastically offered to record the participants. Thus, in addition to Ayler, who continued to be the label's star, ESP-Disk produced LPs by Giuseppe Logan, the New York Art Quartet (headed by Rudd and Tchicai), Paul Bley, Greene, Graves, and Sonny Murray.[37] It is not clear that ESP-Disk records sold well, but they were extensively and positively reviewed in the jazz press. In that regard, they provided valued publicity, if not much remuneration, for the stalwarts of the October Revolution.

Aesthetics

The question inevitably arises: was there any aesthetic commonality or unity to the second wave of the avant-garde, a shared perspective on how to play the music or what to communicate through it? It's clear that they shared economic concerns, were united by having been marginalized in the jazz market and by a rising sense of collective action. Of course, this marginalization was partly due to the unsalable aesthetic that clubs and recording companies perceived them to share. Still, someone not familiar with the jazz field might be struck by the seeming absence of collective statements of aesthetics in the declarations of the JCG. As a first response, it needs to be stressed that traditionally there were no outlets through which jazz musicians could exercise their voices, in sharp contrast to the literary avant-gardes who could speak through their "little magazines" and other forms of publication. Aesthetic discourses were traditionally monopolized by jazz critics, except for the occasional interviews of musicians where critics, however, determined the frame and narrative. This monopoly would be challenged as the second wave gained momentum—indeed this would be one of its defining features.[38] But in the immediate aftermath of the October Revolution, the critics still controlled the discourses, and so I turn to them first.

In its 1965 annual supplement, *Down Beat* continued the debate begun in the Morgenstern-Williams review of the October Revolution, but now expanded to five protagonists: the "anti" position was taken up by Ira Gitler and record producer Don Schlitten, the supposedly middle-of-the-road position by Dan Morgenstern, and the "pro" position by Don Heckman and Martin Williams.[39] Gitler and Schlittin, mainly leveling unsubstantiated charges or expressing personal taste—the music is chaotic, ugly, boring, will never have an audience, unworthy of the Parker tradition—were no match for the theoretically more sophisticated Williams and Heckman who had for years been honing their analytical tools in their support of the avant-garde. It was left to the "centrist" Morgenstern to articulate the theoretical base for the "anti" position, turning what had been expressed as reflective concerns in his "October Revolution" article into polemical thrusts.

The objections that free jazz was chaos, had no form or structure, was all noise, had by early 1965 lost their bite, in the face of the many prevailing accounts about the phrasing and rhythmic patterns, tonal centers, motivic associations, agreed-upon modes of interaction between improvisers, and other practices giving form to the music.[40] The only vestige of this ploy was the oft-heard complaint that the ideology of playing free and the rigorous technical requirements had led to widespread incompetence and charlatanism—a point sometimes conceded by the defenders, but parried as a not relevant critique of the musical ideas themselves.[41] So now that it was agreed on all sides that there was method and form to free jazz, the remaining questions were about their aesthetic value, their proper fit in jazz history, and the kind of public they would draw.

The defenders of avant-garde jazz stressed that it was a natural development of the jazz tradition, the next logical step in the advancement of improvisation, rhythm, phrasing, and so on, and thus part of the jazz mainstream when viewed with broad historical lenses. As Williams put it: "I'm talking about those as natural steps in evolving music. I'm trying to tie the 'new thing' to the past." In this line of argument, Ornette Coleman was the new Charlie Parker, as radical and innovative in his time as Parker was in his. Like Parker and the bebop movement, Coleman and his followers sought to emancipate improvisation, rhythm, and phrasing from some of the prevailing constraints, only now the constraints to be transcended were those imposed by the bebop system.[42]

This is a formidable rhetorical ploy, given that the most active and virulent opponents of the avant-garde (Gitler, Leonard Feather) were in earlier days fervent apologists of Parker and the beboppers in the face of the traditionalist opposition. The only possible retort was to try to disconnect the avant-garde from the Parker legacy, and thus from the jazz tradition, to show, in Morgenstern's phrase, that it is "a much more radical break with the tradition than anything in the past."[43] Gitler and Schlitten contended, for example, that unlike the avant-garde, Parker and Dizzy Gillespie found an audience immediately and sold records—"They didn't sell in the same category as Elvis Presley, but they sold."[44] How can a movement that cannot find a jazz audience be part of the jazz tradition? Morgenstern discounted the "proof" provided by the overflow crowds at October Revolution who (he claimed) were mainly youth who are "easily swayed" and unwilling or unable to pay the much higher prices to sit in a noisy nightclub.[45] Of course, one could mention that the triumph of bebop in the late 1940s was extremely short-lived and followed by a major economic crisis in the jazz field lasting until the mid-fifties, when the more accessible post-bop styles, hard bop and cool jazz, initiated what was called the "jazz renaissance." Perhaps, suggested Williams, easily accessible follow-ups to free jazz might come along, as George Shearing did for bop.[46] Ultimately, for Williams, what the October Revolution proved most powerfully was that a whole new generation of jazz musicians was choosing the path of the avant-garde over the other options.[47]

Morgenstern came up with a theoretically more interesting ploy than the "audience" argument, itself too feeble, for denying the new jazz a place in the tradition. The avant-garde, he claimed, was on its own effectively leaving the jazz field and crossing over into modernist art music. "It is a music that will develop along its own lines and somehow move closer to so-called contemporary classical music—and will lose some of the elements that we think of as peculiar to jazz."[48] A statement of this sort might have been welcomed by many black jazz musicians who disliked the word *jazz* and resented being cordoned off in the jazz field without the kind of recognition given to classical composers. But, they would also stress that they belong to a great tradition of composer-musicians who play what is called "jazz" (e.g., Taylor's allegiance to Duke Ellington). But, for an enthusiastic jazz fan like Morgenstern, strongly committed to maintaining the boundaries, such a crossing-over has the undesirable consequences of losing much of what is valuable in the jazz aesthetic while incorporating some of the objectionable traits of contemporary modernism. The "new thing," like modernist art, has become "terribly serious," he claimed, abandoning the original vocation of jazz as a "refreshing" "entertainment" art, with "broad lyrical expression," "abandonment and freedom," and "beautiful" sound "pleasing to the ear." Listening to Cecil Taylor may be a "tremendous emotional experience" but, rather than providing pleasure, it indulges in "the agony of modern existence." And, like modern art, the jazz avant-garde has "gone away from the idea of direct communication" with the listener and "toward a private means of expression which is available only to those who are 'tuned in' to it."[49]

Were Morgenstern's charges valid, they would unfortunately cut a much larger swath than he would like. For, with regard to jazz's transitioning from a popular art to a serious modernist art, the genie was already out of the bottle with the advent of Charlie Parker and the beboppers. The erstwhile defenders of bebop, notably Barry Ulanov and Leonard Feather, were then already promoting it as an autonomous art form fully informed by the aesthetics of modernism. The opponents to bop, for their part, complained about its obscurity, its disconnect with jazz's populist roots, its excessive Europeanization, its disdain for its audience, and so on.[50] Morgenstern's argument, in an earlier form, had already been defeated in the war over bebop.

The Black Arts Movement

The assassination of Malcolm X on February 21, 1965, set off a series of cultural events that further stimulated and radically transformed the reception and discourses of the jazz avant-garde. It impacted dramatically on the aesthetic practices of the African American bohemia who had gradually been radicalizing politically. Within a month, Amiri Baraka and a number of African American writers and artists, still in shock, left their East Village haunts for Harlem to found the Black Arts Repertory Theater and School (BART/S), whose objective was to bring black poetry, theater, and music to the streets.[51] Out of this emerged the Black Arts Movement (BAM), which spread from New York to other centers, including Atlanta, Chicago, Los Angeles, and the San Francisco Bay Area, and which continued to flourish after the demise

of BART/S in late 1965. The Black Arts Movement, the cultural corre-
lative of the Black Power movement, promulgated an anti-Western,
Afro-nationalist philosophy and aesthetic.[52]

From the beginning, Baraka and the BART/S project received
significant support from the African American free jazz community.
In late March, Coltrane, Shepp, Sun Ra, Grachan Moncur III, and
Charles Tolliver took part in a benefit for BART/S at the Village Gate,
much of it later released on Impulse's compilation, *The New Wave in
Jazz*. A number of avant-garde musicians accompanied Baraka to Harlem or showed up intermittently to participate in various ventures,
including Sun Ra, the house philosopher who led musical parades
down 125th Street, as well as Albert and Don Ayler, Andrew Hill,
Graves, Sanders, and Shepp. "We brought new music out in the streets,
on play streets, vacant lots, playgrounds, parks," where many "of the
newest of the new came up and blew."[53] The black jazz avant-garde
indeed was treated almost as the official music of the BAM, as its
ongoing sound track, as its exemplary art form. The music was cited
frequently in BAM poetry and theater and written about extensively in
black journals of criticism, such as *Liberator, Soulbook, Black Dialogue,*
the *Journal of Black Poetry, Black America*, and *Black Theater*. Thus, a
critical mass was reached sufficient to generate an African American
counter-discourse on the jazz avant-garde (and black music in general),
standing in opposition to the dominant (and virtually all-white) discourses of the jazz press. The resulting bifurcation of these two aesthetic
discourses is made glaringly manifest when comparing the wildly different tones of articles on the same topic in *Down Beat* and *Liberator*—for
example, in contemporaneous interviews, the former revealing an
ethereal and serene Ornette Coleman and the latter a pugnacious
one.[54] According to the counter-discourses of the BAM, the aesthetics
of (black) free jazz is permeated with political and racial significance.

Baraka had articulated the earlier version of this counter-aesthetic
in *Blues People* and his essay "Jazz and the White Critic," also published
in 1963.[55] Against what he viewed as the dominant tendency toward
formalism in jazz criticism, he argued for what I will call a "social-
expressionist" aesthetic as the proper framework for the interpretation
and evaluation of black music. As an aesthetic, expressionism inter-
prets and values artworks, not in terms of mere form, but primarily in
terms of what is connoted or expressed by these forms. We can distinguish between two types of expressionist aesthetics: individualist expressionism, which privileges works that express the deeper stirrings
and perspectives of the artist-creator, the so-called "genius" artist; and
social expressionism, which privileges works that express the ways of
life of the collectivity in whose midst the work arises. It was particularly
in the discourses of folklorists that the social-expressionist aesthetic
emerged, as a way of reading and legitimating the artistic value of
folk music. For Baraka, authentic black music is to be interpreted and

evaluated by reference to the way in which it expresses the evolving philosophies and life forms of African American communities. "Musicological analysis"—typical of avant-garde proponents Williams and Heckman—proves inadequate because of its tendency to look at the notes and sounds in themselves, without reference to their expressive meaning. "Ornette Coleman's screams and rants are only musical once one understands the music his emotional attitude seeks to create [which is a continuous part] of the historical and cultural biography of the Negro."[56] The black jazz avant-garde is "responsible intellectually" but not "emotionally" to the current European classical music whose formal techniques it has appropriated but which it has subjected to the "philosophical attitudes of Afro-American music."[57]

As originally articulated by Baraka, the aesthetic of social expressionism would become a defining feature of the discourses of the BAM. In this updated version, the new music is perceived as expressive of the current frustrations, pains, and anger of African American communities, as well as of new revolutionary aspirations. What the BAM rejected were the bohemian accretions to this aesthetic in *Blues People*, such as passive nonconformism and the appropriation of Western modern art values. The social-expressionist aesthetic had to be supplemented with an aesthetic of political activism and non-Western spirituality. Perhaps the clearest articulator of the BAM values, Larry Neal, argued that it was insufficient for the new writing and music merely to express the conditions of black life—merely to speak *for* black people—but had to speak *to* and rouse the people it spoke for and be understood by them.[58] In addition, he championed musicians, like Milford Graves, who infused jazz with a "non-Western orientation," which for him was equivalent to "shaping the spiritual foundation for revolutionary change."[59]

Thus, with the BAM, the bohemianization of the black avant-garde came to a temporary end, abetted by the hippie takeover of the East Village and the economic deterioration that followed. By no means all black avant-garde musicians were drawn into the ambit of the BAM or otherwise engaged in imparting a racial-political meaning to their music, however sympathetic they may have been on the personal level. Coltrane, Coleman, Dixon, and Tchicai, among others, avoided such direct associations or declarations. But the BAM contributed to a growing social climate encouraging jazz musicians to gain their own voices, to speak out on aesthetics and politics, and to challenge the white critics' monopoly. No one more skillfully exploited this opportunity than Archie Shepp.

The Year of Archie Shepp

The year 1965 was truly the year of Archie Shepp. He wrote and was written about frequently, generating considerable controversy, and recorded frequently with much favorable critical attention. He entered the year well equipped to take center stage. As a playwright and actor, Shepp excelled in the literary turn of phrase, theatrical declamation, showmanship, and the art of provocation. He was fortunate to have Coltrane's and Baraka's full support and Impulse's publicity machine, operating not too discreetly through Bob Thiele's covertly owned *Jazz* magazine. He managed to infuriate and to rouse with his sometimes inflammatory expressions of a racialized and politicized aesthetic—all in the fine tradition of avant-garde shock and self-promotion.

The year began with two articles on Shepp by Baraka: a cover story for *Jazz* magazine, in which he publicizes Shepp's forthcoming *Four for Trane*, and a lengthy interview in *Down Beat*, in which Shepp propounds a social-expressionist aesthetic very much like Baraka's but with a distinctive political-activist twist.[60] "The Negro musician is a reflection of the Negro people as a social and cultural phenomenon," whose "purpose ought to be to liberate America aesthetically and socially from its inhumanity." He is "like a reporter, an aesthetic journalist of America."[61] A few weeks later, Baraka and Shepp, on a Monday night panel at the Village Vanguard with liberal artists Larry Rivers and Jonas Mekas, verbally attacked their friends and made provocative comments about the Holocaust and the death of white civil rights workers.[62]

Meanwhile, Shepp was receiving rave reviews for the two LPs under his name, *Four for Trane* and *Fire Music*, and was basking in the glory of performing on Coltrane's *Ascension* and sharing two LPs with Coltrane's group, *The New Wave in Jazz* and *The New Thing at Newport*. He found room in his recordings for political declamation, an elegy to Malcolm X on *Fire Music*, and a diatribe on heroin and race on *The New Thing*. But Shepp's real tour de force was a scorching political-aesthetic manifesto, "An Artist Speaks Bluntly," appearing at the end of the year in *Down Beat*—a social-expressionist manifesto that denied the separation of art from politics. "My esthetic answer to your lies about me [the collective "me"] is a simple one: you can no longer defer my dream. I'm gonna sing it. Dance it. Scream it." Shepp's politics, his anger, his resistance, is expressed as music: "I am an antifascist artist, my music is functional. I play about the death of me by you. I exult in the life of me in spite of you."[63]

This article elicited a spate of spirited letters for weeks to come, mainly irate or indignant, but some cheering the writer onward. However much this diatribe was found excessive by the jazz press and its fans, it helped legitimate by dint of its implied argument the discussion of race and politics alongside the discussion of music in jazz magazines. Shepp had made his point: for him and many of his cohorts, race and politics were embedded in the music. At the end of 1965, it was no longer a viable position to say that critics should focus only on "the music itself" (as one columnist did in the same issue),[64] as if one could easily separate the musical from the extramusical. *Down Beat*, apparently unperturbed by Shepp's outburst, gave him a major role in the

Music '66 supplement appearing not long after. He participated in a roundtable with other musicians and authored a theoretically imbued essay on the aesthetics and styles of the avant-garde, reflective in tone though with the occasional political pronouncements.[65] This was a clear endorsement of the idea of the musician-critic.

Canonization

By the end of 1965, in little over a year, the second wave of the jazz avant-garde had generated enough of the right kind of momentum, and secured enough of the right kinds of cultural assets, to be assured artistic canonization within the jazz field, an achievement that had eluded the first wave. This second wave would acquire such canonicity once the relevant authorities—in this case, the jazz critics and established musicians—generally recognized it as a legitimate and integral movement within the historical development of the jazz aesthetic, and perhaps even the next logical step. Such had not yet occurred by the end of 1965, when the battle in *Down Beat* over the avant-garde continued to rage. But, enough cultural capital had been secured by then to heavily weigh the battle in favor of free jazz. These piecemeal 1965 victories included a significant growth in the ranks of young and increasingly vocal musicians; canonization by *Jazz* magazine, the only significant rival to *Down Beat* and promoter of Impulse recordings; canonization by the newly radicalized African-American cultural intelligentsia associated with the BAM, some of whose spokespersons (Baraka, Shepp) found writerly outlets in jazz magazines; a high volume of recordings and the generally favorable reviews they received; an upsurge of adulation for Coleman in 1965, effectively the year of his much-delayed canonization; and Coltrane's dramatic embrace of the avant-garde. Perhaps the greatest asset was the emergence of two sophisticated and well-honed aesthetic frameworks supportive of the avant-garde, one rooted in formalism and the other in social expressionism, and the concurrent absence of any viable alternative on the part of the detractors. This meant that at the intellectual level, the debate was already won.

By the end of 1966, the last obstacle was overcome: *Down Beat*, by far the most influential of the North American jazz magazines, had finally given the avant-garde its canonical endorsement. There was of course no final announcement to this effect, given that the magazine, like most, was not a true collective but a heterogeneous mix of different voices under loose editorial oversight. The first sign that such an endorsement was at hand occurred when the opposition began to melt away. The detractors did not necessarily change their minds, they simply pulled out of the debate and changed the subject, while occasionally voicing mild lamentations. Leonard Feather signaled his disengagement from the debate with a genial two-part interview of Archie Shepp in his notorious "Blindfold Test" column, where previously he had provoked musicians (Miles Davis and Oscar Peterson in particular) to lambaste the jazz avant-garde.[66] This freed the defenders from the acrimony of debate, to allow them to author dispassionate disquisitions on the stylistic and formal innovations of the avant-garde and its place in the jazz tradition—a key ingredient in any process of canonization. Thus, *Down Beat*'s resident theorist, musician-critic Don Heckman, celebrated "the year of the breakthrough for the avant-garde" with a magisterial summation of the various musical strains and developments in the avant-garde's short history and the specific contributions of each of the major players.[67] The endorsements spread beyond the jazz field to the major centers of middlebrow culture (e.g., feature articles in *The New York Times, Newsweek*). There was even a small acknowledgment from the "classical" avant-garde music field, when Charlotte Moorman produced the first of the annual "Jazz Nights" at the 1965 Festival of the Avant-Garde at Judson Hall.[68]

Though a story of aesthetic triumph, this is not a triumphalist story. Canonization provided only a small spike in market demand for the jazz avant-garde before its economic blight further deepened. The avant-garde's bleak financial straits were only the most extreme manifestation of a general economic malaise afflicting the whole jazz field, as rock 'n' roll, buoyed by a newfound status among sophisticated adults, was increasingly encroaching into jazz's traditional consumer base. The jazz magazines responded by joining the enemy: in 1967, *Down Beat* decided to cover rock music as well, and *Jazz* magazine, that erstwhile champion of the avant-garde, changed its name to *Jazz and Pop*. Meanwhile a new genre, later called "jazz-rock" fusion, appeared on the scene, pushing the avant-garde from center stage and contesting its claim to be the future of jazz. Even within the BAM, some suggested that it was the pop soul music of James Brown and Otis Redding, and not the avant-garde, that truly spoke to the aspirations of African Americans.[69] Many of the avant-garde left New York in the late 1960s, some for the more receptive climate in Europe, others for academic positions now being made available for the first time. In this period of crisis, the avant-garde did not lose its canonic status, it just got marginalized—another instance of economics trumping aesthetics.

Notes

1. For a helpful history of the 1960s jazz avant-garde, see Iain Anderson, *This Is Our Music: Free Jazz, the Sixties, and American Culture* (Philadelphia: University of Pennsylvania Press, 2007).

2. Ben Young, *Dixonia: A Bio-Discography of Bill Dixon* (Westport, Conn.: Greenwood, 1998), 339–43.

3. Ibid., 344–47; Dan Morgenstern, "The October Revolution: Two Views of the Avant-Garde in Action," *Down Beat* (November 19, 1964): 15.

4. Martin Williams, "The October Revolution: Two Views of the Avant-Garde in Action," *Down Beat* (November 19, 1964): 15.

5. Morgenstern, "October Revolution," 15.

6. Ibid.; Young, *Dixonia*, 344.

7. Young, ibid., 339–43; Morgenstern, "October Revolution," 15, 33; Williams, "October Revolution," 15, 33.

8. Young, ibid., 348.

9. Ibid.

10. On Chicago, see George E. Lewis, *A Power Stronger than Itself: The AACM and American Experimental Music* (Chicago: University of Chicago Press, 2008). On St. Louis, see Benjamin Looker, *BAG: "Point from Which Creation Begins": The Black Artists Group of St. Louis* (St. Louis: Missouri Historical Society Press, 2004). On Los Angeles, see Steven L. Isoardi, *The Dark Tree: Jazz and the Community Arts in Los Angeles* (Berkeley and Los Angeles: University of California Press, 2006).

11. Young, *Dixonia*, 348–50; see also Robert Levin, "The Jazz Composers Guild: An Assertion of Dignity," *Down Beat* (May 6, 1965): 17–18. For the best and most complete history of the JCG, see Benjamin Piekut, "Race, Community, and Conflict in the Jazz Composers' Guild," *Jazz Perspectives*, forthcoming.

12. More research needs to be done on this important African American artistic community in New York's Lower East Side. For a good introductory account, see the special issue of *African-American Review* (27, no. 4 [Winter 1993]) devoted to that topic.

13. LeRoi Jones (Amiri Baraka), *Blues People: Negro Music in White America* (New York: William Morrow, 1963).

14. See Young, *Dixonia*, 29–66, for a wonderfully detailed documentation of Dixon's and Shepp's downtown careers between 1961 and 1963.

15. On the travails of Cecil Taylor, see A. B. Spellman, *Four Lives in the Bebop Business* (New York: Pantheon, 1966), 1–76; Bill Coss, "Cecil Taylor's Struggle for Existence," *Down Beat* (October 26, 1961): 19–21; Nat Hentoff, "The Persistent Challenge of Cecil Taylor," *Down Beat* (February 25, 1965): 16.

16. See George E. Lewis, "Improvised Music after 1950: Afrological and Eurological Perspectives," *Black Music Research Journal* 16, no. 1 (1996): 91–122.

17. See Piekut, "Race, Community," for a detailed account of the inner debates and tensions of the JCG that ultimately led to its demise.

18. "Jazz Composers Schedule '4 Days in December' Fete," *The New York Times*, December 26, 1964, 7. The first night featured the Cecil Taylor Unit and Bill Dixon Sextet; the second the Paul Bley Quintet and the Jazz Composers Guild Orchestra (formed by Carla Bley and Mike Mantler); the third night the Archie Shepp Quartet and the Free Form Improvisation Ensemble; and the final night the Sun Ra Arkestra and the John Tchicai-Roswell Rudd Quartet. See also Young, *Dixonia*, 354–55.

19. John Wilson, "Dig that Free Form Jazz," *The New York Times*, January 24, 1965, X13.

20. John Wilson, "Avant-Garde Jazz Series Offers Cecil Taylor and Dixon Quintet," *The New York Times*, December 29, 1964, 20.

21. John Wilson, "Concert Unveils Free-Form Jazz,"*The New York Times*, December 30, 1964, 14.

22. John Wilson, "Shepp Is Heard in Jazz Concert," *The New York Times*, December 31, 1964, 13.

23. A. B. Spellman, "Jazz at the Judson," *The Nation* (February 8, 1965): 149–51.

24. Ibid., 150–51.

25. Ad in *Village Voice*, December 31, 1964, 6; cited in Young, *Dixonia*, 356.

26. Spellman, "Jazz at the Judson," 149; Wilson, "Dig That Free-Form Jazz," X13.

27. Young, *Dixonia*, 356–68.

28. Williams, "October Revolution," 33.

29. See, for example, Dan Morgenstern, "Caught in the Act," *Down Beat* (February 25, 1965), 15.

30. Blue Note BLP 4225, Blue Note BLP 4224. On Coleman's return from retirement, see John Litweiler, *Ornette Coleman: The Harmolodic Life* (New York: William Morrow, 1992), 108–20; and Peter Niklas Wilson, *Ornette Coleman: His Life and His Music* (Berkeley, Calif.: Berkeley Hills Books), 46–49.

31. See for example, Dan Morgenstern, "Ornette Coleman: From the Heart," *Down Beat* (April 8, 1965): 16–18.

32. John Coltrane, Ascension, Ed. 2, Impulse, 903212–2, 90322–2.

33. On Coltrane and *Ascension*, see Ben Ratliff, *Coltrane: The History of a Sound* (New York: Farrar, Straus and Giroux, 2007), 99–103; Ashley Kahn, *The House that Trane Built* (New York: Norton, 2006), 131–38.

34. Kahn, ibid., 120–23, 135–40.

35. See the Impulse Records Discography Project at http://www.jazzdisco.org/impulse/ (accessed October 6, 2007).

36. Clifford Allen, "Bernard Stollman, the ESP-Disk Story" (interview), http://www.allaboutjazz.com/php/article.php?id=19661 (accessed September 19, 2007). On Ayler at the Cellar Café, see Young, *Dixonia*, 341; and Jeff Schwartz, *Albert Ayler: His Life and Music*, chap. 2, 1963–64, http://www.geocities.com/jeff_l_schwartz/chpt2.html (accessed September 19, 2007).

37. ESP-Disk Records Catalog: 1000, ORO Twelve-inch series, http://www.jazzdisco.org/esp/1000-cat/a/ (accessed October 9, 2007).

38. Unlike the JCG, the Association for the Advancement of Creative Musicians in its initial declarations was already foregrounding aesthetic issues. See Lewis, *A Power Stronger than Itself*.

39. "The Avant-Garde: Pro and Con," *Down Beat* yearly supplement, *Music '65* (1965): 88–95.

40. For an attempt to elaborate the various forms and structures at work in free jazz, see Ekkehard Jost, *Free Jazz* (New York: Da Capo, 1994).

41. Comment by Williams, "The Avant-Garde," 88.

42. Comments by Williams and Heckman, ibid., 90–91.

43. Ibid., 93.

44. See comments by Gitler and Schliltten, ibid., 90, 92.

45. Morgenstern, "October Revolution," 15.

46. Comment by Williams, "Avant-Garde,"92.

47. Williams, "October Revolution," 33.

48. Opening statement, "Avant-Garde," 88. See also, Morgenstern, "October Revolution," 33.

49. "Avant-Garde," 89, 93–94.

50. See Bernard Gendron, *Between Montmartre and the Mudd Club: Popular Music and the Avant-Garde* (Chicago: University of Chicago Press, 2002), 138–57.

51. Amiri Baraka, *The Autobiography of LeRoi Jones* (Chicago: Lawrence Hill, 1997), 293–328.

52. For accounts of the Black Arts Movement, see Larry Neal, "The Black Arts Movement," *The Drama Review* 12, no. 4 (1968): 29–39; Jim Smethurst, *The Black Arts Movement: Literary Nationalism in the 1960s and 1970s* (Chapel Hill: University of North Carolina Press, 2005).

53. Baraka, *The Autobiography of LeRoi Jones*, 307.

54. On Coleman, see Morgenstern, "Ornette Coleman: From the Heart," *Down Beat* (April 8, 1965): 16–18; and Charlie Russell, "Ornette Coleman Sounds Off," *Liberator* (July 1965): 12–15.

55. LeRoi Jones (Amiri Baraka), *Blues People: Negro Music in White America* (New York: William Morrow, 1963); LeRoi Jones (Amiri Baraka), "Jazz and the White Critic," *Down Beat* (August 15, 1963): 16–17, 34, reprinted in Jones (Baraka), *Black Music* (New York: William Morrow, 1968), 11–20. For an excellent account of Baraka as jazz critic, see John Gennari, *Blowin' Hot and Cool* (Chicago: University of Chicago Press, 2006), 264–89.

56. Jones (Baraka), "Jazz and the White Critic," in *Black Music*, 14–15.

57. Jones (Baraka), *Blues People*, 129–30.

58. Lawrence P. Neal (Larry Neal), "The Black Writer's Role," *Liberator* (June 1960): 7–9.

59. L. P. Neal (Larry Neal), "Black Revolution in Music: A Talk with Drummer Milford Graves," *Liberator* (September 1965): 14–15.

60. LeRoi Jones (Amiri Baraka), "Archie Shepp Live," *Jazz* (January 1965): 8–9; LeRoi Jones (Amiri Baraka), "Voice from the Avant-Garde: Archie Shepp," *Down Beat* (January 14,1965): 18–20, 36.

61. Jones (Baraka), *Down Beat*, "Voice from the Avant-Garde," 36.

62. See Harry Gilroy, "Racial Debate Displaces Jazz Program," *The New York Times*, February 10, 1965, 47.

63. Archie Shepp, "An Artist Speaks Bluntly," *Down Beat* (December 12, 1965): 11, 42.

64. Leonard Feather, "Feather's Nest: A Plea for Less Critical Infighting, More Attention to the Music Itself," *Down Beat* (December 12, 1965): 13.

65. "Point of Contact: a Discussion," in *Down Beat* yearly supplement, *Music '66* (1966): 19–31, 110–111; Archie Shepp, "A View from the Inside," *Down Beat* yearly supplement, *Music '66* (1966): 39–42, 44.

66. Leonard Feather, "Blindfold Text," *Down Beat*, part 1 (May 5, 1966): 35; part 2 (May 19, 1966): 39, 41.

67. Don Heckman, "Breakthrough '66," *Down Beat* yearly supplement, *Music '67* (1967): 14–17.

68. Dan Morgenstern, "Caught in the Act," *Down Beat* (October 21, 1965): 32.

69. Laurence P. Neal (Larry Neal), "The Black Musician in White America," *Negro Digest* (March 1967): 53–57.

11

American Cultural Diplomacy and the Mediation of Avant-garde Music

Danielle Fosler-Lussier

During the cold war, many musicians from the United States traveled to distant places under the sponsorship of the U.S. government. They were sent to enhance the reputation of American culture; to compete with Soviet and Chinese performers; to forge personal connections with citizens of other lands; and to create a positive impression of the United States and its foreign policy.[1] The most vigorous government effort to sponsor musicians' tours was the State Department's Cultural Presentations program, which subsidized tours to politically important regions where commercial tours would be financially infeasible.[2] Conductors, composers, and lecturers on music also traveled under the American Specialists program, and some American embassies and diplomatic posts sponsored their own concerts. These efforts, combined with privately funded tours, amounted to a substantial and lasting effort to expose people all over the world to American culture.

As a wealthy nation with a short history, the United States was reputed to favor industry over art: in the words of Congressman Frank Thompson, Jr., the young superpower needed to prove "that we are by no means a Nation of mere 'cultural barbarians.'"[3] From its inception in 1954, therefore, the Cultural Presentations program promoted art music in the classical tradition: several symphony orchestra tours received particular attention and acclaim. Despite the focus on high culture, avant-garde music was absent at the outset, in part due to congressional opposition. (One official noted that "the American Congress hates to think that we are sending Cubist art to the Hottentots."[4])

Even the professional musicians on the Music Advisory Panel, which approved performers and programs, doubted the propaganda value of avant-garde music. When in 1955 the Music Panel considered a proposal by John Cage, David Tudor, and the Merce Cunningham Dance Company, the composer William Schuman "said they are too esoteric, and it would be a gamble to send them."[5] The Music Panel ultimately approved the tour, but the Dance Panel rejected it, and Cunningham would wait until the 1960s for approval to tour under government auspices.[6] Likewise, the pianist Paul Jacobs, a passionate advocate for new music, was rejected in 1960 because "his very limited repertory would appeal to a limited audience": the panel simply did not envision an opportunity to use him.[7]

Although early, narrow definitions of quality remained influential, by the 1960s the range of cultural presentations had widened to include avant-garde music as well as jazz and popular music. Democratic movements in Africa and elsewhere increased the political power of average citizens and students, making it more important for the United States to reach beyond elite audiences; and the civil rights struggle in the United States required explanation abroad.[8] These factors introduced a new emphasis on African American music—including jazz, spirituals, blues, and gospel—and a new willingness to include popular or entertainment music that would not have been considered at the outset of the program. With these urgent propaganda needs to meet and limited funding available, it is all the more remarkable that officials found a niche for avant-garde music in government-funded music programs—a curious role for music that was unlikely to reach these broad target audiences. Using music known for its "outsider" status as propaganda required intensive mediation; when this music was sent from the United States to people elsewhere, it was reframed by its association with the U.S. government, by efforts to explain and promote the music, and by audiences' expectations. The use of avant-garde music in American propaganda therefore offers a new angle on claims that the avant-garde became "institutionalized" during this period, as well as an opportunity to evaluate the music's artistic and political reception both abroad and in the United States.

As we begin, it is important to recognize that U.S. government programs did not represent a coherent or univocal position. Many different individuals and agencies had a stake in the musicians' tours. These included but were not limited to the State Department, the United States Information Agency (USIA), the Operations Coordinating Board and the National Security Council, the Central Intelligence Agency, the Department of Defense, the U.S. Congress, the artists, arts administrators, and patrons who served on the United States Advisory Committee on the Arts, the American National Theatre and Academy, the Music Advisory Panels, ambassadors and other Foreign Service officers at diplomatic posts, impresarios and agents, the hundreds of amateur and professional musicians who asked to tour for the government, the musicians who actually did tour, and their audiences at home and abroad. The interaction among the musical and political agendas of these stakeholders shaped what the tour program would become. For instance, congressional reluctance to fund the tours made the State Department cautious about choosing music that might offend American citizens (who would write to their representatives after reading reports of the tours in the press); Department officials therefore chose performers more conservatively, especially at the outset, than they might otherwise have done. Conflicting aims of this kind resulted in a program that reflected not certainty or coherence, but only a compromise among dozens of people in the fields of intelligence, statecraft, and music.

Regional Aims and Opportunities for Avant-garde Music

The major stimulus for using avant-garde music as propaganda was the need to improve the cultural reputation of the United States in Europe. Attempts to address this issue with more traditional art music during the 1950s had won over a portion of the European public, but had profoundly alienated some intellectuals there.[9] In 1966 the American composer Gunther Schuller wrote to Minister John Calhoun of the U.S. Mission in Berlin that

> official international exchange programs have tended to emphasize to the point of exclusivity the same dozen older and—by advancing standards— more conservative composers, who were the mainstay of American composition in the thirties and early forties, but who no longer represent current activity. Every time we present one of these composers to the exclusion of more recent trends, we damage our cultural image.[10]

State Department officers took such criticisms seriously, for they were well aware that European intellectuals valued avant-garde music. In 1967, when the composer Paul Creston wanted to lecture in Europe on American music under the auspices of the American Specialists program, the Music Panel rejected him as "a very conservative composer" and not representative of current American trends.[11] Some Foreign Service officers actively sought out avant-garde musicians in order to attract audiences of young intellectuals: for instance, the American Embassy in Vienna tried to secure visits from Schuller and Earle Brown during this period.[12]

An ambitious government-funded event that offers some perspective on the State Department's concerns took place in May 1966 when the Centre Culturel Américain in Paris sponsored a festival of American avant-garde music, organized by the American composer Donald Harris (see table 11.1). Reviewers characterized the festival as "probably the first festival of contemporary American music ever to be given in Europe" and called it "an affirmative answer to the question: 'Do the Americans have a culture?'"[13] The American Embassy reported to the State Department that "the Festival achieved an impact vastly more profound than is indicated simply by attendance figures or reviews."[14] Despite the enthusiastic characterization of the festival's artistic success, the ambassador noted:

> It might have been better to hold this Festival in a major European capital other than Paris. Paris is notoriously difficult to impress musically. The voguish anti-Americanism prevalent in some circles affected the press coverage of the Festival. For reasons all their own, the ultra-modernists of Paris (the "Boulez School") virtually boycotted the concerts. . . . The Post believes, nonetheless, that the Festival was a significant landmark in Parisian musical life and that benefits will be reaped for some time to come as a result of such pioneering. However, given the nature of the Paris musical world, the Post does not plan to repeat the Festival.[15]

The Embassy's estimation that cutting-edge composers were not reached seems unfounded, because in fact many well-known advocates of advanced musical styles did attend the concerts, including André Boucourechliev, André Hodeir, Gilbert Amy, Betsy Jolas, Franco Donatoni, Paul Méfano, Jean Barraqué, Alexander Goehr, Francis Miroglio, Henry Barraud, and Henri Dutilleux. Several reviews of the festival reflected negative stereotypes about American music, characterizing some works as uninteresting or banal; but even these contained some praise for the forward-looking style of Charles Ives's Fourth Symphony and the freshness of Stanley Silverman's *Planh* and David Reck's *Number 2*.[16] Other comments were positive: Brigitte Schiffer called the performances "brilliant," "subtle," "bold," and "impressive," and Jacques Bourgeois, who was otherwise caustic, referred to Schuller as "a sort of American Boulez."[17] Elsewhere, the State Department might have considered this a coup, but the Parisian environment raised the political standard for success to an unattainable level.

In addition to the desire to compete with European music according to what was perceived as its predominant scale of value, the other factor that made American avant-garde music suitable for propaganda was its embodiment of desirably American features. In 1966 the University of Illinois Contemporary Chamber Players, a student group, offered "a Happening of assorted electronics, instrumental sounds, and vocal eruptions" in London after stops at the Warsaw Autumn Festival, Darmstadt, Cologne, and Paris. A review from the London press emphasized the music's novelty and insouciance as positive American traits: "If hard pressed to search for the divergencies between the British and the American way of life there is always the University of Illinois to fall back on. The cheerful disregard for academic decorum shown by the Players is as yet unrivaled in music departments over

Table 11.1   Works Presented at the Festival of Contemporary American Music, Paris, 1966

Harvey Sollberger	Variations for 12 instruments and chef d'orchestre
Stanley Silverman	*Planh* [for solo guitar and seven instruments]
David Reck	*Number 2* for 7 musicians
Charles Wuorinen	Chamber Concerto for violoncello and ten instruments
Eugene Kurtz	*Conversations* for 12 instruments
Elliott Carter	Double Concerto for harpsichord, piano and two orchestras
George Rochberg	Duo for violin and cello
Igor Stravinsky	Duo concertante
Donald Martino	Sonata for solo violin
George Crumb	*Night Music* for violin and piano
Charles Ives	Sonata no. 2 for violin and piano
Ross Lee Finney	Three Pieces in Fours
James Randall	*Mudgett*
Leslie Bassett	Three Studies in Electronic Sound
George Wilson	Fragment (1964)
Mario Davidovsky	*Synchronisms no. 1* for flute and magnetic tape
Chou Wen-Chung	*Cursive*
Stefan Wolpe	Piece in two parts
Milton Babbitt	*Relata*
Gunther Schuller	*Spectra*
Samuel Barber	*Knoxville Summer of 1915*
Charles Ives	Symphony no. 4

here."[18] Liberation from conventions sometimes served as a musical analogue for political or social freedom and was an important selling point for American experimental music.[19]

In Eastern Europe, where avant-garde music was long the subject of diatribes and sometimes of state-ordered suppression, U.S. officials could use this music to challenge socialist realist standards and to connect with listeners, particularly young people, who wanted alternatives to socialist realism. As the 1960s progressed, more avant-garde music and jazz was permitted in Eastern Europe; as a result of these styles' suppression, they had acquired an appealing association with freedom that remained potent even after the music had become accessible again.[20] When the La Salle Quartet traveled to Yugoslavia and Poland in 1962, Yugoslav musicians asked them to discuss modern music, especially that of Alban Berg and Anton Webern.[21] Likewise, in 1965, when the Juilliard Quartet was planning a trip to the Soviet Union, the Music Panel encouraged them to choose "more modern" music than Debussy and Ravel, suggesting Webern, Arnold Schoenberg, and Alberto Ginastera as suitable alternatives. (The Panel also named Elliott Carter, Charles Ives, Samuel Barber, Walter Piston, and William Schuman as American options; this relatively conservative list may have reflected their own preferences as well as the likelihood that experimental music would be rejected by the Soviet officials who negotiated the content of tours.)[22] Officials from the USIA provided scores and recordings of new music to conductors and composers in Eastern Europe as a means of encouraging styles that were not officially sanctioned.[23]

American musicians who visited Eastern Europe typically found that some audience members were actively seeking the newest music. The American Embassy in Moscow reported in 1966 that jazz audiences included "the very 'hep,' who inquire why we don't send Charlie Mingus or John Coltrane rather than old timers like Earl Hines."[24] When William Sydeman, a composer of atonal music, visited Eastern Europe on a specialist grant, he brought with him scores and recordings of modern American music (see table 11.2): according to Sydeman, "the more avant-garde the music the better they liked it." Like Schuller, Sydeman criticized the State Department's musical conservatism: "I can guarantee that East European audiences (and I am equally sure west as well) are more than prepared for the work of our younger 'experimental' composers and would welcome it. They have heard the Barber and Copland Sonatas and the Gershwin Rhapsody and should not be led to believe that this is the only compositional activity occurring in America."[25] As composers, of course, Sydeman and Schuller were far from disinterested; their advocacy and that of composers on the Music Panel surely enhanced the role of the State Department as a supporter of new music.

By the late 1960s, American avant-garde performers not only had access to Eastern European stages, but could even achieve acclaim in the press there. The Alwin Nikolais Dance Theatre performed in Budapest in June 1969; the American Embassy reported that the audience was "apparently stunned by the initial piece with its electronic music, abstract rear-projection and emphasis on the linear," but "warmed up" and "showed its amusement at the light-hearted antics of *Tower*, in which the dancers suddenly address the audience with parts of meaningless conversations, spoken simultaneously." An enthusiastic Hungarian newspaper review, quoted in an embassy report, proclaimed: "Nikolais's human, artistic and ethical viewpoint is attractive . . . this is not art for art's sake, nor is it for the sake of sensation, but reflects a true sense of responsibility and strength in art."[26] The review demonstrates how far avant-garde art had come toward acceptance in Eastern Europe: the author applied socialist-realist concepts to Nikolais's radical form of theater and found that the art exemplified all the correct qualities. American officials regarded such successes as indicators of progress in the cultural cold war.

In Asia, Africa, and Latin America, the role of the avant-garde in American cultural diplomacy was much more difficult for officials to define. In these regions, Western art music was unfamiliar to most of

Table 11.2   Works Taken to Eastern Europe by William Sydeman, 1966

Charles Ives	Symphony no. 4
Roger Sessions	String Quartet
Milton Babbitt	Composition for Synthesizer
Aaron Copland	Dance Symphony
Elliott Carter	Double Concerto
Leon Kirchner	Double Concerto
Carl Ruggles	*Sun Treader*
Lukas Foss	*Echoi*
John Cage	*Wonderful Widow*
William Mayer	*Overture for an American*
Alvin Etler	Brass Quintet
Ralph Shapey	*Evocations*
Billy Jim Layton	String Quartet
Larry Austin	Improvisations for jazz group and orchestra
Roger Reynolds	*Quick Are the Mouths of Earth*
Mario Davidovsky	Electronic Studies
Charles Wuorinen	*Electronic Exchanges*
Harvey Sollberger	Chamber Variations
David Del Tredici	*I Hear an Army*
Harold Shapero	Symphony for Strings
Donald Martino	*Parisonata*
Henry Weinberg	String Quartet
William Sydeman	Various works including Music for Flute, Viola, Guitar and Percussion

the population, and the legacy of colonialism meant that vastly different cultural and educational experiences separated the elite social strata from everyone else. The latter situation caused conflicts over what music to send: USIA officials never reached consensus about whether their target for cultural propaganda was a mass or an elite audience.[27] Cultural Affairs officers representing the United States at various diplomatic posts indicated to the State Department that there were "two types of audiences" and that it was "imperative to cater to both." The post in Manila described an "upper class society set—sophisticated, well-educated people thoroughly familiar with the American scene, appreciative of the best" and "in the provinces...more naive, uncritical audiences who are pleased by almost any attraction." An officer in Argentina described an almost identical scene.[28] The problem, then, was finding music that might address both intended audiences, for it was difficult to pinpoint the social implications of any musical style or its attractiveness to audiences according to the simple opposition of mass and elite. (The appeal of a Copland ballet or a modern jazz combo, to name just a few examples, was neither definitively "elite" nor "mass," and the unpredictable tastes of audiences, varying in each locale, would determine how the music was received.)

At some diplomatic posts, officers were willing to take a chance on avant-garde attractions because they themselves liked the music: after Merce Cunningham's visit to Mexico one official expressed excitement about the revelatory performance in a manner that suggested more than a casual familiarity with modernism.[29] Other posts, however, requested only jazz, variety shows, and revues, thinking (rightly or wrongly) that their audiences would not respond to Western art music.

It was often but not always taken for granted that avant-garde music, and even art music in general, could reach only a tiny fraction of the audience in the developing world. From time to time during Music Panel deliberations, the question was raised whether art music could be made accessible to more people. When the Claremont Quartet offered concerts, lecture-demonstrations, and workshops in Kenya, including a range of music from classic to avant-garde, the post reported that "the Quartet revolutionized musical education there by showing that it was possible to interest Africans with no musical education at all in the most sophisticated kind of western music, chamber music."[30] Members of the quartet suggested to a foreign service officer in Peru that "totally unsophisticated audiences can enjoy, appreciate and benefit from excellently performed concerts of chamber music"—but the officer commented to the State Department, "We are doubtful."[31] At a 1963 Music Panel meeting, Mark Schubart, the former dean of the Juilliard School, challenged the idea that only popular music should be sent to Africa. The minutes record this exchange between Schubart and Glenn Wolfe, director of the Cultural Presentations program:

> Mr. Schubart commented that when we talk about sending attractions to Russia or the Orient, we are not instructed to appeal to the lowest tastes; why are we in a different position when sending attractions to Africa? Mr. Wolfe replied because in Africa you have an extremely limited number of educated people; there is an 8% literacy rate.... Mr. Schubart said that when you want to do something about the literacy rate, you don't send comic books. Are we to give the Africans attractions commensurate with their literacy, or win them over to the enjoyment of something better?[32]

Although the Music Panel could guide the State Department, the experts in intelligence and diplomacy would ultimately determine what would be sent. (The Claremont Quartet and the Dorian Woodwind Quintet did travel to Africa with mixed programs including some avant-garde music as a break from the standard fare of jazz and popular music; at times they lightened their programs by playing individual movements rather than entire works. See table 11.3.)[33] The presence of avant-garde music in the Cultural Presentations program was explained as a direct appeal to the most elite audiences; the evaluations of tours by the posts and by the State Department frequently reported that the performances were extremely important to a very small number of influential people.[34]

Table 11.3   Sample Programs, Claremont Quartet

Beethoven	String Quartet op. 18 no. 4
Bartók	*Contrasts*
Mel Powell	*Filigree Setting*
Fauré	Piano Quartet
Haydn	String Quartet op. 76 no. 4 ("Sunrise")
Quincy Porter	String Quartet no. 6
Brahms	Clarinet Quintet

In some cases, it appears that officials considered the provocative quality of avant-garde music a positive feature, much as the music's other advocates did. When the Dorian Quintet included Morton Subotnick's *Misfortunes of the Immortals,* along with works of Mozart and Milhaud on its Asian tour, the reception of the Subotnick work was mixed, with the post in Ceylon calling it "counterproductive" and New Delhi reporting that even lovers of Western music were "bothered and bewildered." In the State Department's estimation, the Subotnick performance could not be called "an artistic success" but it was nonetheless important "because it stimulated debate about the future of the arts."[35] The post in Cairo likewise referred to the "healthy dialogue" instigated by the Paul Taylor Dance Company.[36] One might question whether such dialogue was significant, given the dramatic economic and social problems faced by many of the recipient nations; but officials' comments imply that they considered the kind of open debate fostered by avant-garde music a useful step toward democratization.[37]

The Avant-garde "Gift Economy" in the Developing World

The tours of avant-garde artists under the Cultural Presentations program share some aspects of the "gift economy" that has been described by anthropologists. This tradition of writing includes the following central concepts: the recipient of a gift incurs obligations or a lowering of social status; the circulation of gifts defines social relationships, including power relations; and even gifts that appear to be free can be given with self-interest.[38] A "gift" in this sense is far from altruistic: the giver expects some form of reciprocation, and the recipient's obligation can be weighty and lasting. The ephemeral nature of a musical performance makes it an unusual form of gift for consideration in these terms. As Annette Weiner has pointed out, however, some possessions can be given away and yet kept at the same time: these "are imbued with the intrinsic and ineffable identities of their owners."[39] The music performed on government-sponsored tours can be construed as part of such a gift economy; avant-garde music in particular bore qualities of identity and value that made it an effective instrument for diplomacy.

Certainly the prestige of high culture was a factor in the decision to use it despite its limited appeal. State Department officials thought it wise to send not only popular music but also chamber music to Africa because "it would prove to them that we consider them our cultural equals."[40] Nicolas Slonimsky, a Music Panel member who had traveled to the Soviet Union to evaluate the possibilities for cultural programming, remarked in 1970 that "countries are offended when less advanced composers, such as Barber and Copland, are offered to them."[41] In this context, the music of the avant-garde was participating in a symbolic system where its "advancedness" was important to its value.[42] The very act of sending recondite music was meant to indicate a social judgment about its recipients that was independent of how much enjoyment or intellectual stimulation the actual performance might offer.

In some instances, the compliment was taken in exactly those terms. When the Merce Cunningham Dance Company visited Caracas in August 1968, some audience members walked out on the performance. Nonetheless, the English-language *Daily Journal* reported that the Cunningham group felt that "the Venezuelan audiences understood them better than all the others, were more sophisticated in their reactions and were more sympathetic to experimental and modern techniques—than the audiences in the great capitals of Mexico City, Rio and Buenos Aires." The article's author understood the compliment as elevating Caracas within the order of cities; but his words also reflect a humble willingness to take the Cunningham dancers' opinion as definitive: "We are proud that the Caracas audiences struck them as their best."[43] Likewise, when the Claremont Quartet gave a concert and a seminar in Asyut, United Arab Republic (now Egypt), a student asked them to describe their impressions of the audience at their concert.[44] A critic in Melbourne, Australia, chided the public in his review of the New York Chamber Soloists (see table 11.4). He cited the presence of only 250 people at the concert as a "display of apathy" and stood in judgment over his city: "we disgraced ourselves."[45] In these cases the gift of an avant-garde musical performance brought the abasement of the recipients before the United States as gift-giver. This dynamic was absent from the Western European tours; there, audiences were more likely to stand in judgment over the Americans than to allow themselves to be judged by them. In other cases, the compliment did not necessarily evoke a lowering of social status, but a more neutral acknowledgment of the performers' abilities. When audiences disliked the music, Foreign Service officers often claimed in their reports that the listeners did appreciate the unique skills and effort that went into the performance.

The logistical arrangements preferred by the State Department may have combined with the genre of the music to raise the status of some community members in the recipient countries. Diplomatic posts often arranged concerts together with local impresarios; usually the impresario

Table 11.4   Sample Programs, New York Chamber Soloists

Vivaldi	Concerto in G minor for flute, oboe, violin, cello, and harpsichord
Lester Trimble	Petite Concert, for tenor, oboe, violin, and harpsichord
Mozart	Quartet in D major for flute, violin, viola, and cello, K. 285
Elliott Carter	Sonata for flute, oboe, cello and keyboard
Handel	Three arias from "Acis and Galatea" for tenor, oboe, strings, and continuo
Telemann	Cantata no. 64, "Pache dich, gelahmter Drache" for tenor, violin, cello, and keyboard
Wallingford Riegger	Duo for flute and oboe, op. 35
Riegger	Trio for violin, cello, and piano, op. 1
Handel	"Crudel tiranno Amor," cantata for tenor, violin, viola, cello, and keyboard
Mel Powell	Eight Miniatures for baroque ensemble
Mozart	Quartet in F major, for oboe, violin, viola, and cello, K. 370
Bach	Cantata No. 189, "Meine Seele rühmt und preist"

assumed certain costs and split the proceeds with the State Department. Such an agreement potentially carried prestige as well as financial risk for local presenters. After the Contemporary Chamber Ensemble appeared in Taiwan, "the impresario remarked that although he lost money, he was glad to have been the one to introduce this type of music to Taiwan."[46] When American performances failed, of course, there was a cost both to American prestige and to the local organizers. After a poorly received performance in Arequipa, Peru, by John Eaton, a composer of electronic music, the American ambassador reported to USIA: "I understand that an empresario who puts on concerts in Lima commented that it will take some time for the Eaton performance to be lived down."[47]

The competitive aspect of the program makes it both like and unlike the systems of gift-giving described in the anthropological literature. In those systems, gift-giving was described as competitive in a reciprocal way: individuals would, over time, take both the giver and recipient roles, with the giver temporarily assuming a higher-prestige position. Cold war cultural presentations were generally not reciprocal. The gift-givers were overwhelmingly the superpower nations—the Soviet Union, China, and the United States, with European countries figuring importantly but secondarily—and the recipients were the other nations of the world, whose allegiance to the superpowers was considered to tip the balance of power. The State Department routinely evaluated the success of its tour program by comparison to its competitors. In 1958, officials considered altering their programs toward more popular music because the Russians were winning over audiences with circuses.[48] The aforementioned enthusiastic officer at the post in

Mexico reported jubilantly that the Cunningham Dance Company had shamed the Soviets with a standing-room-only workshop: "In comparison, the 'Stars of the Bolshoi Ballet,' who, tutu-clad, 'pretty,' and swaying to the remembered melodies of Tchaikovsky, were drawing hordes of middle-brows to the cavernous Auditorio Nacional, seemed to be the expression of a dull, conformist and very 'square' 19th century society."[49] Only in the case of U.S.-Soviet exchanges were the tours reciprocal, and then very strictly so, counted ensemble by ensemble, in order that neither nation would gain the upper hand.[50]

Both the vast geographical distances between givers and recipients and the fact that they were not personally acquainted also differentiate this situation from the typical gift economy. Any gift can be construed as a medium that constructs social relations; however, the presentation of avant-garde music in non-Western contexts required not only the performance itself as a medium but also a host of other forms of mediation. The success of these performances invariably relied on a barrage of publicity and explanation, though publicity alone could not guarantee success. When the José Limon Dance Company appeared in Taipei, for example, the American Embassy produced an extensive array of supportive materials and events, including illustrated magazine feature stories, a bilingual souvenir brochure, a special window display in the Embassy's information center, advertising, handbills, posters, newspaper articles and interviews, and letters to important community members. The embassy also organized special music listening hours in the information center along with a lecture-discussion on contemporary music and dance. A television spot, radio announcements, the presentation of taped music and interviews, and live broadcasts of the company's performances ensured adequate attention to the tour both before and during the performances.[51] Other diplomatic posts distributed free tickets or even transported audience members to the theaters: when the New York Chamber Soloists presented a program of classic and contemporary music in Manila in 1969, "ticket sales were slow and center organizers brought busloads of students to fill seats."[52] When the Merce Cunningham company traveled to Rio de Janeiro, the publicity campaign included newspaper advertisements, posters, handbills, people carrying signboards in front of the theaters, radio and TV coverage, press conferences, and interviews. Especially in cases where the music was unfamiliar to local concert reviewers, newspaper coverage for a given concert often relied heavily on the texts of official press releases, making them a particularly important means of disseminating information about American music to publics abroad; new press releases about Cunningham were issued daily to ensure continuing attention throughout the group's stay.[53]

The model of the gift economy cannot completely describe the phenomenon of cold war cultural presentations. Not only the fact of gift giving mattered but also the content of the given performance: officials and musicians alike were eager to make an aesthetic connection with audiences, not merely a political impression. The failure to move audiences aesthetically was sometimes noted explicitly as a difficulty to be overcome. For instance, in a 1963 Music Panel meeting, Glenn Wolfe reported regarding Central Africa, "The fact that we sent them Louis Armstrong was a great compliment and they came by the thousands to see him, but then they walked away. His music did not mean anything to them."[54] Of course, the nature of a musical impression is impossible to ascertain from audiences' outward behavior, and it is difficult to know what precisely was meant by statements that a particular performer was "completely misunderstood" (as was reported about the Martha Graham Dance Company in provincial Asian cities).[55] In most cases, Foreign Service officers seem to have assessed "understanding" according to the general appearance of appreciation on the part of the audience.

"Far Out" Music and Its Official Frame

If the role of an avant-garde is to overturn or break down the norms of an art form, the removal of avant-garde music to distant places presented the challenge of a new context where the relevant norms were not necessarily present.[56] Critics abroad seem to have understood the works mainly as innovations within the Western concert tradition rather than as norm-breaking occurrences. The presentation of mixed programs of classics and avant-garde music may have strengthened this tendency by emphasizing both kinds of music as part of a single tradition. The American avant-garde works may even have seemed supremely normative in their new contexts: because the United States was offering them as its finest and newest art, these presentations may have been understood as representing an American standard of excellence, or rather one standard in an array of normative options that included the variety of representative styles sent to any one region by the program. In this sense, we might conclude that the aesthetic radicalism of avant-garde music was muted both by its geographical displacement and by its presentation as openly acknowledged propaganda.

Any attempt to describe the music sent by the State Department as aesthetically compromised, however, is complicated by the differing perspectives of the numerous constituents involved. The question of co-optation is meaningless from the perspective of recipient audiences who did not necessarily judge art on the basis of its novelty or its independence from politics. The American public and critics did use those terms, but as we shall see, applied them selectively. The State Department intervened in the details of some musical programs much more aggressively than others, depending in part on the genre of the music; and the public's judgments about co-optation were based not on those interventions in artistic decisions, but on perceptions of what social and political roles different kinds of musicians should play. The different treatment of popular music, avant-garde jazz, and avant-garde art music highlights some of the factors involved in perceptions of co-optation.

In at least one instance the association with the State Department was judged to be compromising: the U.S. reputation of the jazz-influenced rock group Blood, Sweat, and Tears was affected by the musicians' decision to tour for the Department. The band had strong antiestablishment credentials: individual members had publicly criticized the government's involvement in the Vietnam War, and the group had performed at a Yippie youth event and at the 1970 Winter Festival for Peace.[57] Before the tour, some of the band members vehemently stated that they were representing American youth, not the State Department, to the extent that some citizens and congressmen complained that they were unfit representatives.[58] The band played many of their hit songs on their wildly successful tour; the only interventions regarding programming came from Eastern European officials seeking to limit the social unrest caused by excited crowds at the concerts. When Blood, Sweat, and Tears returned to the United States, however, they were labeled as co-opted: the Yippies picketed their concert at Madison Square Garden, handed out flyers that called them "pig-collaborators," accused them of "complicity in spreading lies, racism, and imperialism," and called on the public to stop buying albums and attending concerts. A protester also threw a bag of manure onto the stage.[59]

Whereas the Yippies' grounds for protest were clearly political, it is more difficult to pin down the reasons for the decline in critical reputation that followed the tour. Blood, Sweat and Tears had reached a pinnacle of popularity in 1970, beating the Beatles' *Abbey Road* for the Grammy award for best album; but after the tour their appeal waned.[60] Some critics claimed they had never liked the band's sound because it lacked spontaneity and was too commercial.[61] Others objected to the band's appeal to "older, more sedate and straighter folks."[62] These judgments mix elements of political and musical criticism to the extent that the two are difficult to separate. One letter-writer to *The New York Times* explicitly preferred the musical over the political, but did so in a way that shows the relevance of both: "Of course, the group's musical sellout is connected to their growing establishmentarianism in the political field. . . . The reason B, S and T could not play at a rock festival today is not that their politics would be scorned, but that their music, or rather Muzak, would be laughed at."[63] The group's cooperation with the State Department may have contributed to their declining popularity among young people, despite the fact that the Department did not exert control over what they played or what they said.

By contrast, the avant-garde presents the opposite scenario: avant-garde musicians generally avoided accusations in the American press of aesthetic or political compromise, despite some official interventions in the content of the programs. This is particularly evident in the case of avant-garde jazz. Program officials treated jazz as the equivalent of art music in some respects. Much like art music, jazz boasted experts, advanced techniques, and noncommercial respectability; these features made jazz easier to justify to Congress and the public. The Cultural Presentation Committee of the Operations Coordinating Board praised the Dizzy Gillespie and Louis Armstrong tours for attracting "serious music students and lovers of fine music."[64] In Europe, propaganda focused not on jazz's popularity but on its "historical significance," offering "lectures and study groups" to elevate the genre's standing.[65] It is also noteworthy that the music professionals on the Music Advisory Panels tended to refer to both avant-garde jazz and avant-garde art music using the same term, describing music in either genre as "far out."[66]

The 1967 tour of the avant-garde jazz musician Charles Lloyd and his ensemble was evaluated in terms very similar to those used for other avant-garde music in Eastern Europe: a State Department official called the performance

> a huge step away from what Bucharest audiences are used to. No one among the Romanian audience had ever heard anything approaching a program of unrehearsed, extemporaneous musical sounds. Others who considered themselves jazz enthusiasts could not adjust to the non-traditional jazz program without tuneful or clearly recognizable compositions. For something so new to Bucharest, the reaction was remarkably good.[67]

The themes of novelty, difficulty, and success framed in relative terms compare closely with Department evaluations of Cunningham and other avant-garde artists. The diplomatic post in Romania wrote of Lloyd's tour:

> [W]e can say that the U.S. gained by showing the variety of musical expression which thrives there, and that we have enhanced the reputation of the U.S. as a progressive country in the performing arts. This is important particularly among the younger people of Bucharest who would like more freedom of expression.[68]

Here again, the post's emphasis on diversity, progress, and freedom is very similar to typical evaluations of avant-garde art music tours.

Nonetheless, differences in program officials' handling of avant-garde art music and avant-garde jazz suggest that the latter remained the greater challenge to their sensibilities and to their skill as propagandists. In particular, the State Department intervened much more in the programming of jazz musicians; they demanded significantly more flexibility from jazz performers about what music they would play on tour, and they praised those who were "clever enough to sense the preferences and comprehension-level of audiences in each city."[69] In part, this disparity was due to the nature of the art music being performed: while most groups received some guidance about their programs from the Music Advisory Panels and the State Department during the selection process, in the case of fixed scores or choreographed performances the Department knew specifically what it was approving, while the content of jazz performances could be more fluid. At times, however, the Department would approve a jazz attraction, but then ask them to play music that was entirely different from what had been approved. When the Randy Weston Sextet toured in Africa for four months in 1967, this practice caused considerable conflict. The Department reported great frustration that although the Weston group had been told to prepare for "a different situation than they would find in Europe or Japan," the sextet still "preferred to play his own music, which was very sophisticated, even when the posts advised that the audience would like to hear 'When the Saints Come Marching In.'"[70] Weston had been chosen because his compositions reflected African influences; and Georgia Griggs, who traveled with the band, noted with acrimony:

> [T]hose in charge of the program in Washington had seen the group in concert, playing just what they'd be playing on the tour. If they knew what they wanted and knew what they were getting, why did they try to make us feel that the sextet should have been a Dixieland band or a drum troupe?[71]

Griggs characterized the Department's concerns that audiences might not "understand" modern jazz as "patronizing and colonialist."[72] The Department was willing to take advantage of the high-culture associations of sophisticated jazz: in its report to Congress, the Department quoted an assertion by the American Embassy in Rabat, Morocco, that "the Weston group clearly established American superiority in the jazz field."[73] At the same time, even though Weston reportedly succeeded with some audiences, there remained great anxiety about whether avant-garde jazz could reach the right listeners in the right way.[74] Musicians in the art-music tradition, on the other hand, were not generally asked to change programs suddenly in this manner, although they were sometimes criticized by the posts for their failure to be flexible or to choose repertory appropriate to their audiences.[75] Despite these conflicts, it would be overly reductive to speak of systematic and intentional aesthetic co-optation in government music programs, for official efforts to alter the content of performances were sporadic.

It is striking that the collaboration of avant-garde jazz musicians with the State Department did not seem to affect the public's perception of them or give rise to accusations of compromise. Like Blood, Sweat and Tears, Randy Weston was sharply critical of American society; but the jazz press did not respond to his tour by condemning his cooperation with the State Department. Because Charles Lloyd had a wider fan base than most jazz artists, he was vulnerable to the charge of selling out to the market; one writer criticized Lloyd as a "dabbler" in jazz, and another accused him and his manager George Avakian of over-promotion.[76] Yet even though such antigovernment figures as psychedelics and hippies were attending Lloyd's concerts, I have yet found no evidence that connects the musical critiques to Lloyd's role in musical diplomacy.[77] Perhaps jazz was insulated from this kind of criticism by its more consistently marginal social position: far from denouncing the inclusion of jazz in the program, critics had fought for it, both as a means of supporting musicians financially and as a way to publicize good music.[78] Still less were the avant-garde art music tours affected; critics seem to have taken for granted that these products of high culture would be suitable for representing the state, and their presence on the tours generated no special comment from the American press. The unproblematical reception of the musicians' tours by U.S. critics confirms that by the 1960s, music in difficult styles was well integrated into the more general idea of "high art." It retained its connotation of "advancedness," and thereby its usefulness to the State Department, without arousing protest at home.

Avant-garde music was protected from accusations of artistic co-optation by its status of institutionalized outsiderhood; yet its mediation as propaganda also undeniably altered its implications. In hindsight, it would be easy to dismiss the U.S. government's cultural efforts as artistically insignificant because they were propaganda; but to do so would be to deny the intrinsic value of the art and the capacities of the thousands of audience members who attended these performances. It is more fitting to regard the music sent abroad by the U.S. government as both a real effort to reach people artistically and a form of political propaganda.[79] Further study may shed light on the local and personal consequences of these performances in their recipient countries. It seems evident that the presentation of avant-garde music shaped the identities of both its givers and its recipients, defining artistic and political relationships with a vast global reach.

My thanks to Donald Harris for the use of his personal papers; to Angela Hand and Ben Levy for research assistance; and to Emily Abrams Ansari and Steven F. Pond for their thoughtful comments.

Notes

1. See Leo Bogart, *Cool Words, Cold War: A New Look at USIA's Premises for Propaganda*, rev. ed., abridged by Agnes Bogart (Washington, D.C.: American University Press, 1995), 88, 91.

2. Cultural programs were eventually transferred to the United States Information Agency. See Wilson Dizard Jr., *Inventing Public Diplomacy: The Story of the U.S. Information Agency* (Boulder: Lynne Rienner, 2004), 177–78.

3. "Latest Cold War Weapon Widely Supported by United States Press and Democratic Members of Congress," Extension of Remarks of Hon. Frank

Thompson, Jr., in the House of Representatives, 84th Cong., 1st sess., *Congressional Record*, Appendix (June 27, 1955): A4692. See also Thompson, "Are the Communists Right in Calling Us Cultural Barbarians?" *Music Journal* 13, no. 6 (July/August 1955): 5, 20.

4. Bogart, *Cool Words, Cold War*, 30.

5. New York Public Library, Papers and Records of William Schuman, Series I (hereafter NYPL-Schuman), 2/2. Minutes of the Music Advisory Panel, February 8, 1955, 4.

6. Music Panel member Virgil Thomson supported the tour. See Naima Prevots, *Dance for Export: Cultural Diplomacy and the Cold War* (Hanover, N.H.: University Press of New England, 1998), 53–58.

7. NYPL-Schuman, 3/2. Minutes of the Music Advisory Panel, September 14, 1960, 4.

8. See Jeremi Suri, *Power and Protest: Global Revolution and the Rise of Détente* (Cambridge, Mass.: Harvard University Press, 2003); Penny Von Eschen, *Satchmo Blows Up the World: Jazz Ambassadors Play the Cold War* (Cambridge, Mass.: Harvard University Press, 2004); and Von Eschen, "Who's the Real Ambassador? Exploding Cold War Racial Ideology," in *Cold War Constructions: The Political Culture of United States Imperialism, 1945–1966,* ed. Christian Appy (Amherst: University of Massachusetts Press, 2000), 110–31.

9. See Danielle Fosler-Lussier, *Music Divided: Bartók's Legacy in Cold War Culture* (Berkeley and Los Angeles: University of California Press, 2007), 89–93.

10. Gunther Schuller to John Calhoun, U.S. Mission Berlin, February 1966, 1–2. University of Arkansas Library, Special Collections, MC468: Bureau of Educational and Cultural Affairs Historical Collection (hereafter ARK), Group IV, box 147, folder 50 (hereafter abbreviated in the form IV, 147–50).

11. Minutes of the Music Advisory Panel, February 21, 1967, 10; ARK II, 99–20.

12. Guy E. Coriden to Thomas Huff, April 19, 1967; ARK IV, 147–50.

13. Jan Maguire, "Paris Hears 20th-Century U.S. Music." Clipping, Donald Harris papers (privately held, uncataloged).

14. "Educational and Cultural Exchange: Report on 'Festival of Contemporary American Music.'" American Embassy Paris to State Department, September 3, 1966. Donald Harris papers.

15. Ibid.

16. Jacques Bourgeois, "En 1910, Ives avait 40 ans d'avance: Paris découvre sa musique"; Jacques Lonchampt, "Domaine américaine," *Le Monde;* Olivier Alain, "Concert américain d'avant-garde," *Le Figaro*. Clippings, Donald Harris papers.

17. Brigitte Schiffer, "Amerikanische Musik aus erster Hand," *St. Galler Tagblatt,* Sunday edition, no. 258, June 5, 1966; Bourgeois, "En 1910, Ives avait 40 ans d'avance." Donald Harris papers.

18. *Cultural Presentations USA 1966–1967. A Report to the Congress and the Public by the Advisory Committee on the Arts, with an added section on athletic programs* (Department of State Publication 8365, International Information and Cultural Series 95, 1968), 45–46.

19. See "Music from America," clipping enclosed in George D. Henry to Charles M. Ellison, October 7, 1966; ARK II, 81–21. On American experimental music in Europe, see Amy Beal, *New Music, New Allies: American Experimental*

Music in West Germany from the Zero Hour to Reunification (Berkeley and Los Angeles: University of California Press, 2006).

20. See Fosler-Lussier, *Music Divided*, xv, 149–56; and Peter Schmelz, *Listening, Memory, and the Thaw: Unofficial Music and Society in the Soviet Union, 1956–1974* (Ph.D. diss., University of California, Berkeley, 2002).

21. Memorandum of Conversation, Mr. Walter Levin, La Salle Quartet, Mr. Ralph Jones, Mr. James A. Duran Jr., April 8, 1963. National Archives of the United States at College Park, Maryland, Record Group 59, Records of the Department of State (hereafter NARA, RG 59), Subject-Numeric File 1963, box 3255.

22. Minutes of the Music Advisory Panel, March 3, 1965, 3; ARK II, 99–20.

23. See, for example, State Department to American Embassy Bucharest, November 26, 1968. NARA, RG 59, Subject-Numeric File 1967–69, box 327.

24. American Embassy Moscow to State Department, September 6, 1966; ARK II, 66–14. See also Nicolas Slonimsky's remarks in the Minutes of the Music Advisory Panel, December 9, 1966; ARK II, 99–20.

25. William Sydeman, "Report on Tour of Eastern Europe", ARK IV, 148–5.

26. American Embassy Budapest to State Department, June 27, 1969. NARA, RG 59, Subject-Numeric File 1967–69, box 322.

27. See Bogart, *Cool Words, Cold War*, 51–59.

28. "Staff Study on Embassies' Reactions, Suggestions and Comments on Effectiveness of Various Categories and Aspects of Cultural Presentations," 5, 6; ARK II, 94–14.

29. American Embassy Mexico to State Department, September 4, 1968; ARK II, 59–23.

30. State Department to various posts, March 8, 1965; ARK II, 59–2.

31. American Embassy Lima to State Department, September 29, 1965; ARK II, 96–14.

32. Minutes of the Music Advisory Panel, July 24, 1963, 8; ARK II, 99–19.

33. Evaluation Report, Claremont Quartet; ARK II, 96–13; "Chamber Music Is a Hit in Africa," *The New York Times*, May 11, 1964, 38.

34. For examples, see Evaluation Report, Claremont Quartet, ARK II, 96–16; Evidence of Effectiveness Reports, Alvin Ailey in Africa, ARK II, 97–1; American Embassy Buenos Aires to State Department, October 13, 1968, ARK II, 59–23; American Embassy Mexico to State Department, September 4, 1968, ARK II, 59–23. In Tunis, Randy Weston's performance enabled American access to previously unavailable political officials; see USIS Tunis to USIA Washington, September 5, 1967, ARK II, 85–2.

35. Evidence of Effectiveness Report, Dorian Woodwind Quintet, May–June 1970, ARK II, 97–4.

36. American Embassy Cairo to State Department, February 1, 1967, ARK II, 97–11.

37. Sometimes tours were perceived as a waste of resources in the face of dire economic need. See Warner Lawson to Roy Larsen and the Advisory Committee on the Arts, "Report of Tour to Africa, Bonn and Frankfort, Germany and Luxembourg," 3, ARK II, 94–14; and Evaluation Report, Cozy Cole (fy1962), ARK II, 96–12.

38. See Marcel Mauss, *The Gift: The Form and Reason for Exchange in Archaic Societies*, trans. W. D. Halls (1923–24; London: Routledge, 2001); and, on the

subject of reciprocity, *The Gift: An Interdisciplinary Perspective*, ed. Aafke Komter (Amsterdam: Amsterdam University Press, 1996), part 1.

39. Annette Weiner, *Inalienable Possessions: The Paradox of Keeping-While-Giving* (Berkeley and Los Angeles: University of California Press, 1992), 6.

40. Bureau of Educational and Cultural Affairs, "Paper for the Advisory Committee on the Arts on the Fiscal Year 1964 Cultural Presentations Program Planning for Africa," ARK II, 94–14.

41. Minutes of the Music Advisory Panel, May 26, 1970, 5, ARK II, 99–21. A similar point was made at the Music Panel meeting on September 26, 1967, 2, ARK II, 99–21.

42. Philip Ford makes a parallel argument about jazz musicians and political radicalism in *American Popular Music in the Cold War: The Hip Aesthetic and the Countercultural Idea* (Ph.D. diss., University of Minnesota, 2003), 80.

43. "The Caracas Audience: 'Receptive' and 'Sympathetic,'" *Daily Journal*, August 21, 1968, in American Embassy Caracas to State Department, August 27, 1968, ARK II, 59–23.

44. Jay Walz, "Claremont Group Cheered in U.A.R.," *The New York Times*, March 4, 1964, 33.

45. John Sinclair, "Good Music, Free—but No Audience," (Melbourne) *Herald*, September 8, 1969, ARK II, 73–19.

46. American Embassy Taipei to State Department, April 15, 1976, ARK II, 59–15.

47. American Embassy Lima to USIA, August 5, 1974, ARK II, 61–2.

48. James Magdanz, "Recent Developments in the Cultural Presentations Program," page A-19. In Transcript of Proceedings, Third Meeting of the Advisory Committee on the Arts, October 7, 1958. NARA, RG 59, Entry 5079, CU/ACS Records of the United States Advisory Commission on the Arts, 1951–60, box 158.

49. American Embassy Mexico to State Department, September 4, 1968, ARK II, 59–23.

50. U.S.-Soviet exchanges were governed by the Lacy-Zarubin agreement and subject to constant and vigorous negotiation. See Yale Richmond, *Cultural Exchange and the Cold War: Raising the Iron Curtain* (University Park: Pennsylvania State University Press, 2003), 14–19.

51. American Embassy Taipei to State Department, September 3, 1963, in NARA, RG 59, Subject-Numeric File 1963, box 3256.

52. American Embassy Manila to State Department, September 30, 1969, ARK II, 73–19.

53. American Embassy Rio de Janeiro to State Department, received September 12, 1968, ARK II, 59–23.

54. Minutes of the Music Advisory Panel, July 24, 1963, 8, ARK II, 99–19.

55. Edward Mangum to Robert Schnitzer, "Third Tour of Asia for I.E.P.," January 25, 1957, 3, 4, 22, New York Public Library, Billy Rose Theatre Collection, Schnitzer (Robert C.) and Cisney (Marcella) Papers, box 5, folder 10.

56. See Peter Bürger, *Theory of the Avant-Garde*, trans. Michael Shaw (Minneapolis: University of Minnesota Press, 1984).

57. Nicholas von Hoffman, "Yippies Unveil 'Politics of Ecstasy,'" *The Washington Post*, March 20, 1968, A3; Don Heckman, "Pop," *The New York Times*, February 8, 1970, 114.

58. Sally Quinn, "Dissidents As Envoys," *The Washington Post*, June 13, 1970, C1. See the letter from Louise Patterson to Mrs. John Richardson, June 15, 1970, ARK II, 57–2; and John Richardson Jr., "Only if asked" statement, June 16, 1970, ARK II, 57–4.

59. Mark Lewis, "Radical Left—Yippies—Attacks Blood, Sweat and Tears," ARK II, 57–3.

60. A 1973 concert was canceled for lack of ticket sales. See "B,S&T, Mayfield Canceled," *The Washington Post*, June 22, 1973, B12.

61. Peter Gorner, "B, S and T Still Have the Touch of Midas," *Chicago Tribune*, August 23, 1970, F3; Tom Zito, "Blood, Sweat and Tears: No Spontaneity," *The Washington Post*, March 8, 1971, B10; James Lichtenberg, "Making Rock Respectable," *The New York Times*, February 28, 1971, D15.

62. Tom Zito, "B, S, &T: 'Devoid of Feeling,'" *The Washington Post*, September 3, 1971, B1.

63. Tom O'Brien, letter to the *The New York Times*, August 23, 1970, D25.

64. Cited in Kenneth Osgood, *Total Cold War: Eisenhower's Secret Propaganda Battle at Home and Abroad* (Lawrence: University Press of Kansas, 2006), 226. The Operations Coordinating Board was an interagency group that coordinated foreign policy and actions during the Eisenhower administration.

65. "Report on the European Trip of David S. Cooper, September 25–November 9, 1956," 3, NYPL-Schuman, 42/4.

66. See, for example, ARK XIX, 351–2, oral history transcript, interview with Thomas Huff, 164 (regarding Lloyd); ARK II, 99–20 (regarding the Contemporary Chamber Ensemble).

67. Thomas Huff, Memorandum: ACA Monthly Bulletin no. 3 (November 1967), ARK II, 95–1.

68. Ibid.

69. American Embassy Moscow to State Department, September 6, 1966, ARK II, 66–14.

70. Minutes of the Sub-Committee on Jazz, May 12, 1967, ARK II, 98–27. See also American Embassy Libreville to State Department, January 11, 1967, ARK II, 85–1; American Embassy Niamey to State Department, February 11, 1967, ARK II, 85–1.

71. Georgia Griggs, "With Randy Weston in Africa," *Down Beat* 34 (July 16, 1967): 17.

72. Ibid. See also Von Eschen, *Satchmo Blows Up the World*, 170–77.

73. *Cultural Presentations USA 1966–1967*, 38.

74. On Weston's successes, see American Embassy Algiers to State Department, April 13, 1967, ARK II, 84–26; American Embassy Cairo to State Department, April 1, 1967, ARK II, 84–26; Harry Hirsch to Thomas Huff, March 28, 1967, ARK II, 84–26; American Embassy Dakar to State Department, January 20, 1967, ARK II, 84–26; American Embassy Rabat to State Department, April 11, 1967, ARK II, 85–2. The Department's conflict with Weston likely contributed to the decision not to have the prominent avant-garde jazz saxophonist Ornette Coleman tour for the program. Minutes of the Sub-Committee on Jazz, August 30, 1967, ARK II, 101–3.

75. [George West,] "Contemporary Chamber Ensemble East Asian Bicentennial Tour," ARK II, 59–15.

76. Brian Priestley, "Charles Lloyd and Roland Kirk," *Jazz Monthly* 13 (December 1967): 7; Hollie West, "'Jazzman of '67' More of a Dabbler," *The*

Washington Post, January 28, 1968, E2; Chris Albertson, "Charles Lloyd," *Down Beat* 36 (September 4, 1969): 23–24.

77. Bob Houston, "Charles Lloyd: A Song to Sing, Dance to Dance." *Melody Maker* 42 (June 3, 1967): 6.

78. See Robert Sylvester, "Dream Street," *Daily News*, September 8, 1956.

79. The point that an act can be both at once is made by Kenneth Osgood in *Total Cold War*, 185.

12

From Scriabin to Pink Floyd

The ANS Synthesizer and the Politics of Soviet Music between Thaw and Stagnation

Peter J. Schmelz

Leon Theremin (1896–1993), known in Russia as Lev Termen, is the name most often associated with electronic music from the former Soviet Union. In 1920 Theremin developed his eponymous instrument, played by a performer who conjured sounds seemingly "from the ether," gesturing with her hands near, but not touching, a small box with protruding antennae.[1] After securing Lenin's imprimatur and the admiration of Soviet listeners—scientists and workers alike—Theremin predictably embarked on a Soviet agitprop tour. During his Soviet demonstrations, local newspapers touted the Theremin, or the "Termenvox" as it was called by the Russians, as a "musical tractor coming to replace the wooden plough" and proclaimed that "the problem of producing the ideal instrument is solved."[2] Yet upon Theremin's return to the USSR after his decade-long United States residence (from 1927–38) as both inventor and Soviet spy, he was dispatched to the Kolyma Gulag camp and his instrument was all but forgotten. Like many aspects of Soviet society, experiments in electronic music halted under Stalin, and the Soviet Union was not to witness an invention similar to Theremin's until the late 1950s, when the first Soviet synthesizer was developed. And like the Theremin—famously used by the Beach Boys in their 1966 number one hit "Good Vibrations"—this synthesizer, the ANS, was lauded by Soviet officialdom and in the end was appropriated by rock musicians. In the process, it played a unique role in the complicated cultural politics of late Soviet music, "academic" and otherwise.[3]

The ANS was invented and first heard in the years of increasing freedoms spurred on by Khrushchev following Stalin's death in 1953, referred to in Russia as the Thaw or *Ottepel*.[4] The composers who were schooled during this period—including Alfred Schnittke, Edison Denisov, and Sofia Gubaidulina—were able to obtain formerly prohibited scores ranging from Arnold Schoenberg to Pierre Boulez, scores they avidly imitated in their compositions. The 1950s and 1960s also witnessed the development and flourishing of a small but important subculture of unofficial music in the main Soviet urban centers, including Moscow, Leningrad, Kiev, and Tallinn. Audiences were drawn by the novelty, exoticism, and perceived illegality of the new music they heard, and attending these unofficial concerts became a means of circumventing, reinterpreting, and undercutting the dominant socialist realist aesthetic codes. One of the most important venues for unofficial concerts in Moscow during the late 1960s and early 1970s was the electronic music studio at the Scriabin Museum that housed the ANS.

The Scriabin Museum proved an appropriate venue as the synthesizer had been named after Scriabin (Alexander Nikolayevich Scriabin), a hero of its inventor Yevgeniy Murzin (1915–1970).[5] Murzin had been a military engineer in the Second World War, and his friends and former colleagues in both the military bureaucracy and in the Communist Party allowed his studio and its weekly concert series to continue.[6] The history of this machine therefore traces a strange trajectory from its solitary inventor to the highest official supporters at the Union of Composers, the Ministry of Culture, and even the Central Committee of the Communist Party, ending up in the 1970s as a centerpiece for "academic," "avant-garde" experimentation, progressive rock concerts, and Happenings. Leading Soviet unofficial composer Andrey Volkonsky, the first of his generation to write serial compositions, was also one of the first composers to work with the ANS, beginning in 1958 or 1959.[7] By the end of the 1960s, Denisov, Schnittke, and Gubaidulina had tried their hands at composing with the synthesizer. And in the mid-1970s the ANS and a new generation of synthesizer called the Synthi-100 served as instruments for the progressive rock group Boomerang. The story of the ANS and the group of composers and performers attracted to it embodies the paradoxes and contradictions of unofficial Soviet music and its politics during the 1960s. Moreover, it provides an important encapsulation of unofficial concert life in transition between the period of Khrushchev's "Thaw" and that of Brezhnev's "Stagnation." Specifically, the ANS highlights the significant shifts in generations, musical styles, and the possibilities for resistance that took place in Soviet music around 1970.

The electronic studio at the Scriabin Museum illustrates one important aspect of postwar Soviet musical life: the existence of venues that while not wholly official, survived nonetheless thanks to official subsidies. Yet the exceptional history of the Scriabin Museum also offers a necessary refinement and counterexample to anthropologist Alexei Yurchak's recent trenchant critique of binary interpretations of the Soviet "regime." In his anthropological and theoretical examination of the "Last Soviet Generation," Yurchak takes to task writers who emphasize binary oppositions like: "Oppression and resistance, repression and freedom, the state and the people, official economy and second economy, official culture and counterculture, . . . and so on."[8] In response he formulates a more nuanced view of life under what he calls "late socialism," describing those "milieus" that existed at the margins of official Soviet structures—like literary clubs or archaeological circles—with the Russian word *Vnye*. *Vnye* literally means "outside," but for Yurchak it denotes "contexts that were in a peculiar relationship to the authoritative discursive regime—they were 'suspended' simultaneously inside and outside of it, occupying the border zones between here and elsewhere." He elaborates upon *vnye* as follows:

> The meaning of this term . . . is closer to a condition of being simultaneously inside and outside of some context. . . . Being *vnye* was not an exception to the dominant style of living in late socialism but, on the contrary, a central and widespread principle of living in that system. It created a major *deterritorialization* of late Soviet culture, which was not a form of opposition to the system. It was enabled by the Soviet state itself, without being determined by or even visible to it.[9]

Yurchak, himself a former late socialist, recognizes what most Western commentators miss: the fact that Soviet life was never clearly delineated between official and unofficial realms. No single, exclusive group held fast to the dictates of the party while another group doggedly resisted. Particular individuals certainly occupied the extremes, but the majority of Soviets lived in a gray zone in between. Yet because Yurchak's emphasis is on the generation "born between the 1950s and early 1970s," he misses out on the shifting meanings of unofficial Soviet culture of all genres, from progressive rock to "academic" chamber music, during the entire post-Stalin period (from 1953–91).[10] At certain moments during this period, music held more oppositional meanings for its auditors, creators, and performers. Much hinges upon the period under discussion. By the late 1970s and early 1980s, the period Yurchak is primarily describing, the implications and meanings of unofficial locales had altered. The perfectly balanced *vnye* milieus that Yurchak theorizes came into being in music only in the late 1960s, and specifically after 1968 and the Soviet invasion of Czechoslovakia, reaching their fullest form by the mid-1970s.

In the late 1950s and early 1960s when Volkonsky, Denisov, and many other young Soviets retreated into the abstract note counting of serialism, their audiences responded passionately to the novelty of the sounds that resulted, sounds vastly different from the "boring" sonic canvases of most socialist realist music (to borrow Marina Frolova-Walker's apt description).[11] Unofficial concerts of music by the young Soviets of the 1960s enabled listeners to carve out spaces free of official ideology from within venues supported by that very ideology—"suspended within," in Yurchak's formulation, but at that time implying a possibility of change or of some sort of opposition, however contingent. In part this was possible because in the 1960s listeners were more idealistic than they would be a decade later. As Natan Eydel'man has commented about the 1960s: "At that time there was a burning vision and a certain lifting of spirits that today strikes one as funny."[12]

The ANS studio and its changing constituencies (listeners, composers, performers) from the late 1960s to the mid-1970s offer an ideal opportunity to refine Yurchak's generalizations, while thereby further honing our understanding of his "late socialism," which I argue takes shape at this time through a gradual shift that occurs between 1968 and 1975. My previous research on Soviet music of the 1960s has primarily addressed the political and social meanings of its unofficial, "academic" music culture. In the present essay, with the Scriabin Museum's electronic music studio as the locus, I will consider the changing implications and status of both "academic" and more "popular" genres while exploring the tensions and occasional gaps between unofficial and official spheres—the developing nature of being *vnye*—within the Soviet culture of the late 1960s and early 1970s. The Scriabin Museum provides a crucial case study of the formation of Yurchak's "Last Soviet Generation." In particular, it illustrates an important moment of generational change, when the former "young composers" born in the 1930s encountered the tastes of a new musical generation born in the 1940s and early 1950s. Through a more thorough analysis of this generational shift we can observe the changing political meanings of unofficial music of all genres and styles against the backdrop of the Soviet state's final tumultuous decades.[13]

The Musical *Sputnik*

Although Murzin's formal training involved calculating artillery trajectories, "music was always his passion. He worshiped Scriabin."[14] According to official documentation, Murzin had considered building a synthesizer of sound as early as 1938 while still a graduate student.[15] Composer and sound engineer Stanislav Kreychi recalled that some time later Murzin developed and constructed it himself "somewhere at home in his dacha," finishing a working model in 1958.[16] He had been inspired by experiments with movie sound tracks and performances of filmed sound waves done by Russian scientist Evgeniy Alexandrovich Sholpo in the 1930s, experiments that probed the boundary between the aural and visual aspects of sound.[17] As a result, the synthesizer

Murzin developed was unlike any other synthesizer, in that the composer "drew" his composition on the apparatus by erasing portions of a resin-covered glass screen that responded sonically to the light that this erasing revealed (see figures 12.1, 12.2, and 12.3).

The technical aspects of the ANS have been described in detail elsewhere, but I will briefly summarize them before moving on to the broader musical and political ramifications of the instrument.[18] At the heart of the ANS lay a "bank of soundwaves" created by Murzin on a "disk, similar in appearance to a contemporary CD but made of photographic plate, with soundtracks printed on it, similar to those existing on a piece of film" (labeled 3 on figure 12.1).[19] Each disc contained 144

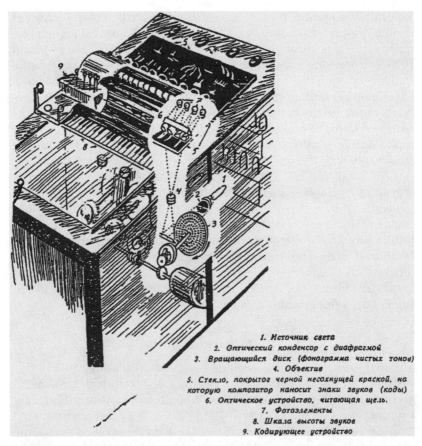

Figure 12.1 Diagram in A. Artem'yev, "Chto takoye ANS," *Sovetskaya muzïka* 2 (1962): 156. Text reads: 1. Light source, 2. Optical condenser and diaphragm, 3. Revolving disc (phonogram of pure tones), 4. Lens, 5. Glass, covered with black nondrying paint on which the composer draws the signs for the pitches (codes), 6. Optical mechanism, reading slit, 7. Photoelectric cells, 8. Scale for determining pitch placement, 9. Digitizing mechanism.

Figure 12.2   The ANS synthesizer (photo taken in 2000 by Peter Schmelz).

sound tracks inscribed in concentric circles, encompassing two octaves divided into 72 equal parts.[20] In all, Murzin created 5 discs containing 720 pure sounds or sine waves (from approximately 20 Hertz to 20,000 Hertz) that rotated at different speeds. These discs were rotated and had light passed through them, and the light was modulated accordingly. The light shining through the five rotating discs passed through a small "slit" (labeled 6 in figure 12.1) and was in turn filtered through the composer's etchings on the ANS's moving "score," the large piece of glass (labeled 5 in figure 12.1) covered by an opaque waxy resin, or mastic, that allowed the composer to target very specific points on the discs and enabled the combination and mixing of the sounds. After encountering the "score," the selected light then hit a photocell (labeled 7 in figure 12.1) and was transformed into an electronic signal that was subsequently realized as a sound. (If the mastic was entirely absent—i.e., the "score" was the clear glass plate—the listener would hear all 720 pitches simultaneously, i.e., ten octaves of twelfth-tones.) The "score" itself could be moved at any speed, either automatically or by hand, forward or backward, creating variations in the duration of sections within a composition or of an entire composition itself. Gleb Anfilov also reported in his primer on electronic music for children that a later development allowed the ANS to be performed "live" by six performers playing six separate keyboards attached to the machine, each keyboard tuned one-sixth of a half-step (i.e., a twelfth-tone) from the others, thereby encompassing all 720 pitches of the machine.[21]

Figure 12.3   The ANS synthesizer (photo taken in 2000 by Peter Schmelz).

Like the Theremin in the 1920s, but now fuelled by cold war concerns, the ANS played into the Soviet fascination with technology and the concomitant desire to keep up with Western scientific advances. The director of the Scriabin Museum, Tat'yana Grigor'yevna Shaborkina, made the point explicit: "The appearance of the ANS in our time, a time of conquering the cosmos, is not a chance occurrence. I think that Murzin's ANS is meant to create new musical rules, to create the music of the COSMOS."[22] Volkonsky made the same point in a letter of support he wrote for the ANS: "The apparatus ANS...is a revolutionary invention, worthy of its century, the century of Sputnik and flights to the cosmos."[23] Such rhetoric appealed directly to Soviet technological pride. Perhaps it is not surprising that the first piece written on the ANS (by Eduard Artem'yev and Kreychi) was called *To the Cosmos* ("V kosmos," 1961), although musically this atmospheric work was a conservative mixture of familiar harmonies interspersed with futuristic sound effects (Artem'yev would later become widely known as the composer of the sound tracks to Andrey Tarkovsky's films *Stal'ker* and *Solaris*).[24]

Not surprisingly, the ANS was taken on tour to London and Paris in 1961, and later in 1964 to Genoa, as a demonstration of the Soviet Union's technical prowess.[25] In correspondence related to funding mass production of the ANS for use throughout the Soviet Union, it was praised because it "surpasses in its capabilities all well-known foreign models of a similar type."[26] A. N. Kuznetsov, the deputy minister of culture of the USSR, made a similar claim in a letter of December 19, 1961, to S. Vladimirsky, the deputy chairman of the State Committee of the Union of Ministers of the USSR for Radioelectronics: "According to the conclusions of specialists, the ANS significantly surpasses well-known foreign achievements in this field."[27] Columbia University Professor and electronic music pioneer Vladimir Ussachevsky confirmed such proud statements in a letter of support he wrote for Murzin during his 1961 visit to the Soviet Union: "I hope that I myself will be able to add to those works that will appear [on the ANS]."[28]

Between 1960 and early 1962, as officials in the Union of Composers (including Dmitriy Shostakovich) and various other government agencies were discussing mass production of the ANS, the press coverage of the synthesizer in the Soviet Union was intense. The following excerpt from the journal *Young Guards* ("Molodaya gvardiya") is indicative:

> On the screen appears some kind of dome, inside of which are rows of chairs. In the chairs are people; elevated before us is an instrument similar to a piano; behind it is a musician. For some reason he delays. But now a man in light-weight clothing walks onto the stage and lifts his hand as if he were the conductor of an invisible orchestra. And immediately...the entire hall is filled with waves of music and light. Sounds, colors, colors as if penetrating the entire space under the dome, as if overflowing, interlacing; they sing a color symphony of all-victorious, multicolored life. And at some moment in the whirlwind of harmony, fire, colors, and sounds appears a voice, reading poems.... The screen slowly fades. The lantern again appears undistinguished, as if it had not just parted the curtain on a not-too-distant future, a future of "synthetic art" which Scriabin predicted half a century ago and which in the near future, possibly, will come true with the help of a new, perfected ANS.[29]

At this time, according to the September 7, 1961, *Moskovskaya Pravda*, a concert of electronic music occurred at the Ministry of Culture of the USSR consisting entirely of pieces written using the ANS: Artem'yev's *Nocturne* ("Noktyurn"); Kreychi's *Echo of the East* ("Otgolosok vostoka") and *On Vacation* ("Na otdïkhe"); and Alexander Nemtin's *Grotesque* ("Grotesk") and *Tears* ("Slyozï").[30] It was the first concert of synthesized music in the Soviet Union—although no doubt it did not resemble the lofty utopian vision of the *Young Guards* article. Recordings of only a sample of these compositions are available, but they reveal a general approach to using the synthesizer emphasizing atmospheric echo effects and other discordant and purposely "electronic" sounds, superimposed upon familiar tonal melodic and rhythmic figurations. Most of these composers blended the conservative and the novel, as Kreychi did in his *Echo of the East* with its snippets of pentatonicism interspersed with space-age blips and bleeps. Other later compositions by this core group of composers were more traditional, as was the case with Nemtin's ANS realization of Bach's C Major Chorale Prelude or Kreychi's tongue-in-cheek *Intermezzo* (which recall similar synthesized versions of canonic masterworks in the United States by contemporary performers like Wendy Carlos).[31]

Unfortunately, the high hopes of its supporters—composers and bureaucrats alike—fell flat when it came to funding, a fact that ultimately allowed the ANS to become a tool of the unofficial composers. In late January 1962 the commission appointed by the Ministry of Culture to investigate and evaluate mass production of the ANS eventually recommended the construction of between forty to fifty ANS machines that were to be distributed to various organizations and republics across the Soviet Union.[32] As revealed by the increasingly terse correspondence between the parties, including the Ministry of Culture and the factories responsible for producing the machines, these projections were ultimately lacking in financial support: the bureaucrats eventually fell to budgetary wrangling. All agreed that the mass production of ANS machines would be a fantastic idea, but no one wanted to pay for it.[33] In the end only one "improved" model was built.

After the construction of this single ANS—which Murzin noted in his scrapbook with a triumphant photograph of the factory-fresh machine annotated "January 1964—the experimental model of ANS is ready!"—the argument now became one of where to install it. The correspondence between the several candidates and the Ministry of Culture indicates that the long-running nominee for housing the new ANS was the Scriabin Museum.[34] In fact, Murzin's original model had been housed there since 1959, when V. A. Popov, the deputy chairman of the Committee for Matters of Inventions and Discoveries for the Union of Ministers of the USSR, had written to the head of the museum, Shaborkina, requesting that the machine be placed there.[35] A later attempt to move the ANS to the Museum of History and Reconstruction of the City of Moscow proved unsuccessful.[36] As noted above, in 1964 the machine was sent to a Soviet industrial trade show in Genoa, Italy. During the 1965 "Russian Winter" festival it was housed "for around a year" (Kreychi's words) at the "Radioelectronics" ("Radio-elektronika") pavilion at VDNKh (Exhibition of National Economic Achievements), an industrial theme park in northern Moscow that in the early 1970s became a venue for unofficial rock concerts.[37] In December 1966, however, supervision of the machine was given to the Melodiya record company and the Scriabin Museum officially became its home.[38] According to Minister of Culture Yekaterina Furtseva's official directive establishing the studio, its purpose was to foster "scientific research work" ("nauchno-issledovatel'skiye raboti").[39] The Scriabin Museum thereby housed the sole electronic music studio in the Soviet Union and the only Soviet synthesizer.

When it was moved to the Scriabin Museum, officialdom more or less lost track of the synthesizer, and the intensive press coverage ceased, although occasional articles did appear after 1966. Murzin also continued to attend foreign exhibitions to demonstrate musical works that had been composed on the ANS, traveling to Florence in 1968, Venice in 1969, and Orange (France) in 1970. After the 1968 demonstration at the

First International Symposium of Centers of Electronic Music ("I Convegno internazionale dei centri di musica elettronica") in Florence, *La Stampa* described with great interest the often "overlooked" electronic music center in Moscow.[40] Artem'yev also remembered that sometime around 1965 a mathematician named Boris Anan'yev even "wrote a code that first studied human speech...I think that in 1965 he greeted the country on the radio with an electronic voice saying 'Happy New Year' created on the ANS synthesizer."[41]

In the last years of the 1960s, concerts of electronic music were held at the Scriabin Museum featuring both Soviet compositions and compositions by Western composers like Karlheinz Stockhausen, György Ligeti, and Boulez.[42] These concerts were open to the public and attracted a wide audience, including students and scientists: "The fact of the matter was that the scientific world was present there all the time, since Murzin attracted people involved in science in order for them to help him further develop and build a new synthesizer....And therefore there were always a lot of scientists there. Of course, they unconditionally supported it."[43] Beginning in 1968 Murzin even allowed Lev Termen to hold seminars there on Wednesdays after he had lost his job at Moscow State University.[44]

At this point the history of the ANS moved from official to unofficial—although not *vnye*. Artem'yev described the not-quite-*vnye* atmosphere at the studio: "It was simultaneously 'underground' and an official studio. The studio was a special organism, therefore it drew everyone who was dissatisfied, who sought something new, wanted to become familiar with something, they came there."[45] It was this discontent among the studio's composers, performers, and listeners that prevented the *vnye* balance that Yurchak theorizes from fully coming into effect there at this time (or ever). Some of the "dissatisfied" young composers that the studio initially attracted included Artem'yev (b. 1937), Kreychi (b.1936), Sandor Kallos (b. 1935), Nemtin (1936–1999), and Oleg Buloshkin. By the early 1970s other Soviet composers like Andrey Eshpai (b. 1925), Gennadiy Gladkov (b. 1935), Yuriy Levitin (1912–1993), as well as Denisov, Gubaidulina, and Schnittke had also explored the machine's capabilities, but as Gubaidulina bluntly stated: "It is impossible to say that our activities [at the studio] turned out very productively. In one year we succeeded in writing only one composition apiece."[46]

The pieces the latter three wrote on the ANS (with Kreychi's invaluable assistance) were as varied as their musical personalities.[47] Schnittke's *Stream* ("Potok") (1969), a brief exploration of the overtone series moving from dissonant pitches to a "continuously varying tone and its overtones," traced a compositional plot of drawn-out crescendo followed by brief subsidence not unlike Schnittke's orchestral *Pianissimo* of the previous year.[48] Gubaidulina's *Vivendi non Vivendi* (1971) meshed ANS's electronic effects with prerecorded sounds, and was clearly inspired by earlier Western electronic compositions like Stockhausen's

Gesang der Jünglinge (1955–56). Gubaidulina described her composition's "subject" as the "opposition of sounds of natural origin with sounds synthesized artificially. Thus a lament, a sigh, a cry, laughter, the ringing of a bell come from natural sources, but are then gradually transformed into artificial sounds" —hence the title of the piece: "living non living." [49]

Denisov's *Singing of the Birds* ("Peniye ptits") (1969) took yet another tack: His composition combined actual birdcalls with electronic sounds and added a live improvised instrumental part to the whole. Like Gubaidulina's composition, Denisov's required the laborious process of splicing recordings of the ANS's synthesized sounds with tapes of recorded birdsong. [50] The instrumental part (the piece may be performed on any instrument) was purely graphic and improvisatory, but also strictly coordinated with the tape part, down to the second. In the graphic score, consisting of six concentric circles, the various signs are left open to the performer's (or performers') interpretation. As the always-rational Denisov tellingly explained: "Here nothing signifies anything, but everything should be logical."[51]

Because of the live performance component, which Denisov added because he felt that electronic music by itself was "dead," Denisov's composition had the widest resonance, especially when performed by young pianist Aleksey Lyubimov (b. 1944). [52] At its official premiere at a concert of the Union of Composers chamber music section at the House of Composers in Moscow on April 28, 1970, Lyubimov wore a bird outfit, a costume not approved of or even suggested by Denisov:

> I was barefoot with my pants cut off at the knees, in two bird masks, one on my face, another in darkness. Little bells were attached to my ankles and wrists. There were several very long, multi-colored ribbons on me that dragged behind me on the stage; they were attached to my arms, legs, and waist. [53]

Lyubimov justified his costumed performances as follows:

> It seemed to me that if there is a visual element to that composition, then you may also realize that visual element externally. *Singing of the Birds* is a piece that is not purely musical, but associative, and I thought that it was possible to present it in the spirit of the theater of the absurd. [54]

When Lyubimov appeared in this attire at the House of Composers, he recalled that "Denisov was in shock. . . . A scandal arose. The public really liked it, but there was unpleasantness in store for Denisov."[55] Denisov recalled that "[t]hey wrote, they appealed to the Central Committee, that it was a mockery of the public for a pianist to be dressed in a bird costume."[56] Denisov took the blame, although the idea had been Lyubimov's alone. As was typical for the time, performers were treated with more leniency than composers. In fact, Lyubimov went on to perform the work several more times in his costumed interpretation without any further repercussions. [57]

Lyubimov's premiere of Denisov's work demonstrates the difference between the atmosphere of the concerts at the House of Composers—because of its delicate balance of official and unofficial, a *vnye* venue par excellence by the early 1970s—and the Scriabin Museum, the source of the composition and by this time a venue far removed from official oversight. That *Singing of the Birds* proved so controversial at the House of Composers shows how far "out" the music at the Scriabin Museum had become, both literally and figuratively. The Scriabin Museum—and, by association, its products, like *Singing of the Birds*—threatened Yurchak's *vnye* balance, not only because it violated socialist realist criteria but also because it stood "outside" ("vnye") official power in a much more direct sense.

Crossing Over

None of the three older composers felt compelled to write additional electronic music using the ANS. Denisov reportedly found it a "device of little interest," and he produced no further electroacoustic composition until the impressionistically titled *In the Shroud of the Frozen Pond* ("Na pelene zastïvshego pruda") for nine instruments and magnetic tape, composed at Paris's Institut de Recherche et Coordination Acoustique/ Musique (IRCAM) in 1991.[58] As Artem'yev summarized: "They only wrote a single composition each. And for various reasons: Schnittke said that in general he didn't 'feel' electronics. Gubaidulina said that the quality of the sound didn't suit her, the sound wasn't alive. And Denisov was more interested in *musique concrete*."[59] As we will see, however, their passing association with the ANS was to remain an important factor in determining its fate.

The electronic music studio at the Scriabin Museum was protected during Murzin's lifetime by his connections within the Soviet government, and especially by a close friend of his, Ivan Kapitonov, who was a member of the Secretariat of the Central Committee of the Communist Party under Brezhnev: "And while Murzin was still alive, everyone was afraid of Kapitonov and were afraid of touching the studio. . . . But when Murzin died, everything immediately went away."[60] Yet the studio was not immediately closed after Murzin's death in 1970. Murzin's death marked a turning point in the studio's fortunes, but for a brief period from 1970 until 1974 Soviet officialdom temporarily abandoned, forgot about, or chose to ignore it. The older generation no longer dominated the events there; the studio actually became *vnye*— "outside"—albeit not in Yurchak's balanced, suspended sense.

By this time a younger generation of composers and performers, including composer Vladimir Martïnov (b. 1946) and violinist Tat'yana Grindenko (b. 1946), had taken over the studio. The tastes of older composers like Artem'yev also began to shift in response to the new musical currents. Murzin, who discovered Scriabin after an early infatuation with Duke Ellington, had encouraged the use of the ANS by "lovers of any music—symphonic or jazz."[61] After Murzin's death the younger generation followed his ecumenical wishes to the extreme, and the concert life at the museum changed drastically. No longer were concerts of electronic music the only offerings; instead, as Artem'yev described it, there were bona fide Happenings:

> They were concerts, the first experiments with light-music. There were laser installations. . . . It was not only our music, but rock music was especially popular. I remember one composition by Emerson, Lake and Palmer [ELP], called "Toccata," such energetic music. The concerts began with it. There were mimes, pantomime, with lasers, with music. . . . That was in the 1970s.[62]

Saxophonist Aleksey Kozlov (b. 1935, and, like Artem'yev, another older figure who kept pace with newer musical trends) recalled the Scriabin Museum's "basement" as "a gathering place for those who were interested in various types of 'meditative art.'" In Kozlov's words, in the early 1970s "there was also a laser installed there, creating various visual effects under a special dome. . . . There I also encountered the pantomiming meditative group of Valeriye [*sic*—Vladimir?] Martïnov, taken from the Pantomime Theater of Gedryus Matskiavichius [*sic*]." Kreychi also described visits to the studio by Marta Tsifrinovich, "a famous puppeteer."[63] Kozlov participated in performances at the museum that he called "our own type of 'crossover' jam ["mezhzhanroviy dzhem"—literally "between genres jam"], attempting to enter into a trance, uniting freely improvised music, psychedelic lights, and meditative rhythmical dance improvisation." The "trance" aspect reportedly eluded him, but for Kozlov "the aesthetic sensation of the completely new [at these events] has remained from that time a vivid memory for my whole life."[64]

Progressive rock became particularly important for the new custodians of the studio. Grindenko vividly described her own initial exposure to the genre:

> In principle I was an extraordinarily academic musician, but once, after a concert at the Scriabin Museum (it was a "normal" concert), I had already put my coat on in the cloakroom and from behind the walls there were these completely phenomenal sounds. I was so floored, was taken by surprise, turned around, and it turned out to be the electronic studio and one of the discs by—I don't remember, either the group Yes or Pink Floyd (it was completely old)—was playing. In general I was floored and generally understood that without that I could no longer exist—quite simply couldn't live. And thus with that music began my general interest in new music, *real* new music—from there [to] Stockhausen [and] Cage.[65]

Artem'yev also described the changing musical tastes of the musicians at the Scriabin Museum:

> Naturally, Pink Floyd was the first such shaker. Then—Genesis, Yes. There was the German group Ash Ra Temple that then became Tangerine Dream,

the same group—Klaus Schulz, [Bryan] Eno, Bryan Adams, Robert Fripp with King Crimson, such intellectual rock music. It was a very strong influence . . . and later, before the closing of the studio [at the Scriabin Museum], that side of the music grew more. Not academic, intellectual music, but more connected with . . . rock.[66]

Artem'yev's changing aesthetic orientation was swayed not only by progressive rock but also by works from other "crossover" genres, specifically Andrew Lloyd Webber's rock-opera *Jesus Christ Superstar* (1971), which was hugely popular in the Soviet Union in the early 1970s because it was perceived as exotic on two counts, both religious and musical. Artem'yev described his reaction to Webber's music to Russian musicologist Margarita Katunyan:

> Webber's opera [*sic*] *Jesus Christ Superstar* demonstrated how one could decide eternal themes on the basis of a democratic language appealing to the masses, not to the intellect but to the heart. I saw that rock musicians were capable of solving large-scale musical problems. All of them dared—and the avant-garde too, they returned music to music ["vernuli muzïku muzïke"].[67]

As a result of these varied influences, in the early 1970s Artem'yev, Martïnov, Grindenko, and others helped form a rock group called Boomerang ("Bumerang"), proudly yet erroneously claimed by Grindenko as "the first rock group in Russia." It was based at the Scriabin Museum, and covered and imitated the same Yes and Pink Floyd that had earlier so struck Grindenko within those very walls and that Artem'yev and Martïnov also noted as a large influence.[68] The central members of Boomerang included Alexander Grabinovich, Artem'yev, Martïnov, and Grindenko, with their instrumentation consisting of electric guitar and electric bass, keyboards (organ, piano), violin, drums, and sometimes synthesizer (the ANS).[69] Some later recordings of this group survive, among them a collection of excerpts from Artem'yev's moody film scores that reveal the degree to which Boomerang was indebted to the aesthetic of progressive rock, not least ELP, whose "Toccata" had been so memorable for Artem'yev.[70] Although they were not the first Soviet rock group, Boomerang was one of the first to cross the boundaries separating "serious," "academic," "intellectual" music from more "popular" genres in the Soviet Union. Audiences responded enthusiastically to their concerts at the Scriabin Museum. The "public was hungry" as Grindenko phrased it:

> And besides that, the majority of music that was in the Soviet Union was music . . . of already dead people, that is to say, Brahms, Bach, Beethoven, Chopin, that assortment in general. But of our [Russian] music there was very little. If it existed, it was [by head of the Soviet Union of Composers Tikhon] Khrennikov, [Rodion] Shchedrin, [Dmitriy] Kabalevsky, or at best, Stravinsky. And therefore, of course, our [Boomerang] concerts were tremendously popular.[71]

For Grindenko, Boomerang and its Western models (ELP, Yes, Pink Floyd), while "popular," also aspired to the status of the composers she named, all primarily "academic," "intellectual" composers.

This attitude was not shared by the older generation of unofficial composers. Grindenko described Denisov's musical tastes:

> He was a tremendous person, but his circle of interests in a great deal of music absolutely did not coincide with ours. He, for example, considered all of the minimalists to be only speculators, [saying] that "I can also write two notes and say that it is a composition, just like that." An absolute lack of understanding.[72]

Martïnov also remembered trying to turn Schnittke and Gubaidulina on to rock groups like Pink Floyd, to which they replied, "It's alien, it's not for us."[73] While it is true that Schnittke incorporated aspects of popular music in his polystylistic compositions, for him it represented the "evil" of the world, a far cry from the liberation it represented for the next generation.[74] Perhaps this was the real reason for the older composers' rejection of the ANS: not only did their lack of technological savvy prove an obstacle, but on a deeper level the ANS had already been marked as an instrument of the young and the "popular"—nonserious, nonacademic, nonintellectual—and therefore seemed suspicious to their "new-music" tastes. Coincidentally, the antipathy felt by the older generation of unofficial composers for the younger generation's more ecumenical musical palette was also shared by Soviet officials. In many ways the upsetting of traditional cultural hierarchies proved the most threatening—and longest lasting—result of the Scriabin Museum's musical activities.

Out of Control

The younger musicians' heady mix of lasers, synthesizers, rock, and improvisation eventually began to draw too much attention and helped force the studio's closure. Despite the more *outré* activities of the younger generation, the involvement of the older generation also proved decisive for the end of the studio. In early 1974 the Ministry of Culture attempted to give control of the studio to the Union of Composers, but the union refused.[75] Instead, at some point between 1974 and April 1975, at the initial stage in its dissolution the studio was "reorganized as a scientific-research laboratory" within the Melodiya record company.[76] Melodiya's governance of the studio obviously had grown increasingly lax after it initially was given control in December 1966; in fact, it is unclear whether their control of the studio before 1974–75 was ever anything other than nominal (another factor that weighs against the studio as a *vnye* milieu: rather than being "suspended," in practice it fell almost fully "outside" official jurisdiction). Most likely, although the company held ownership on paper, while Murzin was still alive he had sole oversight, especially given his higher party connections and the leniency with which scientists were treated generally by the Soviet authorities. After his death, without prompting from above, Melodiya continued to ignore the studio, and the remaining musicians there more or less had free rein. However, at a certain point the authorities decided that intervention was necessary. They were particularly unhappy with its recent popular musical products. In musicologist Alla Bogdanova's words, the Ministry of Culture dismissed their "'applied' ["prikladnoy"] character (for films, theatrical productions, television films)."[77] The "scientific-research work" that had originally been the studio's purpose had clearly fallen by the wayside.

The Ministry of Culture reorganized the studio within Melodiya in order to halt the "avant-garde" experiments there, as exemplified not only by the Happenings, but also by the presence of known suspicious figures, namely Schnittke, Gubaidulina, and Denisov. Artem'yev, forgetting (or unaware) that the studio had always "belonged" to Melodiya, said that the studio was given to the record company in the mid-1970s "in order to quietly close the studio—give it to another organization [that] would shut it down."[78] Kreychi recalled:

> The situation changed with the appearance of Schnittke, Denisov and Gubaidulina, the [official] attitude to whom at the time was well known to everyone. I know that all concert organizations were warned not to include performances of their music in their repertoire, even if a well-known performer wanted to play it.[79]

Melodiya refused to make a decision about the release of a second LP of ANS compositions because, in Kreychi's words, they

> fear[ed] those "odious" names. In fact while reading the names of the composers included [on the LP] the general director—as far as I remember his name was Mokhov (he later became the Deputy Minister of Culture)—said: "Since Schnittke's name is there I won't even listen to it!"[80]

A letter from the Ministry of Culture to the Central Committee from February 12, 1975, confirms Kreychi's report, noting that

> [t]he activities at the studio have ceased to have an authentically scientific character and essentially have been reduced to sufficiently random experiments in the realm of electronic music, around which have united a narrow group of composers (Schnittke, Gubaidulina, Denisov and others). Naturally, neither the administrative leadership of the studio nor the Melodiya firm has been able to evaluate the creative, aesthetic results of these experiments.[81]

Finally, in April 1975, Melodiya was directed by the Ministry of Culture to cede control of the studio to Moscow State University Rector Academic R. V. Khokhlov. The document containing this decision, dated April 2, 1975, echoed the language from the February 12 letter but pinpointed the central issue of control that stood at the basis for the studio's closing:

After the passing of E. A. Murzin the activities at the studio lost an authentically scientific character and essentially have been reduced to experiments that are carried out by a narrow group of composers without any kind of control by governmental institutions and creative organizations.[82]

The Soviet authorities recognized that the studio had somehow fallen through the cracks. While they were no doubt aware of the studio's real excesses—Happenings, "crossover" trance jams, and the like—they instead focused on the familiar violators of official dogma as the assumed ringleaders. But both older and especially younger composers together upset the *vnye* balance pervading most aspects of Soviet life by that time, and thereby required a reassertion of central control. After April 2, 1975, then, the studio was dissolved and the ANS was moved to the Moscow State University building across from the Kremlin where it has resided to the present day (under the auspices of the Laboratory of Structural Linguistics within the Philology Department).[83]

Artem'yev provided a more pragmatic explanation for the studio's closing when he suggested that there were

> two reasons why they closed it. On the one hand, the bosses didn't want it. On the other, it died because there was no kind of support, neither financial, nor any other. . . . Everyone fixed and did everything themselves. That is, it gradually died by its own hand. To create a real studio is an expensive pleasure. Only in serious countries—Holland, America—[is it possible].[84]

Gubaidulina expanded upon this explanation:

> The services [at the studio] were practically at the personal initiative, the personal enthusiasm of the founders of the studio. I remember that [Pyotr] Meshchaninov [Gubaidulina's late third husband, d. 2006] often went to Khrennikov with requests for support, but he showed no interest at all, and so during the whole period financial help was never forthcoming. In the end the studio closed, and each of us went his own way.[85]

Ultimately, a combination of affronts by two generations of unofficial composers led to the Scriabin studio's demise. What had originally portended a period of utopian technological achievements and had inspired music seemingly in harmony with Soviet cold war policy pronouncements had become a nest for eccentric musical experimentation. The technical promise of the ANS at first corresponded with the idealistic aspirations of the Thaw. By the early 1970s however—and especially after the 1968 Soviet invasion of Czechoslovakia—the promise of the Thaw had faded. The other unofficial milieus of the 1960s like Grigoriy Frid's Moscow Youth Musical Club, held at the House of Composers, began to lose their earlier quality of opposition, settling into the more balanced "suspension"—simultaneously immobile and porous—described by Yurchak, with the immobility predominating on the surface.

The unsupervised Scriabin Museum's electronic music studio itself stood outside this type of "suspension" to the end. The crossover jams that Kozlov recalled are suggestive of the paradoxical politics surrounding the disequilibrium there in the late 1960s and early 1970s: a blending of dissimilar, exotic, and taboo musical styles with the goal of inspiring a "trance." They were a provocative way of dropping out, but were without political intent, except in a negative sense. Yet at the same time, indicating the persistence of an oppositional aspect to the studio's "underground," decidedly non-*vnye* status, Artem'yev remembered that the studio "drew everyone who was dissatisfied," suggesting a yearning for novelty that although lacking overt political impetus, and certainly not dissident, nonetheless revealed an underlying "dissatisfaction" with the ordained cultural (and not necessarily only cultural) politics of the state. Regardless of intent, ultimately the experimentation fostered by this sense of "dissatisfaction" did have a political effect: the elimination of the studio.

The studio more successfully effected change through another type of politics: the politics of cultural capital. Thanks to the genre mixing of Boomerang and the "crossover" jams that Kozlov described at the studio, a fundamental realignment began to take place in Soviet aesthetics: popular genres like rock and jazz that were once viewed with suspicion as "nonacademic" or "nonserious" began to be judged by the same criteria as "academic," "intellectual" music. At a basic level, both had returned "music to music," as Artem'yev memorably phrased it. Just as in the United States and Europe, this is one of the most important dividing lines in Soviet music history and one of the most important markers of musical "late socialism." The Scriabin studio became one of its clearest embodiments.[86]

After the studio closed, Boomerang and the ANS took refuge by recording sound tracks for a number of important films (including *Sibiriada* [1979] and *Hot Summer in Kabul*—"Zharkoye leto v Kabule" [1983]). Today there is still a close-knit circle of devotees of electronic music in Moscow, including Artem'yev and Kreychi, who, through his own personal initiative, maintains the ANS. Both composers continue to release recordings of electroacoustic music, some written on the aging synthesizer (like Kreychi's 2000 CD *Ansiana*).[87] The lone ANS machine now stands as a living relic of the Thaw, an emblem of the curious and changing mixture of Soviet politics and music, and the increasingly blurred worlds of official and unofficial, during the late 1960s and early 1970s.[88]

I would like to acknowledge the invaluable assistance of Stanislav Kreychi, Eduard Artem'yev, Tat'yana Grindenko, and Vladimir Martïnov in the research for this project. Richard Taruskin, Katherine Bergeron, Yuri Slezkine, Doug Keislar, and Julian Lim read and commented on various drafts of this material over its long gestation and I am indebted to their advice and suggestions, as well as to the suggestions of the anonymous readers for Oxford University Press. Any mistakes that remain are, of course, my responsibility alone.

Notes

1. See the (London) *Sunday Pictorial* cartoon satirizing Theremin's invention in Albert Glinsky, *Theremin: Ether Music and Espionage* (Urbana and Chicago: University of Illinois Press, 2000), p. 9 of the photo insert between 128 and 129.

2. Ibid., 33.

3. This term "academic" is based on the usage of my informants, Soviet critics, and other Soviet writings that set off one sphere of music as "academic," "serious," or "intellectual"—all labels that describe what commonly is called "art music" or "classical music"—from what in the West would be considered "popular music," a term without a good Russian equivalent (see David MacFadyen, *Songs for Fat People: Affect, Emotion, and Celebrity in the Russian Popular Song, 1900–1955* [Montreal: McGill-Queen's University Press, 2002]). I also explore these issues in Peter Schmelz, "'Crucified on the Cross of Mass Culture' : Late Soviet Genre Politics in Alexander Zhurbin's Rock Opera Orpheus, and Eurydice," *Journal of Musicological Research*.

4. For more on the unofficial "academic" music of the Thaw see Peter J. Schmelz, *Such Freedom, if Only Musical: Unofficial Soviet Music during the Thaw* (New York: Oxford University Press, 2009).

5. Murzin's birth year has been determined from information in A. B., "Musica elettronica di tutto il mondo," *La Stampa*, June 14, 1968, 6; and the transcript for a 1962 "Radio Broadcast for the United States" ("Radioperedacha dlya SShA") included in the ANS scrapbook that Murzin kept from 1960 until his death and that is now located with the ANS itself at Moscow State University (hereafter, Murzin scrapbook). The date of his death is from Anton Rovner, "An Interview with Composer Stanislav Kreychi about the ANS Synthesizer, the Electronic Music Studio at the Scriabin Museum in Moscow (1960–1970), and His Own Musical Activities," *20th Century Music* 6, no. 10 (October 1999): 11. It does not appear in the Russian original at this point: Stanislav Kreychi and Anton Rovnor, "ANS prodolzhayet rabotat'," *Muzïkal'naya akademiya* 4 (1999): 193. All translations throughout are mine unless otherwise noted.

6. Eduard Artem'yev, interview by author, Moscow, September 23, 1999.

7. Russian State Archive of Literature and Art (hereafter, RGALI), fond ("collection," hereafter, f.) 2329, opis' ("inventory," hereafter, op.) 3, yedinitsa khraneniya ("storage unit," hereafter, yed. khr.) 1208, list ("page," hereafter, l.) 7. See also "An Interview with Edward and Artemiy Artemiev" (http://www.eurock.com/features/artemiyindex.html; accessed January 5, 2007); Kreychi and Rovnor, "ANS prodolzhayet rabotat'," 193; Gleb Anfilov, *Fizika i muzïka*, 2nd ed. (Moscow: Detskaya literatura, 1964), 163 (English translation of the first edition: Gleb Anfilov, *Physics and Music* [Moscow: Mir, 1966], 219). For more on Volkonsky, see Peter Schmelz, "Andrey Volkonsky and the Beginnings of Unofficial Music in the Soviet Union," *Journal of the American Musicological Society* 58, no. 1 (Spring 2005): 139–208; and Schmelz, *Such Freedom, if Only Musical*, chapter 3.

8. Alexei Yurchak, *Everything Was Forever, until It Was No More: The Last Soviet Generation* (Princeton, N.J.: Princeton University Press, 2006), 5.

9. Ibid., 127–28. "Deterritorialize" is from Gilles Deleuze and Félix Guattari, *A Thousand Plateaus: Capitalism and Schizophrenia*, trans. and foreword by

Brian Massumi (Minneapolis: University of Minnesota Press, 1987), esp. 10–11. Yurchak's usage varies throughout his book, but "deterritorialize" usually suggests "hollowing out" or "enervating" or doing something otherwise negative to one part of the opposition he creates, borrowing from Bakhtin, between authoritative discourse and individual "authors," though he emphasizes that "it would be wrong to equate this process simply with progressive stagnation or decay" (295).

10. Yurchak, *Everything Was Forever, until It Was No More*, 31.

11. Marina Frolova-Walker, "Stalin and the Art of Boredom," *Twentieth-Century Music* 1, no. 1 (March 2004): 101–24.

12. N. Eydel'man, "Vremya, sulivsheye stol'ko nadezhd," in *Drugoye iskusstvo: Moskva 1956–76; K khronike khudozhestvennoy zhizni*, vol. 1, ed. Irina G. Alpatova and Leonid P. Talochkin (Moscow: Moskovskaya kollektsiya, 1991), 7.

13. For more on the succession and interaction of generations in the Soviet 1970s (and after), see Peter J. Schmelz, "What Was 'Shostakovich,' and What Came Next?" *Journal of Musicology* 24, no. 3 (Summer 2007): 297–338.

14. Artem'yev, interview.

15. RGALI f. 2329, op. 3, yed. khr. 1208, l. 7. The information that follows is drawn from this RGALI material—an entire file in the Ministry of Culture Fond devoted to the ANS—as well as material included in the Murzin scrapbook. See also Anfilov, *Fizika i muzïka*, 156–57.

16. Kreychi and Rovnor, "ANS prodolzhayet rabotat'," 192; Artem'yev, interview; and Anfilov, *Fizika i muzïka*, 157–58.

17. For more on Sholpo, see Anfilov, *Fizika i muzïka*, 139–52. Anfilov also gives a good general account of the creation and early years of the ANS and the Scriabin studio (153–68). Sholpo is also discussed in Kreychi and Rovnor, "ANS prodolzhayet rabotat'," 191.

18. In addition to my own interviews with Kreychi, and Anfilov's discussion in *Physics and Music*, the summary below relies on the following sources: Stanislav Kreichi, "The ANS Synthesizer: Composing on a Photoelectric Instrument," *Leonardo* 28, no. 1 (January/February 1995): 59–62; and Kreychi and Rovnor, "ANS prodolzhayet rabotat'," 191. An early general introduction to the ANS was written by Artem'yev (his first initial is mistakenly identified as A): A. Artem'yev, "Chto takoye ANS," *Sovetskaya muzïka* 2 (1962): 156. See also Mark Vail, "Eugeniy [*sic*] Murzin's ANS: Additive Russian Synthesizer," *Keyboard* (November 2002): 120 (my thanks to Joseph Rovan for bringing this source to my attention).

19. Rovner, "An Interview with Composer Stanislav Kreychi," 9.

20. Rovner's translation states "124 sound tracks," but this is obviously a typographical error (it is not in the Russian original). See Rovner, ibid.

21. Anfilov, *Fizika i muzïka*, 168.

22. Murzin scrapbook. This testimonial lacks a date, but the date on the relevant page of the scrapbook is 1960.

23. Murzin scrapbook.

24. For more on Artem'yev's career see Tat'yana Yegorova, *Vselennaya Eduarda Artem'yeva* (Moscow: Vagrius, 2006).

25. Murzin scrapbook (letter dated August 2/3, 1962, no. 3896–6/29, from Deputy Minister of Culture USSR A. N. Kuznetsov to Chairman of the Executive Committee of MOSSOVET N. A. Dïgay; Po. PS–1553, March 25, 1966, from P. Pleshakov of the MRP ["Ministerstvo Radiopromïshlennosti"] USSR to Deputy Minister of Culture USSR A. N. Kuznetsov).

26. RGALI f. 2329, op. 3, yed. khr. 1208, l. 12. See also the excerpt from a booklet about the ANS found in the Communist Party archives and cited in Alla Bogdanova, *Muzïka i vlast': poststalinskiy period* (Moscow: Naslediye, 1995), 139–40.

27. RGALI f. 2329, op. 3, yed. khr. 1208, l. 16 (appendix no. 2 to the Act of January 24, 1962).

28. Murzin scrapbook.

29. L. Smirnova, "V Moskve, na ulitse Vakhtangova," *Molodaya gvardiya*, January 1, 1963, 295–96; in Murzin scrapbook. The summary of the official communications at this time can be found in RGALI f. 2329, op. 3, yed. khr. 1208, l. 7. This later sheet ("spravka") summarizing the history of the ANS was included with a draft of a Ministry of Culture document ("Resheniye," ll. 1–3) that decided specific details regarding the formation of the studio for electronic music at the Scriabin Museum and the funding for the mass production of the ANS within the Ministry of Culture. It appears to have been drafted after the January 24, 1962, Act (RGALI f. 2329, op. 3, yed. khr. 1208, ll. 8–13; see below). Copies of letters related to the 1960–62 communications are either included as appendices to this Act (esp. ll. 16–17) or are in the Murzin scrapbook.

30. "Muzïka napisana na ANSe," *Moskovskaya Pravda*, September 7, 1961; in Murzin scrapbook. A 1971 recording of Nemtin's *Tears* and Kreychi's *Echo of the East* along with the electronic compositions of Gubaidulina, Denisov, and Schnittke was released on LP in 1990 by Melodiya as *Muzïkal'noye prinosheniye* C-60 30721 000, although Denisov's piece lacked its live instrumental portion and, in fact, was missing an entire section of the tape portion (including only 5'05" of the 7'33" composition); see Edison Denisov, *"Peniye ptits": partitura, fonogramma, materialï, interv'yu*, ed. Margarita Katunyan (Moscow: Kompozitor, 2006), 6. The Melodiya recording was reissued on CD by Electroshock in 1999: *Electroshock Presents: Electroacoustic Music—Volume IV: Synthesizer ANS, 1964–1971* (ELCD 011). For more on Artem'yev's compositions from this period, see Margarita Katunyan, "Eduard Artem'yev: arkhitektor i poet zvuka," in *Muzïka iz bïvshego SSSR*, ed. Valeriya Tsenova, 2 vols. (Moscow: Kompozitor, 1994), 2: 180–207; and Yegorova, *Vselennaya Eduarda Artem'yeva*, 59–64.

31. Recordings of these Nemtin and Kreychi compositions can be found on the Electroshock CD mentioned in the previous note.

32. RGALI f. 2329, op. 3, yed. khr. 1208, l. 10 (January 24, 1962 Act).

33. Much of this correspondence is preserved in Murzin's scrapbook and does not survive in the official Ministry of Culture documents at RGALI. The details can be parsed out by interpolating the material at RGALI (f. 2329, op. 3, yed. khr. 1208, especially ll. 21–23) with the material in Murzin's scrapbook, which continues the correspondence begun in the RGALI documents.

34. RGALI f. 2329, op. 3, yed. khr. 1208, l. 7.

35. Murzin scrapbook.

36. Ibid. (July 30, 1966, letter from the Ministry of Culture RSFSR to the Ministry of Culture of the USSR).

37. Ibid. (March 25, 1966, letter from P. Pleshakov of the MRP USSR to Deputy Minister of Culture USSR A. N. Kuznetsov). For more on the rock concerts at VDNKh, see Hedrick Smith, *The Russians* (New York: Quadrangle/ The New York Times Book Co., 1976), 171.

38. Murzin scrapbook (December 23, 1966, Order of the Ministry of Culture USSR, no. 529). See also Kreychi and Rovnor, "ANS prodolzhayet rabotat'," 193.

39. Murzin scrapbook (December 23, 1966, Order of the Ministry of Culture USSR, no. 529).

40. A. B., "Musica elettronica di tutto il mondo," and Katunyan, "Eduard Artem'yev: arkhitektor i poet zvuka," 188. The program, the Italian translation of Murzin's paper ("Resources of Sound in Electronic Music Techniques and the Establishment of an International System of Notation"), and assorted Italian press clippings are included in the Murzin scrapbook.

41. Artem'yev, interview.

42. Ibid.; Kreychi and Rovnor, "ANS prodolzhayet rabotat'," 194.

43. Artem'yev, interview.

44. Ibid. See also Glinsky, *Theremin: Ether Music and Espionage*, 311.

45. Artem'yev, interview.

46. Valentina Kholopova and Enzo Restan'o [Restagno], *Sofiya Gubaidulina* (Moscow: Kompozitor, 1996), 47 (this is a retranslation from the Italian of Enzo Restagno, *Gubajdulina* [Turin: E.D.T., 1991]); Kreychi and Rovnor, "ANS prodolzhayet rabotat'," 193. A photograph of Artem'yev, Schnittke, Nemtin, Denisov, Buloshkin, Gubaidulina, and Kreychi with the ANS is included on p. 12 of Denisov, *"Peniye ptits."*

47. Stanislav Kreychi, interview by author, Moscow, September 27, 1999; and Kreychi and Rovnor, "ANS prodolzhayet rabotat'," 193.

48. Al'fred Shnitke and Dmitriy Shul'gin, *Godï neizvestnosti Al'freda Shnitke: besedï s kompozitorom* (Moscow: Delovaya liga, 1993), 54. Shul'gin also pointed out the similarities between *Stream* and *Pianissimo* (54–55). For more on *Pianissimo* see Schmelz, *Such Freedom, if Only Musical*, chapter 6.

49. Kholopova and Restan'o, *Sofiya Gubaidulina*, 47. For an analysis of Gubaidulina's composition, see Yuriy Kholopov, "Ob obshchikh logicheskikh printsipakh sovremennoy garmonii," *Muzïka i sovremennost'* 8 (1974): 269–76. See also Michael Kurtz, *Sofia Gubaidulina: A Biography*, trans. Christoph K. Lohmann, ed. Malcolm Hamrick Brown (Bloomington and Indianapolis: Indiana University Press, 2007), 83–84.

50. See Edison Denisov and Dmitriy Shul'gin, *Priznaniye Edisona Denisova: po materialam besed* (Moscow: Kompozitor, 1998), 199; and Edison Denisov, Margarita Katunyan, and V. Serebryakova, "O Penii ptits: interv'yu," in *Svet-dobro-vechnost': pamyati Edisona Denisova, stat'i, vospominaniya, materialï*, ed. Valeriya Tsenova (Moscow: Moskovskaya gosudarstvennaya konservatoriya im. P. I. Chaikovskogo, 1999), 59–67. See also Denisov, *"Peniye ptits,"* 47–71 (and the accompanying CD).

51. Margarita Katunyan, "Peniye ptits E. Denisova: kompozitsiya—grafika—ispolneniye," in *Svet-dobro-vechnost'*, 391. Two versions of the score are included in Denisov, *"Peniye ptits."*

52. Denisov and Shul'gin, *Priznaniye Edisona Denisova*, 200; and Denisov, Katunyan, and Serebryakova, "O Penii ptits: interv'yu," 64–65.

53. Katunyan, "Peniye ptits E. Denisova," 396. Denisov and his biographers provided incorrect dates for the premiere of the work; see Denisov and Shul'gin, *Priznaniye Edisona Denisova*, 202; and Yuriy Kholopov and Valeriya Tsenova, *Edison Denisov* (Moscow: Kompozitor, 1993), 222.

54. Katunyan, ibid., 397.

55. Ibid.

56. Denisov, Katunyan, and Serebryakova, "O Penii ptits: interv'yu," 62; and Denisov, *"Peniye ptits,"* 74.

57. Katunyan, "Peniye ptits E. Denisova," 397. For more information on Lyubimov's subsequent performances of the work, see Schmelz, *Such Freedom, if Only Musical*, chapter 7.

58. Denisov, Katunyan, and Serebryakova, "O Penii ptits: interv'yu," 65. Denisov later recorded his thoughts on electronic music in his essay "Music and Machines" ("Muzïka i mashinï"), in Edison Denisov, *Sovremennaya muzïka i problemï evolyutsii kompozitorskoy tekhniki* (Moscow: Sovetskiy kompozitor, 1986); reprinted in Denisov, *"Peniye ptits,"* 78–90 (he discusses the ANS on p. 89 in a section titled "Music and Painting" ["Muzïka i zhivopis'"]).

59. Artem'yev, interview.

60. Ibid. See also Bogdanova, *Muzïka i vlast'*, 140–41.

61. Anfilov, *Physics and Music*, 224; the version in the second Russian edition is slightly different: Anfilov, *Fizika i muzïka*, 165–66.

62. Artem'yev, interview. Emerson, Lake and Palmer's "Toccata" was based on the Fourth Movement of Ginastera's Piano Concerto no. 1, and appeared on their 1973 LP *Brain Salad Surgery*.

63. Rovner, "An Interview with Composer Stanislav Kreychi," 15.

64. All Kozlov quotations in this paragraph are from Aleksey Kozlov, *'Kozyol na sakse': i tak vsyu zhizn'* (Moscow: Vagrius, 1998), 221–22. A similar atmosphere (dancers, film projections) occurred at some synthesizer concerts in the United States. See Trevor Pinch and Frank Trocco, *Analog Days: The Invention and Impact of the Moog Synthesizer* (Cambridge, Mass.: Harvard University Press, new ed., 2004), 199. I am indebted to my former student Daniel Marin for this reference.

65. Tat'yana Grindenko, interview by author, Moscow, January 12, 2001.

66. Artem'yev, interview. See also Yegorova, *Vselennaya Eduarda Artem'yeva*, 66.

67. Katunyan, "Eduard Artem'yev: arkhitektor i poet zvuka," 182. I address the Soviet reception of *Jesus Christ Superstar* and its Soviet imitators, especially Alexander Zhurbin's rock-opera *Orpheus and Eurydice* (the first in the Soviet Union), in Schmelz, "Crucified on the Cross of Mass Culture."

68. Grindenko, interview; also Vladimir Martïnov, interview by author, Moscow, September 16, 1999; and Artem'yev, interview. See also A. Troytskiy, "Art-rok" in *Rok muzïka v SSSR: opït populyarnoy entsiklopedii* (Moscow: Kniga, 1990), 47. By the mid-1960s there were already numerous Beatles cover groups in the Soviet Union, including *Sokol* (Falcon), *Rebyata* (the Guys), and *Melomanï* (the Melomanes). See Timothy W. Ryback, *Rock around the Bloc: A History of Rock Music in Eastern Europe and the Soviet Union* (New York and Oxford: Oxford University Press, 1990), 62–65; and Artemy Troitsky, *Back in the USSR: The True Story of Rock in Russia* (Boston and London: Faber and Faber, 1988), 23–24.

69. Grindenko, interview.

70. E. Artem'yev, *Kartinï-nastroyeniya*, Melodiya LP C10 21077 002 (this was recorded in 1976, but released in 1980).

71. Grindenko, interview.

72. Ibid.

73. Martïnov, interview.

74. See Al'fred Shnitke and Aleksandr Ivashkin, *Besedï s Al'fredom Shnitke* (Moscow: RIK "Kul'tura," 1994), 155; in English in Alfred Schnittke, *A Schnittke Reader*, ed. Alexander Ivashkin, trans. John Goodliffe (Bloomington and Indianapolis: Indiana University Press, 2002), 22.

75. Bogdanova, *Muzïka i vlast*,' 141–43.

76. Ibid., 143. See also Kreychi and Rovnor, "ANS prodolzhayet rabotat,'" 194.

77. Bogdanova, *Muzïka i vlast'*, 142.

78. Artem'yev, interview.

79. Kreychi and Rovnor, "ANS prodolzhayet rabotat'," 194.

80. Ibid.

81. Bogdanova, *Muzïka i vlast'*, 142.

82. Ibid., 143–44.

83. Kreychi and Rovnor, "ANS prodolzhayet rabotat'," 194.

84. Artem'yev, interview. Kreychi also discussed the financial reasons behind the studio's closure in Kreychi and Rovnor, "ANS prodolzhayet rabotat'," 194.

85. Kholopova and Restan'o, *Sofiya Gubaidulina*, 48.

86. See Schmelz, "What Was 'Shostakovich,' and What Came Next?"; Schmelz, "Crucified on the Cross of Mass Culture"; and A. Tsuker, *I rok, i simfoniya . . .* (Moscow: Kompozitor, 1993).

87. Stanislav Kreitchi [Kreychi], *Ansiana*, Electroshock Records, ELCD 016 (2000).

88. The ANS continues to attract attention from musicians interested in "crossover" experimentation: in 2004 the British industrial group Coil released recordings they had made on the ANS machine in Moscow. Coil, *ANS*, Threshold House CD, 502195841555 (2004).

Index

Davidovsky, Mario
 Electronic Studies, 238
 Synchronisms no. 1, 236
Davis, Angela, 139, 144
Davis, Miles, 228
Davis, Ossie, 121, 127
Debord, Guy
 La société du spectacle, 160
deconstruction, 135
Deleuze, Gilles, 22
Denisov, Edison
 and ANS synthesizer, 10, 263–65, 269
 attitude to minimalism, 268
 electronic music of, 274, 276
 In the Shroud of the Frozen Pond, 265
 and serialism, 256
 Singing of the Birds, 264–65
 and the Thaw, 255
DeNora, Tia, 123
Derrida, Jacques, 135
Detroit, 124
Detroit Artists' Workshop, 186
Deutsche Grammophon, 156
Dixon, Bill, 211–13, 215, 225
 Bill Dixon Sextet, 229
Dockstader, Tod
 Luna Park, 138
Doesburg, Theo van, 19, 20, 22, 27, 28
Dolphy, Eric, 171, 211, 215
Donatoni, Franco, 235
Dorian Woodwind Quintet, 239–40
Down Beat, 213, 220, 221, 224,
 226–28
drugs, 10, 170, 177, 226
Duchamp, Marcel, 145
 Fountain, 84
Dutilleux, Henri, 164, 235
Duyn, Roel van, 72
Dylan, Bob, 4, 50, 219

Eco, Umberto, 104
Eisenhower, Dwight D., 188, 192, 252
Eisler, Hanns, 92
electronic music, 9, 154, 194, 237
 and ANS synthesizer, 254–77
 in Cuba, 59
 of Musica Elettronica Viva, 102,
 105, 106, 108, 111–15
 of ONCE, 170, 172, 174–76, 181, 185
 as "revolutionary" musical means, 66
Ellington, Duke, 266
elitism, 101, 150, 158

Emerson, Lake and Palmer, 266,
 267, 276
Eno, Brian, 267
environmental movement,
 88, 163
Enzensberger, Hans Magnus, 21, 23,
 25, 28
Eshpai, Andrey, 263
Etler, Alvin
 Brass Quintet, 238
Evangelisti, Franco, 103, 105
Evans, Gil, 213
"events," 183, 189, 196, 202, 205
expressionism, 16, 17, 18, 19, 189

Fähnders, Walter, 16, 21
fauvism, 16
Federal Bureau of Investigation
 (F.B.I.), 138
Feldman, Morton, 171, 173–74,
 184, 186, 196, 198
 Atlantis, 195
 Intersection II, 101
feminism, 179, 190
Ferrari, Luc, 8, 14, 145–66
 Hétérozygote, 154
 Presque rien (1970), 8, 145–66
 Société I, 147
 Und So Weiter, 114
film, 83, 171, 177, 179, 188, 193–94, 202
 avant-garde music for, 260, 271
 influence upon avant-garde
 musicians, 184
 as material for avant-garde music,
 175–76, 181
 paranoia in, 138
 as quintessential genre of avant-
 garde, 17
Finney, Ross Lee, 170
 Three Pieces in Fours, 236
First World War, 22, 26
Fluxus, 56, 84, 109, 174
 as collective performance
 movement, 183
 impact in Japan, 188, 195–97, 204,
 207, 208
 involvement in protest against
 Stockhausen, 37–38
 and language, 135
 as "neo-avant-garde" movement,
 16, 17
 relation with Henry Flynt, 38–39